Nathan MacDonald is Lecturer in Old Testament at the University of St Andrews.

NOT BREAD ALONE

Not Bread Alone

The Uses of Food in the Old Testament

NATHAN MACDONALD

OXFORD
UNIVERSITY PRESS

OXFORD
UNIVERSITY PRESS

Great Clarendon Street, Oxford OX2 6DP

Oxford University Press is a department of the University of Oxford.
It furthers the University's objective of excellence in research, scholarship,
and education by publishing worldwide in

Oxford New York

Auckland Cape Town Dar es Salaam Hong Kong Karachi
Kuala Lumpur Madrid Melbourne Mexico City Nairobi
New Delhi Shanghai Taipei Toronto

With offices in

Argentina Austria Brazil Chile Czech Republic France Greece
Guatemala Hungary Italy Japan Poland Portugal Singapore
South Korea Switzerland Thailand Turkey Ukraine Vietnam

Oxford is a registered trade mark of Oxford University Press
in the UK and in certain other countries

Published in the United States
by Oxford University Press Inc., New York

© Nathan MacDonald 2008

The moral rights of the author have been asserted
Database right Oxford University Press (maker)

First published 2008

Figure 2 after J. Milgrom, *Leviticus 1–16*, 722, 725
(Anchor Bible, 3: 1991), Yale University Press. By permission
© 1991 by Doubleday, a division of Bantam Doubleday
Dell Publishing Group, Inc.

British Library Cataloguing in Publication Data

Data available

Library of Congress Cataloging in Publication Data

MacDonald, Nathan, 1975–
Not bread alone : the uses of food in the Old Testament / Nathan MacDonald.
p. cm.
Includes bibliographical references and indexes.
ISBN 978–0–19–954652–7 (alk.paper)
1. Food in the Bible. 2. Food–Religious aspects–Christianity.
3. Bible. O.T.–Criticism, interpretation, etc. 4. Food habits–Israel. I. Title.
BS680.F6M34 2008
221.8'6413–dc22   2008021641

Typeset by SPI Publisher Services, Pondicherry, India
Printed in Great Britain
on acid-free paper by
Biddles Ltd, King's Lynn, Norfolk

ISBN 978–0–19–954652–7

1 3 5 7 9 10 8 6 4 2

Dedicated to
my mother, Ann Josephine MacDonald (1953–)
and in memory of my grandmother, Eva MacDonald (1914–1993)

Two MacDonald mothers and cooks

Preface

The original stimulus for this work was the realization that there was no book on the theology of food in the Old Testament. My initial intention was to produce such a book. Such a volume remains to be written, for as I have worked on food in the Old Testament it became evident to me that there was some very interesting work on food within anthropology that was relevant to the Old Testament. What has resulted, therefore, is a set of preliminary studies that has been stimulated by reading the biblical text in dialogue with works on food and foodways in other cultures.

It will be apparent that the subject matter of this book has required me to stray into areas where my expertise can be described only as that of an interested amateur. I make no apologies for this. The study of the Old Testament is a complex discipline that touches upon many different fields, even before the many issues that relate to food are considered. No one can be an expert in them all and some allowances must be made if the constant call for interdisciplinary work is to be answered (or are they the Sirens' voices?). I can at least console myself with the knowledge that the biblical guild, especially in the United Kingdom and North America, is usually characterized by a generous spirit. New ideas and perspectives on ancient texts are welcomed, whilst also being subjected to critical probing and refining. Disagreement and rigorous correction are friends of academic progress.

In common with many other academic authors I delude myself with the hope that my book will circulate beyond my immediate guild and may be of interest to other academics interested in food and foodways and even to those outside academia. Some guidance on translation and Hebrew words are, therefore, appropriate. Whenever I have quoted the Old Testament I have provided my own translation of the Hebrew text. At some points the versification of the Hebrew text differs from that found in English Bibles. I have provided the English versification only, as scholars with Hebrew are familiar with the points of difference. I have tried to be sparing in my reference to Hebrew, and I have followed a relatively simple system of transliteration whenever it seemed necessary to appeal to points of Hebrew grammar or lexicography. The only exceptions, of course, are when other works are quoted. Here I have remained true to the system employed in the original publication.

I am grateful, as always, to many colleagues in St Mary's and within the wider Old Testament guild for questions, thoughts and ideas. These have

frequently been prefaced with gentle teasing about my chosen topic of research, or with a burning question about some aspect of food in the Bible (Was the fruit in Genesis 3 an apple? What was the manna? Why the pig?). I will, inevitably, omit a name, but those who have been especially helpful have been Mr Peter Altmann, Prof. Craig Blomberg, Prof. Markus Bockmuehl, Prof. Ellen Davis, Dr Jim Davila, Dr Mark Elliott, Dr Walter Houston, Dr Grant Macaskill, Prof. Carol Meyers, Prof. Walter Moberly, Prof. Christopher Seitz, Prof. Alan Torrance, Prof. Jacob Wright. Thanks are also due to Prof. Christoph Levin, who inadvertently helped me to detach this project from another during discussions about an application for an Alexander von Humboldt research fellowship.

Parts of this project were given as papers or lectures at various universities: Aberdeen, Duke, Durham, Emory, Glasgow, Ludwig-Maximillians (Munich), Ruprecht-Karls (Heidelberg), St Andrews and at the SBL meetings in Philadelphia and San Diego. I am grateful to all my interlocutors at those occasions. An earlier version of Chapter 7 appeared as 'Food and Drink in Tobit and Other "Diaspora Novellas"' in M. R. J. Bredin (ed.), *Studies in the Book of Tobit*, LSTS, 55 (London: T&T Clark, 2006), pp. 165–78. The research on Israelite diet was conducted primarily during a trip to Jerusalem funded by a travel grant from the Carnegie Trust for the Universities of Scotland. I am grateful to the trustees for their generous support. I am also grateful to the Kenyon Institute for a pleasant and productive stay as well as to the libraries of the Israel Antiquities Authority, the Albright Institute, the Hebrew University of Jerusalem, Tel Aviv University and Bar Ilan University. A number of Israeli scholars gave generously of their time to hear my ideas and to offer much-needed advice: Profs. Amnon Ben-Tor, Israel Finkelstein, Mordechai Kislev, Amihai Mazar and Pat Smith, and Mr Baruch Rosen. I am grateful to my own institution, the School of Divinity (St Mary's College) at the University of St Andrews for granting a semester's leave in 2006 during which the majority of the book was completed. I am also grateful to the Alexander von Humboldt Stiftung for a research fellowship, which although spent on another related topic, allowed me to check references in the wonderful research environment of the theology library of the Ludwig-Maximillians Universität. Thanks are also due to Jonathan MacKenzie for assistance in compiling the indexes.

Finally, I am indebted to Claire and Callum for their generosity in allowing me to pursue my research and for the constant joy they bring.

Contents

Abbreviations

AB	Anchor Bible
ABD	*Anchor Bible Dictionary* (ed. D. N. Freedman; New York: Doubleday, 1992)
AOAT	Alter Orient und Altes Testament
BASOR	*Bulletin of the American School for Oriental Research*
BBB	Bonner Biblische Beiträge
BETL	Bibliotheca Ephemeridum Theologicarum Lovaniensium
BibInt	*Biblical Interpretation*
BIS	Biblical Interpretation Series
BJS	Brown Judaic Series
BTB	*Biblical Theology Bulletin*
BZ	*Biblische Zeitschrift*
BZAW	Beihefte zur *Zeitschrift für die alttestamentliche Wissenschaft*
CBC	Cambridge Bible Commentary
CBQ	*Catholic Biblical Quarterly*
ConBOT	Coniectanea Biblica Old Testament Series
EncJud II	*Encyclopedia Judaica* (ed. F. Skolnik; London: Macmillan, 2nd edn., 2007)
FAT	Forschungen zum Alten Testament
FRLANT	Forschungen zur Religion und Literatur des Alten und Neuen Testaments
HSM	Harvard Semitic Monographs
HTR	*Harvard Theological Review*
HUCA	*Hebrew Union College Annual*
ICC	International Critical Commentary
IEJ	*Israel Exploration Journal*
Int	*Interpretation*
JBL	*Journal of Biblical Literature*
JPOS	*Journal of the Palestine Oriental Society*
JSJSup	*Journal for the Study of Judaism*, Supplement Series
JSOT	*Journal for the Study of the Old Testament*

JSOTSup	*Journal for the Study of the Old Testament*, Supplement Series
JSPSup	*Journal for the Study of the Pseudepigrapha*, Supplement Series
JSS	*Journal for Semitic Studies*
JTS	*Journal of Theological Studies*
KB	L. H. Köhler and W. Baumgartner, *The Hebrew and Aramaic Lexicon of the Old Testament* (6 vols.; Leiden: E. J. Brill, 1994–2000)
KTU	M. Dietrich, O. Loretz and J. Sanmartín, *The Cuneiform Alphabetic Texts from Ugarit, Ras Ibn Hani and Other Places* (Münster: Ugarit–Verlag, 2nd edn. 1997). First edition published as *Die keilalphabetischen Texte aus Ugarit: Einschließlich der keilalphabetischen Texte ausserhalb Ugarits* (Kevelaer: Butzon & Bercker; Neukirchen-Vluyn: Neukirchener, 1976).
LHBOTS	Library of Hebrew Bible/Old Testament Studies
LSTS	Library of Second Temple Studies
MT	Masoretic Text
NCB	New Century Bible
NEB	Neue Echter Bibel
NIV	New International Version
NRSV	New Revised Standard Version
NSBT	New Studies in Biblical Theology
OBT	Overtures to Biblical Theology
OTL	Old Testament Library
OTS	Oudtestamentische Studiën
PEQ	*Palestine Exploration Quarterly*
SBA	Stuttgarter Biblische Aufsatzbände
SBLDiss	Society of Biblical Literature, Dissertation Series
SBLMS	Society of Biblical Literature, Monograph Series
SBT	Studies in Biblical Theology
SEÅ	*Svensk Exegetisk Årsbok*
SHCANE	Studies in the History and Culture of the Ancient Near East
SNTSMS	Society for New Testament Studies Monograph Series
SWBA	Social World of Biblical Antiquity
TDOT	*Theological Dictionary of the Old Testament* (eds. G. J. Botterweck and H. Ringgren; Grand Rapids: Eerdmans, 1977–2006)
TLZ	*Theologische Literaturzeitung*
UF	*Ugarit-Forschungen*

VT	*Vetus Testamentum*
VTSup	*Vetus Testamentum*, Supplement Series
WBC	Word Biblical Commentary
WMANT	Wissenschaftliche Monographien zum Alten und Neuen Testament
WUNT	Wissenschaftliche Untersuchungen zum Neuen Testament
ZAW	*Zeitschrift für die alttestamentliche Wissenschaft*

Introduction

'Man cannot live by bread alone, but by everything that proceeds from the mouth of YHWH'. In this way Moses summarized the lessons learnt by Israel at the end of forty years in the wilderness, and in the New Testament Jesus quotes these words in his struggle with the devil after his own wilderness experience. Without YHWH and what he provides there is no life for human beings. Yet, that single word 'alone' implies that bread is also necessary for life. Without food human beings will survive little more than a month, without liquid less than a week. 'Give us this day our daily bread' is not an indulgent or otiose request, especially in the vulnerable environment of ancient Palestine.

It is little wonder then that the perennial concern for food makes an impression on the texts that have survived from ancient Israel. Even for the scribal authors who composed the Old Testament, belonging as they did to the social elite, a regular supply of food probably could not be taken for granted.[1] (It should not be forgotten that occasional food shortages were a part of life in Europe even in modern times, and it is only within the last two hundred years that the general population has enjoyed a secure food supply.) The biblical authors express this reality in a number of places by attributing the provision of food to God the creator. In the great antiphonal psalm, Psalm 136, for example, the leader exhorts the worshippers to,

> Give thanks to the Lord of lords,
> His love endures for ever...
> Who gives food to every creature.
> His love endures for ever
>
> (vv. 3, 25)

---

[1] In the following pages I will largely refer to the canon of Jewish scriptures or the first part of the Christian scriptures as the 'Old Testament'. Although some other scholars prefer alternative nomenclatures, the designation 'Old Testament' reflects the author's communal location and that of the large majority of the book's probable readers. 'Old Testament' also has the advantage that in its most capacious sense it includes the books of the Apocrypha, some of which receive attention in Chapter 7. When I make reference to the 'Hebrew Bible' it is particularly when I have in mind the shorter canon and where a reference to 'Old Testament' would be ambiguous.

In the present canonical form of the Old Testament, the divine provision of food is given a central place from the very beginning. According to Genesis 1–11 when God created the world he gave the leafy green plants to the animals as food, whilst he gave the cereals and fruits to humanity. After the deluge human beings are permitted to consume the animals as well. The relation of humanity to this divine provision appears especially in the story of Genesis 3. It is through food that Adam and his wife are tested. They are granted the fruit from every tree in Eden, except for the tree that is in the centre of the garden.

Despite the importance of food to the Old Testament authors, the subject has received surprisingly little attention from modern biblical scholars. The neglect of food in Old Testament scholarship is striking when compared to the number of studies that have been produced on the related subjects of land or agriculture.[2] Land, in particular, has received a great deal of attention, but though much space has been given to the different ideologies of land and its possession, little reflection has been given to how the land might have been used.[3] In the modern world land can be utilized for any number of purposes: residential estates, retail parks, sports facilities, industrial plants, country parks, agriculture. In ancient Israel, except for the small area utilized for villages and towns, land served one purpose only: the production of food. Fertile plains were used for crops, hillsides were planted with olives or vines, and the remaining land was used as pasture for flocks. In the ancient world, land means food. In defence of those who have written studies on land in the Old Testament perhaps this is almost too obvious to mention.

What are the reasons for overlooking the subject of food in the Old Testament? They are, perhaps, not too difficult to discern. First, food is ubiquitous in the Old Testament. There is scarcely a page in the Old Testament where food is not mentioned. It is difficult to know where to begin with a subject that is so broadly represented in the Old Testament corpus. Second, food and drink are so commonplace in the Old Testament and our own human experience that they do not appear to demand particular attention or study. Food is a natural consequence of our physicality that requires little comment. Within the academic study of the Old Testament other perennial problems make more

---

[2] N. C. Habel, *The Land is Mine: Six Biblical Land Ideologies*, OBT (Minneapolis: Fortress Press, 1995); W. Brueggemann, *The Land: Place as Gift, Promise, and Challenge in Biblical Faith*, 2nd edn. (Minneapolis: Fortress Press, 2002); E. W. Davies, 'Land: Its Rights and Privileges', in R. E. Clements (ed.), *The World of Ancient Israel: Sociological, Anthropological, and Political Perspectives* (Cambridge: Cambridge University Press, 1989), 349–69.

[3] Habel, for example, touches on what the land produces on only a few occasions and then only in passing (e.g. Habel, *Land is Mine*, 43, 103).

pressing demands on the biblical scholar. Third, the Bible has traditionally been valued for its profound religious and ethical ideas. Consequently, the focus of much biblical scholarship has been to achieve an understanding of the intellectual and spiritual life of the Israelites, not their bodily appetites. Fourth, two particularly intractable problems in the interpretation of the Old Testament concern food: the meaning and significance of sacrifice and the food laws. One of the principal purposes of sacrifice is to create the appropriate ritual circumstances in which animals might be killed and meat consumed. Yet the possible meanings of sacrifice—if meaning is the right category with which to analyse the issue—has long been an unresolved problem within Old Testament scholarship. The Old Testament dietary laws are also a well-known *crux interpretum*: can we discern their underlying system and logic? These two intellectual problems, dietary laws and sacrifice, have attracted significant scholarly energy and obscured a larger area of potential interest: food. Finally, one of the reasons for the lack of any works on food in twentieth-century scholarship was the comprehensive discussion of food and food-related issues by William Robertson Smith in his *Lectures on the Religion of the Semites*.[4]

A significant part of Smith's celebrated lecture series seeks to show how ideas such as sacrifice, taboo, tithes and covenant had developed out of primitive Semitic communal feasts. Smith's central insight was that 'the fundamental conception of ancient religion is the solidarity of the gods and their worshippers as part of one organic society'.[5] The gods quite literally belong to the same tribe as the worshippers. This community was effected through a communal meal. 'The law of the feast was open-handed hospitality: no sacrifice was complete without guests, and portions were freely distributed to rich and poor within the circle of a man's acquaintance. Universal hilarity prevailed, men ate drank and were merry together, rejoicing before their God.'[6]

Sacrifice in Smith's understanding originated as part of this communal feast in which the whole clan was involved. An essential element of the feast was the consumption of flesh. Indeed, in the early nomadic communities meat was rarely eaten, and it was only at the communal feast that such a special event

---

[4] W. R. Smith, *Lectures on the Religion of the Semites: Their Fundamental Institutions*, 3rd edn. (London: A. & C. Black, 1927). Our concern is primarily with the first series of lectures, since the second and third series of lectures were not published in Smith's lifetime. In addition, the subject matter of the unpublished lectures does not touch on food to the same extent, with the exception of the first lecture from the second series. This lecture addresses the Israelite feasts and is primarily a discussion of calendrical matters (W. R. Smith, *Lectures on the Religion of the Semites: Second and Third Series. Edited with an Introduction and Appendix by John Day*, JSOTSup, 183 (Sheffield: Sheffield Academic Press, 1995), esp. 33–43).

[5] Smith, *Religion of the Semites, First Series*, 32.   [6] Ibid., 254.

took place. Consequently, a feast meant meat, and meat meant a feast.[7] If the consumption of meat creates a community between the gods and men, it also does so between men. A key presupposition of the early Semites was that 'those who eat and drink together are by this very act tied to one another by a bond of friendship and mutual obligation'.[8] The biblical texts that portray the sealing of a covenant by a communal act of eating and drinking bear the imprint of this primitive Semitic idea.[9]

Smith's arguments give historical and logical priority to the communion interpretation of sacrifice. 'The leading idea in the animal sacrifices of the Semites...was not that of a gift made over to the god but of an act of communion, in which the god and his worshippers unite by partaking together of the flesh and blood of a sacred victim.'[10] Sacrifice was a development of the public feast of clansmen, in which the deity is also included.[11] Other theories of sacrifice derive from this as the communal and sacramental theory of sacrifice lost some of its original power. Thus, the interpretation of sacrifice as a gift was a notion transferred from the royal courts of early kingdoms where kings received homage or tribute from their subjects. Similarly, sacrifice as an offering that achieved atonement only developed with later ideas of guilt or obligation. The original Semitic sacrifices were occasions of unalloyed joy and revelry for the tribal community in the presence of their gods.[12]

Smith's ideas about sacrifice also provided an explanation of the Jewish dietary laws. In later forms of Semitic religion a distinction was made between those animals that may ordinarily be sacrificed, and those that were sacrificed only in exceptional circumstances. In the former case, the animal could only be consumed by being brought into the domain of the holy through sacrifice; and, in the latter case, the tabooed animal belonged to the domain of the holy and was prohibited. Behind this distinction Smith perceived a primitive inability to distinguish between the holy and the taboo, which he understood as a relic of early Semitic religion where no distinction was made between ordinary and extraordinary sacrifices, and the killing of any animal was considered a sacrilegious act that could only be done in the presence of the gods and the clan.[13]

Smith's lectures provide a compelling account of the history and development of food and feasting and their relation to key religious ideas and institutions. With a few guiding conceptions Smith is able to produce a comprehensive synthesis that explains sacrifice, public feasting, covenant meals and

---

[7] Smith, *Religion of the Semites, First Series*, 224, 255; cf. 280–1.   [8] Ibid., 265.
[9] Ibid., 271.   [10] Ibid., 226–7.   [11] Ibid., 280.   [12] Ibid., 245–63.
[13] Ibid., 312. For a later critique of this idea, see M. Douglas, *Purity and Danger: An Analysis of the Concepts of Pollution and Taboo* (London: Routledge, 1966), 7–28.

taboo foods. The arguments are supported by evidence drawing widely from classical sources, the Old Testament and nascent comparative anthropology. It is, perhaps, not surprising that subsequent discussions of food, such as the interest in covenant meals, were mere footnotes to Smith's intellectual edifice.[14]

FOOD IN RECENT OLD TESTAMENT SCHOLARSHIP

The credit for observing the absence of food in recent Old Testament scholarship must be given to Rudolf Smend, who as early as 1977 drew attention to this omission. The stimulus for Smend's observation was Walther Zimmerli's considerations of the *Weltlichkeit* of the Old Testament.[15] Zimmerli had argued for the importance of the material world in the theology of the Old Testament and, consequently, for Christian theology. His argument was supported by an examination of the views found in the Old Testament on subjects such as the creation of the world, marriage and sexuality, land and possessions, conduct towards other humans, and life after death. He had, however, omitted any discussion of food and drink in the Old Testament, which Smend identified as a significant lacuna. In Zimmerli's *festschrift* Smend wrote a brief essay on eating and drinking which he offered as an addendum to

[14] See, e.g., W. T. McCree, 'The Covenant Meal in the Old Testament', *JBL* 45 (1926), 120–8; T. H. Gaster, *Thespis: Ritual, Myth and Drama in the Ancient Near East* (New York: Harper & Row, 1950), 372–5; L. Koehler, 'Problems in the Study of the Language of the Old Testament', *JSS* 1 (1956), 3–24, esp. 4–7; D. J. McCarthy, *Old Testament Covenant: A Survey of Current Opinions*, Growing Points in Theology (Oxford: Basil Blackwell, 1972), 30–1, 41–3; A. W. Jenks, 'Eating and Drinking in the Old Testament', in *ABD* 2: 250–4.

   The influence of Smith and the 'covenant meal' are also discernible in Gillian Feeley-Harnik's study of food in early Judaism and Christianity (G. Feeley-Harnik, *The Lord's Table: The Meaning of Food in Early Judaism and Christianity* (Washington: Smithsonian Institution Press, 1981)). Feeley-Harnik's focus is upon the symbolism of food in the Old Testament as it relates to sectarian attitudes to the table in first-century AD Judaism and Christianity. 'The Lord's Table focuses on why and how sectarians in the intertestamental period used dietary rules and other eating practices to address major ethical questions of identity and affiliation in radically changing circumstances' (p. xiii). Controversy over the validity and interpretation of the dietary laws is placed within the wider context of early Jewish food practices. Consequently Feeley-Harnik is interested in the influence of the final form of the Old Testament upon Jewish and Christian thought and the result is a synthetic account of beliefs about food arising from the Old Testament. Feeley-Harnik gives particular attention to the relationships established between God, food and the people consuming it. God demonstrates his power and authority through food, by which he gives life or confers punishment. Those who accept his authority symbolize this through acceptance of his food, whilst rebels seek forbidden food. The eating of the food provided by God is a commensal act, forging relationships with one another and also with God.

[15] W. Zimmerli, *The Old Testament and the World* (Atlanta: John Knox Press, 1976). It should be noted, however, that Zimmerli had briefly considered Israel's ritual feasting.

Zimmerli's work.[16] In his essay Smend warns against interpreting references to eating and drinking in the Old Testament as simply ciphers for the covenant meal, or for a joyful mental state. He considers examples of food as a symbol of distress and happiness, the concerns about sensuality and satiation, and its role in celebrations and other communal events, including the covenant meal.

In recent years the absence of food within the study of the Old Testament, or at least its narrow focus on the questions of sacrifice, food laws and covenant meals, has begun to contrast strongly with other areas of historical study. The subject of 'food and foodways' has become a significant area of intellectual enquiry.[17] Numerous works have been published on food in the classical world;[18] and for the medieval period and onwards the reader is well served with broad surveys and detailed studies.[19] The work on the classical period has even stimulated numerous studies in New Testament. Sustained attention has been given in recent years to issues such as table fellowship, food offered to idols and the application of dietary laws in the nascent Christian church.[20] What has driven this interest in food and drink has not merely been the biological necessity of food as a source of nourishment. Rather it has been the

---

[16] R. Smend, 'Essen und Trinken—Ein Stück Weltlichkeit des Alten Testaments', in H. Donner, R. Hanhart and R. Smend (eds.), *Beiträge zur alttestamentliche Theologie* (Göttingen: Vandenhoeck & Ruprecht, 1977), 447–59.

[17] 'Foodways' are the culinary practices and eating habits of a culture.

[18] Note, *inter alia*, P. Garnsey, *Famine and Food Supply in the Graeco-Roman World: Response to Risk and Crisis* (Cambridge: Cambridge University Press, 1990); P. Garnsey, *Food and Society in Classical Antiquity*, Key Themes in Ancient History (Cambridge: Cambridge University Press, 1999); E. Gowers, *The Loaded Table: Representations of Food in Roman Literature* (Oxford: Oxford University Press, 1993); J. Wilkins, D. Harvey and E. Dobson (eds.), *Food in Antiquity* (Exeter: University of Exeter Press, 1995); J. M. Wilkins and S. Hill, *Food in the Ancient World* (Malden, MA: Blackwell Publishing, 2006).

[19] See, e.g., B. A. Henisch, *Fast and Feast: Food in Medieval Society* (University Park: Pennsylvania State University Press, 1976); S. Mennell, *All Manners of Food: Eating and Taste in England and France from the Middle Ages to the Present*, 2nd edn. (Urbana: University of Illinois Press, 1996); S. W. Mintz, *Sweetness and Power: The Place of Sugar in Modern History* (New York: Penguin Books, 1985); P. Scholliers (ed.), *Food, Drink and Identity: Cooking, Eating and Drinking in Europe since the Middle Ages* (Oxford: Berg, 2001).

[20] See, e.g., C. L. Blomberg, *Contagious Holiness: Jesus' Meals with Sinners*, NSBT (Downers Grove: InterVarsity Press, 2005); W. Braun, *Feasting and Social Rhetoric in Luke 14*, SNTSMS, 85 (Cambridge: Cambridge University Press, 1995); K. Corley, *Private Women, Public Meals: Social Conflict in the Synoptic Tradition* (Peabody, MA: Hendrickson, 1993); J. Fotopoulos, *Food Offered to Idols in Roman Corinth: A Socio-Rhetorical Reconsideration of 1 Corinthians 8:1–11:1*, WUNT, II/151 (Tübingen: Mohr Siebeck, 2003); D. E. Smith, *From Symposium to Eucharist: The Banquet in the Early Christian World* (Minneapolis: Augsburg Fortress, 2003). Note also the SBL unit that in recent years has been devoted to the subject of 'Meals in the Greco-Roman World'. Its aims are described as follows: 'The Greco-Roman banquet, which was a complex and highly influential hellenistic institution, will be explored as a lens into Greco-Roman social bonding and boundaries and as a pivotal consideration in reconstructing the history of early Christianity and Judaism'.

cultural and social uses of food. Food is basic to life, but it is also an important social, cultural and economic marker. In the words of Claude Lévi-Strauss, one of the most important and influential theorists on food and its role in society, food is 'bon à penser'.

In the last decade or so, the possibility that food might not only be good to eat, but also good to think has begun to become apparent to a small number of Old Testament scholars. In 1995 Rolf Knierim observed the absence of the subject in biblical theology.

The lack of biblical studies on food is strikingly evident in the history of Old and New Testament theologies. Despite the biblical evidence, the issues of food has never received attention worthy of a chapter in a theology, let alone the issues of its function in the whole of biblical theology—as if it were theologically irrelevant![21]

In the light of this observation Knierim composed a short essay on the theology of food in the Old Testament relating the subject to two topics that have received far more attention: land and justice. Four years later, Athalya Brenner and Jan Willem van Henten noted that 'hardly any works are to be found on cooking, eating and drinking in the worlds of the Bible'.[22] Consequently they sought to alert the biblical guild to this 'exciting new theme' and edited a *Semeia* volume with essays devoted to food and drink, examining the subject primarily from a social-scientific, a socio-critical or a literary perspective.[23] In recent years the clarion call of Knierim, Brenner and van Henten has been answered with a number of monographs that examine the subject of food in the Old Testament. These studies can be classified according to the different perspectives found in the *Semeia* volume on food.

Food in Social-scientific Perspective: Eleonore Schmitt

The most comprehensive academic study of the material production of food in ancient Israel and its symbolic significance is found in Eleonore Schmitt's *Das*

[21] R. P. Knierim, 'Food, Land and Justice', *The Task of Old Testament Theology: Substance, Methods and Cases* (Grand Rapids: Eerdmans, 1995), 225–43, here 226.

[22] A. Brenner and J. W. van Henten, 'Food and Drink in the Bible: an Exciting New Theme', in J. W. Dyk et al. (eds.), *Unless Someone Guide Me . . . : Festschrift for Karel A. Deurloo*, Amsterdamse Cahiers voor Exegese van de Bijbel en zijn Tradities Supplement Series, 2 (Maastricht: Uitgeverij Shaker Publishing, 2001), 347–54, here 349. This essay is a revised version of A. Brenner and J. W. van Henten, 'Our Menu and What Is Not On It: Editor's Introduction', in A. Brenner and J. W. van Henten (eds.), *Food and Drink in the Biblical Worlds*, Semeia, 86 (Atlanta: Society of Biblical Literature, 1999), pp. ix–xvi.

[23] Social-Scientific perspective: Brumberg-Kraus, Davies, Frick, Matthews, Tomson; Socio-Critical: Brenner, Corley, McKinlay; Literary: Appler, Carroll, Sharon.

Essen in der Bibel: Literaturethnologische Aspekte des Alltäglichen.[24] Schmitt's work, which appeared in 1994 prior to the essays of Knierim, Brenner and van Henten, is the first attempt to draw upon the extensive research on the anthropology of food and apply it to biblical texts other than the food laws and sacrifice. In two chapters anthropological studies on food and biblical scholarship on food are reviewed. Two further chapters examine food in the biblical texts. The first utilizes Goody's model of production–distribution–preparation–consumption–disposal, augmented with the additional category of 'selection', to examine the socio-material context of food.[25] Goody's model allows Schmitt to consider all aspects of food production and consumption in ancient Israel comprehensively. The second is an examination of the religious and social significance of food. Schmitt considers food as a means of character-izing individuals and situations, as a narrative tool to signal scene changes, the use of gastronomic metaphors and its association with other biblical motifs such as poverty, blessing or death.

Schmitt's book is a valuable contribution to the subject of food in the Bible, and its application of the anthropology of food beyond the food laws is an important development. Nevertheless, the attempt to deal comprehensively with food across both testaments in relatively short compass means many interesting topics receive only a brief treatment. In addition, Schmitt's work views food and its symbolism in a static manner, drawing material from across the Bible to produce a synthetic account. The distinctive use by different bib-lical writers or the possibility of historical change finds no place in Schmitt's discussion.

Food in Socio-critical Perspective: Judith McKinlay, Juliana Claassens and Ken Stone

As the title suggests, Judith McKinlay's *Gendering Wisdom the Host: Biblical Invitations to Eat and Drink* is primarily concerned with questions of gender.[26] McKinlay begins with the observation that in Proverbs 9, Ecclesiasticus 24 and

---

[24] E. Schmitt, *Das Essen in der Bibel: Literaturethnologische Aspekte des Alltäglichen*, Studien zur Kulturanthropologie, 2 (Münster: Lit, 1994). Schmitt's volume, originally a doctoral thesis submitted to the University of Mainz, is unfortunately overlooked by Brenner and van Houten, who wrote in 1999, 'To the best of our knowledge, there is no volume on the market—be it a monograph or an anthology—that has food and drink in the Bible and related texts as its center' (Brenner and van Henten, 'Our Menu', p. x).

[25] See J. Goody, *Cooking, Cuisine and Class: A Study in Comparative Sociology*, Themes in the Social Sciences (Cambridge: Cambridge University Press, 1982).

[26] J. E. McKinlay, *Gendering Wisdom the Host: Biblical Invitations to Eat and Drink*, JSOTSup, 216 (Sheffield: Sheffield Academic Press, 1996).

John 4 we have three invitations to eat and drink that appear to stand in an intertextual relationship with one another. Whilst the content of the invitation is relatively constant, the host undergoes significant changes. 'First Wisdom, then Wisdom/Sophia, and third Jesus; not only a change of inviter, but a change of gender. The once host/ess has seemingly become a host.'[27] The one to whom the invitation is issued also changes: the young man of Proverbs 9 becomes the Samaritan woman of John 4.

The feminist reader cannot overlook these changes because they might have important consequences for the perception of gender and sexual relations. McKinlay's study is an attempt to investigate this change and is consequently an examination of the three passages and the portrayal of women in the books of Proverbs, Ecclesiasticus and John. At stake for McKinlay is the question of whether we have an incorporation of the feminine into the divine, or the exorcizing of feminist elements by the masculine Jesus. In her view, 'the use of the Wisdom material in John's Gospel is not so much the Christian statement of the culmination of Wisdom expressing the feminine divine, but the final stage of the long process of the masculinization of Wisdom'.[28] It is apparent, then, that the presence of language about eating and drinking is peripheral to McKinlay's concerns. This is especially clear in her suggestion that the process she discerns in the biblical tradition was already underway in Proverbs 9, where McKinlay suspects goddess language has been appropriated. This is hardly a novel suggestion, and the evidence is well rehearsed along with a detailed examination of what is known about the goddess Asherah. What McKinlay overlooks, however, is the absence of any references to Asherah as a *host*.[29] The alimentary imagery is omitted

---

[27] Ibid., 11.   [28] Ibid., 240.

[29] Esp. ibid., 17–37. The presentation of Athirat in the Ugaritic texts is discussed, *inter alia*, by Binger (T. Binger, *Asherah: Goddesses in Ugarit, Israel and the Old Testament*, JSOTSup, 232 (Sheffield: Sheffield Academic Press, 1997)) and Hadley (J. M. Hadley, *The Cult of Asherah in Ancient Israel and Judah: Evidence for a Hebrew Goddess*, University of Cambridge Oriental Publications, 57 (Cambridge: Cambridge University Press, 2000), 38–53). The only text concerning Asherah that touches upon hosting is peculiarly inapt for McKinlay's argument: 'As soon as El sees her, | he opens his mouth and laughs. | He set his foot on the footstool | and turns his fingers round. | He lifts his voice and sh[outs]: | Why has Athirat, Lady Day, come? | Why has the creatress of the gods arrived? | If you are very hungry and want [to eat] | If you are very thirsty and want [to drink] | Eat or drink! | Eat of the food on the tables! | Drink of the wine in the cups! | Blood of the trees from a golden beaker. | Or is it the 'hand' of the king, of El, that excites | you the love of the Bull that arouses you?' (*KTU* 1.4 IV 27–39; Binger's translation). Here it is El that is host at the feast with food a metaphor for intercourse. The juxtaposition of a feast prepared by El and sexual intercourse is also found in 'The Feast of the Goodly Gods': 'As for El, his staff descends (?) | As for El, his love-shaft droops (?). | He lifts (his hand), he shoots skyward, | He shoots in the sky a bird, | He plucks, sets (it) on the coals; | El indeed entices the two females' (*KTU* 1.23 35–9; Smith's translation). Smith takes the roasting imagery as a metaphor for El's conquest of the two goddesses, an interpretation which is also appropriate for El's enticement of Athirat in *KTU* 1.4 IV (M. S. Smith, *The Rituals and Myths of the Feast of the Goodly Gods*

when it no long serves the socio-critical argument that McKinlay wants
to make.

A more conservative feminist approach is to be found in Juliana Claassens's
analysis of the metaphor of divine provision.[30] Claassens wishes to extend the
metaphorical images for God employed within the Christian tradition and
particularly those images which have female associations. Her study traces the
idea of divine provision from Israel's experience in the wilderness through
the threat of loss as a result of covenant curses and promised restoration.
She argues that the metaphor of provision is not gender neutral, but an
important maternal image that portrays God as a mother caring for her children's needs, whilst also disciplining and teaching. The approach is biblical-
theological and operates on the level of the final form of the text in dialogue with traditional Christian and Jewish interpretations. Claassens's study
is valuable if somewhat restricted in its interests and having a tendency to
interpret even neutral descriptions of divine provision as evidence of female
imagery.

The most sophisticated use of socio-critical hermeneutics is in the work by
the queer theorist Ken Stone entitled *Practicing Safer Texts: Food, Sex and Bible
in Queer Perspective*.[31] His book analyses just some of the many texts in the
Old Testament that juxtapose sex and food, and shows how these two cultural
domains shed light upon each other. In yet another appropriation of Claude
Lévi-Strauss's famous dictum that food is not so much good to eat as good to
think, Stone follows the anthropologist Donald Pollock in arguing that food
and sex are good to think each other. More than that, Stone wishes to argue
that 'food and sex are "good to think" the nature and goals of a safer biblical
interpretation in the contemporary world'.[32]

The chapters of Stone's book do not form a linear argument, but a series of
overlapping studies that touch each other at various points. Stone examines
diet and sexual practices as boundary markers of the community, and argues
that such markers need to be subjected to rigorous interrogation and desta-
bilization. He considers the public implications of sex and food in 2 Samuel
and Genesis in order to undermine the commonly assumed division between

---

of KTU/CAT 1.23: Royal Constructions of Opposition, Intersection, Integration, and Domination,
Resources for Biblical Study, 51 (Atlanta: Society of Biblical Literature, 2006), 83–8). Thus, not
only can the trajectory of female hostess to male host not be sustained by an examination of the
Ugaritic literature that McKinlay uses to support her claims about the presence of a goddess in
ancient Israelite religion, but the hosting is related to El's sexual seduction.

[30] L. J. M. Claassens, *The God Who Provides: Biblical Images of Divine Nourishment* (Nashville:
Abingdon Press, 2004).

[31] K. Stone, *Practicing Safer Texts: Food, Sex and Bible in Queer Perspective*, Queering Theology
Series (London: T&T Clark International, 2005).

[32] Ibid., 22.

public and private life. Through an analysis of 2 Samuel 13 and the Song of Songs he argues that sex and food have the potential to bring pleasure and danger to those who partake. From the portrayal of YHWH in Hosea Stone argues that the provision of food for the family and the control of female sexuality are interrelated matters of male honour. Such agonistic male norms are as endangering to female flourishing as to male, and consequently are in need of deconstruction. Finally, Stone turns to the portrayal of food and sex in the Wisdom literature, arguing that we have in Ecclesiastes a positive message 'that enjoyment of the bodily pleasures of food, drink and sex is one of the best things we can do with our lives, and has been ordained by God'.[33]

Stone's suggestion that food and sex are good to think each other suggests that his reading of the biblical texts will pose ideological and moral challenges to how we think about food and sex. Indeed, in his first chapter he seeks to undermine the tendency of modern biblical readers to overstress the gravity of sexual matters in comparison to food. Examining the story of Adam and Eve in Genesis 2–3 Stone argues that the story is as much about food as it is about sex. Modern scholars and readers of the text overwhelmingly understand the story to be establishing heterosexuality as a creation norm. Yet the story can be seen to be as much about desire for food, as indeed was the case in much early Christian interpretation. The ethical and theological significance of food is a point well made—particularly, one would have thought, in a world where access to food is so inequitable—but Stone's subsequent interpretations of biblical texts and the hermeneutical implications that he adduces from his interpretations prioritize sexuality to the detriment of food issues. This is, perhaps, hardly surprising given Stone's self-identification as a gay man who is also a biblical scholar working in a context where the place of homosexual believers within many Christian denominations is clearly under negotiation. Food is indeed a more important ethical issue than is usually allowed in the Western Christian tradition, but it is difficult for Stone to avoid the existential import of his particular context. In addition, many of the biblical passages that Stone examines use food to speak about sex, rather than the reverse. Thus, Nathan's parable of the poor man's lamb serves to confront David with his crime against Bathsheba and Uriah (2 Sam. 12), whilst in the Song of Songs food items are metaphors of parts of the body, and consumption, of sexual acts. In Stone's book, then, food is really only a vehicle to talk about sex, despite protestations to the contrary.

---

[33] Ibid., 149.

Food in Literary Perspective: Diane Sharon

Diane Sharon's *Patterns of Destiny: Narrative Structures of Foundation and Doom in the Hebrew Bible* seeks to examine the function of eating and drinking within biblical narratives.[34] Utilizing the structuralist methodology of the Russian folklorist Vladimir Propp, Sharon argues that eating and drinking appears as a constant, a structurally constitutive component of the narrative, in two narrative patterns. In the first pattern, the Establishment/Foundation Genre, the eating or drinking event is followed by a positive oracle; in the Condemnation/Doom Genre the eating or drinking event is followed by an oracle of doom. The description of the eating or drinking event provides clues to the nature of the destiny portended.

An example of Sharon's exegesis is her examination of Abraham's entertainment of the three visitors in Genesis 18. The three men arrive at Abraham's tent, where they are given a meal. There is a verbal encounter during which an oracle is given promising Abraham and Sarah a son. The men depart, after which YHWH affirms the oracle in a soliloquy (Gen. 18.18–19). An annuciation does not require an eating or drinking event argues Sharon. Yet here we have a Foundation pattern where Abraham's line is being established through Sarah, thus 'it is no accident that...an eating and drinking event appears in this text'.[35]

Sharon's work makes a valuable contribution to the understanding of the role of eating and drinking, not only in biblical narratives, for she also traces the pattern in ancient Near Eastern texts as early as the third millennium BC. She demonstrates how frequently events of eating and drinking occur in ancient texts and presses for an explanation of this phenomenon. Her work has, however, an involved methodology and it is this, rather than any explorations of the literary role of eating and drinking, that Sharon envisages as the primary contribution of her research. Her work is not immune to the criticism often brought against structuralist theory that its cumbersome methodologies produce relatively modest results.

OUTLINE OF WORK

Our review of recent literature demonstrates the capacity of this subject, food in the Old Testament, to enlighten relatively unexplored aspects of the

---

[34] D. M. Sharon, *Patterns of Destiny: Narrative Structures of Foundation and Doom in the Hebrew Bible* (Winona Lake, IN: Eisenbrauns, 2002).

[35] Ibid., 127.

Israelite world and to provoke new interpretations of familiar biblical texts. Such a survey, however, also highlights certain dangers. First, it is possible for the subject to be overwhelmed by the methodological approach. This issue is especially apparent in socio-critical hermeneutics, where a laudable concern with the ethical or unethical utilization of the text in the present day is the primary stimulus for the hermeneutical method. Food is only interesting to the extent that it sheds light on constructions of gender and sexuality. To describe this as a problem is not, of course, to hold that these matters are unimportant, but only to argue that food's symbolic palette is much richer and more extensive than such studies suggest and worthy of analysis in its own right. Second, the studies that we have examined pay little heed to the historical issues which scholars of the past have felt so pressing. Socio-critical and literary approaches usually engage with the biblical text in its final form and as that text bears on the reader as an ethical or aesthetic being. Historical issues are only of relevance to the extent that they bear on or enlighten the interpretation of the text in the present. In the case of McKinlay's book a critical awareness of historical issues substantially undermines the argument she wishes to make. Schmitt's work, on the other hand, with its socio-scientific methodology, is required to be historically aware, but the assumption underlying the work appears to be that food production and the symbolism of food are fairly static through Israel's history.

The chapters that follow seek to examine some of the many symbolic resonances of food and drink. They make use of both literary and historical approaches. In addition, they utilize some of the numerous anthropological studies of food in human cultures. The nature of the material means that what is offered is not a sustained argument, but a series of interrelated studies. I have prepared, so to speak, a meal with a number of courses, rather than a single dish.

The present state of biblical studies and the questions that we have raised about the existing studies on food in the Old Testament means that the question of methodology cannot be avoided. How have I prepared the meal that you, as reader, are about to enjoy? In seeking to do justice to the insights of anthropological studies, the biblical text's literary nature and the many perplexing historical questions, I wish to propose a methodology that is self-consciously pluralistic. This stems from a belief that no one method produces *the* interpretation of biblical texts and that decisions about the appropriateness of many methods cannot be made *a priori*. Expressed in alimentary imagery it would be a foolish chef who limited himself to one way of cooking or to one set of ingredients. Baking, braising, boiling, frying all have their place, as do

cumin, pepper, oregano and thyme. The culinary creation cannot be judged
on the basis of its components or the methods of cookery used. The proof of
the pudding is in the eating.

The first chapter, therefore, seeks to articulate a methodological approach
to the study of food in the Old Testament that is fully responsive to research on
the anthropology of food, the literary form of the biblical text and historical-
critical biblical scholarship. The necessity of all these aspects will be demonstrated through an analysis of work on the Israelite dietary laws in Leviticus 11
and Deuteronomy 14. For this classical interpretative puzzle Mary Douglas's
work, *Purity and Danger*, has been a decisive turning point. Her analysis
has stimulated many biblical scholars, but this has required her own views
to be re-articulated in light of closer readings of the text and the work of
historical-critical scholarship. The conversation not only shows the need for
well informed use of anthropological research, literary analysis and historical-
critical scholarship, but also the necessity of moving beyond tired debates
between materialists and structuralists, or, in the usual terms of biblical scholarship, diachronic and synchronic.

The second chapter demonstrates how a careful coordination of historical
and literary issues might enlighten our understanding of an issue such as
the diet of the ancient Israelites. The Old Testament portrayal of Canaan as
a 'land flowing with milk and honey' has determined many assessments of
the Israelite diet. These fail to take into account the literary and rhetorical
nature of the biblical materials. They also fail to make critical use of the many
available resources from archaeology, palaeopathology, archaeozoology and
comparative anthropology. The more realistic assessment of Israelite diet that
is offered owes much to Peter Garnsey's studies of food issues in the classical
world. Garnsey pioneered the utilization of nutritional anthropology in the
study of Graeco-Roman diet and society, convincingly demonstrating the
frequency of food scarcity and the poor diet of most subjects of the Roman
empire.

The third chapter applies recent anthropological work by David Sutton
on the relationship between memory and food to the book of Deuteronomy.
Rhetorically poised between the wilderness and the Promised Land, Deuteronomy uses food as a vehicle for articulating Israel's memory of exodus, wilderness and conquest. In doing so it takes a number of radical departures from
the book of Exodus in its description of the Canaanite cult and in defining
Israelite religion focused around pilgrimage feasts to the chosen cultic place.
The book also defines the identity of the chosen people through narratives of
hospitality or inhospitality that underline its requirement to offer food to the
poor and vulnerable.

The fourth chapter utilizes Mary Douglas's theories of *matter out of place* to consider the use of food in the book of Judges. According to Douglas the Israelite dietary laws catalogued animals according to their physical domains. Clean animals had certain characteristics appropriate to those domains. Animals lacking those characteristics are *out of place* and deemed unclean. In Deuteronomistic ideology sacrifice, food, warfare and sexual intercourse occupy separate domains that should not be confused. The book of Joshua is exemplary in maintaining the boundaries between these domains. In Judges, however, these boundaries are frequently transgressed. In this way the book conveys the dissolution of Israelite society prior to the establishment of the monarchy.

Although food is often viewed as a conservative element in society it can also have a role in social change as recent work on feasting has sought to demonstrate. In Chapter 5 the development of Israel from a segmentary society to a monarchy is re-examined. Whilst early proponents of the use of social-scientific methods made significant gains in their analysis of early Israelite society, their work had numerous gaps. One of these was the use of agricultural surpluses and how these were controlled and invested to drive forwards technological and social change. Recent anthropological work on feasting allows this lacuna to be filled, whilst also highlighting that the Old Testament literature was conscious of the importance of food circulation in the social and political economy of the Israelite kingdoms.

The sixth chapter examines the symbolism of the table as the context for divine and human judgement. The association of the table with the feasting of the king and his officials may lie behind this idea. The use of the symbolism and its inversion will be examined especially in the books of Samuel and Kings. This motif may provide an explanation for the otherwise mysterious conclusion of the Deuteronomistic History with Jehoiachin's elevation to the table of Evil-Merodach. The relationship between table and judgement is also expressed in imagery such as the 'cup of wrath' and Psalm 23's overflowing cup. An important development for later Jewish and Christian thought is found in Isaiah 25, where the image of the table is transported into the eschatological future.

The post-exilic period is often thought to see important developments in the food consciousness of the Israelites, usually in relation to the dietary laws. In Chapter 7 the fascination with the feasting habits of the Persians will demonstrate that there was another aspect to this developing religious consciousness. The Persians indulge in conspicuous consumption, which both fascinates and repels the writers of Jewish narrative. The characterization of the Persians is important for establishing the nature of Jewish identity, which

is exhibited in a moderate attitude towards food. Similar ideas in relation to Greek identity are found in the work of Greek historians. In the Jewish writings this theme is combined with the idea of divine judgement at the table. The table, thus, becomes the place at which ungodliness or righteousness is expressed and punished or rewarded.

The volume concludes with a brief consideration of how some of the aspects of food in the Old Testament find resonance in the books of the New Testament.

1

Food, Anthropology, Text and History

Food is a subject that has rarely been examined within the Old Testament. It is, indeed, an 'exciting new theme', but how is such a theme to be approached? As we have already seen, there exist a small number of studies that examine aspects of the subject. These, however, do so from particular hermeneutical standpoints that narrow the field of enquiry or from the perspective of another theme. In such studies food is displaced from the centre of enquiry, and becomes a means to another end rather than a subject of study in its own right. This is perhaps not surprising since the ubiquity of the subject within the biblical text means that some method must be employed to make the material manageable.

If our aim is to place food at the centre of academic investigation and to be sensitive to its various symbolic resonances, how might this be done? In the following pages I wish to examine the scholarship on the biblical food laws in Leviticus 11 and Deuteronomy 14 in order to ground a methodological pluralism. Since Mary Douglas's seminal work in the 1960s there have been numerous studies of the dietary laws, some of which have disputed her conclusions and offered alternative construals, others that have sought to correct or supplement her work. Some of the discussion has been focused around two methodological extremes: a structuralist approach, on the one hand, and a materialist approach, on the other hand. Additionally, there have been other aspects to the discussion stemming from the particular issues raised by the biblical texts: the problem of two related versions of the dietary laws in Leviticus and Deuteronomy, the questions of historical criticism and the use of archaeological and other historical research. I will examine this discussion and show how light has been shed on the dietary laws from a variety of theoretical perspectives. In this way it can be seen that various methodological approaches are needed in order to understand a complex and intriguing biblical text.

The purpose of this chapter, consequently, is not to provide a comprehensive survey of the different theories about the food laws. These exist in abundance, and there is surely no need to duplicate information that can be found elsewhere. The challenge of the biblical dietary laws does not lie in a

lack of efforts to describe the problem.[1] Nor do I intend to add to the list of theories. Milgrom is tempted into hyperbole when he remarks that 'there are as many theories as theorists',[2] but not without justification when some scholars are able to propose more than one theory.[3] My purpose is merely to argue for the importance of a plurality of methodological approaches when examining a subject such as food in the Old Testament.

EARLY MARY DOUGLAS

Mary Douglas's interpretation of the dietary laws is, without question, the most influential contribution to the subject in modern times. Her impact on biblical studies would have been considerable if limited to this subject alone but, as it is, her work on impurity is wide-ranging and relevant to a number of biblical texts. Douglas's work on the dietary laws divides into two clear phases. The first exposition of the laws occurs in her seminal work on pollution and taboo, *Purity and Danger*, published in 1966.[4] The limitations of this first brief discussion necessitated extending and clarifying her exposition in a number of essays appearing in the early 1970s.[5] After about twenty years Douglas returned to the dietary laws and to the priestly material in the Old Testament more generally.[6] There are strong continuities with her earlier work, but there

---

[1] See, e.g., Feeley-Harnik, *Lord's Table*, 6–18; G. J. Wenham, 'The Theology of Unclean Food', *Evangelical Quarterly* 53 (1981), 6–15; K.-K. Chan, 'You Shall not Eat These Abominable Things: An Examination of Different Interpretations on Deuteronomy 14.3–20', *East Asian Journal of Theology* 3 (1985), 88–106; W. J. Houston, *Purity and Monotheism: Clean and Unclean Animals in Biblical Law*, JSOTSup, 140 (Sheffield: JSOT Press, 1993); J. Duhaime, 'Lois alimentaires et pureté corporelle dans le Lévitique: L'approche de Mary Douglas et sa réception par Jacob Milgrom', *Religiologiques* 17 (1998), 19–35; J. Moskala, *The Laws of Clean and Unclean Animals in Leviticus 11: Their Nature, Theology and Rationale, an Intertextual Study*, Adventist Theological Society Dissertation Series (Berrien Springs, MI: Adventist Theological Society Publications, 2000), 15–159; J. Moskala, 'Categorization and Evaluation of Different Kinds of Interpretation of the Laws of Clean and Unclean Animals in Leviticus 11', *Biblical Research* 46 (2001), 5–41; W. J. Houston, 'Towards an Integrated Reading of the Dietary Laws of Leviticus', in R. Rendtorff and R. A. Kugler (eds.), *The Book of Leviticus: Composition and Reception* (Leiden: Brill, 2003), 142–61; S. D. Kunin, *We Think What We Eat: Neo-Structuralist Analysis of Israelite Food Rules and Other Cultural and Textual Practices*, JSOTSup, 412 (London: Continuum, 2004), 31–83.

[2] J. Milgrom, *Leviticus 1–16*, AB, 3 (New York: Doubleday, 1991), 718.

[3] I am thinking, of course, of Mary Douglas, who proposed at least three different theories.

[4] Douglas, *Purity and Danger*.

[5] M. Douglas, *Natural Symbols: Explorations in Cosmology* (London: Routledge, 1970; rev. edn. 1996), 37–41; M. Douglas, 'Deciphering a Meal', in *Implicit Meanings* (London: Routledge, 1975), 249–75; M. Douglas, 'Self-Evidence', in *Implicit Meanings* (London: Routledge, 1975), 276–318.

[6] M. Douglas, 'The Forbidden Animals in Leviticus', *JSOT* 59 (1993), 3–23; M. Douglas, *Leviticus as Literature* (Oxford: Oxford University Press, 1999); M. Douglas, 'The Compassionate

has been some considerable rethinking of the function of the dietary laws in ancient Judaism. This second phase of Douglas's work will be considered later in this chapter, but at this point we will examine her initial contributions to the subject.

Mary Douglas's 'The Abominations of Leviticus'

Douglas's first foray into the subject of the biblical dietary laws is a chapter entitled 'The Abominations of Leviticus' in *Purity and Danger*. Her concern in that celebrated work is to understand concepts of contagion in non-Western cultures and to demonstrate the rationality of primitive ritual. Two principles inform Douglas in this exercise. First, it is necessary to approach concepts of defilement as entire systems, and not in a piecemeal fashion. Second, Douglas follows Durkheim in understanding ritual as symbolic of social processes.

If we are to understand primitive understandings of contagion Douglas argues that we must eschew medical materialism. This understands rituals either as inchoate and intuitive expressions of hygiene, which can be explained by scientific means, or as incoherent attempts to deal with pollution that need to be replaced by scientific insight. In the first case the symbolic and religious significance of ritual have been degraded into a bare medical functionalism, and in the second case the clear similarities between primitive and modern practices of purification are obscured. To move beyond these unsatisfactory positions, Douglas argues, we must view pollution as a contravention of an ordered set of relations. Pollution, or dirt, is 'matter out of place': 'To conclude, if uncleanness is matter out of place, we must approach it through order. Uncleanness or dirt is that which must not be included if a pattern is to be maintained. To recognise this is the first step towards insight into pollution.'[7]

It is in this context that Douglas introduces her interpretation of the biblical dietary laws. The dietary laws are not only a well-known textual puzzle, but the various solutions that had been proposed illustrate the flawed approaches to primitive understandings of contagion that Douglas had identified. The avoidance of the prohibited animals was either taken to have a

---

God of Leviticus and his Animal Creation', in M. O'Kane (ed.), *Borders, Boundaries, and the Bible*, JSOTSup 313 (London: Sheffield Academic Press, 2002), 61–73; M. Douglas, 'Impurity of Land Animals', in M. Poorthuis and J. Schwartz (eds.), *Purity and Holiness: The Heritage of Leviticus* (Leiden: Brill, 2000), 33–45; M. Douglas, *Jacob's Tears: The Priestly Work of Reconciliation* (Oxford: Oxford University Press, 2004).

[7] Douglas, *Purity and Danger*, 41.

sound medical basis, with ingenious attempts to provide a scientific justification of the rules,[8] or was understood as an arbitrary and irrational divine commandment.[9] Douglas's own interpretation of the food laws is brief and is merely meant to illustrate the benefits of viewing the laws as a coherent system.

Douglas places the dietary laws in the context of the priestly theology of holiness. Holiness means both separateness and wholeness. Wholeness means physical perfection: sacrifices must not be blemished and those with bodily discharges are excluded from the temple until they are purified. The concern for wholeness is also expressed in the rejection of hybrids and other confusions. Bestiality is prohibited, as are breeding different animals, sowing a field with two crops, or wearing a garment with mixed fibres. Holiness is completeness and 'requires that individuals shall conform to the class to which they belong'.[10] In the priestly view, these classes are derived from creation.

The dietary laws develop the theology of holiness along the same lines. Working with the common assumption at the time that the early Israelites were originally pastoralists, Douglas begins with the livestock the Israelites kept. Cattle, sheep and goats were the livelihood of the Israelites and were, by definition, proper food. Wild animals were not hunted frequently, but if they were they needed to have similar habits. In other words, they needed to be ruminants. Wild animals that failed to correspond, that is, neither having cloven hooves nor chewing the cud, were unclean. In this way domesticated animals that were not ruminants, such as the pig or the camel, were also excluded. The rest of the animal world is dealt with according to the three domains described in the Genesis 1 creation story: the earth, the waters and the sky. Every animal belongs to one of these domains, and each domain is defined, in Douglas's view, by a distinctive form of locomotion. Animals

---

[8]   See, for example, the attempt by D. I. Macht to demonstrate the relative toxicity of the muscle juices of forbidden animals (D. I. Macht, 'An Experimental Pharmacological Appreciation of Leviticus 11 and Deuteronomy 14', *Bulletin of the History of Medicine* 27 (1953), 444–50).

[9]   Douglas's instincts to see a single system are apparent in her understanding of earlier attempts to explain the dietary laws. In her presentation of the history of scholarship Douglas notes the tradition amongst Anglo-Saxon Old Testament scholars 'to say simply that the rules are arbitrary because they are irrational' (Douglas, *Purity and Danger*, 46). In support Douglas quotes R. S. (*sic*) Driver's commentary on Deuteronomy. Driver writes, 'No single principle, embracing all the cases, seems yet to have been found, and not improbably more principles than one co-operated. Some animals may have been prohibited on account of their repulsive appearance or uncleanly habits, others upon sanitary grounds; in other cases, again, the motive of the prohibition may very probably have been a religious one...' (Douglas, *Purity and Danger*, 46). In Douglas's eyes 'more principles than one' means none, and the rules are arbitrary and irrational. This is undoubtedly a misreading of Driver, but illustrates well Douglas's objection to reading the dietary laws in a piecemeal fashion.

[10]   Douglas, *Purity and Danger*, 54.

that do not exhibit an appropriate form of movement are unclean. On the earth four-legged animals ought to hop, jump or walk. Those animals which creep, crawl or swarm on the earth are unclean (Lev. 11.41–4). As are those animals endowed with hands that use those hands for walking: the weasel, the mouse, the crocodile, the shrew, lizards, the chameleon and the mole (vv. 27–31). In the waters clean animals should swim. Fish with scales and fins are deemed clean, whilst all other marine animals are unclean (vv. 9–12). Animals that live in the air must have two feet and fly. Douglas offers little comment on the list of unclean birds (vv. 13–19) because no criteria for determining clean and unclean are given, and many of the names are uncertain. The situation is clearer with insects. Winged insects with four legs that fly are unclean, whilst insects that hop, locusts, crickets and grasshoppers, are clean because they are denizens of the land, and not of the air (vv. 20–3).

The Strengths and Weaknesses of 'The Abominations of Leviticus'

Our purpose in this chapter is to show the kinds of consideration that must be brought to bear on the biblical texts when studying the subject of food in the Old Testament, it is not to provide a comprehensive interpretation of the biblical dietary laws. Therefore, it is not necessary to consider in detail every criticism or modification of Douglas's theory. As an original and suggestive interpretation it has naturally received a great deal of attention. Her theoretical approach and her consistency in applying it have been examined by anthropologists.[11] Aspects of her exegesis have been shown by biblical scholars to be based on misunderstandings or in need of adjustment.[12] Nevertheless, Douglas's work is a decisive moment in the interpretation of the dietary laws and a number of biblical scholars have accepted her interpretation as

[11] See, *inter alia*, M. Harris, *Good to Eat: Riddles of Food and Culture* (London: Allen & Unwin, 1986), 67–87; Kunin, *We Think What We Eat*, 29–66.

[12] Milgrom lists a number of technical mistakes in Douglas's exegesis (Milgrom, *Leviticus 1–16*, 720–1; cf. J. Milgrom, 'Ethics and Ritual: The Foundations of the Biblical Dietary Laws', in E. B. Firmage, B. G. Weiss and J. W. Welch (eds.), *Religion and Law: Biblical-Judaic and Islamic Perspectives* (Winona Lake, IN: Eisenbrauns, 1990), 159–91). Various other problems with 'The Abominations of Leviticus' as an interpretation of the biblical text are noted by R. Alter, 'A New Theory of Kashrut', *Commentary* 68 (1979), 46–52; H. Eilberg-Schwartz, 'Creation and Classification in Judaism: From Priestly to Rabbinic Conceptions', *History of Religions* 26 (1987), 357–81; M. P. Carroll, 'One More Time: Leviticus Revisited', in B. Lang (ed.), *Anthropological Approaches to the Old Testament*, Issues in Religion and Theology, 8 (Philadelphia: Fortress Press, 1985), 117–26; E. B. Firmage, 'The Biblical Dietary Laws and the Concept of Holiness', in J. A. Emerton (ed.), *Studies in the Pentateuch*, VTSup, 41 (Leiden: Brill, 1990), 177–208; Houston, *Purity and Monotheism*, 93–114.

essentially correct.[13] That someone who is not a specialist biblical scholar should make such a contribution is noteworthy and the reasons for it merit attention.

First, the success of Douglas's work stems from her close attention to the biblical texts. She quotes extensively from Leviticus and Deuteronomy and discusses relevant texts besides those that concern clean and unclean foods. This attention to the wider biblical context is matched by an attention to the detailed interpretation of particular words and phrases. Sparse in references to secondary material, it, nevertheless, exhibits familiarity with the work of biblical scholars. Second, and closely related, Douglas places the food laws in the intellectual world of the priestly writer (P). Douglas showed herself to be sensitive not only to the historical-critical work of the previous century, but also to its manner of operation. This is combined with an intuitive feeling and respect for the ritual concerns of the priestly school. By prefixing her discussion of the food laws with an account of the intellectual history of anthropological work on primitive ritual she effectively allowed the pervasive influence of the nineteenth century's anti-ritualism to become apparent without directly confronting its frequent manifestation in Old Testament scholarship. The point that P needed to be taken more seriously is made graciously and effectively. Third, Douglas's work came to prominence at one of those periodic moments when there was dissatisfaction in the biblical guild with treating the biblical texts in an atomized and fragmented manner. Where hygiene theories make the dietary laws a historical singularity and theories of their arbitrary nature make them an undigested bolus from an earlier period, Douglas's dietary laws have a place as part of a coherent symbolic universe created by the priestly writer. At the level of the dietary laws alone Douglas's interpretation largely succeeds in seeing the laws as a unified system. Locomotion is a persuasive account of the laws' unity that can appeal to certain textual details.

For all its advantages, and an almost uncritical acceptance by some biblical scholars, Douglas's interpretation does suffer from a number of weaknesses. First, locomotion is not only questionable in its details—*kaf*, 'paw', is incorrectly rendered as hands in the case of the eight land-based animals that walk on all fours (vv. 27–31)—but also fails to account for the prohibition of the larger land animals (vv. 4–8) as well as the list of twenty winged creatures (vv. 13–19). In the case of the camel, the hare and the hyrax it is unclear why their failure to have cloven hooves should result in their exclusion as food. Perhaps land animals require cloven hooves in order to move appropriately, but this would not explain the prohibition of the pig,

---

[13] See, e.g., G. J. Wenham, *The Book of Leviticus*, New International Commentary of the Old Testament (Grand Rapids: Eerdmans, 1979); Wenham, 'Theology of Unclean Food'.

which is excluded only because of its failure to chew the cud. Birds pose a particular problem for Douglas's scheme as she herself confesses: 'birds I can say nothing about because, as I have said, they are named and not described and the translation of their name is open to doubt'.[14] Twenty species are listed as unclean, but no criteria are given to assist in the identification of clean birds.

A broader and much more important methodological criticism is Douglas's failure to describe the relationship between the dietary regulations and the structure of Israelite society. It is certainly commendable that Douglas integrates the theory of the food laws into the wider dimensions of priestly thought, but the theology of the priestly authors remains peculiarly abstract in Douglas's account despite her explicit Durkheimian concerns. Arguably Douglas's consideration of the dietary laws is merely intended to demonstrate the importance of considering pollution as a comprehensive system, and is not a complete anthropological exercise. Nevertheless, as we shall see, this criticism was recognized by Douglas as cogent and deserving further discussion. In fact, the social context of the priestly writers does receive attention in *Purity and Danger*, but only tangentially in a discussion of the Coorgs in the Hindu caste system.

When rituals express anxiety about the body's orifices the sociological counterpart of this anxiety is a care to protect the political and cultural unity of a minority group. The Israelites were always in their hard-pressed minority. In their beliefs all the bodily issues were polluting, blood, pus, excreta, semen, etc. The threatened boundaries of their body politic would be well mirrored in their care for the integrity, unity and purity of the physical body.[15]

This is suggestive, if brief, and with its concern for bodily discharges more applicable to Leviticus 12–15 than to the dietary laws of chapter 11.

Third, although Douglas recognizes that the dietary laws occur in both Leviticus and Deuteronomy, they are not analysed separately.[16] Instead, Douglas oscillates between regarding them as virtually identical and devoting attention almost exclusively to the laws as found in Leviticus. On the one hand, after citing both versions of the laws, Douglas treats them as a single set of rules. In proposing divine holiness as the conceptual background for the Israelite food laws, Douglas can appeal promiscuously to Leviticus or

[14] Douglas, *Purity and Danger*, 56.
[15] Ibid., 125. Again this exemplifies Douglas's tendency in *Purity and Danger* to use the biblical material as examples for modern anthropological problems. It is arguably the case that at this stage Douglas did not fully appreciate the distinctive problems associated with the biblical material that demand concentrated attention in themselves.
[16] Cf. Kunin, *We Think What We Eat*, 39–40.

Deuteronomy as suits her argument.[17] On the other hand, the preference for Leviticus is apparent in Douglas's entitling her chapter 'The Abominations of Leviticus'. This prioritizing of Leviticus may well be the result of the assumption that the dietary laws are more fitting to Leviticus than Deuteronomy. Certainly, Douglas argues along these lines for the interpretative priority of the dietary laws in Leviticus in a more recent study: 'It seems fair to ask that impurity be studied according to Leviticus, and not according to Deuteronomy which is, after all, not a book especially concerned with ritual.'[18]

Fourth, there exists a tension between Douglas's attempt to consider the food laws as a coherent system and her appeal to the historical circumstances that give rise to the prohibition of pork. Douglas's ostensive purpose is the former: to provide a plausible account of the priestly ideas of defilement. Yet at the point where her attempt proves problematic—accounting for the exclusion of certain land animals—she moves unannounced to a diachronic explanation. As pastoralists, she informs her readers, the Israelites would have regarded domesticated ruminants as the model of proper food. The only wild food that could be consumed would have to have similar characteristics, such as the antelope or the wild goat. Since pigs were not kept by Israelite pastoralists the exclusion of pork must have been on the basis of the exclusion of wild boar. 'I suggest that *originally* the sole reason for [the pig] being counted as unclean is its failure as a wild boar to get into the antelope class.'[19] Recent work on Israelite origins reveals a number of difficulties with this as a historical account.[20] Israel's origins were not as an exclusively pastoral people, and the earliest evidence suggests a small amount of pig-breeding was practised by the

---

[17] For the differences between the theology of holiness in the priestly writers and Deuteronomy see, *inter alia*, J. B. Gammie, *Holiness in Israel*, OBT (Minneapolis: Fortress Press, 1989) and J. B. Wells, *God's Holy People: A Theme in Biblical Theology*, JSOTSup, 305 (Sheffield: Sheffield Academic Press, 2000)

[18] Douglas, 'Compassionate God of Leviticus', 62. See also Douglas, 'Self-Evidence', 39, where Douglas attributes the dietary laws in Leviticus *and* Deuteronomy to P. We should also note that this is a surprisingly promiscuous use of the term 'ritual'. The dietary laws are concerned with purity and impurity, but are not strictly speaking concerned with ritual.

[19] Douglas, *Purity and Danger*, 56. My italics.

[20] Kunin makes a similar point. 'She also suggests that the preference for domesticated animals over game was perhaps analogous to a similar preference among another 'pastoral' people, that is, the Nuer. This point, however, ignores the evidence which challenges the pastoral understanding of Israelite culture. At the time of composition of the texts the Israelites were primarily settled agriculturalists, with some aspects of a pastoral ideal in certain quarters. Thus, the analogy with the Nuer is probably not supportable, nor is the use of that model sufficient as an explanation' (Kunin, *We Think What We Eat*, 46). Kunin's criticism of Douglas is not entirely fair, for when Douglas was writing in the 1960s a number of biblical scholars did believe Israel's origins to be pastoralist. More apropos is Kunin's comment about the 'time of composition' which neatly highlights the shift that has taken place in Douglas's argument.

Israelites. A more significant problem is the dependence upon a diachronic explanation in what is otherwise a synchronic account.[21]

Early Corrections and Clarifications

The initial response to Douglas's work on the biblical dietary laws appeared primarily from fellow anthropologists, rather than biblical scholars. At the beginning of the 1970s Douglas produced a number of essays that clarified and extended her original discussion in *Purity and Danger*. In *Natural Symbols* Douglas briefly addresses Bulmer's question of why the pig is singled out for such abhorrence in Judaism.[22] She rightly observes that neither Leviticus nor Deuteronomy draw any special attention to the pig. Historically, Douglas argues, it is only in the Maccabean period that the avoidance of pork becomes such a powerful symbol of allegiance to Judaism. More importantly there is a new attention to the dietary rules as an expression of Jewish society. Temple, nation and body are coordinated symbols. Alongside defence of the re-consecrated Temple comes an insistence on the purity of the body, especially the refusal of defiling pork.[23]

The response to Bulmer's question reflects a heightened sensitivity to the question of the social context of the dietary laws. This concern stems from Douglas's acceptance of the critique of Bulmer and also Tambiah.[24] They had observed that Douglas's work remained on the level of classification and thought alone. As Douglas confesses 'it was even against the whole spirit of my book to offer an account of an ordered system of thought which did not show the context of social relations in which the categories had meaning'.[25] Providing a fully-orbed description of the patterns of social relations is one of the principal aims of Douglas's essay 'Self-Evidence' and more fully her essay 'Deciphering a Meal'.

Douglas explores the social relations of the Israelites in two different directions, first in relation to temple service, and second, following the lead of Bulmer and Tambiah, in relation to permissible marriage partners. In the case of temple service Douglas suggests that there exists a similar structure between the animals suitable for the altar and those Israelites fit for temple service.

---

[21] Douglas's appeal to multiple explanations as demanded by the biblical material, and the limitations of her model emphasize the injustice of her attack on S. R. Driver's attempt to understand the dietary laws.

[22] R. Bulmer, 'Why is the Cassowray not a Bird?' *Man* 2 (1967), 5–25.

[23] Douglas, *Natural Symbols*, 37–41.

[24] S. J. Tambiah, 'Animals are Good to Think and Good to Prohibit', *Ethnology* 7 (1969), 423–59.

[25] Douglas, 'Deciphering a Meal', 261.

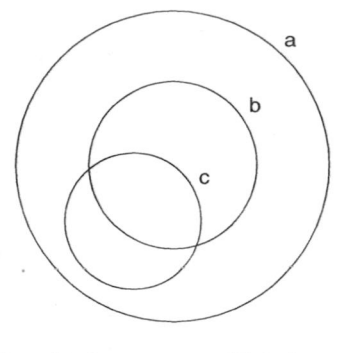

Figure 1. The Israelites (a) under the covenant; (b) fit for temple sacrifice: no blemish; (c) consecrated to temple service, first born. Their livestock (a) under the covenant; (b) fit for temple sacrifice: no blemish; (c) consecrated to temple service, first born (after Douglas, 'Deciphering a Meal', 268).

All Israelite livestock are kept under the conditions of the covenant, but a small number of these are unblemished and not suitable for sacrifice. Overlapping both categories are the firstborn animals, which are dedicated to YHWH. Similarly for Israel all the descendants of Abraham are under the covenant, but uncleanness may exclude them from the temple courts, and consequently sacrifice. The firstborn of Israel are dedicated to YHWH, and the Levites are consecrated to YHWH in their stead. These relationships can be represented diagrammatically (Figure 1). At first glance the relation of altar and temple service appear to have nothing to do with the dietary laws. Douglas argues, however, that the most important covenantal boundary between Israelites and non-Israelites is analogous to the division between clean and unclean animals. Additionally, there is the requirement that domesticated animals are sacrificed and the blood returned to YHWH before being consumed. Israel's own practice was a reminder of the analogy that existed between altar and table.

The analogy drawn between table and altar does not itself provide any explanation of the anomalous animals, which were so important in Douglas's earlier examination of the dietary laws. For this Douglas gives consideration to the question of permissible marriage partnerships. The work by Tambiah on north-east Thailand and Bulmer on the Karam in New Guinea had shown a strong relationship between table and bed. 'Both demonstrate how the classification of animals is imbued with strong social concerns. In each case the taxonomy organizes nature so that the categories of animals mirror and reinforce the social rules about marriage and residence.'[26] In Israelite society

[26] Douglas, 'Self-Evidence', 30.

endogamy was strongly encouraged. Whilst marriage with a captive from a distant land is allowable, marriage to a woman from Israel's near neighbours is particularly threatening. In a similar way, Douglas argues that animals such as the pig, camel, hare and hyrax, which sit on the boundary between clean and unclean, having only one of the two characteristics required to be clean, are particularly worrying for the priestly authors.

The classification which counts abominable the beasts which either chew the cud or cleave the hoof but not both is isomorphic with the other classification of Israelites which does not object to inter-marriage with female captives of far distant foes (Deut. 20:14–18) but worries about the prospect of intermarriage with half-blooded Israelites. The pig attracts, with the camel, the hare, and rock-badger, the odium of half-eligibility for table and sacrifice.[27]

Douglas appeals to the Canaanites as an example of the threat of intermarriage.

How else did the resident Canaanites come to be absorbed? In the relevant periods, betrothal to a foreigner was certain to be celebrated with feasting in breach of the Mosaic rules. But far more likely to appear on the table than the camel, the hare and the rock badger was the domesticated pig. So we move towards understanding its special taxonomic status.[28]

In a change from her position in *Natural Symbols* Douglas now suggests the pig had a special status in the original dietary laws. It suffers from multiple pollutions: it defies classification, it eats carrion and it is reared by non-Israelites who would use it at their betrothal feasts.

Douglas's pursuit of a structural analogy between Israel's social relationships and the food laws is an important development of her interpretation. This basic insight has proved a decisive one for many subsequent interpreters. As we will see Milgrom also recognizes an analogy between the non-Israelites and animals unclean for food, though he suggests that further analogies are between Israel and animals clean for food and between the Levites and animals suitable for sacrifice, rather than the ones Douglas chooses. There are problems, however, with Douglas's discussion of the anomalous pig. There is no evidence for Douglas's suggestion that pork would be on the menu at betrothal or wedding feasts. More significantly, Douglas has confused recognizing similar patterns of thought between food laws and intermarriage, with finding the two at the same social occasion. Given that Douglas concurs with biblical scholarship's usual dating of the priestly writers to the post-exilic period her arguments about the purity laws would neatly cohere with Ezra and Nehemiah's concerns about intermarriage. With such a comparison, however,

---

[27] Ibid., 38.   [28] Ibid., 39. Cf. Douglas, 'Deciphering a Meal', 272.

it would be better to see all foreign intermarriage as prohibited as all unclean animals are, with special concern over groups such as the Samaritans.

OTHER COMPARATIVIST CONTRIBUTIONS

Douglas's work is strongly comparativist in approach, informed by her own anthropological work among the Lele people of the Congo and the anthropological work of others. We will also consider two other scholars working with a comparativist method: Frederick J. Simoons and Marvin Harris. In contrast to Douglas, who focuses on the dietary laws as part of a wider system of priestly thought, Simoons and Harris are concerned only with the prohibited animals and, in particular, the pig.

Frederick J. Simoons's *Eat Not This Flesh*

Simoons's *Eat Not This Flesh: Food Avoidances in the Old World* is a broad exercise in cultural geography that seeks to map food avoidances throughout the world, with the exception of the Americas, from the earliest historical records to the present.[29] Relying primarily on literary sources he documents the avoidance of pork, beef, chicken, horse, camel and dog in various cultures. Collating the relevant data from such a varied array of sources is itself a Herculean undertaking, but Simoons also seeks to review the explanations offered.

Although the Jewish dietary laws exclude a number of animals that Simoons examines, it is, perhaps naturally enough, pork of all the food avoidances that receives the most attention. Simoons observes widespread use of pork in the Neolithic period that declined in subsequent periods. This shift in taste is attributed to the influence of pastoralists. In the arid regions that these nomads occupied the pig was unsuitable. It requires shade and moisture, and cannot be driven like cattle, sheep and goats. The antagonism between pastoralists and agriculturalists led to the pastoralists associating pork with their sedentary neighbours. 'From these facts it is logical to suppose that pastoralists living in arid regions developed contempt for the pig as an animal alien to their way of life and symbolic of the despised sedentary folk, and came to avoid its flesh for food.'[30]

---

[29]   F. J. Simoons, *Eat Not This Flesh: Food Avoidances in the Old World* (Madison: University of Wisconsin Press, 1961).

[30]   Ibid., 41.

In his discussion of other animals that are prohibited in the dietary laws, Simoons has little to say about Jewish practice. His discussion of horsemeat concentrates primarily on the use of horsemeat in central Asia and the reasons for the avoidance of horseflesh in medieval Europe. Muslim views on horse-flesh are mentioned briefly, but the exclusion of the horse within Judaism receives no comment.[31] Simoons rightly observes that although the camel becomes an important marker between Muslims and non-Muslims, the rejec-tion of camel meat in Judaism and other groups predates Islam. He concludes, however, that 'the origin of the avoidance of camel flesh is not known, and does not seem likely now to be determined'.[32] Simoons notes the prohibition of dog flesh amongst the Zoroastrians and other Near Eastern groups, but omits to mention Jews. He advances the intimate association among pastoral-ists between working dogs and their masters as a reason for the avoidance of dog flesh.

In assessing Simoons contribution to understanding the Jewish dietary laws we might say that his explanation of the avoidance of pork is certainly plau-sible. However, the appeal to a strong contrast between pastoral nomads and agriculturalists is overstated. In the Levant, caprovines were kept in significant numbers by sedentary farmers as well as by transhumant semi-nomads. In addition, the relationship between agriculturalists and pastoralists is often one of mutual coexistence and interdependence, rather than antagonistic oppo-sition. What Simoons's work does suggest is that Israel's avoidance of pork could potentially be part of a wider cultural phenomenon. To demonstrate this requires Simoons to work over a large canvas with inevitable consequences. In particular, his historical sources are primarily literary, with other forms of evidence, such as archaeological or iconographic, usually absent.

Marvin Harris's *Good to Eat*

Marvin Harris's *Good to Eat: Riddles of Food and Culture* is far more polemical in tone than Simoons, though like him he examines food avoidances from across the world.[33] Harris is a combative advocate of a cultural materialist approach to food, and he sets himself against the symbolist and structuralist schools of thought represented not only by Mary Douglas, but also by Claude Lévi-Strauss.[34] Lévi-Strauss famously claimed 'that natural species are chosen

---

[31] Ibid., 79–86.   [32] Ibid., 87–90.   [33] Harris, *Good to Eat*.

[34] It is impossible to deal with Lévi-Strauss's vast contribution to the structuralist analysis of food. His influential and vast work on myth, the four volumes of *Mythologiques*, frequently discuss food as the titles of the individual volumes bear witness (C. Lévi-Strauss, *The Raw and the Cooked* (New York: Harper & Row, 1969); C. Lévi-Strauss, *From Honey to Ashes* (New York:

not because they are "good to eat", but because they are "good to think".[35] Harris's response is robust.

The theory that foods are selected primarily because they are good to think rather than because they are good to eat...mocks the hungry living and dead by transforming the struggle for subsistence into a game of mental imagery. The idea that cooking is primarily a language is food for thought only among those who have never had to worry about having enough to eat.[36]

According to Harris food prohibitions can be explained exclusively by means of a cost–benefit analysis. Religions prohibit dietary patterns that would be economically disastrous. 'Preferred foods (good to eat) are foods that have a more favourable balance of practical benefits over costs than foods that are avoided (bad to eat).'[37]

Harris begins by reviewing traditional theories of the reason for the pig prohibition in Judaism, such as the idea that the prohibitions stemmed from concerns about hygiene or health. With Douglas he agrees that such theories are unsatisfactory, but he finds himself equally unimpressed with her own arguments about classification and anomaly, which he finds circular. According to Douglas the pig is regarded as abominable because it is out of place, and consequently 'dirty'. But the pig is only 'matter out of place' according to the taxonomy the Israelites have created. 'To observe that the pig is out of place taxonomically is merely to observe that Leviticus classifies good-to-eat animals in such a way as to make the pig bad to eat. This avoids the question of why the taxonomy is what it is.'[38] The classification results from the way in which the Israelites used animals, and not the converse.

To explain the rejection of the pig Harris turns initially to the Israelite preference for ruminants. Passing over the specification of cloven feet, why should animals that chew the cud be preferred by the Israelites? His answer is that cattle, sheep and goats are simply better suited to the Near Eastern environment. They are herbivores that thrive on plant foods with a high cellulose content that are indigestible for humans, such as grass, hay, leaves. Cud chewing is an observable characteristic of those animals with a compartmentalized stomach

Harper & Row, 1973); C. Lévi-Strauss, *The Origin of Table Manners* (New York: Harper & Row, 1978); C. Lévi-Strauss, *The Naked Man* (New York: Harper & Row, 1981)). The famous culinary triangle is found in C. Lévi-Strauss, 'The Culinary Triangle', *Partisan Review* 33 (1965), 586–95. As perhaps the most influential theorist on food his work is frequently discussed in surveys of scholarship on food and foodways. See, e.g., S. Mennell, A. Murcott and A. H. van Otterloo, 'The Sociology of Food: Eating, Diet and Culture', *Current Sociology* 40 (1992), 1–152.

[35] C. Lévi-Strauss, *Totemism* (Boston: Beacon Press, 1963), 89.

[36] M. Harris, *Cultural Materialism: The Struggle for a Science of Culture* (New York: Random House, 1979), 189.

[37] Harris, *Good to Eat*, 15.   [38] Ibid., 72.

designed to digest grasses. Ruminants can transform grasslands, which would otherwise be unproductive, into meat that can be consumed by humans. The pig, on the other hand, as Simoons had argued, is not suited to the climate and ecology of the Near East. It needs shade and wallow, which due to deforestation were in increasingly short supply in the Levant. Additionally pigs do not thrive on grass, and although they are omnivores many of the foods that they eat are those that humans use. Unlike the ruminants, the pig had no other benefits, such as providing traction, milk or hides, and was easily condemned. What purposes did the prescription of animals with undivided hooves serve? In Harris's view this criterion was the means by which the priestly author codified the traditional avoidance of the camel. In Israel the camel played little role except for crossing the desert. Reproduction is very slow, and consequently camels were rare and valuable commodities which it made no sense to slaughter for food.

In his earlier work *Cannibals and Kings* Harris attempted to explain all the prohibitions in the dietary laws with a cost–benefit analysis.[39] His discussion in *Good to Eat*, on the other hand, appears to allow some role for prohibition on symbolic and taxonomic grounds. He suggests that some of the sea birds are listed in order to demonstrate the priestly writer's knowledge of the natural world. The land-locked Israelite readers or hearers would probably never have seen the exotic sea birds that the priestly writer named. A similar case is made for the list of prohibited sea creatures. Nevertheless, Harris is unable to resist appealing to an economic analysis. The lists of prohibited birds and fish would hardly be worth wasting time trying to catch for food. Thus even in this instance the capacity of the priestly writer to work on an aesthetic or symbolic level is effectively overruled by economic considerations.[40]

The principal strength of Harris's interpretation of the food laws is the attention it gives to the particular ecological constraints that Israelite society faced during its history. This aspect has frequently been overlooked, but under the influence of Harris, cultural materialism has been developed by Old Testament scholars such as Norman Gottwald.[41] The difficulty with Harris's approach is that this emphasis excludes the possibility of any other

---

[39] M. Harris, *Cannibals and Kings: The Origins of Cultures* (New York: Random House, 1977), 193–208.

[40] At this point Harris's arguments resonate with the thinking of Origen. 'And to come to the Mosaic legislation, many of the laws, so far as their literal observance is concerned, are clearly irrational, while others are impossible ... the griffin, which the lawgiver forbids to be eaten, there is no record that it has even fallen into the hands of man' (Origen, *De Principiis* 4.3.2 in the Greek; translation according to Origen, *On First Principles*, trans. G. W. Butterworth (New York: Harper & Row, 1966), pp. 290–1).

[41] N. K. Gottwald, *The Tribes of Yahweh: A Sociology of the Religion of Liberated Israel, 1250– 1050 BCE* (Sheffield: Sheffield Academic Press, 1979; 2nd edn. 1999).

explanation, and is ultimately reductionistic.[42] The relationship between ecology and human culture is one of complex interaction and cannot be analysed by paying attention to one direction of influence. Ecology creates conditions which may be altered by human activity, and which may also give rise to a variety of social and cultural possibilities. Harris's discussion of marine life and birds illustrates the inadequacy of appealing to one type of solution. The inclusion of these species appears to be more an exercise in priestly categorization, in Harris's words 'a taxonomic principle that has been somewhat overextended',[43] than traditional taboos that arise from environmental constraints. As such they demand that attention be paid to the kinds of logic and symbolism with which the priestly school worked. Harris, however, needs to produce a materialistic basis, but it does not convince. After all, what need is there to prohibit animals that take too much effort to hunt? The case of the camel is even more difficult to justify, for Harris's cost–benefit analysis can be used to undermine it. It is easy to accept Harris's arguments that camels are difficult to breed and hardly make for a regular supply of meat. Yet, why should economically unproductive animals, the sick or old, not be consumed or sold? Indeed, Simoons observes that in Islamic communities, where the camel is permitted, it is ordinarily only injured or diseased animals that are eaten.[44]

Harris makes a better case for the prohibition of pork. Indeed, it was received with some enthusiasm by John Rogerson.[45] Pigs are not as readily suited to the Near East as ruminants. However, if we move beyond the truth of this general statement we find many examples of pig-keeping in the Near East. There are a number of regions in the Middle East and in Palestine in particular that can support pigs. This is especially true when we remember that the deforestation of the region was not as severe as in modern times.[46] Consumption of pork was never as common as beef or lamb, but archaezoological evidence from the Levant shows that pork was consumed especially in the Bronze Age and also along the coastal plain in the Iron Age.[47] Thus, whilst Harris's arguments cannot explain why pork was prohibited, they can show why it was pork that could be prohibited and not sheep or goat.

---

[42] See Houston, *Purity and Monotheism*, 90–3.   [43] Harris, *Good to Eat*, 62.

[44] Simoons, *Eat Not This Flesh*, 87–90.

[45] J. Rogerson, 'Anthropology and the Old Testament', in R. E. Clements (ed.), *The World of Ancient Israel: Sociological, Anthropological and Political Perspectives* (Cambridge: Cambridge University Press, 1989), 17–38, here 33.

[46] Houston argues with others that deforestation may be the result of the decline of the pig rather than its cause. He notes the case of Albania, where Christians and Muslims occupy land adjacent to one another, but the Christian areas are better wooded than the Muslim ones (Houston, *Purity and Monotheism*, 87–90, see esp. literature cited on p. 88).

[47] See N. MacDonald, *What Did the Ancient Israelites Eat? Diet in Biblical Times* (Grand Rapids: Eerdmans, 2008).

Developmentalism and Structuralism

Harris's controversy with Douglas brings to the surface the sharp theoretical divide between developmentalists and structuralists.[48] It is, perhaps, little surprise that the biblical dietary laws should have seduced proponents from both sides of one of the most fundamental controversies in the anthropology of food into explaining the laws from their theoretical perspective. The food laws are one of the most well known problems in the study of food and one of the most resistant to simple explanation.

In addition to Mary Douglas, the structuralist approach to the study of food is associated with Claude Lévi-Strauss, Roland Barthes and Pierre Bourdieu. Lévi-Strauss approached a society's cuisine as a language in which he sought to uncover its essential grammar. This grammar is the unconscious attitudes of the society, which also find expression in other spheres such as art, social codes and mythology. Ultimately Lévi-Strauss hoped to uncover the underlying structures of human thought. The concern with encoded structures is clearly shared by Douglas, though her own work lacks Lévi-Strauss's universalistic expectations. The earlier part of another of Douglas's works, 'Deciphering a Meal', is concerned with the pattern of meals in British households and how they express hierarchies and boundaries. The 'grammar' that Douglas seeks is culturally specific. Barthes examined French taste with similar concerns. Bourdieu, on the other hand, relates 'individual' tastes to the expectations of social class, rather than examining society as a whole.

Structuralist concerns with the aesthetics of food, rather than its nutrition value, together with analyses of structure that did not allow for historical change, led to a growing chorus of criticism and new theoretical approaches.[49] As we have seen, Marvin Harris stresses the role that securing nutrition plays in dietary choices. Environmental constraints can result in changes to human diet. Stephen Mennell examines the changes in taste and manners in France and England since the Middle Ages. He pays attention to how broader social, political and economic changes impact culinary culture.[50] Sidney Mintz traces the interaction between economic factors, nutritional needs and symbolic meanings in the exponential rise of sugar consumption in the modern world. In the area of Roman history Peter Garnsey has examined the strategies

---

[48] Mennell, Murcott and van Otterloo classify Harris, Goody, Mennell and Mintz as 'developmentalists' (Mennell, Murcott and van Otterloo, 'Sociology of Food', 14). Harris's own preferred self-designation would be 'materialist', though Mennell is unhappy with the term. This difference in terminology highlights the differences that exist between these different theorists. Nevertheless, in their opposition to structuralists and their attempts to discern the causes of change in food habits they share a common cause.

[49] See, e.g., Mennell, *All Manners of Food*, 1–19; Goody, *Cooking, Cuisine and Class*, 10–39.

[50] Mennell, *All Manners of Food*.

that individuals and governments employed to cope with periodic food crises.[51]

The contrast between these two different approaches has sometimes been over-emphasized. Harris, for example, appears to allow some role for symbolic meanings. 'For my part, I do not wish to deny that foods convey messages and have symbolic meanings.'[52] Yet, as we have seen, even where Harris allows for the possibility that some of the prohibited animals may have been prohibited on the basis of scribal symbolism, he immediately backtracks and finds an economic basis. Douglas, as we have seen, ostensively explains the dietary laws as a systematic whole without recourse to piecemeal historical explanations. Yet, not only does she appeal to historical explanations for the prohibition of the pig, but she also recognizes that historical events, such as the Maccabean revolt, can effect shifts in the grammar of diet.

Recent writers have been more circumspect in their assessment of structuralism and developmentalism. 'Each of the "twofold values" of food, as nutrition and as protocol, merits discussion in a study of food in ancient societies. It is indeed difficult, and ultimately I suspect unnecessary, to make a rigid distinction between the two roles or "values" of food.'[53] From the perspective of biblical scholarship, the debate between structuralists and developmentalists is another instance of the contrast between synchronic and diachronic approaches. In biblical studies too a polarized debate has resolved itself in recent years to something of an uneasy truce as the validity of both sides has been recognized.[54]

The dietary laws neatly illustrate the tensions, for anywhere beyond the ideological extremes we have to engage with both the intellectual coherence of the dietary laws to the final editors and their location in a historical continuum. Even Harris and Douglas, who appear to represent opposite ends of the spectrum, appeal to arguments that move them outside their theoretical position. Harris's 'overextended taxonomic principle' and Douglas's Israelite pastoralists suggest that there is more to discuss than immediately meets the eye. The productiveness of the discussion depends, at least partially, on the avoidance of two errors. First, the reductionism that we have seen in Harris's work must be rejected. Second, we must avoid the confusion of arguments that

---

[51] Garnsey, *Famine and Food Supply.*   [52] Harris, *Good to Eat*, 15.

[53] Garnsey, *Food and Society.* Mintz and Du Bois's review of recent work on food barely touches upon the disagreement between structuralists and developmentalists (S. W. Mintz and C. M. Du Bois, 'The Anthropology of Food and Eating', *Annual Review of Anthropology* 31 (2002), 99–119), though these divisions were staples of earlier analyses (e.g. Mennell, Murcott, and van Otterloo, 'Sociology of Food').

[54] Cf. Sutton's judgement that 'these debates, which stimulated the field earlier, seem to have run their course' (D. E. Sutton, *Remembrance of Repasts: An Anthropology of Food and Memory* (Oxford: Berg, 2001), 6 n. 5).

occurs in Douglas's discussion of the pig. Her appeal to the origins of the pork taboo in ancient Israel is at odds with her claim to be analysing the dietary laws as a coherent system of priestly thought. She immediately exposes herself to the genetic fallacy: arguing that the grounds for the priests prohibiting the pig were the same grounds as led to the original avoidance of pork by the Israelites.

TWO CONTRIBUTIONS FROM BIBLICAL SCHOLARSHIP

Biblical scholarship has traditionally been more attentive to the historical depth of the biblical material and less attentive to its literary coherence. The introduction of new literary methodologies has effected significant changes. Jacob Milgrom and Walter Houston attempt a comprehensive evaluation of the dietary laws and, consequently, give attention to both aspects. Though differing from one another in various ways, they both show themselves responsive to anthropological work and its theoretical issues, but also engage with the biblical text with a clarity and precision that could not be expected from Douglas and Harris. They both demonstrate the importance of detailed textual analysis as the final arbiter to the insights derived from anthropological comparisons. In addition, Milgrom will illustrate the importance of literary-critical analysis, and Houston, the value of archaeological work.

Jacob Milgrom

No other scholar has done more to understand the much maligned writers of the priestly school and present them to the modern reader than Jacob Milgrom. His earliest contribution to this lifetime task was an essay on the dietary laws, 'The Biblical Diet Laws as an Ethical System', published in 1963. The discussion of Leviticus 11 in his massive commentary on Leviticus has considerably more detail and the argument is more substantial and mature than the original essay. Nevertheless, Milgrom's understanding of the chapter remains essentially the same as that which he proposed thirty years earlier.

Two central convictions characterize Milgrom's understanding of the dietary laws. First, their principal purpose is ethical by teaching respect for life. Second, they are part of a coherent system of dietary regulations that are

found not just in Leviticus 11 but throughout the priestly material.[55] Milgrom approaches the forbidden animals through the prohibition against ingesting blood. This restriction was placed upon man after the flood together with the permission to kill animals for meat. 'Humanity', writes Milgrom, 'has a right to nourishment, not to life.'[56] Israel is called to discipline its appetite to a greater degree in the dietary laws of Leviticus 11 and Deuteronomy 14. In his 1963 essay Milgrom notes the stress on holiness and the imitation of God as the reasons for the dietary laws. Through the dietary laws Israel is called to share God's reverence for life. The dietary laws also effect Israel's separation from the other nations, called to a special holiness as befits the chosen people of God.

With his emphasis on the dietary laws as a didactic tool for disciplining the appetite, Milgrom owes much to Philo, the rabbis and Maimonides. There are also emphases which are congruent with the approach taken by Douglas. Both agree in seeing the dietary laws as a coherent system, rather than incoherent vestiges of early Israelite taboos. In addition, they share a positive appreciation of the priestly writer's theology, and for both the concept of holiness is central to their exposition of the dietary laws. It is little surprise that there has been a reciprocal relationship between their scholarship.[57] Their initial contributions to the subject were published independently, but as early as her 'Self Evidence' and 'Deciphering a Meal', both published in 1972, Douglas was having her understanding of the biblical texts informed by Milgrom. Milgrom, for his part, acknowledges Douglas's seminal contribution in his recent work on the dietary laws.

The insights of the Durkheimian school, especially as exemplified in the work of Mary Douglas, have led to the disclosure of the intricate connections between Israel's animal taxonomy and aspects of its value system, specifically, the requirement to separate itself from the nations by refraining from their meat and women and to separate itself to God by following his commandments along the road to holiness. In particular, Douglas has uncovered the basic postulate that underlies the criteria for permitted animals: each species must exhibit the locomotion that fits its medium.[58]

---

[55] Houston rightly draws attention to the term 'system' in the title of Milgrom's 1963 article, 'The Biblical Diet Laws as an Ethical System' (Houston, 'Integrated Reading of the Dietary Laws', 142).

[56] Milgrom, 'Ethics and Ritual', 169.

[57] Duhaime's discussion of Milgrom and Douglas would suggest that the relationship has merely been one of critical reception by Milgrom, and appears to be ignorant of Milgrom's early contribution to the study of the dietary laws (J. Milgrom, 'The Biblical Diet Laws as an Ethical System', *Int* 17 (1963), 288–301) and its essential continuity with the arguments presented in Milgrom's commentary on Leviticus (Duhaime, 'Lois alimentaires').

[58] Milgrom, *Leviticus 1–16*, 726. Milgrom's ambiguous 'refraining from their meat' could be understood to mean that pork was a characteristically non-Israelite meal or that Israelites were invited to non-Israelite ritual meals. For Milgrom's discussion of Douglas's proposals see 719–26.

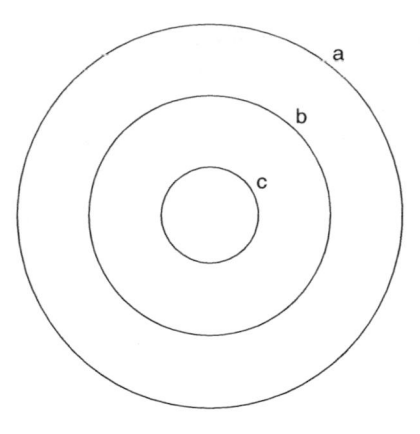

Figure 2. Humans: (a) humanity; (b) Israel; (c) Priests. Animals: (a) all animals; (b) fit for the Israelite table; (c) suitable for sacrifices to YHWH. Space: (a) Earth; (b) the land of Israel; (c) the sanctuary (after Milgrom, *Leviticus 1–16*, 722, 725).

As we will see Douglas's recent contributions to the study of the dietary laws exhibit her debt to Milgrom by consistently stressing the ethical importance of the laws.

Whilst accepting Douglas's basic insights into the purity laws, Milgrom does subject them to modification. The correspondence between the human and animal worlds supports Milgrom's analysis of priestly thought, which he envisages modelling the world as a series of concentric circles (Figure 2).

The three human divisions are matched by three animal divisions. All animals are permitted to humans for food (Gen. 9.3–5), only clean animals are allowed for Israel, with a limited number of domesticated animals fit for the altar. To these threefold divisions also corresponds the threefold priestly ordering of space.

There are clear similarities to Douglas's understanding, but her interest in anomaly has been abandoned. For Milgrom the emphasis in the dietary laws is that Israel's choice of meat has been severely circumscribed in order to teach the Israelites reverence for life. An interesting comparison can be made, at this point, to the alternative construal of Seth Kunin. More avowedly structuralist in his approach, Kunin places a greater emphasis on the anomalous animals and their clear assignment into the category of prohibited animals. Whilst the determining theological structure for Milgrom is Jewish ethics and divine command, for Kunin it is divine election. God has chosen Israel, and excludes any liminal peoples, just as liminal animals have been excluded.[59] The different interpretations offered by Milgrom and Kunin are, in my view,

---

[59] Kunin, *We Think What We Eat.*

potentially compatible. The different emphases are determined not primarily by theory, but by the biblical intertexts that each deems most relevant. In the case of Milgrom this highlights the extent to which his understanding of the dietary laws depends on his argument that they are part of a larger concern with shedding blood and animal slaughter. The ethical rationale is found explicitly in the concern about shedding blood, 'the blood is the life', a rationale which is absent from the dietary laws themselves.

Perhaps the most interesting contribution from Milgrom is his effort to distinguish between the dietary laws as they are found in Leviticus and Deuteronomy. It is far too common, as we have already seen, for interpreters to assume that the two versions of the dietary laws are identical. That there are differences between Leviticus 11 and Deuteronomy 14 has long been apparent to Old Testament scholarship as it is has sought to determine the literary relationship between the two passages. That there must be some relationship is clear, but is Deuteronomy derived from Leviticus, Leviticus from Deuteronomy, or do they both stem from a common source? The solution offered in the nineteenth century—that Leviticus expanded Deuteronomy—has been accepted by most interpreters since. Milgrom puts forward a detailed case arguing that, in fact, Deuteronomy abridged Leviticus.[60]

An important part of Milgrom's argument is that Deuteronomy has simplified the terminological distinctions found in Leviticus. Leviticus 11 uses two terms to classify animals. The term *sheqets* is used of prohibited fish, birds, swarming animals of the air and some swarming animals of the land. The term *tame* 'impure' is used of the prohibited land animals and the remaining land swarmers. In Leviticus, then, the prohibited animals fall into two categories. 'Animals termed *sheqetz* may not be eaten but they do not convey impurity, whereas animals termed *tame* are both forbidden to be eaten or touched.'[61] This distinction suggests that animals that are *sheqets* are pure. For Milgrom this calls into question the usual translation of *sheqets* with 'detestable' in Leviticus 11, and he favours a more functional translation such as 'prohibited as food'. The reason this distinction has been obscured is because Deuteronomy regards all the prohibited animals without distinction as *to'evah*. This term is used elsewhere in Deuteronomy with the sense 'abominable'.

Whether or not Milgrom's arguments about the vocabulary of the dietary laws can be maintained, his close attention to it underlines the need to consider Leviticus 11 and Deuteronomy 14 independently as well as in their relationship to one another. The biblical text has a complex literary history

---

[60] Milgrom, *Leviticus 1–16*, 698–704.

[61] J. Milgrom, 'Two Biblical Hebrew Priestly Terms: *Sheqetz* and *Tame*', *MAARAV* 6 (1992), 107–16, here 108.

that needs to be examined in all its aspects. Too much discussion has taken place that assumes the dietary laws are just a single entity, or gives one passage interpretative priority.[62]

Walter Houston

Walter Houston's *Purity and Monotheism* is a monograph treatment of the biblical dietary laws, and is consequently the most detailed discussion currently available. Houston's work includes a review of the various explanations offered. It is Houston's judgement, with which we concur, that neither materialist nor structuralist explanations are sufficient in themselves for fully understanding the biblical dietary laws in their present form. 'Although no one theory has proved completely satisfactory, all have suggested aspects that need to be taken into account. No full explanation is possible that does not take account of both the material and the social contexts of the code.'[63] Houston's work is marked by a clear methodology in which he sets out the material and cultural context within which the dietary laws arose, before seeking to explain the logic of the classifications in Leviticus and Deuteronomy.

The advantage of Houston's clear methodology is that it keeps the historical and literary-structural aspects of the problem separate for the purposes of analysis, but allows them to be mutually informative. As such he avoids Douglas's genetic fallacy and Harris's reductionism. His eclectic approach

---

[62] It is most common to assume that the purity laws are more at home in Leviticus with the priestly concerns for purity and ritual. Douglas, for example, writes, 'it seems fair to ask that impurity be studied according to Leviticus, and not according to Deuteronomy which is, after all, not a book especially concerned with ritual' (Douglas, 'Compassionate God of Leviticus', 62). Such assumptions need to be established. Mayes, for example, argues that the dietary laws envisage a different social system to that found elsewhere in Deuteronomy, which allows for the inclusion of outsiders. He views the dietary regulations as a priestly creation inserted into Deuteronomy in the post-exilic period (A. D. H. Mayes, 'Deuteronomy 14 and the Deuteronomic World View', in F. García Martínez et al. (eds.), *Studies in Deuteronomy: In Honour of C. J. Labuschagne on the Occasion of his 65th Birthday*, VTSup, 53 (Leiden: Brill, 1994), 165–81). However, Milgrom's analysis demonstrates that Deuteronomy 14 has been redacted so that it is a constituent part of Deuteronomy. Nelson rightly notes that with its concern for food, the resident alien and the foreigner, Deuteronomy 14 is very much a part of Deuteronomy 12–15 (R. D. Nelson, *Deuteronomy*, OTL (Louisville: Westminster John Knox Press, 2002), 176; cf. P. M. Ventner, 'The Dietary Regulations in Deuteronomy 14 within Its Literary Context', *Hervormde Teologiese Studies* 58 (2002), 1240–62). Indeed, it is arguably the case that with its concern for ethical and ritual purity, Leviticus 11 is less suited to the immediate context of Leviticus 12–15, where the concern is with ritual purity. Consequently some have argued that Leviticus 11 stems from the hand of the holiness writer (H) (see J. Klawans, *Impurity and Sin in Ancient Judaism* (Oxford: Oxford University Press, 2000), esp. 31–2, and Houston, 'Integrated Reading of the Dietary Laws', 143). For further discussion of Deuteronomy 14, see Chapter 3.

[63] Houston, *Purity and Monotheism*, 122.

also allows him to present a nuanced and, in my view, persuasive answer to the hoary question of whether taboo or criteria are prior. The material and cultural context suggests that certain animals were not commonly eaten in the Near East, nor used for sacrifice. The pig, for example, was an impractical animal in economies having a strong pastoral element and they had a low status relative to the ruminants. The reduced evidence of pigs in Iron Age Palestine suggests that pigs were tabooed by the Israelites. Thus, in this instance the taboo preceded the criteria. The development of the criteria led to the tabooing of other animals. In the priestly attempt to schematize the various spheres of the cosmos and determine what was clean and unclean, many animals were assigned a place in the schema. Some of these animals the ordinary Israelites may never have eaten or contemplated as a source of meat. Thus, in this instance the criteria preceded the taboo.

In his examination of the dietary laws as a symbolic reflection of societal ideals Houston emphasizes their role as a theological and ethical statement.

It stands for the order and peace of civil society over against the disorder and violence of the wild; for the just and traditional ordering of society against anarchy; for the purity of the sanctuary against the permanent threat of pollution; for the holiness of the people of God as his devoted ones; for their protection against pressures from without, and their separation from all that would threaten their dedication to their one God; for the possibility, not confined to Israel alone, of living in peace with God's creatures and in the experience of his presence. It does not merely symbolize these things; by the constant practice of the rules it actually inculcates them.[64]

There is a great debt here to Douglas's argument that animals are part of the Israelite community, and much in common with Milgrom's conclusions about the ethical import of the dietary laws.

It is in his attention to the material context, however, that Houston makes a distinctive and decisive contribution to the study of the dietary laws. Simoons and Harris demonstrated the importance of ecology and climate as factors in food prohibitions, but to prove useful for biblical studies their sweeping, occasionally erroneous, assumptions about the Near East need to be given greater precision by close study of the region of Palestine. Houston does this in two ways. First, he utilizes the findings of archaeozoology to provide a detailed picture of the meat consumption habits of the inhabitants of Palestine. Archaeozoology is the scientific study of animal remains recovered from archaeological sites. In the archaeological study of the Levant it has only been utilized in a systematic way in excavations since the 1970s. In earlier excavations animal remains, the most common material recovered, were usually considered of little value and were discarded. Advances in archaeozoology

---

[64] Ibid., 258.

mean that animal bones can reveal a variety of useful information including the proportions and types of species represented at a site. Houston coordinates the animal proportions discovered at a site with other archaeological evidence for the site's use and with geographical and climatic information. He not only documents the relative infrequency of the pig in the Levant, but also examines evidence for other animals. Second, Houston examines literary sources for evidence of sacrificial practice throughout the ancient Near East, particularly the possibility that pigs were sacrificed. This is in order to establish whether there is a relationship between the animals eaten by humans and those permitted on the altar.

For our purposes Houston demonstrates the benefits of incorporating a number of theoretical perspectives when examining the subject of food. The choice and uses of food are influenced by material *and* cultural realities. Failure to give attention to one aspect results in a lopsided portrayal. Houston also demonstrates the importance of utilizing archaeological discoveries. Food as it passes from production to waste, through preparation and consumption, frequently leaves traces of its journey in the archaeological record. Tools, storage jars, ovens, kitchen implements, animal bones, to name but a few, have all formed part of the archaeological deposit. The examination of food in the Bible will need to have recourse to this evidence as appropriate.

LATER MARY DOUGLAS

In her latter years Mary Douglas returned to the interpretation of the dietary laws with a series of publications. The priestly system of thought was no longer merely an example to be furnished as part of wider arguments, but the centre of attention. This new perspective is apparent in Douglas's 1993 essay, 'The Forbidden Animals in Leviticus',[65] in which she sets out a literary structure for the whole of Leviticus that proves crucial for her understanding of the dietary laws. Leviticus, Douglas argues, has a chiastic structure pivoting around chapter 19, which pairs chapters 11–15 with chapters 21–2. In Leviticus 21–2 those with a blemish are forbidden from approaching the altar, whilst blemished animals are forbidden from being offered on it. Douglas takes these chapters, together with Milgrom's arguments about the ingestion of blood, as her interpretative key for understanding Leviticus 11. The prohibited animals, argues Douglas, are excluded from the Israelite diet for one

---

[65] Douglas, 'Forbidden Animals'; cf. Houston, 'Integrated Reading of the Dietary Laws', 150–2.

of three reasons. First, on the basis of the blood prohibition, carnivores are excluded. Second, animals that lack criteria to be deemed clean are seen as blemished. Appealing to Lev. 24.19, which demonstrates that a blemish can be understood as the result of an assault, Douglas argues that blemish connects the animals with those that suffer injustice. Third, the fish without scales or fins lack defence and are also excluded from the table. According to Douglas, then, the priestly authors excluded from the Israelite table predators and those animals that were preyed upon. As Douglas herself appreciates, this interpretation is a form of allegory in which the forbidden animals symbolize the oppressors or the victims of injustice. Its message is inculcated to the people as they appreciate its symbolic figuration. Houston is probably generous in arguing that 'readings of this kind cannot be proved or disproved, only felt as convincing or unconvincing'.[66] The comparison to blemish lacks any genuine verbal parallel, and depends on how convinced the reader is of Douglas's chiastic structure. Arguably Douglas did this interpretation no disservice by quietly abandoning it.

Douglas's last analysis of the dietary laws appeared in her monograph-length literary analysis of Leviticus.[67] Accepting Milgrom's arguments about *sheqets* and *tame* she considers land animals separately from other animals. Reflecting her arguments in *Purity and Danger* she argues that the only permitted land animals are domestic and included under the covenant. Since the life is in the blood, animals may only be killed on the altar. Israel's actions both are ethical and demonstrate loyalty to the one covenant God of Israel by sacrificing at his altar. Moving beyond the land animals, Douglas argues that the other animals are to be eschewed because they are swarmers and so express fertility. We might say that both sides of Leviticus 11 express the identification of YHWH, the God of Israel, with life, and his opposition to death.

There are a number of problems with Douglas's most recent interpretation of the food laws. Douglas's arguments only cover some of the animals in Leviticus 11. No explanation of the list of unclean birds is offered, though alternative explanations are dismissed as moralistic. It is unclear why fish with fins and scales should be permitted to the Israelites. They are not covered by the covenant. Further, as Houston has shown, fish are included in Genesis 1 amongst those animals that swarm in the water.[68] Consequently, Douglas's equation of swarming with fecundity, and consequently with prohibition as

---

[66] Houston, 'Integrated Reading of the Dietary Laws', 152.

[67] Douglas, *Leviticus as Literature*, 134–75; Douglas, 'Compassionate God of Leviticus'.

[68] Houston, *Purity and Monotheism*, 104–5; Houston, 'Integrated Reading of the Dietary Laws', 156.

food, cannot be sustained. Finally, the distinction between *sheqets* and *tame* is undermined by Lev. 11.43–5. In his exegesis of Leviticus, Milgrom ascribes these verses to the editorial activity of the Holiness school (H). Douglas's appeal to H's redaction is at odds with her attempt to read Leviticus as a coherent literary work.[69]

Though Douglas offered more than one interpretation of the food laws in recent years, there are certain common features that can now be seen to characterize her later work. First, there is a strong emphasis on the ethical concerns of the dietary laws and their priestly authors. The influence of Milgrom's ethical reading of the laws is clearly in evidence, especially in the important role that the prohibition against the ingestion of blood now plays. Second, Douglas is no longer convinced that the dietary laws symbolize the external boundaries of the community. The purity laws in Leviticus do not attribute impurity to any group inherently, rather impurity afflicts everyone, irrespective of class or status, at some stage. Third, there is a new emphasis on the literary and rhetorical form of Leviticus. The dubious appeal to the historical origins of the prohibition of pork has now been fully excised and Douglas concentrates on the priestly theology as expressed in the text of Leviticus. In particular, Douglas accepts Milgrom's attempt to distinguish between the priestly term *sheqets* and the Deuteronomic term *to'evah*. She, therefore, recognizes the differences between the dietary laws in Leviticus 11 and Deuteronomy 14.

APPROACHING FOOD IN THE OLD TESTAMENT

The modern discussion about the interpretation of the Old Testament dietary laws, initiated by Douglas in 1966, has seen the influence of a number of different methodological approaches. It is evident in the most recent discussions by Milgrom and Houston that this issue, like so many others in the Old Testament, is complex, and the interpreter will need to take account of a number of different issues in reading the text.

Like myself, both Milgrom and Houston have been schooled in the discipline of Old Testament interpretation, a schooling that brings with it certain insights if also its own particular blind spots. Both recognize the need for the discipline to be informed by external perspectives, in this case by the work of anthropologists. Since anthropology provides some of the most stimulating

---

[69] See ibid., 152–7.

reflections on food and culture this will be an important resource for our exploration of food in the Old Testament. The benefit of anthropology or social-scientific research to the study of the Old Testament is its ability to represent the Old Testament in all its familiarity to the interpreter as something 'other'. Conversely, it frequently has the ability to make the 'otherness' of the Old Testament more explicable by placing it within the context of other cultures.

The controversy between structuralists and developmentalists is clear warning that the Old Testament scholar, by appropriating the insights and tools of another academic discipline, cannot receive them uncritically or without recognition that they frequently exhibit theoretical perspectives that might be contested. Whilst keeping this in mind, the value of anthropological comparisons is the way they help the Old Testament scholar interpret the text. Ultimately the reading of the text that the comparison produces is the arbiter.

Within anthropology, the tension between structuralist and developmentalist methodologies has largely been spent. Our comparison of Douglas and Harris shows that whilst there was significant distance rhetorically between the approaches, the reality was often more complex. Food is, evidently, both good to eat and good to think. Attention must be paid to the ecological, material and historical context of food production, but the constructions of human societies are as significant in determining how foods are used and interpreted.

Within biblical studies, what I want to suggest is that an analogous tension between diachronic and synchronic methods has largely resolved itself with the recognition that in exploring the complex reality of the biblical text both aspects are needed. Thus, in the pages that follow, attention will be given to historical aspects of food and its symbolism, and to the literary aspects. The historical aspect includes such things as diachronic change, and the historical context and the historical-critical complexity of the biblical materials. The literary aspect includes the artistry and overarching logic of biblical books and passages. These two broad ways of approaching the biblical material are mutually informing, but must often be separated for methodological consistency and heuristic clarity. Consequently, in the chapters that follow we will move from historical issues to literary issues and back again, whilst also seeking to make clear what sort of argument is being pursued at any point. Thus, historical-criticism, archaeology, anthropology and social-scientific methods, and literary analysis are all utilized as the subject matter demands.

The second chapter, in particular, illustrates how the two approaches might inform one another, and also how they can be misused. Some recent

archaeologists have attempted to argue that the ancient Israelite diet was a very healthy one. In this analysis they have been too influenced by biblical rhetoric and have not attended to the literary and ideological purposes of this rhetoric. The archaeological evidence is then overinterpreted on the basis of a poorly informed interpretation of the biblical text. In addition, evidence that might inform a reconstruction of Israelite diet has been neglected. In contrast I offer a brief reconstruction of the Israelite diet that gives attention to the full gamut of biblical and archaeological evidence. In addition, careful consideration is given to what we do and do not know from biblical and archaeological evidence.

Subsequent chapters also attend to historical and literary aspects of the subject of food. The third chapter considers the representation of the relationship between food and memory in the book of Deuteronomy. To fully appreciate how Deuteronomy understands this relationship attention must be paid to how Deuteronomy reformulates texts from Exodus to Numbers. Thus, the historical analysis undergirds the appreciation of the book's argument. The fourth chapter analyses the confusion of food, sex, death and sacrifice in the stories of the Judges. Although operating on the literary level, giving attention to the symbolism of food and the use of punning within the book, this analysis seeks also to address the issue of why the biblical judges with all their imperfections were utilized by Deuteronomistic writers to further their own views. In this way the analysis makes use of the historical-critical observation that a distinction exists between the stories of the judges and the Deuteronomistic editorial framework.

The fifth chapter presents a historical argument that feasting was an important catalyst for state formation in pre-monarchic Israel and remained an important component of the monarchy's operation. This argument draws on anthropological evidence that feasting had such a role in other cultures, archaeological evidence and biblical texts that reflect the importance of feasting in the Israelite states. Given the importance of feasting in the Israelite monarchies, the sixth chapter explores how this is reflected in some Israelite literary works. In particular it is argued that the table is the locus at which divine condemnation or vindication is demonstrated. The seventh chapter examines how this literary motif is developed in the Second Temple period, when it is united with the Greek fascination with Persian alimentary indulgence. In this way attention is given to the literary motif of divine judgement at the table, but also the way this changing motif represents a development in Jewish food consciousness.

In the chapters that follow I have sought to give appropriate attention to the historical and literary aspects of food, respecting the integrity of each

methodological approach, but bringing them into constructive and, hopefully, fruitful dialogue as well. In my view, there is no simple formula for deciding which methodological approach will prove most useful or should be employed first in particular exegetical instances. Cookery and exegesis possess their scientific aspects, but for all that, both are, in a very real sense, arts. For me, and I hope for you as reader, the most important issue is whether at the end of my interpretation the biblical text is served well.

2

Milk and Honey: the Diet of the Israelites

To appreciate aspects of the symbolic grammar of food in the books of the Old Testament it is valuable to have some understanding of Israelite diet. What can be known about the diet of the ancient Israelites? What were its mainstays, and what would have been considered a rare luxury? Did diet vary according to social class, geographical location, or historical period? Is it possible to assess the nutritional value of the Israelite diet? In recent years attempts have been made to assess the diet during the period of the Israelite monarchy and in later periods. We will examine these attempts and subject them to critical probing. I will argue that to gain a true assessment of Israelite diet a broad set of evidence needs to be taken into consideration. This includes archaeological evidence that has not previously been utilized in the discussion about Israelite diet, such as archaeozoology and palaeopathology.

Amongst the sources of information on Israelite diet is, of course, the Old Testament, since the Old Testament frequently touches upon the foods that the ancient Israelites ate. That the information the Old Testament provides needs to be treated with critical consideration should be clear, for the Old Testament at no point purports to provide us with an objective account of Israelite diet. Indeed, as we shall see, some of the descriptions of food in the Old Testament are rhetorically marked. In assessing Israelite diet, therefore, it is necessary to engage with the tension between historical and literary approaches that we observed in the previous chapter. In other words, the Old Testament provides useful information about the historical diet of the Israelites, but the text needs to be examined critically because that information is presented in a literary manner.

POSITIVE APPRAISALS OF THE ANCIENT ISRAELITE DIET

Models of the Israelite Rural Economy and Israelite Diet

How well did the Israelites eat? The conclusion of much biblical scholarship of the last centuries has been that the Israelite diet was, by modern standards, barely adequate. There were a limited array of foods, meat was rarely eaten

and there was the constant threat of famine. The *Interpreter's Dictionary of the Bible* informs its readers that,

The Hebrews and early Christians did not enjoy as extensive a variety of foodstuffs as their modern descendants. Furthermore the danger of famine due to crop failure was much greater in ancient times.... In biblical times meat was not a regular part of the diet.[1]

Such views owed something to a careful reading of the biblical text, which makes occasional reference to famine, and to Robertson Smith's comparative work at the end of the nineteenth century. Smith had observed the occasional nature of meat in the nomadic diet.

Animal food—or at least the flesh of domestic animals, which are the only class of victims admitted among the Semites as ordinary and regular sacrifices—was not a common article of diet even among the nomad Arabs. The everyday food of the nomad consisted of milk, or game, when he could get it, and to a limited extent of dates and meal.... Flesh of domestic animals was eaten only as a luxury or in times of famine.[2]

Nomadism was, in Smith's time, taken to be the original social form of the Israelite tribes and their patriarchal ancestors. Smith's views, however, were slightly more nuanced than those expressed in the *Interpreter's Dictionary*, for whilst he held that, for later Israel, flesh was ordinarily consumed on feast days and holidays,[3] he also noted that sacrifices began to be multiplied on trivial occasions, and that flesh became 'a familiar luxury'.[4] It was, though, his observations about the rarity of meat in nomadic diets that became the most influential characterization of Israelite diet for subsequent scholarship.

In recent years a number of Israeli archaeologists have sought to reassess the consensus within critical biblical scholarship. Thus, Shimon Dar observes that, 'it used to be commonly thought that the inhabitants of the eastern Mediterranean basin did not eat much meat in ancient times. But the most recent excavations do not support this theory.' Instead, recent archaeological work 'teaches us about the varied and satisfying diet which the inhabitants of Palestine enjoyed in ancient times. It appears that the calorific value did

---

[1] J. F. Ross, 'Food', in *The Interpreter's Dictionary of the Bible* (New York: Abingdon Press, 1962–76), 2: 304–8.

[2] Smith, *Religion of the Semites, First Series*, 222–3. Cf. Wellhausen: 'the life of which the blood was regarded as the substance (2 Samuel xxiii.17) had for the ancient Semites something mysterious and divine about it; they felt a certain religious scruple about destroying it. With them flesh was an uncommon luxury, and they ate it with quite different feelings from those with which they partook of fruits or of milk' (J. Wellhausen, *Prolegomena to the History of Israel* (Edinburgh: Adam & Charles Black, 1885), 63).

[3] Smith, *Religion of the Semites, First Series*, 238.   [4] Ibid., 346.

not fall short of that of the present day.'[5] Dar's confidence about the ancient Israelite diet is based upon the attempts by himself and others to model the agricultural economy, population and, consequently, the diet of Israelite villages using empirical data derived from excavations.

Such an approach to modelling the rural economy of ancient Palestine is Baruch Rosen's examination of the early Iron Age site at 'Izbet Ṣarṭah.[6] In an essay included with the excavation reports, Rosen used the capacity of the silos discovered at stratum II of 'Izbet Ṣarṭah to calculate the amount of land under cultivation. At the same time, the number of families at the site allows the number of cattle available for ploughing to be estimated. Taken together with the animal proportions at the site known from faunal remains the pattern of animal husbandry can be modelled, and the contribution of milk and meat in the human diet determined.[7] Rosen makes allowances for spoiling and the need to keep seed for sowing in the following year. Similarly for the herd numbers, Rosen assumes a cull pattern that would allow the herd to be maintained. With such assumptions Rosen finds that the majority of the calories needed by the population would have come from cereals, with protein supplied by legumes. The area under cultivation would have provided a harvest that exceeded the villagers' needs, and the surplus could have been exchanged for olive oil, wine and other foodstuffs. The animal resources were less abundant. Nevertheless, Rosen concludes that this village of a hundred people could have owned around 22 cattle and 130 sheep or goats, and that the village's livestock would have supplied about 0.45 litres of milk and 44 grams of meat per person per day.[8] The population at 'Izbet Ṣarṭah, Rosen argues, enjoyed a diet that supplied all their calorie, protein and mineral needs. The only possible deficiency was a lack of vitamin C sources, which he speculates

---

[5] S. Dar, 'Food and Archaeology in Romano-Byzantine Palestine', in J. Wilkins, D. Harvey and E. Dobson (eds.), *Food in Antiquity* (Exeter: University of Exeter Press, 1995), 326–36, here 333.

[6] Dar's own attempt at modelling was with Qarawat bene Hassa, a significant regional centre of Samaria in the Hellenistic and Roman periods. Dar's model shows a community with cereal crops sufficient for local consumption, but with a wine and oil production capacity that far exceeded local needs, with the excess sold at market. A few observations are merited. First, it may be questioned whether a significant rural regional centre provides a sufficient basis from which to make claims about the diet of ancient Palestine. Second, Dar assumes that the community of Qarawat bene Hassa would have enjoyed the benefits of the generated surpluses. The question of who owned the land and labour and would receive the fruits of that labour is not addressed. There are good grounds for thinking that in the Roman-Byzantine economy a small urban-based elite would have benefited from any rural profitability. (S. Dar, *Landscape and Pattern: An Archaeological Survey of Samaria, 800 BCE-636 CE*, 2 vols. (Oxford: BAR, 1986)).

[7] B. Rosen, 'Subsistence Economy of Stratum II', in I. Finkelstein (ed.), *'Izbet Ṣarṭah*, BAR International, 299 (Oxford: BAR, 1986), 156–85.

[8] Ibid.

could have been supplied from wild or cultivated greens.[9] In a later essay, Rosen worked in the opposite direction. By estimating the population from the size of the buildings, the overall nutritional requirements of the villagers can be determined. With this information Rosen calculates the land under cultivation and the number of animals needed and determines whether such a local economy would have been feasible.[10]

The potential weakness of Rosen's models lies in their estimation of the animal population. A plausible estimate of the human population can be made from the area of buildings excavated and an area survey can suggest the amount of land available to a population centre. The proportion of caprovines to bovines can be estimated from animal bone remains, but the number of animals kept by a community must be calculated from these other estimated figures. This is a significant weakness because livestock numbers affect the estimates of the amount of land that can be ploughed and the amount of meat in the diet. In order to address this methodological weakness Aharon Sasson has recently developed a model that incorporates ethnographical data from censuses of Palestine during the British mandate. Using the census figures, he calculates the average number of animals per inhabitant for a Palestinian village that is located close to the ancient site he is investigating. In this way calculations of human population also provide an estimate of the animal population. From the number of animals available to a community, Sasson is able to calculate the meat and milk provision per person, the potential area ploughed by the cattle and the level of grain production. Comparing the food production capabilities of a village to the nutritional requirements of its inhabitants can establish the basis of the agricultural economy. He concludes that the Iron Age villages of 'Izbet Ṣarṭah and 'Ai had high pastoral components and produced a surplus of grain. The village of Naḥal Rephaim, on the other hand, had an economy based on orchards. The grain and animal products generated were for self-consumption and had to be supplemented by trade. Sasson argues that none of the sites produced a surplus in animal products, although they do provide for each individual in the village between 30 and 77 grams of meat per day and between 149 and 224 millilitres of milk per day.[11]

The exercise of estimating the amount and type of food consumed in ancient Palestine is valuable, but the figures must be treated with considerable

---

[9] B. Rosen, 'Subsistence Economy in Iron Age I', in I. Finkelstein and N. Na'aman (eds.), *From Nomadism to Monarchy: Archaeological and Historical Aspects of Ancient Israel* (Jerusalem: Israel Exploration Society, 1994), 339–51.

[10] Ibid.

[11] A. Sasson, 'The Pastoral Component in the Economy of Hill Country Sites in the Intermediate Bronze and Iron Ages: Archaeo-Ethnographic Case Studies', *Tel Aviv* 25 (1998), 3–51.

caution, for such models are only as good as the assumptions they make. First, it is possible to develop different models and, consequently, to reach different results. This is most apparent in Rosen's development of two models for the same location. In Rosen's first model the herd of 'Izbet Ṣarṭah is a relatively modest size. The villagers possess 120 caprovines and 22 cattle. In Rosen's second model, however, there are 300 caprovines and 12–15 cattle. In this second model about the same amount of land is used by the villagers, but a smaller area is devoted to crops.[12] Second, all of the data used is estimated on the basis of archaeological finds or comparative evidence: the amount of land worked, the proportion devoted to arable, horticulture and pastoral use, crop yields, population and so forth. Not only could individual figures and estimates be disputed, but also each figure introduces a margin of error that must be taken into account when using these estimates. This is especially apparent with the estimations of animal numbers since these are calculated on the basis of estimations that already carry with them a margin of error. Third, Rosen and Sasson assume that sowing and ploughing are the principal inhibitors to more extensive cultivation. However, Halstead has argued that in the ancient Near East food production capacity was limited by harvesting and post-harvest processing.[13]

Fourth, the estimation of animal numbers remains problematic even in Sasson's models. The modern Palestinian villages examined by Sasson are considerably larger than the ancient ones. Within these modern villages the number of animals per villager varies from 0.28 to 3.3, that is, by more than a factor of ten. There are numerous different ways in which animal herders can respond to their environment, and the difference in animal numbers for modern Palestinian villages is a demonstration of that. Fifth, the models of Rosen and Sasson assume that all the cattle are utilized maximally for traction. The potential for this to increase the calculated production of wheat is clear when the estimated wheat production per person of the Iron Age villages is compared to the figures for wheat production from the British censuses. Sasson estimates that 'Izbet Ṣarṭah and 'Ai produced 590 and 520 kgs of wheat per person, but the four twentieth-century villages that Sasson examines could only produce between 50 and 175 kgs of wheat per person.

Sixth, the analyses undertaken by Rosen and Sasson assume that all meat is consumed within the village, and none of it is used in exchange for other commodities. This is a puzzling assumption when set alongside the idea that some villages aimed to generate a grain surplus that could be traded. Thus, the

[12] Rosen, 'Subsistence Economy in Iron Age I', 347–9.
[13] P. Halstead, 'Plough and Power: The Economic and Social Significance of Cultivation with the Ox-drawn Ard in the Mediterranean', *Bulletin of Sumerian Agriculture* 8 (1995), 11–22.

models appear to be working with an idea of subsistence or trade in a manner that is not consistent or whose logic is unexplained. Animal remains from excavations are assumed to be representative of the diet consumed, with an identity between producers and consumers. However, when a surplus of crops is produced by the calculations it is assumed that they are traded out of the village population. It is possible, then, that the utilization of animal products, including important proteins, vitamins and minerals, within the villages has been overestimated. Sasson appears to assume that, since the animal protein needs of the community would only just be met by their own animals, they cannot have been traded outside. This assumes the priority of nutritional requirement over any political or economic need that may have existed to exchange. Additionally, it is more likely that animals will be marketed than grain, since cereals are difficult to transport and have a relatively low value. If cereals were traded it would only have been economically viable within a small area. Animals, however, are not only a valuable resource with their products highly prized, but are also easily driven to another district. Seventh, all models calculate the production capabilities of the whole village and then the figure per person. This assumes an equal division of fields, labour and animals, or an equitable distribution of agricultural produce. The latter two criticisms are particularly significant since what is assumed is a certain under-standing of early Israelite society—essentially egalitarian and with very little trade between or within districts—that is not uncontested.[14]

What such models show at their best is the probable way in which land was utilized in different locations in Palestine in response to different environmental niches.[15] We should not be surprised to discover that in an average year the Israelite villages had access to sufficient agricultural resources, and that for certain products the village could not only supply its own needs, but also produce a trading surplus. Dar, Rosen and Sasson show, as David Hopkins has argued elsewhere, that most villages in the Israelite highlands would have had a mixed farming strategy so minimalizing their risk.[16] Sasson also shows that, because of the extensive nature of pastoralism, a significant pastoral factor could not have existed in the central Israelite highlands. What these models arc not able to provide, it seems to me, is conclusive arguments about the nature and sufficiency of Israelite diet.

---

[14] See, e.g., R. B. Coote and K. W. Whitelam, *The Emergence of Early Israel in Historical Perspective*, SWBA, 5 (Sheffield: Almond Press, 1987).

[15] For a recent detailed description of the environmental niches in the central highlands, see R. D. Miller II, *Chieftains of the Highland Clans: A History of Israel in the Twelfth and Eleventh Centuries B.C.* (Grand Rapids: Eerdmans, 2005), pp. 52–63.

[16] D. C. Hopkins, *The Highlands of Canaan: Agricultural Life in the Early Iron Age*, SWBA, 3 (Sheffield: JSOT Press, 1985).

Other Assessments of Israelite Diet

Whatever their methodological problems, the attempts to examine Israelite diet by Dar, Rosen and Sasson seek to be logical, rigorous and transparent. They also utilize a number of sources, especially archaeological ones. The assessment of the land of Israel and its productivity has not always been so dispassionate. The rhetorical assessment of Palestine's fecundity is found as early as the Middle Egyptian story 'The Tale of Sinuhe', where the land of 'Yaa' is described.

It was a good land called Yaa. Figs were in it and grapes. It had more wine than water. Abundant was its honey, plentiful its oil. All kinds of fruit were on its trees. Barley was there and emmer, and no end of cattle of all kinds.[17]

The Old Testament is no less glowing in its description of the land of Canaan:

YHWH your God is bringing you into a good land, a land with flowing streams, with springs and underground waters welling up in valleys and hills, a land of wheat and barley, of vines and fig trees and pomegranates, a land of olive trees and honey, a land where you may eat bread without scarcity, where you will lack nothing, a land whose stones are iron and from whose hills you may mine copper. You shall eat your fill and bless YHWH your God for the good land that he has given you.   (Deut. 8.7–10)

Most memorably, the land is described to the oppressed Israelite slaves as 'a land flowing with milk and honey' (Exod. 3.8). For Ezekiel such descriptions are not sufficiently superlative. It is not only a land flowing with milk and honey, it is also 'the most glorious of all lands' (Ezek. 20.15).

The biblical descriptions have, quite understandably, been taken up by Jewish and Christian writers. It is hardly surprising that ancient Israelite and Jewish writers spoke of their homeland in exalted terms. Rarely did they have any experience of other lands, and when they did some of Israel's neighbours would have provided a favourable comparison. The rocky and arid hills of Edom, or the deserts of Sinai and Egypt, make Israel look like a veritable paradise. Still more influential was the ideological conviction that the land had been given by God, and could hardly be less than very good. For Christians too the abundance of the Promised Land confirmed the generosity of God and promised a more exalted spiritual inheritance to them. According to the early Christian historian Hegessipus,

The land is rich and grassy: it is adorned with every kind of crop, and dotted with trees. Indeed it would charm any one, and would attract even a lazy man to think about working on the land. ... The ground is easy to work with implements, and fairly

---

[17] M. Lichtheim, *Ancient Egyptian Literature: A Book of Readings*, vol. 1: *The Old and Middle Kingdoms* (Berkeley: University of California Press, 1973), 226–7.

soft, which makes it good for corn, and second to none for its fertility. . . . The region is wooded, and thus rich in cattle, flowing with milk, and there is positively no other place where cows have udders so full of milk. Fruit, whether wild or cultivated, is more abundant in this region than in any other.[18]

Some scholars have accepted such portrayals as essentially true. Oded Borowski, for example, begins his book-length treatment of Israelite agriculture with the biblical idealizations, which he affirms as basically accurate.

Eretz Israel was regarded by the OT as 'a land flowing with milk and honey' (Exod 3:8). A more detailed description of its agricultural richness and mineral resources is presented to the Israelites with the words [of Deut 8:7–9]. . . . Although some of the details in this description are idealized, the portrayal of the agricultural versatility of Palestine is accurate.[19]

The accuracy of the biblical account is 'evident from historical documents and archaeological discoveries'. The overlap between the 'Tale of Sinuhe' and Deuteronomy 8, for example, appears to be more than happy coincidence. When Borowski discusses the diet of the ancient Israelites in his account of daily life in biblical times, he is similarly positive.

It is assumed that the ancient Mediterranean diet was a healthy one, and many modern references are made to this effect. Although there is evidence that some of the ancient inhabitants of the region were not slim and trim, most of the available information suggests that most people were not overweight, due to their diet and the strenuous physical activities in which they were engaged.[20]

The extent to which we can we draw conclusions from the rhetorical biblical descriptions of the land of Canaan must be questioned. It is immediately apparent that the biblical texts do not purport to provide a scientific account of Israelite diet. Some descriptions of the produce of the land in the Old Testament are undoubtedly representative. Deuteronomy's repeated references to the so-called Mediterranean triad of 'grain, wine and oil' maps accurately to the three main Israelite crops. On the other hand, the description of the 'land flowing with milk and honey' is a rhetorical creation.[21] The exact significance of the two foodstuffs is debated, but, if a comparison with Isa. 7.22 is apt, it

---

[18] J. Wilkinson, *Jerusalem Pilgrims: Before the Crusades*, 2nd edn. (Warminster: Aris & Phillips, 2002), 94–8, 216–30.

[19] O. Borowski, *Agriculture in Ancient Israel* (Winona Lake: Eisenbrauns, 1987), 3.

[20] O. Borowski, *Daily Life in Biblical Times* (Atlanta: Society of Biblical Literature, 2003), 63. The implication that the Israelites might have been overweight had it not been for their many physical activities cannot be supported. As with other ancient populations, the true risk was under-nourishment.

[21] Lohfink writes: 'one problem is that the well-being and wealth is painted in colors that really do not fit the land of Israel' (N. Lohfink, '"I am Yahweh, Your Physician" (Exodus 15:26): God, Society and Human Health in a Postexilic Revision of the Pentateuch (Exod. 15:2b, 26)', in

may be a reference to the land's natural fecundity and not to its agricultural production.[22] One characteristic of the expression deserves particular notice, and that is its teleological function. The use of 'the land flowing with milk and honey' always anticipates the reality of a land not yet experienced. Most uses of the expression are to be found in the Pentateuch, and even those in the prophets are part of projections back to Israel's wilderness experience. We should also observe that Borowski's account lacks any references to the other side of the biblical portrayal of food and diet. There are frequent references in the Bible and later literature to the periodic famines that were experienced in Palestine.

If the use of biblical references is problematic in Borowski's account, so is his reference to the 'Mediterranean diet'. The virtues of the Mediterranean diet have been widely publicized in the media, especially in contrast to the consumption patterns of Western societies. The low incidence of heart disease and cancer in the peoples of southern Europe is generally attributed to their healthy diet. Since the basic elements of the diet are unchanged—cereals, oil and wine—it is tempting to draw similar conclusions about the healthiness of the ancient Mediterranean diet. However, there are good grounds, as the classical scholar Peter Garnsey has argued, for hesitancy at this point.[23] For one thing the Mediterranean diet has not remained static. Tomatoes, potatoes and many other fruit and vegetables have been introduced over the centuries. As the diet has diversified so the dominance of the 'Mediterranean triad' has diminished. The narrowness of the ancient diet must be reckoned with, and it is now widely recognized that only a varied diet will provide all the vitamins and minerals that humans need.

If citing biblical rhetoric about the fecundity of the Promised Land is an exercise vulnerable to serious misunderstanding so also is listing the potential foodstuffs available to the Israelites. Borowski employs such an approach in his book on *Daily Life in Biblical Times*. King and Stager do likewise in their *Life in Biblical Israel*, alongside biblical and Egyptian accounts of the land's fecundity and diverse produce.[24] On the one hand, such lists make a clear contribution as a form of responsible lexicography and have a long academic heritage.[25] The Old Testament presents a bewildering array of flora and fauna

---

Theology of the Pentateuch: Themes of the Priestly Narrative and Deuteronomy (Edinburgh: T&T Clark, 1994), 35–95, here 84 n. 137).

[22] This makes Borowski's appeal to it, in a book on *Agriculture in Ancient Israel*, somewhat inapt.

[23] Garnsey, *Food and Society*, 12–21.

[24] P. J. King and L. Stager, *Life in Biblical Israel*, Library of Ancient Israel (Louisville: Westminster John Knox Press, 2001), 85–107.

[25] A. Macalister, 'Food', in *A Dictionary of the Bible*, ed. J. Hastings (Edinburgh: T&T Clark, 1899), 2: 27–43.

that the Israelites consumed. Many of these items are of uncertain meaning, and by listing them and discussing their possible meanings a valuable service is rendered to the reader of the Bible. On the other hand, it easily becomes an extension of the rhetoric of Deuteronomy 8; it provides the fullest possible listing of items that were on the Israelite menu. The impression is easily given that each of the foods listed were available to the average Israelite and potentially contributed to their diet. In reality the weekly menu of the average Israelite covered a narrow range of foods, and many of the items mentioned in the Old Testament may never have passed their lips. Variety is not the only issue, for access to food is also significant. We cannot assume that all Israelites, especially the poor, were able to obtain a varied diet. A diet may contribute sufficient calories for survival, but be deficient in vitamins and minerals with serious consequences for human health. Indeed, as we shall see, a diet consisting of grain, legumes and olive oil has significant deficiencies.

INVESTIGATING BIBLICAL DIET

Our critical analysis of the work by Borowski, Rosen and Sasson has begun to reveal how complex and multi-faceted any investigation into the Israelite diet must be. The different writers begin from different places and utilize different sources and data in attempting to assess Israelite diet. For an account of Israelite diet to be compelling it must be comprehensive and integrate the various sources of knowledge about life in ancient Palestine. Thus, Robertson Smith's comparison of Israelite diet with Bedouin diet raises a number of issues that merit critical probing, but the use of comparative anthropology has a place in a critical consideration of Israelite diet. Dar's rejection of an earlier consensus about the place of meat in Israelite diet replaces one source of knowledge with another, but without justification or explanation of that choice. Additionally, as we will see, there are important sources of information about Israelite diet that none of these writers incorporate into their work.

The first set of sources for our understanding of the diet of the ancient Israelites is the surviving written documents from the period. This means primarily, but not exclusively, the documents that constitute what is known as either the Old Testament or the Hebrew Bible. The problems of using the Old Testament as a source of any form of historical information are well known and the consumption of food by the Israelites is no exception. A basic issue in the case of diet is the security of our lexicographical knowledge. There are numerous foodstuffs that are mentioned in the Old Testament, not all of

which can be identified with confidence. Comparative Semitics, the translation instincts of the early versions, a knowledge of the ecological possibilities in ancient Palestine might all contribute to our knowledge in what is often a difficult field.[26]

A problem that attends any historical work on the Old Testament is the compositional complexity of the biblical texts. The issues can hardly be understated, and the present text reflects not only oral traditions but a lengthy process of composition and redacting. As a great deal of recent scholarship has emphasized, most of the books in their final form are the result of the activities of a scribal elite based in Jerusalem in the Persian and Hellenistic periods. We should expect the books to bear the impress of their values and judgements, but also to some degree those of their literary predecessors.

A quite different problem, that is just as fundamental, is that the Old Testament does not address the questions of diet that we wish to pose to it. In other words, it does not provide an objective, statistical account of the diet of a variety of Israelites from different periods, places and social groups. References to food, when they occur in the Old Testament, serve to further the various intentions of the authors and editors. On many occasions the Old Testament writers may unconsciously reflect valuations of food that were held in Israelite society. Vegetables, for example, were not regarded highly, and this is reflected in Prov. 15.17: 'Better is a dinner of vegetables where love is than a fatted ox and hatred with it.'[27] Pulses, too, which may have had an important place in the Israelite diet, are hardly mentioned at all. Other unconscious biases are likely to be towards male, elite, urban diets, and we have little sense of how this may have differed from the diet of women and children, the poor, and rural inhabitants.

Written documents other than the Old Testament that touch upon diet in ancient Israel are limited in number. The meagre epigraphic finds from ancient Palestine do include ostraca from Samaria and Arad, which describe the distribution of flour, bread, wine and oil. Unlike the Old Testament there are no problems of a complex editorial history. Such material, however, is not without its own interpretative challenges. For example, to what extent are such snapshots representative of conditions during the Israelite monarchy?

---

[26] For the latter, see especially J. M. Renfrew, *Palaeoethnobotany: The Prehistoric Food Plants of the Near East and Europe* (London: Methuen, 1973); D. Zohary and M. Hopf, *Domestication of Plants in the Old World: The Origin and Spread of Cultivated Plants in West Asia, Europe, and the Nile Valley*, 2nd edn. (Oxford: Clarendon Press, 1994).

[27] The low opinion of vegetables continues to be found in some rabbinic texts. In *b. Pes.* 42a coarse bread, new beer and raw vegetables are considered unhealthy, whilst sifted bread, fat meat and old wine are considered beneficial (M. J. Geller, 'Diet and Regimen in the Babylonian Diet', in C. Grottanelli and L. Milano (eds.), *Food and Identity in the Ancient World*, History of the Ancient Near East Studies, 9 (Padua: Sargon, 2004), 217–42).

The second group of sources for reconstructing the Israelite diet are archaeological remains discovered during excavations. Dar, Rosen and Sasson make particular use of many of the results of traditional archaeological research. Population numbers are estimated from the size of buildings used for human occupation. The remains of agricultural installations and storage facilities provide evidence of land use and can give some idea of the level of food production.

In their models Rosen and Sasson also make some use of animal bones, which provide evidence not only of meat consumption, but also of the nature of the economy. The ratio of sheep to cattle can indicate whether a community was pastoral or agricultural, since cattle were primarily kept for traction. There are, however, other ways that the evidence of animal bones can shed light on the ancient Israelite diet. It is now possible for archaeozoologists to determine the age of mortality. Cull patterns can suggest how herds were used. Unfortunately, although this specialized area of archaeology has produced an impressive array of results from a number of archaeological sites across Israel, there have been little more than a few *ad hoc* attempts at synthesis. The abundance of faunal remains contrasts strongly with the poverty of floral remains. Interesting results from the studies of plants are frequently the result of chance findings due to carbonization or dessication. However, where palaeobotanical remains, such as seeds or wood, exist, they can give important information about plant cultivation. Unfortunately, such results are not frequently utilized in surveys of Israelite diet. Also under-utilized is the study of human remains, palaeopathology, which has much promise for the reconstruction of ancient diet, since bones and teeth can provide evidence of environmental stress.

The discoveries of archaeologists need critical interpretation no less than ancient texts. A few detailed examples are sufficient to illustrate specific issues related to the question of the Israelite diet. The discovery of animal bones (such as camel bones) need not imply consumption, and some remains that are difficult to detect, such as fish bones, have been missed in earlier excavations. We cannot determine what quantity of meat was consumed by individuals, although the ratio of one animal to another may indicate proportional contribution to diet. Cereal and fruit seeds and wood from fruit trees have been found frequently at archaeological sites, but vegetables almost never. Absence from the archaeological record does not imply absence from the Israelite diet.

Our third set of sources is comparative evidence of diet in other related cultures. There is a great deal of epigraphic and archaeological information available for many of Israel's ancient Near Eastern neighbours. These include the Egyptian empire and the various empires that dominated Mesopotamia.

Sharing similar geographical and climatic constraints, there are Israel's immediate neighbours, such as the Syrian kingdoms and evidence from states such
as Ugarit. Chronologically proximate are the Bronze Age and the Hellenistic,
Roman and Byzantine periods. Recent scholarship has shown that the boundaries between these historical periods should not be overemphasized, and that
in each case there was significant material and cultural continuity. This is
especially the case with food, for whilst new foodstuffs were introduced at
various points the dietary mainstays remained fairly constant. Nevertheless,
the same critical judgements that are necessary in analysing the written and
archaeological evidence for the Israelite period also apply to other historical
periods.

Comparative evidence of a quite different sort is provided by modern
anthropological research into non-industrialized societies. The diet and nutrition of contemporary pastoralists, for example, can provide a useful comparison to some sections of Israelite society. The problems attending the critical
use of modern anthropological models and data are now well known. Chronological and spatial distance require careful handling. Anthropological research
on modern communities in Palestine is useful for observing responsiveness
to similar ecological constraints, but the relationship between man and his
environment is not unidirectional. The environment of ancient Israel had
been managed/mismanaged by the time of the settlement and has continued
to change under human use to the present. Another important problem concerns the models that explicitly or implicitly inform reconstructions. Thus, for
example, Robertson Smith's assumption of the nomadic origins of Israel and
the relevance of a comparison with nineteenth-century Palestinian Bedouin is
questionable and requires reformulation. Moving further afield, other primitive societies potentially provide evidence of societal structure, patterns of
exchange, food distribution and the use and generation of surpluses.

A fourth set of sources that must be brought into the dialogue is scientific
knowledge on food production and consumption. A number of different areas
of scientific study are relevant to our investigation. First, food production
is made possible and constrained by the environment of Israel. The various
branches of geography—meteorology, geology, soil science—contribute to
our understanding of agricultural possibility. Second, nutritional science aids
in considering the effect of individual food items in the diet and the overall
healthiness of a diet.

There are, then, a number of sources that can help in our reconstruction of
the diet of the ancient Israelites and our assessment of its nutritional value.
Since we do not have direct access to data about the consumption of the
Israelites, it is necessary to make use of all these sources, giving careful consideration to their strengths and weaknesses, and, consequently, the weight they

can bear. Even where this is done, we are likely to find that the evidence for the Israelite diet is fragmentary, and it will be necessary to accept the uncertainties that exist.

TOWARDS A CRITICAL ACCOUNT OF ISRAELITE DIET

To adequately consider Israelite diet, doing justice to all the relevant sources, would require a treatment far larger than this chapter.[28] Nevertheless, in shorter compass, it is possible to sketch out a critically reconstructed diet of the ancient Israelites which utilizes the various sources of information already outlined. This includes sources that have been under-utilized and provide new perspectives on, and pose fresh questions about, the diet of the ancient Israelites.

The Components of the Israelite Diet

The main components of the ancient Israelite diet were certainly the so-called 'Mediterranean triad'. Not only do biblical texts refer to 'the grain, the wine and the oil' (for example Hos. 2.8), but its importance can be seen in non-biblical texts, such as the Arad inscriptions,[29] and in the agricultural installations, such as olive and wine presses, discovered in archaeological excavations. Probably the vast majority of Israelite land under cultivation was given over to the Mediterranean triad.

The most important of the triad in terms of its contribution to diet was grain. For the typical Israelite, bread or other grain-based foods such as porridge probably contributed over half their calorific intake, with estimates varying between 53 and 75 per cent.[30] In the North the main grain crop was

---

[28] For a more thorough examination of the diet of the ancient Israelites, see MacDonald, *What Did the Ancient Israelites.*

[29] Y. Aharoni, *Arad Inscriptions* (Jerusalem: Israel Exploration Society, 1981), 11–118, 141–51; A. F. Rainey, 'Three Additional Texts', in Y. Aharoni, *Arad Inscriptions* (Jerusalem: Israel Exploration Society, 1981), 122–5; J. Naveh, 'The Aramaic Ostraca from Tel Arad', in Y. Aharoni, *Arad Inscriptions* (Jerusalem: Israel Exploration Society, 1981), 153–76; G. A. Reisner, C. S. Fisher and D. G. Lyon, *Harvard Excavations at Samaria, 1908–1910*, vol. 1 (Cambridge, MA: Harvard University Press, 1924), 227–46; B. Rosen, 'Wine and Oil Allocations in the Samaria Ostraca', *Tel Aviv* 13–14 (1986–7), 39–45.

[30] It is impossible to provide exact quantities for ancient societies, and this is especially the case for ancient Israel. It is worth outlining some of the comparative evidence that may inform our understanding of the role of cereals in Israelite diet. The ration lists from Egypt and Mesopotamia consistently indicate the prominence of cereals (see, for example, R. Ellison,

wheat, whilst in the drier South it was barley. In Israel, as in many other parts of the ancient world, wheat was valued higher than barley.[31] Wine is ubiquitous in the Old Testament and the vine or its fruit was often used as a symbol of Israel by the prophets. The frequent references to wine in the Old Testament suggest that it was the principal drink. Whether it was usually watered down before consumption, as was the practice of the Greeks and Romans,[32] or drunk undiluted is uncertain. Isaiah's disparaging comparison of Judah's righteousness as 'wine mixed with water' (1.22) might suggest that there was a preference for undiluted wine. Olive oil had a number of uses, including as a dietary component. It was part of the mishnaic food basket that the rabbinic sages required to be provided for an estranged wife, where it contributed 11 per cent of the overall calories.[33] The Old Testament, though, says little of it as a foodstuff. In the story of Elijah and the widow of Zarephath the oil is mixed with flour to make a cake (1 Kgs. 17.12–13). Other uses suggest it was a valuable product associated with good eating (Ezek. 16.13, 19; Isa. 25.6).

Breads and porridges were probably supplemented ordinarily by vegetables, pulses and fruit. To what extent is unclear as these foodstuffs rarely leave a trace in the archaeological record. In addition, their appearance in the Old Testament may not be representative; a low value was placed on vegetables, but fruit was highly esteemed. Those who ate vegetables in significant amounts may have been at the extremes of Israelite society: the few who could afford to set aside land for a vegetable garden (cf. 1 Kings 21), and the poor who may have used wild vegetation and other foods to supplement their diet: leafy plants, bulbs, wild fruits and nuts, roots, mushrooms.[34] In the Iron

'Diet in Mesopotamia: The Evidence of the Barley Ration Texts (c. 3000–1400 B.C.)', *Iraq* 43 (1981), 35–45). For the diet of Roman Palestine, Magen Broshi takes the food basket that the Mishnah required be given to an estranged wife as representative. On this basis he calculates that 'bread supplied half the daily calories (53–55 per cent)'. This compares favourably with the proportions consumed by the modern Arab population in Israel and Palestine (M. Broshi, 'The Diet of Palestine in the Roman Period: Introductory Notes', in *Bread, Wine, Walls and Scrolls*, JSPSup, 36 (London: Sheffield Academic Press, 2001), 121–43, here 123). On the other hand, Foxhall and Forbes suggest a figure of 70–75 per cent for the Roman empire (L. Foxhall and H. A. Forbes, '*Sitometreia*: The Role of Grain as a Staple Food in Classical Antiquity', *Chiron* 12 (1982), 41–90). Either figure is far higher than the bread consumption in modern Western economies.

[31] See 1 Kgs. 4.28; 2 Kgs. 7.16; cf. *m. Ket.* 5.8 (Broshi, 'Diet of Palestine', 124).

[32] Broshi assumes the wine was diluted in the Roman period. M. Broshi, 'Wine in Ancient Palestine: Introductory Notes', in *Bread, Wine, Water and Scrolls*, JSPSup, 36 (London: Sheffield Academic Press, 2001), 144–72, here 161–2).

[33] Broshi, 'Diet of Palestine', 122. The amount of oil to be provided depends on the conversion rate used for a 'log' of olive oil.

[34] Rosen notes that 'there is occasional evidence of the use of wild plants in the Iron Age. Traces of *Malva* sp. in Beer-Sheba attest to their role as contributors of calories and vitamins to

Age significant parts of Palestine were still covered by thick forests, especially in the north of the country. These forests would have provided ideal
environments for foraging for wild vegetation. Various pulses are mentioned
in the Old Testament, including the lentil and broad bean, and others have
been found in archaeological excavations. It is possible that they played a
more substantial role in Israelite diets than the Old Testament or archaeology
might lead us to suspect.[35] The Israelites were familiar with a number of
fruits, the most important of which were grapes, the fig and the pomegranate
(cf. Deut. 8.8–9). Fruits are mentioned frequently in the Old Testament, but
may have played a relatively minor role in Israelite diet. The exception is
the fig, which is mentioned frequently in the Old Testament, particularly
alongside other staples in food assemblages (e.g. 1 Sam. 25.18; 30.12; 2
Sam. 16.1–2).[36]

Assessing the place of animal products in the ancient Israelite diet is an area
fraught with controversy, especially in relation to meat. As we have seen, critical Old Testament scholarship has maintained that meat was consumed only
on rare occasions, though this has been challenged in some recent scholarship.

the nutritional intake of the contemporary peasant' (Rosen, 'Subsistence Economy in Iron Age
I', 342).

On the Roman period, Broshi observes that, 'a considerable number of the vegetables consumed in our period... were wild (as they are for the modern Palestinian Arab peasant)... a
close reading of the Talmudic literature and of modern ethnobotanical literature reveals the
important contribution of wild vegetables to the diet' (Broshi, 'Diet of Palestine', 131; cf. J. M.
Frayn, *Subsistence Farming in Roman Italy* (London: Centaur Press, 1979)). To a large degree
the use of wild plants by the Israelites to supplement their diet is a matter of critical conjecture
because of the limitations of our sources. For another ancient society for which there is greater
literary evidence, see J. M. Frayn, 'Wild and Cultivated Plants: A Note on the Peasant Economy
of Roman Italy', *Journal of Roman Studies* 65 (1975), 32–9.

[35] First, in societies where meat is a rarity, pulses are an important source of protein. 'In
traditional agricultural communities pulses served—and still serve—as a main meat substitute'
(Zohary and Hopf, *Domestication of Plants*, 86). Second, legume rotation could have played an
important role agriculturally. Wheat and barley quickly exhaust the soil's fertility and its supply
of nitrogen. Leguminous crops utilize nitrogen from the air and ultimately return it to the soil.
This form of crop rotation was certainly employed extensively during the Roman empire (K. D.
White, *Roman Farming: Aspects of Greek and Roman Life* (Ithaca: Cornell University Press, 1970),
113, 121 3). The question is whether the same is true of Iron Age Palestine. Hopkins suggests that
the possibility of legume rotation should remain open, though the Old Testament only makes
mention of fields left fully fallow (Hopkins, *Highlands of Canaan*). Third, in Roman Palestine
there is evidence that pulses played a significant role in the diet (Broshi, 'Diet of Palestine', 122;
Y. Feliks, 'Jewish Agriculture in the Period of the Mishnah', in Z. Baras (ed.), *Eretz Israel from
the Destruction of the Second Temple to the Muslim Conquests* (Jerusalem: Yad Ben Zvi, 1982),
419–41), and this may have been true for earlier periods.

[36] Borowski notes that 'the importance of the fig tree as one of the mainstays of biblical
economy cannot be overemphasized' (Borowski, *Agriculture*, 114). The fig was also part of the
mishnaic food basket (Broshi, 'Diet of Palestine').

Nevertheless, as we have seen, there are a number of difficulties with the models proposed by Dar, Rosen and Sasson.

One of the most important and under-utilized sources of information on ancient Israelite diet is archaeozoology, the scientific examination of animal bones recovered from archaeological excavations. Archaeozoology provides not only evidence of the proportion of animals kept at a site, but also the age at which animals were culled. The cull profile of a herd can suggest how the animals were primarily used: as sources of meat, or for their secondary products—milk, wool or traction. Over the last thirty years a valuable and nuanced picture of meat consumption and animal husbandry practices in ancient Israel has been built up.[37]

The archaeozoological evidence suggests that the main animals consumed were the four domesticated animals—cows, pigs, sheep and goats. In the north of Israel wild animals were occasionally killed and eaten. Although there is evidence of some pig consumption in Iron Age Palestine this was unusual outside of early Iron Age Philistia. Sheep and goats were more common than cows, but since one cow provides a large amount of meat, in areas where cows were kept more beef was consumed than sheep or goat meat. Cull data suggests that animals were frequently kept for secondary products, such as milk and wool, rather than as sources of meat. Nevertheless, animals do have to be culled and at those points make meat available for consumption within the community or for the market.

There is evidence for changing cull patterns and, together with what we know about Israel's social and historical development, this suggests changing patterns of animal consumption. In early tribal Israel animals were kept primarily for their secondary products, but the lack of significant social stratification meant that when they were culled the meat was probably distributed within the community and in a relatively equitable manner. The development of Israelite society during the monarchy sees a slight shift towards animals being butchered at prime ages. Greater social stratification means that probably an elite enjoyed this greater consumption of meat more than the average Israelite. With the rise of Assyrian empire, however, it has been suggested that the Assyrians may have exploited the animal economy in Palestine. Prime age animals were exported to Mesopotamia.[38] This is certainly likely as we have evidence of the exploitation of Palestine's horticultural resources

---

[37] Unfortunately this data has been scattered in technical archaeological reports and has only rarely been brought together to provide a comprehensive picture. For my own attempt see MacDonald, *What Did the Ancient Israelites*.

[38] P. Wapnish, 'Archaeozoology: The Integration of Faunal Data with Biblical Archaeology', in A. Biran and J. Aviram (eds.), *Biblical Archaeology Today, 1990: Proceedings of the Second*

through industrial-scale wine and olive oil production facilities discovered in Ashkelon, Gibeon and Ekron during this period.[39] If this were the case, then meat would have become far less common for most Israelites during this period.

Unfortunately, animal remains cannot inform us about how much meat was consumed per capita over a given period of time. Dar is probably right to question the assumption that the Israelites rarely ate meat, for animals have to be culled to maximize the flock's productivity. The models employed by Dar, Rosen and Sasson suggest that not insignificant quantities of meat may have been available. Yet, the possibility of Assyrian exploitation during one period of Palestinian history highlights the fact that factors of distribution as well as production must be considered.[40] We have no evidence for how socio-economic status would have affected the amount of meat consumed in ancient Israel, but it would not be unreasonable to assume that it played a role and that males and elites had greater access to food resources. Thus, whilst we should hesitate to assume meat was rarely eaten, it would be unwise to regard it as a regular part of the average Israelite's diet.

Domesticated animals were important not only for providing a supply of meat, but also for the secondary products that they provide. Goats and, to a lesser extent, sheep were particularly valuable because they provided fresh milk for part of the year. Since milk quickly soured in the heat, it was often processed into ghee or 'cheese'. Since a mixed farming economy was pursued in many parts of Palestine dairy products were probably an important part of many Israelites' diets, but especially so for pastoralists in the south and east of Palestine.

Our assessment of the place of fish in the ancient Israelite diet also needs to take into account recent archaeological finds. One of the most surprising discoveries of recent excavations is the extensive evidence for the consumption of fish. It has often been assumed that, with no direct access to the sea during their history and very few perennial rivers, ancient Israelites rarely ate fish, particularly in the early periods. Further justification for this argument appeared to be provided by the absence of fish from the Israelite sacrificial regulations. The discovery of fish remains from almost every recent excavation requires these conclusions to be abandoned. The fish include not only freshwater fish from the Sea of Galilee or the few perennial rivers in Palestine, but also

---

International Congress on Biblical Archaeology (Jerusalem: Israel Exploration Society, 1993), 426–42.

[39] L. E. Stager, 'Ashkelon and the Archaeology of Destruction: Kislev 604 BCE', *Eretz Israel* 25 (1996), 61–74; J. B. Pritchard, *Winery, Defenses and Soundings at Gibeon* (Philadelphia: Pennsylvania University Museum, 1964).

[40] Goody, *Cooking, Cuisine and Class.*

freshwater fish from the Nile and marine fish from the Mediterranean Sea and the Red Sea. The discovery of fish that originated in the Nile or the Red Sea suggests that there existed throughout the Eastern Mediterranean an extensive trading network in fish, to which even inland Israelite cities belonged.[41] As the Iron Age progressed fish appears to have become readily available, but it was probably expensive and restricted to urban elites and to those who lived along the Jordan valley or other major rivers.

The Healthiness of the Israelite Diet

Our critical description of dietary components has shown that different items made varying contributions to the Israelite diet. The ancient Israelites were not presented with a choice of foods from which they could choose as they wished. For the vast majority of Israelites food was determined by availability. Probably only a small elite was able to make limited choices about its diet, and even for them the principal component would still have been grain-based. We have also seen that diet was not fixed, but varied over time. In addition, diet varied according to location. The diet in the south and east where there was a larger pastoral component to the economy would have been significantly different from the hills and valleys of the north where crops and fruit trees were cultivated. Finally, diet would have varied according to social location, varying not only between the extremes of wealthy elite and the landless poor, but probably also between males and females. Thus, diet varied according to axes of time, place and social location, such that we can only speak of Israelite *diet* to the extent that we recognize this dietary variation.

How healthy was the diet of the ancient Israelites? As we have seen, models of the agricultural capacity of Israelite settlements suggest that the land under cultivation could have provided sufficient calories for their populations. Yet there are other constraints that the environment of Palestine imposes, not least a variable climate. The pages of the Old Testament make frequent reference to the regularity of famine induced by low rainfall, and modern records show that rainfall in the Levant is highly variable.[42] David Hopkins notes that 'for Jerusalem...three years out of ten will experience accumulation of rainfall about 16 percent less than the mean and that one or two of these years will

---

[41] See W. Van Neer et al., 'Fish Remains from Archaeological Sites as Indicators of Former Trade Connections in the Eastern Mediterranean', *Paléorient* 30 (2004), 101–48.

[42] Aharoni writes, 'years of drought and famine run like a scarlet thread through the ancient history of Palestine' (Y. Aharoni, *The Land of the Bible: A Historical Geography*, 2nd edn. (London: Burns & Oates, 1979), 14).

experience more than 25 percent less'.[43] In addition, the timing of the rains—Deuteronomy 11's 'early' and 'later' rains—is also essential. It is likely that only in the most extreme cases a pattern of poor years would lead to catastrophic famine with starvation, but lean years could result in poor nutrition, a perilous situation for the particularly vulnerable—especially young children and lactating mothers.[44]

Nutrition means more than calorific intake. The possibility that ancient diets, dominated by cereal consumption, might give rise to nutritional deficiencies was first raised by Rosemary Ellison in relation to Mesopotamian diet.[45] Assuming that the diet of workers who received barley rations was not supplemented with any other food, she concluded that 'the most obvious nutritional deficiencies in the barley rations were those of vitamin C and vitamin A'.[46] Good sources of vitamin A are dairy products, animal livers and the green leaves of plants; vitamin C is found in fruit and vegetables as well as fresh meat. In the ancient Near East, where diets may well have been low in animal foods, fruit and vegetables, serious deficiencies could occur. Vitamin A deficiency is associated with a variety of eye diseases, including night-blindness, xerophthalmia and blindness.[47] Vitamin C deficiency can lead to scurvy, though occurrences of scurvy may well have been seasonal.[48] As Peter Garnsey notes in his study of Roman diets, another possible nutritional deficiency in diets with a high cereal content is iron deficiency anaemia. Bran has a very high content of phytate, which inhibits iron absorption.[49] In ancient Israel cereals were probably frequently consumed as chapattis made from flour with a high extraction rate (under-sieved) and thus the bran and phytate intake of ancient Israelites would have been high. Consequently iron deficiency anaemia may have been common, particularly among children and pregnant women. Iron deficiency affects brain function and the immune system and can reduce working capacity. Even in the present, it is the most common nutritional deficiency disorder, and is particularly prevalent in non-industrialized countries.[50]

---

[43] Hopkins, *Highlands of Canaan*, 89. See also J. Neumann, 'On the Incidence of Dry and Wet Years', *IEJ* 5 (1955), 137–53.

[44] For famine and nutrition in the Graeco-Roman world note Garnsey, *Famine and Food Supply*.

[45] Ellison, 'Diet in Mesopotamia'; R. Ellison, 'Some Thoughts on the Diet of Mesopotamia from c. 3000–600 B.C.', *Iraq* 45 (1983), 146–50.

[46] Ellison, 'Some Thoughts on the Diet of Mesopotamia', 149.

[47] D. S. McLaren et al., 'Fat-Soluble Vitamins', in J. S. Garrow and W. P. T. James (eds.), *Human Nutrition and Dietetics*, 9th edn. (Edinburgh: Churchill Livingstone, 1993), 208–38, here 212.

[48] Ellison, 'Some Thoughts on the Diet of Mesopotamia', 149.

[49] Garnsey, *Food and Society*, 20–1.

[50] L. Hallberg, B. Sandström and P. J. Aggett, 'Iron, Zinc and Other Trace Elements', in J. S. Garrow and W. P. T. James (eds.), *Human Nutrition and Dietetics*, 9th edn. (Edinburgh: Churchill Livingstone, 1993), 174–207, here 182.

Critical reconstruction of Israelite diets and comparison with contemporary pre-industrialized diets provides some basis for suspecting that the nutritional status of ancient Israel's population may have fallen short of the ideal. A degree of substantiation can be provided by palaeopathology, the scientific study of human skeletal remains. Modern advances in palaeopathology mean that skeletal remains can provide evidence of a limited number of nutritional diseases and deficiencies.

Unfortunately there have been relatively few findings of human remains from Iron Age Palestine and only some of these have been submitted to palaeopathological investigation. For Iron Age Israel the most important study undertaken was upon the skeletal remains of 60 individuals found in Jerusalem and dated to the seventh century BC.[51] In this group there were 17 examples of a condition known as cribra orbitalia (31.5 per cent). Cribra orbitalia and the closely related porotic hyperostosis are pathologies of the cranium that have often been discussed as possible indicators of iron deficiency. Both terms are used to describe lesions on different parts of the skull.[52] The condition occurs in childhood and results from iron-deficiency anaemia: a reduction below normal in the concentration of haemoglobin or red blood cells.[53] It has been common to associate this condition with an inadequate diet, though caution must be exercised here, for there are a number of possible causes of iron-deficiency anaemia. In particular, it has been suggested that iron deficiency is part of the body's defence against infection, and consequently is better judged as evidence of a high exposure to infectious diseases.[54] It may not be necessary to choose between inadequate diet and high exposure to infection. Vulnerability to disease and poor nutritional status have a symbiotic relationship. Thus evidence of chronic iron deficiency may still provide indirect evidence of poor nutrition.[55] The

---

[51] The remains were unearthed from a burial cave on the western slopes of Mount Zion. The date and location of the remains would strongly suggest these were Judahite burials, as also do the other archaeological finds (B. Arensberg and Y. Rak, 'Jewish Skeletal Remains from the Period of the Kings of Judaea', *PEQ* 117 (1985), 30–4).

[52] 'These lesions are characterized by pitting of the compact bone, usually associated with an increase in the thickness of the adjacent diploic bone. The lesions can vary in size from less than 1mm in diameter to large, coalescing apertures, and are found on the orbital roof and skull vault, particularly the frontal, parietal, and occipital bones' (P. L. Stuart-Macadam, 'Nutritional Deficiency Diseases: A Survey of Scurvy, Rickets and Iron-Deficiency Anemia', in M. Y. Işcan and K. A. R. Kennedy (eds.), *Reconstruction of Life from the Skeleton* (New York: Liss, 1989), 201–22, here 217).

[53] Ibid., 212.

[54] Ibid. For a statement about the current state of knowledge, see A. C. Aufderheide and C. Rodriguez-Martin, *The Cambridge Encyclopaedia of Human Palaepathology* (Cambridge: Cambridge University Press, 1998), 1–10, 348–51.

[55] Stuart-Macadam, 'Nutritional Deficiency Diseases', 219–20; Garnsey, *Food and Society*, 43–61; N. Scrimshaw, C. E. Taylor and J. E. Gordon, *Interactions of Nutrition and Infection* (Geneva: World Health Organization, 1968). Stuart-Macadam concludes her article on

occurrence of cribra orbitalia in the Iron Age population of Jerusalem is in no way unusual for historical Palestine. Similar levels are found in other historical periods.

Together with the evidence for iron-deficiency anaemia we should also note that life expectancy at Iron Age sites in Palestine is markedly lower than in the Bronze Age or the Hellenistic and Roman periods. Only further discoveries will confirm whether or not these sites are representative, but such evidence would again suggest the population did not enjoy a good health status. These demographic patterns are consistent with those from many other pre-modern agricultural communities. They suggest that most people had a short life, with a high level of infant mortality, and few adults surviving beyond the age of fifty.[56] This cannot be attributed to nutrition alone, but there are good grounds for thinking that poor nutrition played a contributory role.

CONCLUSION

The discussion of the *realia* of Israelite diet has revealed that an apparently simple subject is extremely complex. A comprehensive account of Israelite diet is extremely difficult, but a number of different sources of information do provide important evidence of its nature. I have argued that we cannot

nutritional deficiency diseases in the following manner. 'It is true that nutrition is an important aspect of the relationship between a population and its environment. However, a comprehensive survey of scurvy, rickets, and iron-deficiency anemia illustrates the importance of other culturally and environmentally determined factors involved in this relationship. There are complex adaptations between the human body, its nutrient requirements, and its environment. It is vital to have an appreciation of these complexities in any consideration of a "nutritional deficiency" disease' (Stuart-Macadam, 'Nutritional Deficiency Diseases', 220).

[56] Pat Smith notes that 'most adults from all the archaeological sites appear to die before 50 years of age. The Iron Age seems to be the lowest and the Hellenistic the highest, from the point of view of percentage of older adults.' For the Iron Age period less than 20 per cent of adults survived beyond the age of fifty. Smith notes further that 'even the data for the Hellenistic period differ markedly from that calculated from death registries for a 20th century rural district in Egypt (nearly 60% surviving beyond 50), while WHO statistics for England report over 85% surviving beyond 50 years of age. Either conditions in the Hellenistic period were incomparably worse than those of rural Egypt at the present time, or our data are too incomplete to provide an accurate assessment of longevity' (P. Smith and L. Kolska-Horowitz, 'Culture, Environment and Disease: Palaeo-Anthropological Findings for the Southern Levant', in C. L. Greenblatt (ed.), *Digging for Pathogenes* (Rehovot: Balaban, 1998), 201–39, here 226–7; cf. P. Smith, 'An Approach to the Palaeodemographic Analysis of Human Skeletal Remains from Archaeological Sites', in A. Biran and J. Aviram (eds.), *Biblical Archaeology Today, 1990: Proceedings of the Second International Congress on Biblical Archaeology* (Jerusalem: Israel Exploration Society, 1993), 2–13).

afford to ignore or marginalize any of these sources of information. If we do we may gain a view of Israelite diet that is unrepresentative of the historical reality. The variety of different sources that need to be taken into consideration demonstrate the importance of the pluralistic methodology outlined in the previous chapter. It is only by giving attention to all our potential sources of knowledge—textual, archaeological and comparative—that a nuanced and critical account of Israelite diet can be reached.

3

Chewing the Cud: Food and Memory in Deuteronomy

In one of the earliest readings of the Jewish dietary laws, the *Letter of Aristeas* interprets the instructions about clean animals in the following manner: 'all cloven-footed creatures and ruminants quite clearly express, to those who perceive it, the phenomenon of memory. Rumination is nothing but the recalling of (the creature's) life and constitution, life being usually constituted by nourishment.'[1] *Aristeas* then goes on to blend two quotations from the book of Deuteronomy, 'Thou shalt remember the Lord, who did great and wonderful deeds in thee' (Deut. 7.18; 10.21).[2] *Aristeas* interprets 'in thee' from Deut. 10.21 as a reference to the human body, which offers the believer the opportunity to meditate on God's wonderful works. In calling these to mind God,

has ordained every time and place for a continual reminder of the supreme God and upholder (of all). Accordingly in the matter of meats and drinks he commands men to offer first fruits and to consume them there and then straightaway. Furthermore in our clothes he has given us a distinguishing mark as a reminder, and similarly on our gates and doors he has commanded us to set up the 'Words', so as to be a reminder of God.[3]

With these words *Aristeas* maintains its focus on Deuteronomy and his creative blending of texts, bringing together the Deuteronomic emphasis on feasts as

---

[1] *Letter of Aristeas* 153–4 (translation from R. J. H. Shutt, 'Letter of Aristeas', in J. H. Charlesworth (ed.), *The Old Testament Pseudepigrapha*, vol. 2: *Expansions of the 'Old Testament' and Legends, Wisdom and Philosophical Literature, Prayers, Psalms, and Odes, Fragments of Lost Judeo-Hellenistic Works* (New York: Doubleday, 1985), 7–34). In his discussion of the Jewish dietary laws in *De Specialibus Legibus* Philo presents a similar understanding of the clean land animals. 'For just as a cud-chewing animal after biting through the food keeps it at rest in the gullet, again after a bit draws it up and masticates it and then passes it on to the belly, so the pupil after receiving from the teacher through his ears the principles and lore of wisdom prolongs the process of learning, as he cannot at once apprehend and grasp them securely, till by using his memory to call up each thing that he has heard by constant exercises which act as the cement of conceptions, he stamps a firm impression of them on his soul' (*Spec. Leg.* 4.107 (translation from Philo, *Philo VIII*, trans. F. H. Colson, Loeb Classical Library (Cambridge, MA: Harvard University Press, 1960))). Philo appears to be indebted to the *Letter of Aristeas* or, at the very least, a common Jewish exegetical tradition.

[2] *Letter of Aristeas* 155.   [3] Ibid. 157.

locations of memory and the instruction to physically display the commandments on clothing and buildings.

In choosing Deuteronomy to illustrate the importance of 'a continual
reminder of the supreme God' *Aristeas* certainly chose well. The importance of
memory to the Deuteronomic paraenesis has also been observed by modern
Old Testament scholars. In his examination of the theological development of
the subject of memory in ancient Israel, Brevard Childs begins with Deuteronomy: 'in the preaching of the Deuteronomist the word [*zakar*] is used with
a theological significance which goes beyond the general psychological'.[4]
E. P. Blair also draws attention to the importance of 'the memory motif in
Deuteronomy'.[5] Neither observes any particular association between memory
and food, although Blair notes that in the Old Testament generally 'the feasts,
ceremonies, and memorial objects of Israel were designed to help the people
"remember"'.[6] *Aristeas*, on the other hand, whilst certainly mistaken in understanding the dietary laws to be teaching the importance of memory, has an
intuitive grasp of the close connection between memory and food in the book
of Deuteronomy. Food is a central means by which to remember YHWH's 'great
and wonderful deeds', not in relation to the human body as divine creation as
Aristeas understands them, but as Deuteronomy clearly intends, in relation to
YHWH's actions in Israel's history.

FOOD AND MEMORY

In recent historical research, as we have seen, food and foodways have become
important areas of study. Food is not merely a matter of the nutritional
health of historical populations. Among other things, it reveals significant
and changing attitudes about social structure, national identities, gender roles
and religious beliefs. Consequently food is an important source of historical
knowledge. Yet food is not merely a part of the past; it is also a means of
remembering the past. As David Sutton puts it, 'if "we are what we eat", then
"we are what we ate" as well'.[7] Memories are formed within communities, and
food is one of the ways in which communities structure the past.

---

[4] B. S. Childs, *Memory and Tradition in Ancient Israel*, SBT, 37 (London: SCM Press, 1962),
50.

[5] E. P. Blair, 'An Appeal to Remembrance: The Memory Motif in Deuteronomy', *Int* 15 (1961),
41–7.

[6] Ibid., 44. This is also true of the most recent discussion of memory and Deuteronomy by
R. P. O'Dowd: 'Memory on the Boundary: Epistemology in Deuteronomy', in M. Healy and
R. Parry (eds.), *The Bible and Epistemology: Biblical Soundings on the Knowledge of God* (Milton
Keynes: Paternoster, 2007), 3–22.

[7] Sutton, *Remembrance of Repasts*, 7.

Taste and smell are the most imprecise of the senses and have the least developed vocabulary. It may be precisely for this reason that they are the most evocative of the senses with the ability to awaken memories.[8] A sustained study of the relationship between memory and food from an anthropological perspective is to be found in Sutton's *Remembrance of Repasts: An Anthropology of Food and Memory*. We will outline some of the arguments made by Sutton and briefly consider a recent application of his ideas to the field of New Testament studies before returning to the subject of food and memory in the book of Deuteronomy.

David Sutton's *Remembrance of Repasts*

David Sutton's work on food and memory stems from fieldwork undertaken on the Greek island of Kalymnos. There he found food to be an important repository of communal memory, leading him to examine the interrelationship between culture, food and memory amongst the islanders. In describing the forms taken by memories generated by food, Sutton utilizes a distinction made by Paul Connerton between 'inscribed' and 'incorporated' memories. The former are concerned with any practices of storing and retrieving information, especially through textualization, whilst the latter focus attention on the embodiment of memory.[9] Since food concerns the consumption of physical objects by the body the memories that it creates are best thought of as incorporated memories. Whilst inscribed memories are often performed only occasionally in acts of writing down and rereading, incorporated memories result from habitual repetition. Thus, embodied memories are concerned with performance and active appropriation, rather than passive reception.

One of the most obvious places in which food is a vehicle for memory is in ritual acts of eating. Ritual feasts mark the passing of the agricultural year and the cycle of life from birth to death. Nevertheless, Sutton avoids drawing a strong distinction between ritual and quotidian acts of eating. Drawing upon Mary Douglas's work on patterns of meals he suggests that 'mundane and extraordinary eating are connected: mutually entailed in systems of meaning, metaphors of each other'.[10] Thus, even everyday meals reflect the agricultural cycle as certain foods associated with particular seasons are consumed. It is not only past and present that are related by the system of meals, the future

[8] T. J. Gorringe, *The Education of Desire: Towards a Theology of the Senses* (London: SCM Press, 2001), 22–6. Cf. Sutton, *Remembrance of Repasts*, 88–90.

[9] Sutton, *Remembrance of Repasts*, 10–11, with reference to P. Connerton, *How Societies Remember* (Cambridge: Cambridge University Press, 1989), 72–104.

[10] Sutton, *Remembrance of Repasts*, 20, with reference to Douglas, 'Deciphering a Meal'.

is also anticipated. 'Food is equally important in the creation of *prospective memories*, that is, in orientating people toward future memories that will be created in the consumption of food.'[11]

A second area where Sutton examines food's ability to generate and structure memory is the exchange of food. Anthropologists have long been fascinated by the circulation of gifts through exchange, but food is often bracketed out of the discussion because it is consumed and cannot continue to circulate within the society. Sutton reminds his readers that food too is exchanged, and what is circulated is reputation in the form of stories about generosity, hospitality or even inhospitable behaviour. Since the food is itself consumed after exchange it is a potent medium of 'embodied' memory 'because it *internalizes* the debt to the other'.[12] The memories that are generated are important both as expressions of social relations and as constructions of identity. This is true not only for the individual, but also on the level of the community. Kalymnian narratives claim hospitality to be characteristic of Greeks and especially Kalymnians. Such memories as configurations of the past in relation to the present are usually concerned with hospitality in the recent past, but Sutton also observes that food generates nostalgia for a distant past when, it is held, communal relations were closer and hospitality more generous.

A third area that Sutton examines is the capacity of food to construct 'worlds'. For members of the Greek diaspora particular foods—their taste, texture and smell—evoke memories of home. Such food can become a localized cultural 'whole' that provides a brief sense of comprehensive identification for the culturally displaced. For those who remain at home sending food to family members is a way of maintaining such memories and the incorporation of those relatives within the community. A second aspect of world construction appears in a proclivity towards synaesthesia, the use of different senses to describe one another. According to Sutton these assist memory, underscore the sense of embodiment, and ensure identification with the totality of the national homeland.

Finally, Sutton analysed the embodiment of memory that finds expression in the transmission of culinary skill. In Kalymnos, as in so many cultures, cooking is traditionally learnt by observation and practice, rather than by following instructions from a recipe book. Such an approach to food production allows for constant adjustment through the process of cooking, and for variation within a recognized theme. It is an embodied memory. Those trained in its practice treat with disdain culinary technology and those who rely on it. However, according to Sutton, since the Second World War there has been a shift amongst Greeks from embodied learning to textual instructions. This

---

[11] Sutton, *Remembrance of Repasts*, 28. Italics original.   [12] Ibid., 46. Italics original.

does not dissolve the role of memory in food production, it only reconfigures it. This can be seen amongst the Kalmynian diaspora in America where there is considerable appetite for 'nostalgia cookbooks', where recipes are interspersed with personal reflections and other cultural reminiscences.

Food and Memory in 1 Corinthians

Sutton's achievement is to describe the numerous relationships that exist between food and the memory of the past. The potential of bringing Sutton's anthropological work to bear upon biblical texts is demonstrated by Louise Lawrence's examination of 1 Corinthians.[13] As Lawrence observes, 'food appears with notable frequency in 1 Corinthians and serves as a powerful and evocative image for debate on other issues'.[14] Lawrence gives particular attention to Paul's instructions about the Lord's Supper in 1 Corinthians 11, observing that, of the New Testament writers, Paul is unique in making memory a key element of the ritual.

For Paul the ritual of the Lord's Supper brings Christ's Passion, the worshipping Christian community and the eschatological future together in an act of memorialization and anticipation: 'for as often as you eat this bread and drink the cup, you proclaim the Lord's death until he comes' (1 Cor. 11.26). The meal memorializes a narrative of generosity, Jesus' giving of his flesh for his disciples, which Paul contrasts with the inhospitable behaviour of some of the Corinthians. The meal is to be an act of identification with the crucified Lord and an imitation of him. The sensory elements of the rite—taking and eating—expresses the community that should result from participation. It is, Lawrence notes, also significant that Paul places particular emphasis on a practice that is embodied, rather than inscribed. Consequently, any interpretation of 1 Corinthians 11 must give attention not only to what the meal symbolized or meant—the typical concern of interpreters—but also to what the meal physically accomplished.

Memory in Deuteronomy

Lawrence's study shows that food and memory can be closely configured in biblical texts, and that there is value in introducing Sutton's analysis to interpret this configuration. If 1 Corinthians 11 is a prime text for such a

---

[13] L. J. Lawrence, *Reading with Anthropology: Exhibiting Aspects of New Testament Religion* (Milton Keynes: Paternoster Press, 2005), 172–86.
[14] Ibid., 178.

convergence of food and memory in the New Testament, I wish to suggest the same is true of Deuteronomy in the Old Testament.[15] As we have seen this was grasped intuitively by *Aristeas*. More recently I attempted to draw attention to the relationship between food and memory in Deuteronomy 8, noting that, 'in Deuteronomy 8 . . . food is the vehicle through which Deuteronomy envisages Israel expressing her remembrance of YHWH. Through hunger and the manna she is to express her humble dependence on YHWH, and through the abundance of bread in the land she is to express thankfulness to YHWH'.[16] What is required is to extend the analysis beyond Deuteronomy 8 to the book as a whole.[17] In the rest of this chapter we will examine Israel's memory of her *heilsgeschichte*, the memory of the Canaanites and the memory of her encounter with other nations. Finally we will return to Connerton's distinction between inscribed and incorporated memory and ask whether it is appropriate when it comes to the book of Deuteronomy.

MEALS IN DEUTERONOMY AND THE MEMORY OF ISRAEL'S *HEILSGESCHICHTE*

The origins of the book of Deuteronomy are usually placed sometime around the middle of the seventh century BC, towards the end of the Judaean kingdom. Within this context the book is intended as a blueprint for the reform of the

---

[15] There has been recent interest in memory amongst Old Testament scholars, although it seems to me that this has often been used to negotiate the perennial tension in modern scholarship between critical reconstructions of Levantine history and Israel's own account of its history (see, e.g., M. S. Smith, *The Memoirs of God: History, Memory, and the Experience of the Divine in Ancient Israel* (Minneapolis: Fortress Press, 2004), esp. 124–58; J. Assmann, *Moses the Egyptian: The Memory of Egypt in Western Monotheism* (Cambridge, MA: Harvard University Press, 1997); R. S. Hendel, *Remembering Abraham: Culture, Memory, and History in the Hebrew Bible* (New York: Oxford University Press, 2005)). Much closer to the concerns of this chapter is the essay by Blenkinsopp (J. Blenkinsopp, 'Memory, Tradition, and the Construction of the Past in Ancient Israel', *BTB* 27 (1997), 76–82). Blenkinsopp observes that 'social memory is shaped, sustained, and transmitted to a great extent by non-inscribed practices including rituals of re-enactment, commemorative ceremonies, bodily gestures, and the like' (78). He notes particularly the importance of feasting and fasting as sites of memory. Unfortunately Blenkinsopp's treatment of the subject is very brief.

[16] N. MacDonald, *Deuteronomy and the Meaning of 'Monotheism'*, FAT, II/1 (Tübingen: Mohr Siebeck, 2003), 139. Additionally, I observed that 'the chapter does not describe the "passive response of covenant loyalty" in contrast to the "active response" of chapter 7. . . . Remembrance in Deuteronomy is not something passive. Instead, both chapters describe the active ways in which "love" to YHWH is to be expressed.' The resonances with Sutton's discussion of embodiment and the performative nature of memory are apparent enough.

[17] At the time I observed in a footnote: 'with its emphasis on food as a vehicle for expressing love to YHWH, Deuteronomy 8 shares in a theme that runs throughout the book (see, for example, chapters 12 and 14)' (ibid., 139 n. 80).

social, religious and political life of the nation. This Deuteronomic reform programme has many different facets, but an important part of the structure for this programme and its theological values is a coherent account of the historical experience of the people of Israel. According to Deuteronomy Israel is a well-defined body of people that have known the election of YHWH. In the distant past their ancestors enjoyed a special relationship with YHWH. At a later period the people experienced the saving power of YHWH in Egypt, his address at Horeb, where they entered into a covenant with him, and his sustenance during the wilderness wanderings. In the literary presentation of the book as an address by Moses on the borders of the Promised Land, the last major component of that history is the anticipated conquest of the land.

For the book of Deuteronomy this account of Israel's origins though YHWH's saving actions, her *heilsgeschichte*, is not just true, but so central to Israel's identity and calling that its memorization is crucial to the Deuteronomic reform programme. Fathers, exodus, wilderness and conquest together articulate Israel's relationship to YHWH, his law and his land. Whether this Deuteronomic history presupposes an alternative account of Israel's experience is uncertain,[18] but we would be mistaken to imagine Deuteronomy's assumed audience already knew the Deuteronomic historical outline in the manner deemed necessary by the proponents of the reform programme. Rather through obedience to the Deuteronomic law the hearers of the book participated in practices of memorialization, and the memorized history in turn provided justification for the law that had generated it.

To examine the relationship between meals and Deuteronomy's account of Israel's *heilsgeschichte* we will turn first to the so-called 'small historical *credo*' in Deut. 26.5–11, before turning to the Deuteronomic festive calendar in Deuteronomy 16, and finally to Deuteronomy's concerns about satiation leading to forgetfulness of Israel's *heilsgeschichte*.

The 'Small Historical *Credo*'

A justly famous example of the Deuteronomic account of Israelite history is the so-called 'small historical *credo*' in Deut. 26.5–11:

---

[18] It has often been suggested that the Deuteronomic movement combated a belief that had an interest in fertility as one of its central elements. Earlier scholarly characterizations of 'Canaanite fertility religion' were frequently unguarded and unduly polemical. Nelson's recent account of the background to the 'small historical credo' in Deut. 26.5–11 makes use of the fertility motif of pre-Deuteronomic Israelite religion, but is more nuanced in its description. 'The text intends to unify the events of national history in terms of Yahweh's saving action and to concretize them in the fertility of the land. ... Fertility is centered firmly on Israel's history with Yahweh, perhaps as a way of devaluing competing, problematic ceremonies or ideologies of fertility' (Nelson, *Deuteronomy*, 310).

My father was a wandering Aramean. He went down to Egypt and sojourned there as an alien, little in number. There he became a great, powerful and numerous nation. The Egyptians ill-treated and oppressed us, and imposed harsh labour upon us. We cried to YHWH, the god of our fathers. YHWH heard our voice and saw our affliction, trouble and oppression. YHWH brought us up from Egypt with a strong hand and an outstretched arm, with great terror and signs and wonders. He brought us to this place and he gave us this land, a land flowing with milk and honey. So now, see, I bring the firstfruits of the ground that you have given to me, O YHWH.

Although von Rad sought to argue that this was an ancient creed that predated Deuteronomy, it is now generally taken to be a late theological summary.[19] It includes many of the elements of the Deuteronomic account of national history, omitting only those that are unnecessary for its contrast between Israel's historical experience and that of the grateful Israelite farmer. The creed is to be recited during the offering of the firstfruits at the sanctuary, and is presumably presented to the hearer of Deuteronomy as something to be memorized for that event. Although the declaration is to be made by the individual Israelite, the creed links the 'I' of the present and the future with the 'we' of Israel's national past. More importantly for our concerns, this particular moment of memorialization occurs at the offering of food to YHWH.

The recital is to take place at the offering of the firstfruits of the harvest to YHWH.[20] Whether envisaged as a regular annual offering or a foundational obligation for the initial harvest after the conquest the firstfruits are emblematic of the possession of the land. The memorialized history itself reflects this with the contrast between Israel's earlier landless existence and the situation of the offerer. Whether as wandering Aramean or as landless alien in Egypt, Israel's national life prior to the conquest lacked possession of land. Lack of land means neither more nor less than a precipitous existence without

---

[19] See, e.g., G. von Rad, 'The Form-Critical Problem of the Hexateuch', *The Problem of the Hexateuch and Other Essays* (Edinburgh: Oliver & Boyd, 1966), 1–78; N. Lohfink, 'The Small Credo of Deuteronomy 26:5–9', in *The Theology of the Pentateuch: Themes of the Priestly Narrative and Deuteronomy* (Edinburgh: T&T Clark, 1994), 265–89; L. Rost, 'Das kleine geschichtliche Credo', in L. Rost (ed.), *Das kleine Credo und andere Studien zum Alten Testament* (Heidelberg: Quelle & Meyer, 1965), 11–25.

[20] It is unclear whether this would be an offering at the Feast of Weeks or the Feast of Tabernacles. Firstfruits is connected with the Feast of Weeks elsewhere in the Pentateuch (Exod. 23.16; 34.22; Num. 28.26) and would be the obvious context (so, e.g., J. G. McConville, *Law and Theology in Deuteronomy*, JSOTSup, 33 (Sheffield: JSOT Press, 1984), 120), but the reference to a basket, which suggests the offering of fruit and not just grain, could suggest the Feast of Tabernacles (so, e.g., G. Braulik, *Deuteronomium II 16:18–34:12*, NEB (Würzburg: Echter, 1992), 196). Nelson suggests that 'to cut through this impasse, the interpreter must realise that Deuteronomy was more interested in promoting theology than in establishing a coherent liturgical system' (Nelson, *Deuteronomy*, 307). As we will see in our examination of Deuteronomy's festive calendar, the book makes no sharp distinction between the two festivals, both of which celebrate the gift of the land.

a secure source of food. What is offered to YHWH, the giver of the land, is food, the produce of the land. Consequently the firstfruits are not themselves consumed by the donor, but are left at the altar (26.10) to be consumed by the priests (18.4).[21] Nevertheless, the offering of the firstfruits is the context for a celebratory meal for, as we shall see, 'rejoicing' with the Levite and the resident alien (26.11) is a reference to a communal meal.

Within Deuteronomy 26 the 'small historical *credo*' is related closely to the instructions that follow concerning the triennial tithe, a matter already discussed in Deuteronomy (vv. 12–15; cf. 14.28–9).[22] Following the distribution of the tithe to the poor and other dependants, the farmer is to visit the sanctuary and make a declaration. The declaration that he has completed the distribution in the required manner is followed by an appeal: 'Look down from your holy habitation, from heaven, and bless your people Israel and the land that you gave to us just as you swore to our fathers, a land flowing with milk and honey' (26.15). On this occasion distribution of food is linked to a historical confession about the land, by implication the conquest, and the memory of the nation's ancestors.

We may justly question, with Aeldred Cody, whether it might not be more appropriate to describe these historical recollections as examples of anamnesis rather than *credo*. That is, through the Israelite's statement YHWH's historial dealings with Israel are recalled and become part of his identity in the present. The land which he has farmed and from which he has collected his crops is identified as the land promised by YHWH to his ancestors, now possessed.[23] With this recollection the individual Israelite farmer becomes part of the Deuteronomic account of history.

---

[21] *Contra* D. T. Olson, *Deuteronomy and the Death of Moses: A Theological Reading*, OBT (Minneapolis: Fortress Press, 1994), 115.

[22] The two offertory prayers belong together in the final form of Deuteronomy 26 (cf. Rad, 'Form-Critical Problem', 3).

[23] A. Cody, ' "Little Historical Creed" or "Little Historical Anamnesis"?' *CBQ* 68 (2006), 1–10. Cody poses the obvious question about the difference between a creed and an anamnesis: 'Is not an anamnesis a statement of belief, like a creed? Not really. In an anamnesis, belief in the reality or truth of what is recalled is presupposed, but the primary purpose of an anamnesis is to recall, not to state belief in the truth of what is recalled. In a ritual anamnesis, what is recalled, what we identify with, what is perhaps actualized, may be an object or a person, as Senn says in his definition, but it may also be an event' (5, with reference to F. C. Senn, 'Anamnesis', in *The New Dictionary of Sacramental Worship*, ed. P. E. Fink (Collegeville: Liturgical Press, 1990), 42–3). We may well wonder whether this understanding of a creed is not a little attenuated. Mere belief does not seem to be what von Rad intended by speaking of Deuteronomy 26 as a *credo*: 'The whole might be called a confession of faith, or rather an enumeration of the saving facts which were the constitutive element of the religious community. The speaker divests himself of all his personal concerns and aligns himself with the community' (Rad, 'Form-Critical Problem', 4–5) Nevertheless, anamnesis seems more closely to approximate the emphasis on national memory.

Deuteronomy's Festive Calendar

The historical memory that Deuteronomy seeks to instil in its hearers is an important expression of its novel imagination of the cult. The Deuteronomic cult is centred around communal acts of eating which connect the memory of the past actions of YHWH with the present experience of divine generosity in the Promised Land. The memory of the past and the experience of the present are united in acts of joyful celebration, which are central to the Deuteronomic concept of worship. Compared to the Canaanite cults with all their paraphernalia, the Deuteronomic cult appears relatively spartan with only a single altar at the sanctuary where sacrificial offerings are made. It is perhaps because of this that the book so emphasizes the joy of worship centred around a communal feast: 'You shall eat there in the presence of YHWH, your god, and rejoice in every undertaking of your hands in which YHWH, your god, has blessed you, both you and your households' (12.7).[24] Indeed, this is so much the case that in Deuteronomy 'to rejoice before YHWH' is shorthand for celebrating a cultic meal (14.26; cf. 16.11, 14).

The Deuteronomic writer's positive assessment of the cultic feast is characteristic of his general attitude towards food and sustenance. The danger that food poses is that it is so good and abundant that it results in forgetfulness.[25] This positivity contrasts with Exodus 34, where there is concern that the people of Israel may be tempted to join the cultic feasts of their Canaanite neighbours and so be lead into idolatry and intermarriage. Deuteronomy shares the concerns about idolatry and intermarriage, but does not relate them to the observance of Canaanite festivals (7.1–5). With the exception of the 'bread of affliction' eaten at the feast of Passover–Unleavened Bread, it seems that food in Deuteronomy is always a cause for rejoicing. The abundance of the Promised Land is a sign of the divine generosity which is to be freely enjoyed.

Joyful worship at the sanctuary is focused around the pilgrimage feasts that are outlined in chapter 16. 'Three times a year all your males shall appear before YHWH, your god, in the place that he will choose: at the Feast of Unleavened Bread, at the Feast of Weeks and at the Feast of Tabernacles. He shall not appear before YHWH empty handed' (16.16). It has often been observed that the Deuteronomic festival calendar is a reworking of earlier calendars (e.g. Exodus 23), which makes a number of significant changes to its precursors.

---

[24] See T. M. Willis, "'Eat and Rejoice before the Lord": The Optimism of Worship in the Deuteronomic Code', in M. P. Graham, R. R. Marrs and S. L. McKenzie (eds.), *Worship and the Hebrew Bible: Essays in Honour of John T. Willis*, JSOTSup, 284 (Sheffield: Sheffield Academic Press, 1999), 276–94.

[25] It is interesting to observe, for example, that in the Deuteronomic retelling of the incident of the Golden Calf any mention of the people being made to drink from the stream into which the desiccated calf had been scattered is omitted (Deut. 9.21; cf. Exod. 32.20).

Most significantly the feasts are given a central role in Israel's recollecting of the past.

The Deuteronomic festival calendar emphasizes the combined festival of Passover and Unleavened Bread. This combination has a particularly important place within scholarship because the Passover slaughter and the Feast of Unleavened Bread appear to have had an independent history prior to Deuteronomy's integration of them.[26] Tracing the origins and development of the two celebrations prior to their integration by Deuteronomy has proved difficult and scholarly disagreements remain on various details.[27] According to Exodus 23 the Feast of Unleavened Bread is already a celebration held in the same month as the Israelites left Egypt (v. 15). The old idea that Unleavened Bread was originally a celebration of the barley harvest cannot be squared with a date in the month of Abib (March–April), when the crop is still immature.[28] The evening Passover slaughter, on the other hand, is associated with the tenth plague, the destruction of the firstborn *prior* to the exodus from Egypt, according to Exodus 13. In Deuteronomy the Passover and the Feast of Unleavened Bread are not only related, but both are associated with the exodus. Thus, the moment of the Passover slaughter becomes in Deuteronomy the exact time of the exodus. 'There you shall sacrifice the Passover at evening, when the sun goes down, the time when you went out of Egypt. Boil it and eat it' (16.6).[29] For Exodus the Passover is an apotropaic rite that protects the life of the firstborn, in Deuteronomy it has become a meal of remembrance. Observing the shift Levinson comments, 'remarkably, in Deuteronomy, the Passover proper—the deliverance from the tenth plague—remains entirely without cultic commemoration!'[30] Not quite so remarkable, perhaps, because the deliverance from the tenth plague plays no part in the Deuteronomic recitations of Israel's history of salvation, whilst the exodus from Egypt is crucial.

In the Deuteronomic code the Feast of Unleavened Bread and the Passover overlap, for the Passover is not to be eaten with leavened bread (v. 3), and like the Feast of Unleavened Bread commemorates the exodus. The consumption

---

[26] Levinson provides a detailed discussion, see B. M. Levinson, *Deuteronomy and the Hermeneutics of Legal Innovation* (Oxford: Oxford University Press, 1998), 53–97.

[27] On Passover, e.g., compare ibid., 53–97 and A. D. H. Mayes, *Deuteronomy*, NCB (London: Oliphants, 1979), 254–7.

[28] For a review of the arguments see Mayes, *Deuteronomy*, 254–7. Occasionally the older view is uncritically assumed, e.g., J. A. Soggin, *Israel in the Biblical Period: Institutions, Festivals, Ceremonies, Rituals*, trans. J. Bowden (Edinburgh: T&T Clark, 2001), 93–4.

[29] Boiling the meat is the appropriate procedure if the Passover animal is understood as a sacrifice. Exod. 12.9 forbids boiling in water and prescribes roasting. As is well known 2 Chron. 35.13 seeks to resolve with 'they boiled the Passover in the fire'.

[30] Levinson, *Deuteronomy and the Hermeneutics of Legal Innovation*, 78.

of unleavened bread is explained as arising from the haste with which the people exited Egypt, but it is also given a unique symbolic interpretation as 'bread of affliction'.[31] 'Affliction' is one of the ways the oppression of the Israelites in Egypt is described (Exod. 3.7, 17; 4.31). This symbolic association is all the more striking since food bearing negative connotations is unusual in Deuteronomy.[32] In addition, as Braulik observes, the unleavened bread has been placed at the heart of the Feast of Passover–Unleavened Bread.[33]

The historical symbolism of Passover and Unleavened Bread may not be restricted to eating alone. Attention should also be given to the command in v. 7 to depart the morning after the sacrifice of the Passover. This is a well-known interpretative problem: 'return to your tents' may be an instruction for the Israelites to leave the sanctuary and return to their own homes. The Feast of Unleavened bread and the concluding 'solemn assembly' would then be celebrated at home. This argument stumbles on the unusual use of 'tents', for Deuteronomy otherwise consistently portrays the Israelites dwelling in houses. Alternatively, the Deuteronomic author may have presupposed the presence of camps around Jerusalem during the festival to which the worshippers departed.[34] It is unclear though why the celebrants would have to leave the sanctuary for nearby tents on the first day of Unleavened Bread. Additionally the celebration of a 'solemn assembly' (*atsereth*; 16.8), rather than a feast (Exod. 13.6), on the final day suggests that Deuteronomy envisages the people in their own local settings and not at the sanctuary. This problem may be resolved if the author of Deuteronomy was deliberately seeking to relate the conclusion of the Passover feast with Israel's experience of the wilderness.[35] In common with their ancestors the celebrating Israelites leave the Passover and move immediately into an existence of living in tents.

---

[31] G. Braulik, 'Leidensgedächtnisfeier und Freudenfest: "Volksliturgie" nach dem deuteronomischen Festkalender (Dtn 16,1–17)', in *Studien zur Theologie des Deuteronomiums*, SBA, 2 (Stuttgart: Katholische Bibelwerk, 1988), 95–121.

[32] Interestingly, Veijola argues that the 'bread of mourning' in 16.3 is part of a post-priestly layer (T. Veijola, 'The History of the Passover in the Light of Deuteronomy 16,1–8', *Zeitschrift für altorientalische und biblische Rechtsgeschichte* 2 (1996), 53–75).

[33] Braulik, 'Leidensgedächtnisfeier', 104.

[34] For the 'tents' as homes see, e.g., Levinson, *Deuteronomy and the Hermeneutics of Legal Innovation*, 89, and as temporary camps for the festival see, e.g., Mayes, *Deuteronomy*, 259. McConville sees the expression as a theologically motivated equivocation (J. G. McConville, 'Deuteronomy's Unification of Passover and Massot: A Response to Bernard M. Levinson', *JBL* 119 (2001), 47–58, esp. 54), though Levinson argues that this is not a 'coherent alternative' (B. M. Levinson, 'The Hermeneutics of Tradition in Deuteronomy: A Reply to J. G. McConville', *JBL* 119 (2000), 269–86, here 276).

[35] Cf. Braulik, who writes that, 'Ja die kultische Bewußtseinsveränderung greift so sehr auf das alltägliche Leben über, daß die eigenen "Stadtbereiche" (v. 5) in der Symbolik der Wanderung nun zu "Zelten" (v. 7) werden, zu denen man zurückgeht' (Braulik, 'Leidensgedächtnisfeier', 107).

The detailed attention directed towards Passover–Unleavened Bread contrasts with the relative paucity of information about the Feast of Weeks and the Feast of Tabernacles (vv. 9–15). No doubt the lack of liturgical details points in part to the assumption of previous practice. Nevertheless, in Deuteronomy both festivals appear to have lost much of their individual colour. As Weinfeld puts it, 'the feast of unleavened bread still retains some distinctiveness because of the paschal sacrifice, but the feast of weeks and the feast of booths have been generalized to such an extent that they are hardly distinguishable from each other'.[36] Both festivals celebrate points in the agricultural calendar. The Feast of Weeks celebrates the completion of the grain harvest; the Feast of Tabernacles the storage of both grain and vintage.[37] The historicization of these festivals—Weeks with the giving of the law at Sinai and Tabernacles with the wandering in the desert—is not to be found in Deuteronomy. Yet, neither is lacking some role in the formation of Israel's memory for the celebration of both feasts with the poor and impoverished leads to reflection on the relation of past and present for the community.

In contrast to Unleavened Bread's solemn consumption of the 'bread of affliction' the Feast of Weeks and Tabernacles are focused around a joyful communal repast. The landowning Israelite, whom Deuteronomy addresses, is to celebrate the goodness of God by inviting his whole family and household servants, the Levites, aliens, fatherless and widows to a feast at the sanctuary. This is expressed with the elliptical 'rejoice before YHWH, your god' (vv. 11, 14). The justification for this generosity in the case of the Feast of Weeks is the remembrance of Egypt: 'remember that you were a slave in Egypt, and keep and do these statutes' (v. 12). In the case of the Feast of Tabernacles the justification is the blessing received in the land. 'For YHWH your god will bless you in all your produce and in all the work of your hands. You will surely rejoice' (v. 15). These are not two separate explanations, rather both are aspects of a celebration of the reception of the land. The Israelite landowner remembers Egypt from the vantage point of the land which has yielded the produce with which he can be generous. Thus, the feasts of Weeks and Tabernacles celebrate the gift of the land.

Through the course of the festival calendar, therefore, Deuteronomy prescribes an annual performance of Israel's historical experience. This possibility was raised by McConville in relation to the combined feast of Passover–Unleavened Bread:

[36] M. Weinfeld, *Deuteronomy and the Deuteronomic School* (Oxford: Clarendon Press, 1972), 220.
[37] Thus, not merely the harvest of the vines (cf. Judg. 9.27; 21.19–21). See Nelson, *Deuteronomy*, 209–10.

The reason for Deuteronomy's conscious and emphatic amalgamation of Passover and Massot in 16.1–7 is an intention to bring together that theme which was supremely expressed in the Passover (viz. memory of the exodus) and one which, according to some biblical traditions was present in Massot (as in Josh. 5.10–12 and Ex. 13.5), viz. the enjoyment of Canaan's plenty.[38]

The appeal to 'some biblical traditions' betrays the indebtedness of this thesis to a synthetic reading of the festival calendars, rather than Deuteronomy's distinctive calendrical logic. Deuteronomy's calendar does move Israel from slavery to the Promised Land but this takes place over the whole festive calendar and not in the combined feast of Passover–Unleavened Bread alone. Israel begins with the feast of Passover–Unleavened Bread in slavery in Egypt, from where it moves to a wilderness experience before receiving the gifts of the Promised Land in the festivals of Weeks and Tabernacles. The different foods characterize this historical movement as one from sorrow and affliction to unalloyed joy.

Food and Forgetfulness

In the lawcode at the heart of Deuteronomy (chapters 12–26) the abundance of the land offers a cause for joy at the generosity of YHWH. Celebration takes place at the great annual feasts, but also at other times, for according to Deuteronomy food can now be consumed freely without concern. If an Israelite desires to eat meat but lives at some distance from the chosen sanctuary site, Deuteronomy permits the consumption of meat 'as much as you desire' (12.20, 21). It is noteworthy that Deuteronomy even uses a word for 'desire' (*'avah*) that has negative connotations in other passages: the sinful craving at Kibroth-hattavah (Num. 11.4; cf. Pss. 78.30; 106.14) and the Deuteronomic version of the commandment against coveting (Deut. 5.21). Similarly capacious in its permissiveness is the description of the meal that results from the triennial tithe. The purpose of the tithe is to provide for the marginalized in society so that they eat and are sated (14.28–9).[39]

In the framework to the lawcode (Deuteronomy 1–11; 27–34) eating and being sated are not positive descriptions of Israel's feasting. Instead, the abundant food of the Promised Land constitutes a threat to Israel's memory for which 'eating and being sated' is the harbinger. If food is a means of remembering Israel's *heilsgeschichte* in the lawcode, it is also a means of forgetting

---

[38] McConville, *Law and Theology*, 115.

[39] The only exception to this picture of the lawcode is the law concerning the rebellious son (Deut. 21.18–21). The son is brought before the elders because the parents find him not only 'stubborn and rebellious' but also 'a glutton and a drunkard'.

it. The danger of forgetfulness greatly exercises those who composed the lawcode's framework, for Israel's religious loyalty to YHWH is vulnerable and easily transferred to other deities. The danger of forgetfulness is a matter of such concern that it appears as the first item in the catalogue of expressions concerning loyalty to YHWH in 6.10–19:

When YHWH your god brings you to the land that he swore to your forefathers, to Abraham, Isaac and Jacob, he would give to you—fine, large cities that you did not build, houses full of every good thing that you did not fill, hewn cisterns that you did not hew, vineyards and olive groves that you did not plant—and you eat and are sated. Take care to yourselves lest you forget YHWH that brought you up out of the land of Egypt, from the house of slavery.   (vv. 10–12)

It it noteworthy that it is the history of salvation that is perceived to be under threat, the remembrance that YHWH brought the Israelites out of Egypt.

The concern about future forgetfulness is also found in 11.13–17, where eating and being sated leads to worshipping other gods, but it is in chapter 8 especially that the theme of memory and forgetting receives extended exposition: Israel is to remember the wilderness (8.2–4); she is not to forget YHWH (8.11, 14), but to remember him (8.18); following other gods is to forget YHWH (8.19). Deuteronomy 8 utilizes the liminal setting of the book of Deuteronomy to view the past experience of the wilderness and the future experience of the Promised Land. The Promised Land is described in an exuberant, almost poetic, manner that draws attention to the land's abundant supply of food.

For YHWH your god is bringing you into a good land, a land of flowing streams, springs and waters pouring out of valleys and hills, a land of wheat and barley, of vines, figs and pomegranates, a land of olive oil and honey, a land which has no scarcity of bread for you to eat, in which you will lack nothing, a land whose stones are iron and from whose hills you may mine copper.   (8.7–9)

As a description of the land it has a similar flavour to the better known 'a land flowing with milk and honey', which is also a favourite in Deuteronomy (6.3; 11.9; 26.9, 15; 27.3; 31.20). It is a parabolic description of an abundant ideal. The danger is that the abundance of the land will result in forgetfulness where the people attribute the possession of the land to their own strength and not to the actions of YHWH.

The solution that Deuteronomy offers is that the people thoroughly appropriate the lessons of the wilderness. The wilderness that the people have experienced is the extreme opposite of the Promised Land: 'the great and terrible wilderness with fiery serpents and scorpions, a desert with no water' (Deut. 8.15). In this situation the Israelites learn dependence on YHWH who supplies them with water from flinty rock and manna. The recognition of

this dependence expresses itself in humility that contrasts to self-exaltation (8.14).[40]

If inspiration is to be sought for Deuteronomy's concern with satiation in the land we may not need to go any further than the Song of Moses in Deuteronomy 32. The song is usually held to have had a history independent of the book, and evidence of this is provided by the distinctive way in which its ideas are expressed.[41] Here too we find a contrast between the experience of the howling waste of the wilderness and the Promised Land with its oil and honey, milk and curds, sheep and goats, wheat and wine (32.10, 13–14). The result of the rich land is that Israel grew fat and abandoned YHWH.

With the concern about satiation and forgetfulness, the framework of Deuteronomy creates prospective memories for life in the land. These concur with the lawcode that the Israelite experience in the land is to be characterized not by care for where the next meal is going to come from, but by abundance. For the framework this abundance offers a threat to which the lawcode makes no reference. The framework also differs from the lawcode in having a concern not only for specific cultic acts of eating, but for all acts of eating. In this way the framework places the cultic meals of the lawcode in a broader framework that views their abundance as a threat as well as a blessing and coordinates them with the quotidian meals of the Israelites. Though they do not explicitly refer to Israel's *heilsgeschichte*, which is the perspective of the cultic meals, the daily meals in the Promised Land do nevertheless offer a challenge to the Israelites to remember YHWH and to cultivate the humility that they learned when consuming the manna (8.2–5).

THE MEMORY OF THE CANAANITE CULT

Israel's loyalty to YHWH is threatened not only by forgetfulness that results from satiation in the land, but also by the memory of the Canaanite cult. As we have already seen, Deuteronomy's festival calendar, with its emphasis on memorializing the acts of YHWH through feasting, is an alternative imagination of the Israelite cult and a bulwark against other cultic practices, which Deuteronomy characterizes as 'Canaanite'. This 'Canaanite' cult is considered by most modern scholars to be other forms of Israelite worship that existed in the seventh century BC, but which were rejected by the writers of

---

[40] Nebuchadnezzar's pride is described with the same expression (Dan. 5.20). Humility only returns after he is driven mad, turned out of human society and eats grass with the beasts.

[41] For discussion of the song's provenance see P. Sanders, *The Provenance of Deuteronomy 32*, OTS, 37 (Leiden: Brill, 1996) and MacDonald, *Deuteronomy*, 140–2.

Deuteronomy. It is not impossible that the cult that Deuteronomy is seeking to replace had its own account of the past, against which Deuteronomy's own historical memory has consciously been composed. If this was the case, Deuteronomy has not left a clear sense of its content. However, the memory of the Canaanite cult is important for Deuteronomy for it functions as a negative foil against which it sets its own re-conceptualization of the cult.

The Deuteronomic lawcode begins in chapter 12 with instructions to conduct sacrificial worship only at the sanctuary 'that YHWH will choose from among your tribes'. Deuteronomy's positive instructions about sacrificial worship are framed by descriptions of Canaanite worship (vv. 2–4, 29–31). That worship is said to have taken place at various places: on mountains, on hills and under trees. These cultic sites together with all their paraphernalia—altars, standing stones, asherah poles, idols—are to be destroyed by the Israelites. The reason that these relics of Canaanite worship are to be destroyed is that they may be a snare to the Israelites. Consequently the instructions about sacrificial worship are followed by the instructions in Deuteronomy 13 that concern the strenuous efforts that must be taken to ensure that no hint of Canaanite practice is found within the borders of Israel.[42]

The threat of the Canaanite cult results from its use of particular forms of incorporated memory. The cultic paraphernalia of altars and standing stones cannot be merely abandoned, since they possess in their very bodily existence a memory that always threatens to reawaken in Israel if not thoroughly destroyed. The durability of incorporated memory is, perhaps, particularly evidenced in the requirement that the apostate Israelite city be treated to a more thorough destruction than that demanded of the Canaanite cities (13.12–18). The threat is so deep-rooted that even objects spared in the conquest of the land must now be destroyed. All that remains is a ruin that acts as an embodied memory of the apostate city and the act of its destruction (cf. 13.9).

The possibility of apostasy is very much alive not only because of the seventh-century BC context of the writers of Deuteronomy, but also because the writers of Deuteronomy have placed themselves in the paradoxical position of requiring that the memory of the Canaanite cult be obliterated, whilst the existence of this memory is central to the construction of their own alternative memory. A similar paradox might be found in Deuteronomy's use of Exodus, which Levinson has sought to argue involves an appeal to

---

[42] 'Structurally, chapter 13 is linked to the preceding chapter by 12:29–13:1 (ET 12:32), which provides a transition from the demand to worship only in the ways commanded in chapter 12 to the concerns of chapter 13. The question asked in 12:30 points to the service of "their gods", which is the theme of chapter 13' (Nelson, *Deuteronomy*, 165).

authoritative texts whilst subverting the meaning of those texts,[43] and in the response to Amalek, whose memory Israel is to blot out whilst never forgetting them (25.17–19). Although paradoxical it seems that this is a necessary component of attempts to make a fresh start and obliterate earlier memories. In his work on social memory Connerton observes the importance of a particular memory of the monarchy in the French Revolution, despite the Republic's claim to be making a completely fresh beginning. He notes that 'the rejection of the principle of the dynastic realm . . . was still an account of, and a recalling of, the superseded dynastic realm'.[44] The same dynamics are clearly present in Deuteronomy's memory of the Canaanite cult.

According to Deuteronomy the practices of the Canaanites are an 'abomination (*to'evah*) to YHWH' (12.31; cf. 13.14). As it occurs in the book of Deuteronomy the term 'abomination' becomes an important means of bringing together various practices that the book finds detestable and linking them to the memory of the Canaanites.[45] These include idolatry (7.25–6), child sacrifice (12.31; 18.10), sacrificing defective animals (17.1), sorcery and witchcraft (18.9–12), cross-dressing (22.5) and cult prostitution (23.18). In each case the practices are prohibited for the Israelites, but a memory of these actions is retained in the book of Deuteronomy.

The characterization of the Canaanite cult with the term 'abomination' also includes the consumption of prohibited animals (14.3–21). As Milgrom has observed, Deuteronomy does not employ the vocabulary of *sheqets*. In Leviticus' version of the food laws *sheqets* and *tame* denote different categories, and *sheqets* lacks the negative connotations usually attributed to it.[46] In its appropriation of the food laws Deuteronomy places all prohibited animals under one category: they are unclean (*tame*). In a further departure from Leviticus' reception of the food laws the prohibited animals are also characterized as an abomination (*to'evah*).[47] Through its use of *to'evah* the consumption of unclean animals is associated with the memory of the Canaanite cult.[48]

---

[43] Levinson, *Deuteronomy and the Hermeneutics of Legal Innovation*.

[44] Connerton, *How Societies Remember*, 6–13, here 9.

[45] R. P. Merendino, *Das deuteronomische Gesetz: Eine literarkritische, gattungs- und überlieferungsgeschichtliche Untersuchung zu Dt 12–26*, BBB, 31 (Bonn: Peter Hanstein, 1969), 327. For the term *to'evah* in Deuteronomy and literature influenced by it see H. D. Preuss, 'תּוֹעֵבָה *tô'ēbâ*', *TDOT* 15: 591–604. The term appears to have originated in a wisdom context and Deut. 25.16 still bears that imprint (see Weinfeld, *Deuteronomy and the Deuteronomic School*, 260–74).

[46] Milgrom, 'Priestly Terms'.

[47] Milgrom argues that the food laws in Deuteronomy are a revision of the laws in Leviticus. Many interpreters have argued that we should posit a common source. For the most recent detailed discussion see C. Nihan, *From Priestly Torah to Pentateuch: A Study in the Composition of the Book of Leviticus*, FAT, II/25 (Tübingen: Mohr Siebeck, 2007), 283–99.

[48] The distinctive Deuteronomic appropriation of the dietary laws means that it is not surprising that interpreters since Maimonides have sought to associate the laws with pagan practices.

The discussion of prohibited animals in chapter 14 occurs logically after the instructions to worship at the chosen site—and the related concerns about apostasy from the Deuteronomic cult in chapter 13—because slaughter outside the chosen sanctuary is now not controlled by the priestly authorities and consequently needs legislation.[49] The authors of Deuteronomy place all Israelites, whether sacrificing at the chosen sanctuary or slaughtering animals in Israelite towns,[50] under the obligation to observe the laws about clean and unclean animals. Thus, the joyful feasts that the Israelites consume not only provide a positive memory of the gift of the land and YHWH's acts of salvation, but also make the Israelites remember *and* forget the Canaanite cult through the absence of forbidden meat. Thus, in Deuteronomy not only do the dietary laws have a role, but they have been placed within the context of Deuteronomic concerns with feasting, memory and the Canaanite cult.[51]

ISRAEL'S MEMORY OF ITS ENCOUNTER WITH OTHER NATIONS

In his work on the Kalymnians, Sutton observed how narratives about hospitality were used to express social relations and construct identity. These observations offer a valuable perspective from which to assess some of Deuteronomy's accounts of Israel's history. Israel's encounter with other nations in Egypt, the wilderness and the entrance to the Promised Land is told in a distinctive manner—often at variance with traditions known elsewhere in the Pentateuch. This retelling places particular emphasis on expressions of hospitality or inhospitality.

---

[49] The laws in Leviticus 11, on the other hand, occur in the context of instructions that relate to the conduct of the Israelites and priests in relation to the sanctuary.

[50] It is common to use the shorthand 'sacred' and 'secular', but these terms are a little misleading since even slaughter of animals outside the chosen sanctuary has sacred elements such as the pouring of the animal's blood onto the ground.

[51] *Contra* Mayes, who holds that 'the dietary regulations are not an original part of the deuteronomic lawcode' (Mayes, 'Deuteronomy 14', 181). Mayes's interpretation rests on the argument that because the dietary laws codify a social system with a clear division between outsiders and insiders they must originally have been priestly and not Deuteronomic. They do not fit the Deuteronomic worldview and are a late interpolation in the book. However, such an understanding of the dietary laws rests on the work of Douglas who assumes that the laws more naturally have their home in a priestly context, rather than Deuteronomy. The argument is, thus, circular.

For a discussion of the different theories about the role played by Deuteronomy 14 in the book see Ventner, 'Dietary Regulations', 1249–61.

A useful starting point is offered by the Deuteronomic laws of admission in Deut. 23.1–8. According to the classic analysis of these laws by Galling we have a collection of admission laws that originated from different Israelite sanctuaries (vv. 1, 2a, 3a).[52] These have been considerably expanded in their appropriation by the book of Deuteronomy. In this process of appropriation they have been transformed to serve Deuteronomy's rhetoric of communal formation and instruction.[53] What is particularly interesting is the important role that narratives of hospitality have in the Deuteronomic appropriation of these laws. These narratives provide a justification for the exclusion of certain nationalities from the community. Nevertheless, the purpose of the narratives is not merely to explain the boundaries of the Israelite community, but also to describe what membership of the community consists in: hospitality; and does not consist in: inhospitality.

According to Deuteronomy 23 the Ammonites and the Moabites are to be excluded from the assembly in perpetuity because they failed to show hospitality to the Israelites during their journey to the Promised Land. 'No Ammonite or Moabite may enter into the assembly of YHWH; even the tenth generation of their descendants may never enter the assembly of YHWH. For this reason: they did not meet you with bread or water on the way when you came out of Egypt, and he hired Balaam son or Beor, from Pethor of Aram Naharaim, to curse you' (vv. 3–4). This is an account of Israel's encounter with Moab that is somewhat difficult to square with the description of the same episode in Deuteronomy 2. After passing through Edom, Moab and Ammon, Moses sends emissaries to Sihon, king of Heshbon, asking for similar treatment as the Israelites have received in the other countries of Transjordan: 'You shall sell me food for silver that I may eat, and give me water for silver that I may drink. Only allow me to pass through on foot—just as the descendants of Esau who live in Seir and the Moabites who live in Ar have done for me—until I cross the Jordan into the land that YHWH, our god, is giving to us' (2.28–9). Although various solutions to the problem have been offered, it is most likely that we have different traditions that have not been fully harmonized within the book of Deuteronomy.[54] This seems particularly likely in light of the varying Old

---

[52] K. Galling, 'Das Gemeindegesetz in Deuteronomium 23', in W. Baumgartner (ed.), *Festschrift Alfred Bertholet zum 80. Geburtstag* (Tübingen: Mohr, 1950), 176–91.

[53] This does not mean that they have lost their role as communal boundary markers, though the noun *qahal* has been transformed from the worshippers at individual Israelite sanctuaries into the national community. The use of this passage for determining the boundary markers of the national community can be found in the application of them in Neh. 13.1–2.

[54] The two alternative solutions are problematic. First, it has been argued that we can harmonize the two passages by understanding Ammon to have shown inhospitable behaviour, whilst Moab hired Balaam to curse Israel (M. Weinfeld, *Deuteronomy 1–11: A New Translation with Introduction and Commentary*, AB, 5 (New York: Doubleday, 1991), 171–2). The difficulty with

Testament traditions about the hospitality or lack of hospitality to be found in the transjordanian kingdoms. According to Genesis 19 Lot, the ancestor of the Moabites and Ammonites, shows hospitality to the two strangers that appear in Sodom despite the hostile behaviour of his neighbours. In 2 Samuel 10, however, Hanun the Ammonite king acts in an inhospitable manner to the messengers that David sends bearing his condolences on the death of Hanun's father.[55]

Deuteronomy's transformation of Israelite laws of admissions reflects a high valuation of hospitality, and finds it absent amongst the Moabites and Ammonites. This is reflected not in observations about contemporary transjordanian inhospitality, but in an appeal to Israel's memory of her wilderness journey. Interestingly this account of Israel's encounter with Moab and Ammon is found nowhere else in the Old Testament and appears to be part of Deuteronomy's creative remembrance of the past.

Similarly novel is the book's memory of Israel's experience with the Edomites. According to Deut. 23.7–8 a third-generation child of an Edomite may enter the Israelite community: 'You shall not abhor an Edomite for he is your brother. . . . Children of the third generation that are born to them may enter the assembly of yhwh.' The particular treatment of the Edomites appears to have in view the account of Edom in Deuteronomy 2, and it is striking that both chapters refer to a brother relationship between Israel and Edom (2.8; 23.7).[56] According to Deuteronomy 2 the Israelites purchased food and water from the Edomites: 'You shall buy food from them for silver so that you may eat, and also purchase water from them for silver so that you may drink' (2.6;

this suggestion is that whilst the singular verb in 23.4b (*shakar* 'he hired') appears to have only Moab in view, the plural verb in v. 4a (*lo qidmu* 'they did not meet') must refer to both the Ammonite and Moabite of v. 3 (Mayes's literary critical level harmonization recognizes this issue. He argues that 23.4b refers to the king of Moab, whilst 23.4a is an addition to the chapter that presupposes the silence about the Ammonites in 2.29 (Mayes, *Deuteronomy*, 316)). Second, Weinfeld argues that 2.28–9 may be merely Mosaic rhetoric intended to induce an inevitable rejection from Sihon. 'It is also possible that the facts mentioned here have no historical basis and are just diplomatic devices in an address that is not sincerely meant' (Weinfeld, *Deuteronomy 1–11*, 172). However, the book of Deuteronomy gives no indication that Israel bypassed Moab. On the contrary, it is possible that the other references to Moab in Deuteronomy 2 understand Israel to have passed through Moab (vv. 8–9, 18) (for the translation of 2.18, see Mayes, *Deuteronomy*, 139). We must avoid assuming that Deuteronomy understood Israel to have bypassed Moab just because she is said to have done so with Edom in Num. 21.10–20.

[55] There are a number of interesting parallels between the stories in Genesis 19 and 2 Samuel 10, which have generally been overlooked in the scholarship on these passages. First, there is the use of the verb *hafak* 'to overthrow' (2 Sam. 10.3; Gen. 19.21, 25, 29; and elsewhere of the cities of Sodom and Gomorrah). Second, both stories concern messengers, with the inhabitants of the town uncertain of their intents and seeking to sexually humiliate the messengers (I have considered the parallels between these two passages more fully in N. MacDonald, 'Genesis 19 and 2 Samuel 10: An Unexplored Parallel', paper given at International SBL, Vienna, 2007).

[56] J. R. Bartlett, *Edom and the Edomites*, JSOTSup, 281 (Sheffield: JSOT Press, 1989), 92.

cf. 2.28). This is an account that is at odds with Num. 20.14–21 where Edom refuses Israel entry into its land.[57] Again not only does Deuteronomy offer a distinctive memory of Israel's history, but it is also one that emphasizes the hospitality shown to Israel.

According to Deuteronomy 23 the Egyptians are to be treated in a similar manner to the Edomites: their descendants are to be permitted into the Israelite community in the third generation. This appears to break the pattern of acceptance into the community based on historical instances of hospitality. The justification stems from a memory of the past: 'You shall not abhor the Egyptian because you were a resident alien in his land' (23.8), but this memory would hardly seem to be hospitality, because in the book of Deuteronomy Egypt is remembered as the house of slavery (e.g. 4.20; 7.8; 26.6).

Why should the Egyptian be treated so generously? The answer appears to be found in the Deuteronomic laws of release. According to Deuteronomy 15 the Israelite freeman is to release Israelite slaves after six years of labour. In doing so they are instructed not to send them out empty-handed (*reqam*; v. 13): 'Generously bestow on him from your flock, your threshing floor and your winepress. Give to him just as YHWH, your god, has blessed you. Remember that you were a slave in the land of Egypt' (15.14–15). The gifts at the departure of the slave are all, of course, foodstuffs. This pattern of slave release has its parallel in the departure of the Israelites from Egypt. This is the case not because the motivation clause appeals to the Israelites' experience of slavery, but also because according to Exod. 3.21, 'I will give this people favour in the eyes of Egypt so that when they go out, they will not go out empty-handed (*reqam*).'[58] The use of *reqam* in Deut. 15.13 may be a conscious echo of Exod. 3.21, suggesting that Deuteronomy understands the Egyptians to be generous owners who provided liberally for their released slaves.[59] They are, consequently, allowed to enter the assembly of YHWH in the third generation.

Within the book of Deuteronomy the memory of Egypt has an important role in Deuteronomy's theology of hospitality, particularly in relation to the motivation clause 'because you were a resident alien in his land' (23.8). This clause clearly originates in the Covenant Code (Exod. 22.21; 23.9; cf. Lev. 19.34). However, the book of Deuteronomy appropriates this clause and makes it a distinctive bearer of Deuteronomic theology (5.15; 15.15; 16.12;

---

[57]   Ibid., 91.

[58]   According to Exod. 12.35, however, the Israelites received silver, gold and clothing from the Egyptians. The Egyptians provide only when request is made by the Israelites, and the result is presented more negatively as the 'plundering' of the Egyptians.

[59]   *Reqam* occurs only sixteen times in the Old Testament. A particular instance of Israelite generosity is found in the story of Ruth when Boaz insists that Ruth take back six measures of barley to her mother-in-law Naomi with the words 'do not return to your mother-in-law empty-handed (*reqam*)' (Ruth 3.17; cf. Job 22.9).

24.18, 22). This is achieved in a couple of ways, which can best be illustrated by comparing Exod. 23.9 with Deut. 24.17–18. In Exod. 23.9 we read: 'You shall not oppress the resident alien; you know the experience of a resident alien, because you were resident aliens in the land of Egypt.' Deuteronomy reformulates this command: 'You shall not subvert justice for the resident alien or the orphan, and you shall not take a widow's garment in pledge. Remember that you were a slave in Egypt and YHWH, your god, redeemed you from there; therefore I am commanding you to do this thing.' Three changes are worth noting. First, here and in the other uses of the motivation clause Deuteronomy places the Egyptian experience within its theology of memory through the addition of 'remember'. Second, the Israelite experience is that of being slaves, rather than of being resident aliens. This is in order to emphasize, third, the historical act of divine redemption as the basis of motivation rather than empathy with the experience of resident aliens.

In Deuteronomy the experience of Egyptian slavery and redemption is used to motivate actions towards the poor and vulnerable in Israel, particularly through the provision of food. The exceptions are the Sabbath commandment in 5.15 and the reformulation of Exod. 23.9 in Deut. 24.17–18. In 5.15 salvation from Egypt justifies Sabbath rest for the Israelite freeman, but also for all his workers.[60] The Sabbath commandment makes no mention of any special meal on the day, it is merely a day in which the whole community and their livestock are 'to do no work' (5.12).[61] In 24.17–18 the concern is justice rather than provision of food for the vulnerable widows, orphans and resident aliens.

---

[60] The Sabbath command (5.12–15) aptly illustrates the importance of historical memory for the author of Deuteronomy. The Exodus version, which is probably original, enjoins the people to 'remember the Sabbath day' (Exod. 20.8). The author of the Deuteronomic Decalogue has orientated Sabbath observance away from creation towards the exodus. In doing so he has substituted the imperative 'keep', a word more characteristic of Deuteronomy's commandments. 'Remember' has been reutilized in Deuteronomy's justification of the Sabbath command, which recalls Israel's historical experience in Egypt. 'Remember that you were a servant in the land of Egypt, but YHWH, your god, brought you out from there with a strong hand and outstretched arm' (Deut. 5.15). In Deuteronomy it is the past that is remembered, rather than the commandment (Nelson, *Deuteronomy*, 82).

Weinfeld argues instead that the author of Deuteronomy changed the verb 'on purpose in order to avoid the allusion to sacred commemoration' (Weinfeld, *Deuteronomy 1 11*, 303; cf. Weinfeld, *Deuteronomy and the Deuteronomic School*, 222). For Israel's sacral traditions to 'remember' the Sabbath was a sacral act that redramatized the act of creation. Here as elsewhere, according to Weinfeld, Deuteronomy makes a decisive departure from the accepted tradition. Weinfeld's argument requires reading Deuteronomy's version of the Sabbath commandment against a cultic alternative. Not only is this cultic alternative conjectural, but it fails to recognize the positive intent of Deuteronomy's reformulation.

[61] Nevertheless, there are a number of linguistic affinities between the Sabbath commandment and Deuteronomy's law about Passover-Massot, not least the requirement to do no work, which suggests that 'Deuteronomy intends to bring these two commands into close relationship' (McConville, *Law and Theology*, 118).

In 15.15, as we have seen, the Israelite freeman is to send out the former slave with gifts from 'your flock, your threshing floor and your winepress'. As we have already observed these gifts are all foodstuffs. In 24.22 the Deuteronomic lawcode requires that the fields, vineyards and olive groves are not completely harvested. Instead, the vulnerable elements of society—the widow, the orphan and the resident alien—are allowed the opportunity to access the staple products of grain, wine and olives. Finally, the 'slaves in Egypt' motivation clause also occurs in the Deuteronomic instructions about the celebration of the Feast of Weeks, where it occurs in relation to the communal feast which the Israelite freeman throws not only for his household, but also for the Levite, the resident alien, the orphan and the widow (16.11–12). These last two examples demonstrate that the 'slaves in Egypt' motivation clause is closely related to the widespread Deuteronomic theme of showing generosity to the marginalized triad of widow, orphan and resident alien (with the Levite occasionally added to their number).[62] This generosity is particularly shown through acts of hospitality where the Israelite freeman provides for those who cannot provide for themselves (12.12, 18–19; 14.28–9; 16.9–15; 26.1–11, 12–15).

Behind Israel's own generous hospitality lies, of course, YHWH's own example of gracious provision. This is apparent in the appeal to YHWH's own act of redeeming Israel from Egypt as the basis of these acts of generosity, and also in Deuteronomy's theology of *imitatio dei*. It has often been observed that Deuteronomy has a developed notion of the imitation of God.[63] The most sustained reflection upon this theme is found in 10.12–22, where YHWH is portrayed as the divine king. In this role he defends the orphan and widow and provides food and clothing for the resident alien. This portrayal leads to the exhortation that Israel herself is to love the alien, 'for you yourselves were resident aliens in the land of Egypt' (v. 19). Elsewhere too YHWH is the archetypal host. This is apparent especially in the gift of the land and all its produce. It is this generosity that underlines YHWH's requirement that Israelite

---

[62] For a discussion of these terms see most recently H. V. Bennett, *Injustice Made Legal: Deuteronomic Law and the Plight of Widows, Strangers and Orphans in Ancient Israel* (Grand Rapids: Eerdmans, 2002), 23–71.

Ramírez Kidd rightly observes that in Deuteronomy the triad 'are clustered around the theme of *food*' whilst pre-Deuteronomic and post-Deuteronomic references to the triad 'are not related to *eating* measures but with *legal* matters'. This he relates to an 'effort to counteract the growing poverty of the population due to the process of urbanisation, and to the emergence of large numbers of immigrants in Israelite society during the VIII century BC' (J. E. Ramírez Kidd, *Alterity and Identity in Israel*, BZAW, 283 (Berlin: de Gruyter, 1999), 35, 42, 43).

[63] See most recently W. J. Houston, 'The Character of YHWH and the Ethics of the Old Testament: Is *Imitatio Dei* Appropriate', *JTS* 58 (2007), 1–25. Houston writes, 'in Deuteronomy…there are a number of texts which suggest the theme of imitatio dei, though in a less explicit way than in [the] H[oliness Code]' (ibid., 10).

freemen are generous to those without: 'give to him just as YHWH, your god, has blessed you' (15.14). YHWH's generosity is also seen in his provision for Israel during the wilderness. Though Israel ate no bread and drank no wine during her forty years of wandering (29.2–5; cf. 8.2–5), she 'lacked nothing' (2.7; cf. 8.9) and was blessed in 'all the work of your hands' (2.7). This last expression relates elsewhere in Deuteronomy to agricultural products and must be used in an extended sense in 2.7.[64]

For Deuteronomy 23 the question of acceptance into the Israelite community clearly turns on the historical memory of hospitality. A spectrum is mapped with descendants of the Edomites and Egyptians permitted in the third generation, but the descendants of the Ammonites and Moabites forever excluded. In the book of Deuteronomy one end of this spectrum is occupied by Israel. She is *de facto* the assembly of YHWH and ought to exhibit exemplary hospitality in imitation of YHWH. The other end of the spectrum, I want to suggest, is occupied by the Amalekites. The Deuteronomic account of the Amalekites is found in 25.17–19. Although removed from Deut. 23.1–8, the passage about the Amalekites concludes the laws of chapters 23–5. Thus, as Nelson observes about 25.17–19, 'from a structural perspective this passage functions as a bracket along with 23:4–7 to enclose the various laws of chapters 23–25'.[65]

The importance of the Deuteronomic memory of the Amalekites is asserted in a striking, almost paradoxical, way: 'Remember what Amalek did to you…wipe out the memory of Amalek from under heaven; do not forget' (25.17, 19). Deuteronomy's memory has, again, novel elements in comparison to other Pentateuchal accounts, in the case of Amalek, Exod. 17.8–16.[66] Exodus 17 records only that the Amalekites attacked Israel at Rephidim, whilst Deuteronomy 25 portrays the attack as a cowardly action against those who were struggling at the rear.[67] The Israelites are described, according to the

---

[64] Cf. Mayes, *Deuteronomy*, 136.

[65] Nelson, *Deuteronomy*, 302. Mayes also observes that 23.1–25.19 is a single section with the lawcode, which has two concerns '(a) the purity of the people of Yahweh and (b) the humanitarian behaviour which is required of the people of Yahweh' (Mayes, *Deuteronomy*, 313). In his view the first concern dominates 23.1–8, though it is my contention that the two are closely interlinked around the theme of hospitality.

[66] 'Israel is to remember the tradition of a paradigmatic battle similar to, but not exactly equivalent to, the one narrated in Exod 17:8–16' (Nelson, *Deuteronomy*, 302).

[67] An attempt at harmonization has been offered by Propp. He takes the reference to Moses striking the rock at Horeb in Exod. 17.6 as evidence that Moses and the elders have left Israel in Rephidim and moved on to Horeb. Propp claims to take the narrative sequence in Exodus 17 at 'face value'. In his view the 'redaction (i.e., 19:1–2 (P, R)) has confused the fairly clear sequence of events within E. At Rephidim, the people demand water, and Moses and the elders go on to Horeb to produce the springs of Massah-Meribah. As the Israelites bring up the rear, they are attacked by Amalek between Rephidim and Horeb. Moses sends back Joshua to muster the first army of the once timorous people…he himself stands on Horeb, channeling divine power

NRSV, as 'faint and weary'. This translation obscures the implicit reference to food and drink, for parallel uses of *ayep* 'faint' show that it is most commonly used of fatigue resulting from lack of food or drink. As a result Tigay offers the translation 'famished'.[68] *Yaga*', on the other hand, is used of exhaustion, especially that which results from physical labour.[69] As a result Deuteronomy's interpretation of Amalek's action is more than a justification of why a nation can be annihilated,[70] it coheres with Deuteronomy's emphasis on hospitality towards Israel. Thus, Amalek, rather than supplying food and water (as did the Edomites) or refusing to supply them (as did the Moabites and Ammonites), actually seeks to take advantage of Israel's vulnerability and attack her. It is because of this hostility towards the weak that it is to be shown no mercy.

In a discussion of Deuteronomy 23 David Frankel poses the rhetorical question, 'Is the failure of the Ammonites and Moabites to present the Israelites with food and water a sufficient reason to ban their descendants from entering the congregation of the Lord for all time?'[71] In the light of our examination of Deuteronomy 23, the implied answer 'no' could not be further from the truth of the matter. In the book of Deuteronomy, narratives of past hospitality and inhospitality provide an important means of expressing social relations and constructing identity. Deuteronomy may well appropriate traditions of sanctuary admission, but has transformed them so that they not only express the relations that Israel has to neighbouring nations, but also configure internal

through the rod. After routing Amalek, Israel camps at the mountain and presumably drinks' (W. H. C. Propp, *Exodus 1–18: A New Translation with Introduction and Commentary*, AB, 2 (New York: Doubleday, 1999), 620–1; cf. E. Zenger, *Israel am Sinai: Analysen und Interpretationen zu Exodus 17–34* (Altenberge: CIS Verlag, 1982), 56–75). This is clearly a reading of Exodus 17 informed by the parallel in Deut. 25.17–19 and not a reading of Exodus 17 at 'face value'.

[68] J. Tigay, *Deuteronomy* דברים: *The Traditional Hebrew Text with the New JPS Translation*, JPS Torah Commentary (Philadelphia: Jewish Publication Society, 1996), 237, 392; Hasel similarly observes that 'in a number of passages, it is clear that physical fatigue is occasioned by actual bodily weakness caused by lack of food (Gen. 25:29f.; Jdgs 8:4f.; 1 S. 14:28, 31; 2 S. 16:2, 14) and/or drink (2 S. 16:2; Job 22:7; Prov. 25.25; Isa. 29:8; 44:12)' (G. F. Hasel, 'עָיֵף y'p I', in *TDOT* 6:148–56, here 153).

[69] There may also be another subtle reference to the provision of food in the opening expression 'remember what Amalek did to you' (25.17). 'Remember', as we have seen, is frequently used with reference to food, but in addition the phrase 'they did to (*'asah l^e*)' is also used elsewhere in Deuteronomy in relation to food provision. Moses refers to what Moab and Edom 'did for us' (2.29) and the divine provision in the wilderness is described as 'what he did for you in the wilderness' (11.5; cf. 8.15–16).

[70] 'The deuteronomic author, whose national conscience was highly developed, could not tolerate the notion that a nation should be wiped out just because of its having proclaimed a war. He had therefore to supply an explanation which changed the picture of the whole event. According to this reinterpretation Amalek had to be blotted out, not because he attacked Israel in war, but because he chose a cruel, inhuman way of doing so' (Weinfeld, *Deuteronomy and the Deuteronomic School*, 275).

[71] D. Frankel, 'The Deuteronomic Portrayal of Balaam', *VT* 46 (1996), 30–42, here 40.

social relations. Israelite society is to be characterized by generous hospitality towards the vulnerable and, as Deuteronomy presents it, this is a crucial component of Israelite identity that derives from the example of YHWH himself. For Deuteronomy narratives of hospitality structure the experience of the past and create expectations for the manner in which future hospitality in the land is to be expressed.

CONSUMING THE TEXT

Sutton and Connerton make a strong distinction between what they label 'inscribed memories' and 'incorporated memories'. Incorporated memories are embodied experience, whilst inscribed memories are those that are held on physical devices. As Connerton recognizes, it is not possible to maintain an absolute distinction between the two, since many practices of inscription have an element of incorporation. Thus he notes that 'writing, the most obvious example of inscription, has an irreducible bodily component'.[72] Nevertheless, he argues that the distinction is valid as a heuristic device.[73]

However valid the distinction between inscribed memories and incorporated memories may be as a general rule, it scarcely does justice to Deuteronomy, which holds together inscribed and incorporated memories, seeing them as mutually supportive. At a fundamental level this is because, as we have seen, food and communal meals are the basic means by which Deuteronomy establishes its particular memory of the past amongst the Israelites. This is achieved, however, through a literary text, the book of Deuteronomy itself. Yet it is also an essential component of Deuteronomy's strategy of memorialization, for in Deuteronomy it appears that inscribed memories only truly become possessed as memories when they are incorporated. The most apt example is the *Shema* in Deut. 6.4–9, whose words are to be placed as amulets on the hands and forehead, and written on the door-frames of houses and on the city gates. The purpose of these actions is to impress the commandment in the memories of the Israelites.

Food is also an incorporated memory that furthers Deuteronomy's inscribed memory. This is true of the feasts, which embody a memory about exodus, wilderness and the Promised Land, that can also be expressed in textual form (e.g. Deut. 26.5–11). They are not, therefore, bodily habits of the type that Connerton discusses, such as the bodily memory of how to swim or of posture as social expression, since these cannot be placed in textual form.

---

[72] Connerton, *How Societies Remember*, 76.   [73] Ibid., 79.

Nevertheless, it is clear for the strategy of Deuteronomy that inscription is not sufficient on its own.

The relationship of these two forms of memory to one another finds apt expression in the instructions concerning the construction of the altar at Mount Ebal (27.1–8). On the day that the Israelites arrive in the land they are to inscribe the words of the law upon plastered stones, build an altar for sacrifices and celebrate a cultic meal. This text is usually reckoned to have a complex literary history,[74] which in its final form has brought the stones (*even*) of the altar into close relationship with the stones (*even*) upon which the law has been inscribed.[75] Indeed, in the fulfilment of this instruction in Joshua the two sets of stone are no longer distinguished from one another (Josh. 8.30–2). On one set of stones are the written words that are to be read and on the other the sacrifice that is to be consumed. The words and the meal are mutually informing acts of remembrance.

Acts of forgetfulness can also be mutually informing, as is apparent in the law about the rebellious son (21.18–21). The son is characterized in two ways. He is both 'stubborn and rebellious refusing to obey his father and mother' and 'a glutton and a drunkard'. These separate descriptions of the son belong together. They do also in Israel's experience, for as we have seen, eating and being sated may lead to forgetfulness of yhwh and his commandments.[76]

The most conscious reflection upon food and word is, of course, the famous aphorism that 'one does not live by bread alone, but on every thing that proceeds from the mouth of yhwh' (8.3). As Perlitt has shown the impression that bread and manna are being contrasted is mistaken, rather the point is that it is not possible to live by bread *alone*, that which yhwh decrees is also needed.[77] What yhwh decrees includes the manna in the wilderness and ordinary bread in the Promised Land, but more especially 'what proceeds from the mouth of yhwh' is the commandments. These are what is truly life-giving. The aphorism expresses then the extent to which food and law belong together—they both stem from yhwh and give life—and do not belong together—man depends most fundamentally on the divine commandments. Humble

---

[74] M. Anbar, 'The Story about the Building of an Altar on Mount Ebal: The History of its Composition and the Question of the Centralization of the Cult', in N. Lohfink (ed.), *Das Deuteronomium: Entstehung, Gestalt und Botschaft*, BETL, 68 (Leuven: Leuven University Press, 1985), 304–9.

[75] This occurs because v. 8 resumes the topic of the plastered stones after a discussion of the altar stones in vv. 5–7. This is usually judged to be the result of the interpolation of vv. 5–7 into vv. 2–4, 8.

[76] It is possible that the intent is that 'the theologically sensitive reader will draw a parallel to Israel as Yahweh's rebellious son' (Nelson, *Deuteronomy*, 261). Certainly 'stubborn and rebellious' is used elsewhere in the Old Testament to describe Israel (Jer. 5.23; Ps. 78.8).

[77] L. Perlitt, 'Wovon der Mensch lebt (Dtn 8:3b)', in *Deuteronomium-Studien*, FAT, 8 (Tübingen: Mohr Siebeck, 1994), 74–96.

dependence is required to experience the gift of the land's prosperity and to receive the commandments obediently. The memory of both is mediated through the manna, and the forgetfulness of both may result from being sated with the land's goodness.

From a historical perspective the reasons Deuteronomy views 'inscribed memories' and 'incorporated memories' together could be explained with reference to its important role in the development of textualization in Israel.[78] The book of Deuteronomy has numerous references to recording the law textually, references that are entirely explicable given the book's putative setting just before the death of Moses. The Ten Commandments are written on tablets of stone (4.13; 5.22; 10.4) and the entire law is itself written down—'the book of the law' (28.61; 29.20; 30.10)—and deposited with the Levites (31.9). The Song of Moses too is committed to writing (31.19). The importance of writing is additionally seen in Deuteronomy's conscious use of a literary precursor—the Book of the Covenant (Exod. 20.22–23.33). The stress on the written character of the divine revelation may not be the starting point of having authoritative scriptures, but is certainly an important milestone in the process. Thus, one way of making sense of memory in Deuteronomy would be to hold that it stands at a distinct juncture within Israel's history with a primarily oral religious culture in one direction and a primarily textual religious culture in the other. Inscribed memories and incorporated memories are related to one another, because there is no other way in which to think at this point. An alternative way of understanding the question of memory would be to see it as a compromise sought between the textual habits of a literate elite and the oral culture of the majority. Thus, as Schaper observes, 'textuality, in ancient Israel and Judah, cannot do without orality. ... Deuteronomy and Joshua provide us with numerous references to the written Torah being brought to life through recitation, meditative murmuring and public readings'.[79] Thus, the text is read by Levites to an illiterate majority who maintain habits of incorporated memorization. On the other hand, it can be claimed that Deuteronomy has seized upon a perceptive theological instinct to hold together inscribed and incorporated memories, since both are essential to an appropriation of the law that for Deuteronomy makes demands upon the whole person, mind and body.

---

[78] For a discussion of orality and literacy in Deuteronomy and its context in seventh-century BC Judah, see J. Schaper, 'The Living Word Engraved in Stone: The Interrelationship of the Oral and the Written and the Culture of Memory in the Books of Deuteronomy and Joshua', in S. C. Barton, L. T. Stuckenbruck and B. G. Wold (eds.), *Memory in the Bible and Antiquity: The Fifth Durham–Tübingen Research Symposium (Durham, September 2004)*, WUNT, 212 (Tübingen: Mohr Siebeck, 2007).

[79] Ibid.

CONCLUSION

In the book of Deuteronomy food is an important vehicle for memory. Deuteronomy's account of the Exodus from Egypt and the gift of the land are a particular memory of Israel's history, and one that may not have been universally shared in ancient Israel. This memory celebrates Israel's dependence on YHWH and the existence of a covenant between YHWH and Israel, and as such it affirms the importance of obedience to the Deuteronomic law. The memory of the past thus legitimates the Deuteronomic social order.

The Israelite festivals are a particularly important expression of Israel's historical memory as understood by Deuteronomy. Through the course of the year the journey from Egypt to the Land is memorialized and celebrated. Through the consumption of the bread of affliction and the sacrifice of the Passover lamb at the precise moment of the exodus the Israelites embody the memory of their salvation. By giving communal meals to the disenfranchised they not only act for the social good, but embody the fact that they are no longer resident aliens themselves. Thus, for Deuteronomy life in the land in the present can only truly be appreciated through a memory of the past.

The memory of the past must, according to Deuteronomy, influence present action in other ways. Narratives of past hospitality or inhospitableness not only inform Israelites about the social order beyond Israel's borders, they also define how membership of the community is to be expressed. Thus, Deuteronomy does not merely command generosity to the disenfranchised in the community, it shows through an appeal to communal memory that it should be a national characteristic. The use of narratives of hospitality to define the international social order is an interesting variation on the use of genealogy to achieve the same effect (e.g. Genesis 10). Deuteronomy does not subscribe to Robertson Smith's idea of Semitic hospitality where sharing a meal makes the companions kin. For Deuteronomy the resident alien remains a resident alien. Nevertheless, it does recognize meals and hospitality as important expressions of social relations.

4

Mixed Menus: the Confusion
of Food in Judges

Readers of the book of Judges will know that it has a strange texture. A series of stories recounts the exploits of heroic figures who deliver the Israelite people from oppressive neighbouring nations. At many points, however, there are elements which are more sinewy. They place the stories of the Judges within a tight framework that portrays Israel's existence prior to the monarchy as a pattern of historical cycles. The Israelites do what is evil in the sight of YHWH, for which they are punished with foreign oppression. YHWH hears their cry and sends a 'judge' who delivers the people. When the judge dies the people return to their former ways. The account of Othniel's deliverance of Israel in Judg. 3.7–11 is a succinct example of the complete cycle. Israel begins to worship Baal and as a punishment is delivered into the power of Cushan-Rishathaim. When the Israelites appeal to YHWH they are delivered by Othniel, who secures peace in the land for forty years.

These sinewy elements have been identified as evidence of a Deuteronomistic editing of the book which often has few links with the actual stories about the judges.[1] Indeed, the ingredients are so markedly different that it has been considered relatively easy to strip away the book's Deuteronomistic framework. When this is done what remains is a collection of stories about Israel's heroic deliverers. Although these are the judges of the popular imagination—Gideon, Samson and so forth—their stories contribute more than narratives about deliverance. They frequently introduce material that places the judges in an ambivalent light, making them far from ideal representatives of Deuteronomistic values. We may wonder, then, why these stories, rather than any others that may have existed, have been selected for inclusion in the book of Judges. To pose the problem in succinct fashion: Why are the judges in the book of Judges?

---

[1] For the most recent discussion of the literary criticism of Judges see R. G. Kratz, *The Composition of the Narrative Books of the Old Testament*, trans. J. Bowden (London: T&T Clark, 2005). References to the literature on the redaction of Judges can be found there.

WHY ARE THE JUDGES IN THE BOOK OF JUDGES?

In relation to the famous story of the sacrifice of Jephthah's daughter, Thomas Römer asks, 'Why would the Deuteronomists tell about the sacrifice of Jephthah's daughter?' Römer argues that it is difficult to conceive of a Deuteronomistic historian attributing such an act to one of Israel's judges. Elsewhere in the Deuteronomistic History child sacrifice is viewed as an abhorrence, and the absence of censure appears inexplicable. Römer's solution is to attribute the story to the later Hellenistic period when there were different sensibilities.[2] The action of Jephthah is a particularly problematic example, but it is not the only one. As the book develops the judges appear increasingly unheroic and their actions morally ambiguous or reprehensible.

In responding to Römer's question David Janzen rightly observes that the story of Jephthah's daughter 'fits quite well into one of the dominant structuring motifs of the book of Judges: the decline of Israel and its judges'.[3] This decline can be seen in the Deuteronomistic cycle, which becomes more disjointed as the book progresses. When the Ammonites oppress Israel her cry of repentance is initially met with rejection by YHWH (10.10–15). After Gideon the land is no longer said to have any rest. In the judgement of Cheryl Exum, 'the political and moral instability depicted in Judges is reflected in the textual instability. The framework deconstructs itself, so to speak, and the cycle of apostasy and deliverance becomes increasingly murky.'[4] Thus, the refrain 'the Israelites did evil in the eyes of YHWH' (2.11; 3.7, 12; 4.1; 6.1; 10.6; 13.1), which introduces each wave of oppression and divinely appointed deliverer, eventually disappears. In its place the judgement is given that 'there was no king in Israel; everyone did what was right in their own eyes' (17.6; 21.25).[5] This dissolution of the framework appears to parallel the increasingly chaotic lives of Israel's deliverers. Indeed, the decline in the Deuteronomistic framework cannot be accounted for in terms of the framework alone, rather stories like that of Jephthah's daughter are needed.

---

[2] T. C. Römer, 'Why Would the Deuteronomists Tell about the Sacrifice of Jephthah's Daughter?' *JSOT* 77 (1998), 27–38.

[3] D. Janzen, 'Why the Deuteronomist Told about the Sacrifice of Jephthah's Daughter', *JSOT* 29 (2005), 339–57, here 341.

[4] J. C. Exum, 'The Centre Cannot Hold: Thematic and Textual Instabilities in Judges', *CBQ* 52 (1990), 410–31, here 412.

[5] Veijola suggested that the formula in Judg. 17.6 relates to Deut. 12.8–12 (T. Veijola, *Das Königtum in der Beurteilung der deuteronomistischen Historiographie: Eine redaktionsgeschichtliche Untersuchung*, Annales Academiæ Scientiarum Fennicæ, 198 (Helsinki: Soumalainen Tiedeakatmia, 1977), 24–9; cf. J. A. Soggin, *Judges*, OTL (London: SCM Press, 1981), 265; Braulik, *Deuteronomium II*, 96–7); but note Becker, who relates to the similar formula in Kings (U. Becker, *Richterzeit und Königtum*, BZAW, 192 (Berlin: W. de Gruyter, 2000), 294–6).

In this chapter I wish to examine how the stories about the judges contribute to the evolution of the Deuteronomistic framework throughout the book. In other words, some rationale will be given for the inclusion of these stories in the book of Judges. To do so I will utilize Mary Douglas's structuralist approach to the food laws. Douglas, as we have already seen, famously argues that the dietary laws reflect a structuring of the animal world where clean animals have locomotion appropriate to the sphere to which they belong. A failure to conform to this classification results in the animal being deemed unclean. The food laws, then, evidence an attempt to categorize the world: animals must belong either to the heavens, to the earth, or to the waters under the earth. Within this system hybrids are rejected as 'matter out of place'. The maintenance of these 'natural' boundaries by the Israelites reflects concern within the community about 'social' boundaries.

In Judges I wish to suggest that the social dissolution within pre-monarchic Israel is represented by the collapse of natural and cultural domains where great effort was made to avoid confusion. The natural domains include the division between animal and human, the cultural domains include the distinctions between food, sex, killing and sacrifice. Just as the pig's failure to conform to the class of ungulates is considered a threat, so also the confusion of sacrifice and murder, of animal sacrifice and human child, in the story of Jephthah's daughter is evidence of a dangerous threat to the social and natural order.[6] As the book progresses, the stories of the judges portray these crucial natural and cultural distinctions being lost. The loss of these category distinctions points to a societal malaise which results by the end of the book in a society where anything goes: 'everyone did what was right in their own eyes'.

It might be thought that these ideas would be too abstruse for a biblical writer to operate with, and so it may be helpful to draw a modern parallel. Social commentators frequently express concern about the number of families that eat only 'TV dinners'. The consumption of food on the sofa in front of light entertainment poses no risks to a person's health, except perhaps an increased likelihood of indigestion (even if, combined with other factors, it is part of the rise in obesity). It has, however, become a powerful symbol for many of family life having gone awry. The failure to eat at a proper location (the dining room) in the proper way (seated at a table with plates and cutlery) is powerfully expressive of larger concerns about societal changes, such as the

---

[6] The analysis offered here is congruent with the arguments of Stavrakopoulou, who sees child sacrifice as an ideological boundary marker (F. Stavrakopoulou, *King Manasseh and Child Sacrifice: Biblical Distortions of Historical Realities*, BZAW, 338 (Berlin: W. de Gruyter, 2004)). My application of Douglas's 'matter out of place' explains why this might have been so in the circles that composed the Deuteronomistic History.

loss of familial interaction and the pervasiveness of passive entertainment in modern society.

Before turning to the stories that have been incorporated into the book of Judges it will be desirable to take two preliminary steps. First, evidence of a distinction between humans and animals needs to be demonstrated in the Old Testament. Second, it has to be shown that the Old Testament writers considered food, sex, killing and sacrifice to be incommensurable domains. Having taken these preliminary steps it will be useful to delay examining Judges by turning to the book of Joshua. It will be argued that in the book of Joshua, which is an important counterpoint to the book of Judges, there is a concern with orderliness in which cultural domains are kept distinct.

Humans and Animals in the Old Testament

Old Testament texts assume a distinction between animals and humans. The clearest expression of this is to be found in Genesis 1. Land animals and humans are created on the sixth day but in distinct creative actions. Human beings are distinguished by their creation 'in the image of God' (1.26), which sees them exercising rulership over the animal world (1.27–8). The distinction between animals and humans is expressed concretely in the diet assigned to each. The land animals and the birds are given the green vegetation as food, whilst human beings are given cereals and fruit.[7] The distinction is maintained after the flood, when animals are given to humans as food. Humans may kill animals, but animals may not kill humans (9.5). It is little wonder, then, that the priestly laws governing sexual relations in Leviticus 18 prohibit sexual intercourse with animals. Bestiality entails crossing natural boundaries determined by God.[8]

Food, Sex, Killing and Sacrifice in the Old Testament

The Old Testament describes the cultural domains of food, sex, killing and sacrifice in a manner that preserves the integrity and independence of each domain. No confusion of them is allowed. Such assumptions are never articulated explicitly in any one place, but evidence for them can be found in many biblical texts. The boundaries between the different domains are not

---

[7] C. Westermann, *Genesis 1–11: A Commentary* (Minneapolis: Augsburg, 1984), 162.

[8] 'The cosmology of the OT places barriers between the divine realm and the human realm and between the human realm and the animal realm; any mixing of these barriers is considered unnatural, a confusion' (J. E. Hartley, *Leviticus*, WBC, 4 (Nashville: Thomas Nelson, 1992), 298).

all policed with the same level of anxiety. In Israel's historical and religious context certain boundaries were under greater threat. As is well-known a number of Old Testament texts refuse to collapse sacrifice and killing, but concern about the confusion of eating with sexual intercourse, for example, appears less frequently.

It makes good sense to begin with clearer examples and, thus, we naturally turn to the boundary between sacrifice and killing. Sacrifice involves, of course, the slaughter of domestic animals, but cultic killing of humans is prohibited as numerous Old Testament texts demonstrate. The most famous example is the story of the non-sacrifice of Isaac in Genesis 22, but there is also the account of the sacrifice by Mesha, king of Moab, of his son, which results in great anger coming upon Israel (2 Kings 3). In the eyes of the Deuteronomistic writers of Kings the worst act committed by the kings of Israel and Judah was the sacrificing of their children in the fire (2 Kgs. 16.3; 17.17; 21.6). Deuteronomy prohibits these acts and characterizes them as Canaanite and an 'abomination'. In the context of war, Deuteronomy avoids any equation of killing with sacrifice. This includes the legislation for killing the Canaanites. Deuteronomy employs a specific term, *cherem*, for how the Israelites are to deal with the Canaanites. This term indicated the devotion of an object to someone. Although this might easily be taken as a form of sacrifice, Deuteronomy never describes the annihilation of the Canaanites as a sacrifice. This is confirmed in Deuteronomy's instructions concerning an apostate Israelite city. Although the destruction of the buildings and the livestock is described as a 'whole burnt offering' (*kalil*) to YHWH, the humans are placed under the *cherem*. *Cherem* may share common features with sacrifice, but for Deuteronomy it is not a sacrifice.[9]

If human beings cannot be killed as a sacrifice, neither can they be killed for food. In the cosmology of Genesis, humans may consume animals, but the possibility of humans eating humans is not entertained. Indeed, it is possible to understand the permission to eat animals as a solution to the problem of human violence that originally led to the flood. Restricted access to the animal world provides an outlet for human aggression. The rest of the Old Testament shares with Genesis an unwillingness to entertain the idea

---

[9] *Contra* S. Niditch, *War in the Hebrew Bible: A Study in the Ethics of Violence* (Oxford: Oxford University Press, 1993), 28–64; J. J. Collins, 'The Zeal of Phinehas: The Bible and the Legitimation of Violence', *JBL* 122 (2003), 3–21, here 4–10. Note, e.g., Collins's assertion that 'Deuteronomy does not eradicate the sacrificial aspect of the ban, but it seeks to rationalize the practice by justifying it' (7). Niditch spends a great deal of time seeking to show the *cherem* is a sacrifice. According to her, we find 'no clearer description of the ban as sacrifice' than in 1 Kgs. 20.39–43 (36). Yet, the prophetic parable shows only that the king must take the place of the *cherem* he has released. Niditch and Collins assume that if the *cherem* looks like sacrifice to our modern eyes (it involves killing, a vow, a victim and the divine) it must be a sacrifice.

of humans consuming other humans. When it does it occurs at the very limits of human destitution. Thus, when Deuteronomy envisages the wrath of YHWH against a disobedient Israel, it includes parents consuming their own children (28.53). This starvation is so desperate that the mother consumes her own children and the afterbirth in secret so that her own family do not share her feast (28.56–7). Such desperate straits occurred in the siege of Samaria described in 2 Kings 6. In a shocking inversion of the famous story of Solomon's wisdom, a woman comes to the king with a case of a female companion and their two sons. The woman recounts how she and the other woman made a pact to kill and eat their sons at successive meals, but after they had eaten her own son, the other woman had hidden her child. On hearing of such a monstrous act the distressed king tears his clothes.

As we have seen killing in war is not to be confused with sacrifice, nor, according to Deuteronomy, are war and sexual intercourse to be confused. The rape of the women of defeated populations would have been known by the Israelites. This is the implication of the Deuteronomic curse where defeat by enemies leads to betrothed women being enjoyed by others (28.30). In Israel's own practice, however, a wedge is to be driven between war and sex. In the infamous commandment to destroy the Canaanites the Israelites are to utterly destroy the people of the land, and they are not to intermarry with them. For nations outside of the Promised Land if one of the victorious Israelites finds a desirable woman he must allow a month before he marries her (21.10–14). Whilst Nelson is right to argue that 'the law is hardly the humanitarian breakthrough in gender relations that some interpreters have imagined it to be',[10] it does seek to place violation of women outside the sphere of war, even whilst it assumes male hegemony. In common with Deuteronomy's other humanitarian war laws, such as the ban against cutting down fruit trees, this law imagines war as a tidy exercise where ethical concerns can and should be prioritized. For Deuteronomy, in theory at least, sex is not to be found on the battlefield.

The relationship between sacrifice and food is complex. Sacrifices are, of course, food, at least for the priests and those who bring the offering. Sacrifice as food for the deity is a much more complex problem. As we have already seen in Deuteronomy's vision of the Israelite cult the sacrifices are to be consumed at the sanctuary. 'You shall eat there before YHWH, your god, and you and your household will rejoice in all your undertakings in which YHWH, your god, has blessed you' (Deut. 12.7). Eating before YHWH is neither eating with him nor providing him with food. The question of whether in fact Israelite sacrifice originated as the provision of food for YHWH and to what extent evidence

---

[10] Nelson, *Deuteronomy*, 259–60.

for this can still be found in the Old Testament have long been discussed by students of Israelite religious history. What is certainly the case is that there is at least one biblical text that explicitly distances Israel's god from such ideas. Psalm 50 famously has YHWH declaring,

> If I were hungry, I would not tell you,
> For the world and its fullness belong to me.
> Do I eat the flesh of bulls
> And drink the blood of goats?
>
> (vv. 12–13)

More often, though, we can merely observe the reticence of Old Testament texts compared to the widespread idea of sacrifice as food for the gods in other ancient Near Eastern texts.[11]

The most difficult cases are to demonstrate that Old Testament texts seek to maintain a clear distinction between sexual intercourse and sacrifice, and sexual intercourse and food. Concerns about the potent mix of these three cultural domains are to be found in Deuteronomistic characterizations of Canaanite cultic feasts. Recent scholarship has rightly questioned the accuracy of early scholarly understandings of Canaanite fertility cults. These took biblical portrayals as first-hand evidence and failed to give due regard to the considerable theological reflection that had shaped them over time. Deuteronomy itself does not show undue concern with the Canaanite feasts, instead its energies are expended on prescribing correct sacrificial practice at the sanctuary and the procedures for animal slaughter elsewhere. The book's rhetoric suggests to its readers the self-evident attractiveness of its own cultic meals as celebratory occasions.

A quite different note is struck in the summary recapitulation of the Covenant Code after the sin of the Golden Calf (Exod. 34.11–26), a passage which, in other respects, has a number of important resonances with some of the theological ideas of Deuteronomy.[12] The Israelites are warned not to make a treaty with the Canaanites, and to destroy their cultic paraphernalia. If they fail to do so Moses imagines a situation where the Israelites are drawn into

---

[11] W. G. Lambert, 'Donations of Food and Drink to the Gods in Ancient Mesopotamia', in J. Quaegebeur (ed.), *Ritual and Sacrifice in the Ancient Near East*, Orientalia Lovaniensia Analecta, 55 (Leuven: Peeters, 1993), 191–201.

[12] There is no little disagreement in Old Testament scholarship between those who regard Exod. 34.11–26 as a very early, if not the earliest, Israelite lawcode (e.g. J. Halbe, *Das Privilgerecht Jahwes*, FRLANT, 114 (Göttingen: Vandenhoeck & Ruprecht, 1975); F. Crüsemann, *The Torah: Theology and Social History of Old Testament Law*, trans. A. W. Mahnke (Edinburgh: T&T Clark, 1996), 115–43) and those who regard it as a late Deuteronomistic creation (e.g. L. Perlitt, *Bundestheologie im Alten Testament*, WMANT, 36 (Neukirchen-Vluyn: Neukirchener Verlag, 1969), 216–32). In my own view, the latter position is the most persuasive.

idolatry. The Canaanites engage in worship of their gods and offer sacrifices. They invite their Israelite allies to the feast, who share the sacrificial meal. Children are betrothed to one another and thus the following generation is drawn into apostasy (Exod. 34.11–15). As if to counter such temptation there follows an account of the three annual Israelite festivals (vv. 17–26). Exodus 34 produces a prospectus for the occupation of the land in which the Canaanites are to be vanquished, their cultic places destroyed, Yahwistic festivals celebrated and only endogamy permitted. Exodus 34 plays an important role in characterizing not only the Canaanite cult. Additionally, it shapes how the apostasy of the Golden Calf is understood, bringing it closer to the other act of cultic apostasy in the wilderness: the sin at Baal Peor (Num. 25).[13]

ORDERLINESS IN THE BOOK OF JOSHUA

The Deuteronomistic account of Israelite apostasy that introduces the book of Judges (1.1–3.6) clearly has Exodus 34 in view. After the death of Joshua the concerns expressed in Exodus 34 come to pass, its sense of order is lost and the Israelites are ensnared in Canaanite idolatry and intermarriage. In contrast to the apostasy during the period of the Judges the lifetime of Joshua is depicted as a time of faithfulness: 'the people served YHWH all the days of Joshua and all the days of the elders who outlived Joshua, who had seen all the great deeds YHWH did for Israel' (Judg. 2.7). We might, therefore, expect the conquest under Joshua to exhibit the order that I will argue is lacking in the book of Judges. Therefore, I want to delay our examination of the book of Judges by giving a little time to consider Joshua as a counter-example to Judges.

In the book of Joshua the sense of orderliness is apparent from the moment the Israelites cross the river Jordan in Joshua 4. The people who cross the Jordan are characterized as a new generation of Israelites who had not see the wonders in Egypt, but had been born in the wilderness (5.2–7). The book of Joshua affirms the distinction between the old and the new generation that is found in the Pentateuch.[14] The boundary is now set by the Jordan,

---

[13] N. MacDonald, 'Recasting the Golden Calf: The Imaginative Potential of the Old Testament's Portrayal of Idolatry', in S. C. Barton (ed.), *Idolatry: False Worship in the Bible, Early Judaism, and Christianity* (London: T&T Clark, 2007), 22–39.

[14] For example in Numbers (see D. T. Olson, *The Death of the Old and the Birth of the New: The Framework of the Book of Numbers and the Pentateuch*, BJS, 71 (Chico: Scholars Press, 1985)) and Deuteronomy 1–3.

with the new generation on one side and the old generation perishing on the other (5.6). Joshua 5's emphasis on order established by the Jordan boundary continues with the cessation of the manna. On the fourth day after the crossing of the Jordan the people celebrate Passover at Gilgal, and the following day they eat some of the land's crops.

The day after the Passover—that very same day—they ate from the produce of the land, unleavened bread and parched grain. The manna ceased the day after they ate from the produce of the land, and the Israelites no longer had manna; they ate from the harvest of the land of Canaan that year.   (Josh. 5.11–12)[15]

Unleavened bread and parched grain require the least amount of time from harvesting to consumption and are entirely appropriate for the Israelites' first meal in the land of Canaan. The emphasis is not on the nature of the meal, but the transition from wilderness to the Promised Land.[16] The repetitions underline the orderliness of the transition as does the emphatic 'that very same day'. The cessation of the manna and the consumption of the land's crops reflect precise timing. This well-defined boundary finds further confirmation in the book of Joshua's only reference to 'the land flowing with milk and honey' (5.6). With the exception of a few verses in the prophets, which themselves refer back to Israel's wilderness experience, this well-known expression makes its final appearance. As a teleological expression it exists only in anticipation, and its final use is rightly found immediately before the Israelites enjoy the bounty of the land.

The majority of Joshua is not concerned with the fruit of the land, but its conquest. Here too Joshua expresses a clear sense of order. The book of Joshua portrays Israel's settlement in the land as a faithful implementation of Moses' instructions in Deuteronomy 7 to annihilate the Canaanites.[17] All of the inhabitants of the cities that the Israelites encounter are put to the sword (6.21; 8.26; 10.28–38; 11.11–15), and the majority of the land has been conquered during Joshua's leadership. A large part of the book is devoted to the allocation

---

[15] For a recent discussion of the literary criticism of these verses and their relationship to Exodus 16, see J. A. Wagenaar, 'The Cessation of Manna: Editorial Frames for the Wilderness Wandering in Exodus 16.35 and Joshua 5.10–12', *ZAW* 112 (2000), 192–209.

[16] T. C. Butler, *Joshua*, WBC, 7 (Waco, TX: Word, 1983), 60.

[17] My concern here is to follow the narrative presentation of Deuteronomy and Joshua. In light of the ethical questions that the biblical *cherem* poses, it is worth noting that *cherem* in Deuteronomy 7 should be understood as a metaphor for religious devotion. See MacDonald, *Deuteronomy*, 108–22. This has implications for how Joshua should be read and understood— as metaphor writ large. See the readings of Joshua by L. G. Stone, 'Ethical and Apologetic Tendencies in the Redaction of the Book of Joshua', *CBQ* 53 (1991), 25–36; G. Mitchell, *Together in the Land: A Reading of the Book of Joshua*, JSOTSup, 134 (Sheffield: Sheffield Academic Press, 1993).

of this land amongst the different tribes (chs. 13–21). With their attention to the exact boundaries of tribal territory, the chapters describing the land's allocation underscore the book's obsession with order. Closer attention to the text reveals a number of exceptions that threaten to subvert the orderliness of Joshua's account. Nevertheless, in each case the book manages to resolve the problem. Rahab the prostitute hides the Israelite spies and receives a promise from them that her life and the lives of her family will be spared. What would appear to be a breach of the divine commandment is resolved by a confession of YHWH's supremacy (2.9–11) and the incorporation of Rahab within the people of Israel (6.25). Achan disobeys the command to devote everything in Jericho to YHWH. His disobedience brings defeat upon Israel at Ai. Resolution is achieved by executing Achan and his family. Finally, the Gibeonites deceive the Israelites into making a treaty with them. Unable to undo a treaty of peace Joshua sentences the Gibeonites to a menial task of service within the people of Israel. In each case the threatened disorder is destroyed or domesticated.

The book of Joshua is only concerned with sacrifice when the two and a half Transjordanian tribes build an altar on the other side of the Jordan (ch. 22). This provokes a national crisis, since it contradicts the Deuteronomic command that YHWH only be worshipped at a unique divinely chosen sanctuary. An internecine war is averted only when the Transjordanian tribes affirm that the altar is a memorial for future generations rather than for sacrificial use. Again, an apparent rupture in Joshua's, or rather Deuteronomy's, sense of order is resolved. Sexual relationships also appear infrequently in the book of Joshua. Joshua's concluding speeches to Israel include a reaffirmation of the prohibition of intermarriage (23.12). The implication of Joshua's speech is that there has been no intermarriage during the time of his leadership. Restraint in sexual relationships is exhibited at exactly the place where we might suspect it would occur in the story of Rahab (ch. 2). The entrance of the spies into the house of a prostitute is inauspicious, and the reader's suspicions increase when Rahab goes up to the spies just before they went to sleep (2.8). The anticipated intercourse does not occur for Rahab has come to the men's beds to make a confession of faith in YHWH.

In conclusion the book of Joshua presents an orderly account of Israel's conquest of the Promised Land. Food, warfare, sacrifice and sex all appear (or more accurately in the case of the latter two do not appear), but do not threaten the orderliness of the book. Even those cases that touch the boundaries are resolved clearly and with no room for doubt. Nevertheless, the threat to these four areas already anticipates the disorder that will result in the book of Judges.

DISORDERLINESS IN THE BOOK OF JUDGES

Joshua presents a society in which everything is in order. The laws of Moses are obeyed and the conquest of the land proceeds with divine blessing. The land is taken and divided with geographical precision amongst the twelve tribes. In the book of Judges neither animals and humans, nor the four domains of warfare, food, sacrifice and sex, can be separated from one another, and as the book develops they increasingly collapse into one another. We will examine the book sequentially observing how the disorder increases as the book moves towards its chaotic end. Initially the confusion of the natural and cultural domains is utilized as a means of mocking Israel's enemies. Increasingly, though, the confusion penetrates the life of the Israelites and their judges. In the story of Samson an attempt is made to reassert the boundaries between the different domains, but the boundaries cannot hold and the denouement of Samson's life occurs in the kind of non-Yahwistic sacrificial feast envisaged in Exodus 34. In the chapters that follow, the social life of Israel appears to be in utter disorder and there is no longer a judge to resolve a messiness that results not from an external threat, but from within Israel itself.

The suggestion that Judges be examined with the areas of warfare, food, sacrifice and sex having a prominent role, and with each collapsing into the other, suggests a role for food within the book that has not been observed by other interpreters. Since the biblical books have been so thoroughly explored the reader can be excused scepticism at such a claim. It is appropriate then to observe the way that the issue of food is foregrounded in the book itself by examining the opening story about Adoni-bezeq. There we will discover the disintegration of some of these cultural distinctions as well as the natural distinction between humans and animals.

The book opens with an attack by the tribes of Judah and Simeon in which they defeat the Canaanites and Perizzites and capture the king Adoni-bezeq (1.1–8). The description of this victory follows a pattern found elsewhere in the former prophets, except for the addition of two elements.[18] In the first, Judah is chosen to lead the fight when the Israelites seek divine guidance. The importance of this positive portrayal of Judah has often been observed.[19] The second addition has largely been overlooked and is the description of how

[18] As observed by B. G. Webb, *The Book of Judges: An Integrated Reading*, JSOTSup, 46 (Sheffield: Sheffield Academic Press, 1987), 84–5. This pattern of narration has the following structure: the joining of the battle; the outcome; the casualties suffered by each side; an account of the death of an important person or persons on the defeated side.

[19] See, e.g., Y. Amit, *The Book of Judges: The Art of Editing*, BIS, 36 (Leiden: Brill, 1999), 145–8.

Adoni-bezeq receives his just deserts.[20] When captured Adoni-bezeq has his thumbs and big toes amputated, a treatment he recognizes as divine justice. 'Seventy kings with their thumbs and big toes cut off used to glean under my table; as I have done, so God has paid me back' (1.7). Although parallels from the classical world have often been adduced, these are not especially pertinent since their concern is preventing the conquered from bearing arms in the future, an issue absent from Judges 1.[21] Adoni-bezeq's actions appear to parody the political council. The traditional membership of the council— whether divine or human—in ancient Near Eastern or biblical texts is seventy.[22] This number may be equivalent to those who traditionally ate at the king's table. Certainly in Exodus 24 seventy elders are selected to accompany Moses, Aaron, Nadab and Abihu onto Mount Sinai, where they conclude the covenant and eat a meal before YHWH.[23] In Adoni-bezeq's feast, however, the kings are not advisors who share the table, but defeated foes who scrabble for food.

The macabre humour of this feast would be further enhanced if the name Adoni-bezeq is indeed a deliberate misspelling of Adoni-zedek intended to make a pun on *bzq*, a 'pebble' or 'fragment'.[24] Would this be their lost digits or the food they are scraping from underneath the table?[25] We can only guess at any intended pun—if indeed there is one to be found—but the picture of mutilated human flesh at a royal feast is suggestive enough even without it. Alternatively, the reduction of five digits to four may transform the kings

[20] Old Testament scholarship has largely been concerned with the question of whether the tradition represented in Judges 1 is a variant of that found in Josh. 10.1–3.

[21] See G. F. Moore, *Judges*, ICC (Edinburgh: T&T Clark, 1895), 17–18.

[22] Ugaritic texts attest to the belief that there were seventy deities ('the seventy sons of Athirat' (*KTU* 1.4.vi.46)), and this idea seems to be reflected in altered form in Deut. 32.8–9 and in some later Jewish traditions (see Sanders, *Provenance of Deuteronomy 32*, 158 n. 294). Gideon had seventy sons, whom Abimelech represents as ruling jointly (Judg. 9.2). In the wilderness Moses is aided by a spirit-anointed committee of seventy elders (Numbers 11). The seventy-seven officials and leaders of Succoth is a variation of this tradition (Judg. 8.14). See J. C. de Moor, 'Seventy!' in M. Dietrich and I. Kottsieper (eds.), *'Und Mose schrieb dieses Lied auf': Studien zum Alten Testament und zum Alten Orient*, AOAT, 250 (Münster: Ugarit-Verlag, 1998), 199–203. Unfortunately, de Moor overlooks the example in Judges 1.

[23] See Chapter 6.

[24] The difficulties of discerning 'humour' in the ancient texts of the Bible often give rise to scepticism about its existence. Many of the conscious confusions of food and other cultural domains can be paralleled in ancient Greek comedy. For this see the exhaustive study by Wilkins: J. Wilkins, *The Boastful Chef: The Discourse of Food in Ancient Greek Comedy* (Oxford: Oxford University Press, 2000).

[25] 'The title Adoni-bezek, "Lord of the crumbs" may then be announcing the final destiny of the king who ended up picking crumbs under his own table (Judg. 1.7)' (P. Guillaume, *Waiting for Josiah: The Judges*, JSOTSup, 385 (London: T&T Clark International, 2004), 91 n. 66; cf. KB, 118).

from powerful rulers into dogs who hunt around the table for scraps. If this is the case Adoni-bezeq treats humans as though they are dogs, deliberately confusing the human and animal worlds.[26]

The Deuteronomistic Introduction to Judges

The remainder of the introduction to the book has many of the marks of the Deuteronomistic editing that we have already noticed (1.1–3.6). Its texture and the nature of its concerns are markedly different from the epic stories about the judges that constitute the rest of the book. Some observations should be made about how the introduction relates to the stories of the judges. As we will see, Israel's social and moral collapse is seen in the stories through the failure to maintain natural and cultural boundaries. Although there is little evidence of the collapse of these boundaries in these first three chapters, we do have the appearance of the Canaanite cult, a characteristic Deuteronomistic concern. After the passing of Joshua the Israelites fail to remain faithful to YHWH. 'The Israelites did evil in the eyes of YHWH and served the Baals. They forsook YHWH, the god of their fathers, who had brought them out of Egypt and followed other deities from among the gods of the peoples around them' (2.11–12). The Canaanites are not exterminated nor is their cult expurgated; instead, the Israelites conclude treaties and intermarry with them. Although Judges 1–3 describes neither sacrifice nor feasting, the allusions to Exodus suggest that its account of the Canaanite cult and its threat are presupposed.[27] Additionally, sacrifice and feasting were integral parts of the ancient cult as seen, for example, in the Philistine festival described in Judg. 16.23–7. The failure of the Israelites to keep the Pentateuchal law and their intermingling with the Canaanites results in the conquest of the land coming into disorder. The Israelites fail to drive out the autochthonous inhabitants of the land, and eventually find themselves oppressed by their enemies.

---

[26] I am grateful to Carol Newsom for drawing my attention to this potential significance of the four remaining digits. Note Moore's comment: 'We are not, therefore, to imagine the kings actually under the table, but as gathering up from the ground, like dogs (Matt. 15.27, *Odyss.* xvii.309)' (Moore, *Judges*, 18).

[27] The Israelites have disobeyed YHWH's instructions not to make treaties with the Canaanites and to tear down their altars (2.2; cf. Exod. 34.12, 14). Consequently the Canaanites have become a snare to the Israelites (2.4; cf. Exod. 23.33). Such actions are viewed as prostituting themselves to other gods (2.17; cf. Exod. 34.15, 16).

The Stories of Ehud and Jael

In the story of Adoni-bezeq the confusion of food with human bodies, or animals with humans, is a macabre and humorous way of communicating the retributive side of divine justice at the hands of the faithful Israelite tribes. The stories of Ehud and Jael continue in a similar vein, collapsing boundaries between cultural domains that are kept separate in more untroubled times. These stories redound to the glory of the Israelite judges, reducing the leaders they oppose to cuts of meat or human sacrifices.

Ehud's deliverance lifts the oppression of the Israelites stemming from Eglon, king of Moab. Ehud's stratagem to deliver Israel depends on using the opportunity offered by the presentation of Israel's agricultural tribute to their oppressor.[28] The term used for the tribute, *minchah*, can describe both the tribute offered to a political superior and an agricultural sacrifice. The story plays on this ambiguity between food and sacrifice. Those responsible for bringing the tribute are described as 'the bearers of the tribute' (*noshe minchah*), a term commonly used in the context of offering political tribute (e.g. 2 Sam. 8.2, 6). Yet the actual presentation of the tribute sees a shift to cultic language: 'he *offered* the tribute to Eglon' (*wayyaqrev et-hamminchah lᵉ'eglon*).

The ambiguity surrounding the nature of Ehud's offering affects our assessment of Eglon in the story. Is Eglon a king receiving tribute or a deity receiving a sacrificial offering? In fact neither is the case, rather the king himself is part of the sacrificial offering. When Ehud offers the tribute to Eglon, the narrator sees fit at this point to observe that 'Eglon was a very fat man' (3.17). Eglon's obesity has a central role in the development of the story and the king's humorous demise, yet this does not explain its position here and this observation about Eglon's corpulency might easily have been located elsewhere.[29] In its present position, however, it has been carefully juxtaposed with the cultic language of the offering. That this is not accidental is confirmed by the unusual description of Eglon's obesity not with the typical Hebrew word for human fatness, but with a word usually reserved for a fattened

---

[28] For the role of food appropriation and distribution in the political economy of the small states in Palestine see Chapter 5.

[29] Moore notes, 'a circumstance of importance in the sequel of the story is parenthetically introduced by anticipation at the first meeting of Ehud and Eglon, instead of in v. 20 or 22' (Moore, *Judges*, 93). Cf. Anderson, 'both of these details, the sword and the mention of corpulence have no narrative role in this first scene' (G. A. Anderson, *Sacrifices and Offerings in Ancient Israel: Studies in their Social and Political Importance*, HSM, 41 (Atlanta: Scholars Press, 1987), 62–3, 69). Richter rejects suggestions that the clause be relocated (W. Richter, *Traditionsgeschichtliche Untersuchungen zum Richterbuch*, BBB, 18 (Bonn: Peter Hanstein, 1966), 14).

animal.[30] Ehud has brought along a cereal offering to accompany a choice cut of meat. As it happens this offering of meat is beef, for the king—surely no accident—bears a name that means 'calf'.[31] As the narrative develops, then, the king's anticipated death is presented as a sacrificial offering, and more than that the human king has become an animal.

Taken in by Ehud's ploy the dim-witted Eglon cuts a strikingly bovine pose, but the narrator is hardly finished making the king a figure of fun. His voracious appetite is not satisfied with the generous offering and he seizes keenly on Ehud's secret message. We are not told what the king hoped would be the content of this message, but we may, perhaps, suppose he desired yet more food. That he is a man concerned primarily with his belly is suggested by his gruesome death. He is constituted by nothing more than fat and faeces.

Perhaps, though, he had an appetite for more than just food. Some interpreters have wondered whether there might not also be sexual innuendo alongside the sacrificial imagery and toilet humour. This is a story where it is not only sacrifice and killing that are confused, but where food and sex are also brought into the mix. In the opinion of Marc Brettler there is a 'use of scatology and sexual innuendo [that] is atypical of the Hebrew Bible'.[32] Ehud 'comes to' the king in his bathroom thrusting into him a small straight dagger, a grisly penetration.[33]

The case for sexual innuendo is stronger in the story of Jael's killing of Sisera. This is but one of many common themes between the stories which give the impression that Ehud and Jael form a literary diptych.[34] Certainly we find sex and murder coming together in complex and suggestive ways, in the story of Jael even more explicitly in relation to food. This is true in both the narrative version of the story (Judg. 4.17–22) and its poetic retelling (5.24–30).[35] Jael's part in the story begins with the defeat of Sisera's army and the fleeing of the

[30] I.e., *bari*. It is only otherwise used of human beings in Ps. 73.4 and Dan. 1.15. For detailed discussion see Anderson, *Sacrifices*, 67–8.

[31] Anderson details a number of these arguments to support such an interpretation. He notes, however, that 'one argument against this understanding of Eglon as a "fatted calf" is that it serves to portray Ehud's act of political assassination as a human sacrifice' (ibid., 68). The reading of Judges that we are undertaking removes any strength to this objection.

[32] M. Z. Brettler, 'Never the Twain shall Meet? The Ehud Story as History and Literature', *HUCA* 62 (1991), 285–304, here 298.

[33] Ibid.; R. Alter, *The Art of Biblical Narrative* (New York: Basic Books, 1981), 37–41.

[34] O'Connel notes the following similarities: use of satire to mock Canaanite nobility, use of deception by the protagonists, almost identical wording of the discovery scene (3.25; 4.22), use of disjunctive syntax (R. H. O'Connel, *The Rhetoric of the Book of Judges*, VTSup, 63 (Leiden: Brill, 1996), 126–8). Webb includes: a murder followed by discovery, use of *tq'*, wording of the discovery (Webb, *Book of Judges*, 136).

[35] The question of the historical priority of one account over another need not distract us at this point. In the present form of the material the narrative precedes the song of Deborah and Barak, even if the historical order is the reverse.

Canaanite commander on foot. Jael offers Sisera hospitality and when he has settled down to sleep she drives a tent peg through his skull.

Scholars disagree about how to assess Jael's hospitality. Yairah Amit regards Jael's actions prior to Sisera's death as exemplary. She provides hospitality to the visitor, going out of her tent to meet him and persuade him in. When he asks for water she gives him milk and provides him with somewhere to sleep. Victor Matthews, on the other hand, thinks Jael and Sisera violate numerous elements of the hospitality code. She usurps her husband's role and he breaks with convention by asking for water. Finally, rather than offering her guest protection Jael murders him.[36] The choice between the two is an unhappy one, for what Judges emphasizes is excess; this excess suggests something unusual, but its implications for the narrative cannot be decided prematurely. It alerts the reader to suspect the occurrence of something unexpected. It is only when the final blow is struck that the reader can be certain that this is not how hospitality should be offered. Here then we have a different boundary being breached, not between separate cultural domains but between appropriateness and excess.

There seems little doubt that sexual imagery is employed in Judges 5, particularly in the lingering portrayal of Sisera's death in v. 27.[37] Sisera is described as falling between Jael's feet, a posture that suggests intercourse when used with the word feet (*rᵉgalim*), a common biblical euphemism for the sexual organs. The remaining verbs that describe the collapse of Sisera's body—*krʿ*, *npl* and *shkb*—can be used for intercourse as well as being applied to death.[38] With Niditch we can conclude that 'the language in Judg 5.27 is double, evoking simultaneously death and eroticism'.[39] The use of this evocative language is ironic as made clear by the distress of Sisera's mother. She fears for his safety when he does not return quickly. Her companions seek to pacify her by suggesting that Sisera is merely tarrying over the spoil, ravishing the women of the conquered. The truth is the inverse: Sisera himself has been conquered and lies at the feet of a woman. Alongside this sexual imagery there

[36] Y. Amit, 'Judges 4: Its Content and Form', *JSOT* 39 (1987), 89–111; V. H. Matthews, 'Hospitality and Hostility in Judges 4', *BTB* 21 (1991), 13–21.

[37] It has been suggested that this is the case in Judges 4 too. Jael's initial invitation has been compared to the seductress of Proverbs 7 who goes out to meet a man and invite him to her home (Y. Zakovitch, 'Sisseras Tod', *ZAW* 93 (1981), 364–74). Like the woman of Proverbs 9 she offers him refreshment. When he enters Jael's tent he immediately lies down. Finally, the story ends with an act of penetration with the tent-peg interpreted as a grisly parody of intercourse.

Lindars expresses some reserve with this interpretation of Judges 4, although he is willing to recognize sexual imagery in Judges 5 (B. Lindars, *Judges 1–5* (Edinburgh: T&T Clark, 1995), 197–201).

[38] See Lindars, *Judges 1–5*, 279; S. Niditch, 'Eroticism and Death in the Tale of Jael', in P. L. Day (ed.), *Gender and Difference in Ancient Israel* (Minneapolis: Fortress Press, 1989), 43–57.

[39] Niditch, 'Eroticism and Death', 51.

is also a careful use of maternal imagery. Jael is a mother figure, alongside Deborah and Sisera's mother. The mortally wounded Sisera falls between her feet like a child at birth (5.27).[40] Possibly chapter 4 reflects this view of Jael by portraying her covering Sisera with a blanket and providing him with milk.[41] The employment of maternal imagery accentuates the terrible breach of hospitality. The killer is not merely a host, but a mother.

The provision of food works in a slightly different way in the poetic and narrative retellings, though in both cases a link is provided between sex, death and the consumption of food. In the narrative of Judges 4 Sisera is provided with milk whilst reclining and covered with a blanket. The connection is spatial: the bed is the place to receive the maternal milk, but also the place of sex and death. In the poem of Judges 5 Sisera's death occurs at the moment when he is drinking from a lordly bowl. The connection is temporal: the moment when the commander quenches his thirst is the point of his death. Whether the link is spatial or temporal the consumer has become the consumed; bed, battle and bowl have become hopelessly confused.

Gideon and Abimelech

In the stories of Ehud and Jael the confusion of food, sex, sacrifice and killing and the confusion of animals and humans are used to full comic effect at the expense of Israel's enemies. When the tale of heroic deliverance has ended the foe lies sliced, diced and sexually humiliated. With Gideon, however, that confusion begins to touch Israel and whilst Israel's enemies bear most of the brunt of culinary metaphors, the violence does not leave Israel unscathed. This darker possibility reaches a premature climax with Gideon's son Abimelech. Not described as a judge, a celebrated deliverer, within the book of Judges he symbolizes the terrifying prospect that the violent possibilities of confusion might be as devastating within Israel. His socially corrosive reign will soon come to an end, but not before many people have been ground, threshed or sacrificed.

[40] See A. Brenner, 'A Triangle and a Rhombus in Narrative Structure: A Proposed Integrative Reading of Judges 4 and 5', in A. Brenner (ed.), *A Feminist Companion to Judges* (Sheffield: Sheffield Academic Press, 1993), 98–109.

[41] Questions have been raised about why Judges 4 and 5 picture Jael giving Sisera milk rather than other drinks with erotic connotations or having a soporific effect, such as wine or milk and honey (Songs 4.10–11; although note C. F. Burney, *The Book of Judges* (London: Rivingtons, 1918), 93 and R. G. Boling, *Judges*, AB, 6A (New York: Doubleday, 1975), 97–8, who argue that some goat milk products are strongly soporific). Milk and honey, as already observed, do not occur as a pairing once the Israelites enter the Promised Land. Nevertheless, both milk and honey do appear separately in the book of Judges but in surprisingly ambiguous ways (Judg. 4.19; 5.25; 14.8–9).

Before we encounter these more troubling occasions in which boundaries between natural and cultural domains are crossed we might also note that these can occur in apparently more benign forms. One of these occurs during the appearance of a mysterious visitor to Gideon. The identity of the visitor, who could be either a prophetic figure or an angel, does not become apparent to Gideon until the end of the commissioning. Gideon's own uncertainty is, perhaps, indicated by his request to bring the messenger a *minchah*, which as we have seen is most often used in the Old Testament of a sacrificial offering, but can also be used of a gift.[42] Gideon, as a good host, brings to his guest a generous meal of a kid and unleavened bread.[43] All ambiguity disappears when the messenger requests the broth be poured out like a libation, and the offering is consumed by fire (6.20–2).[44] The story's refusal to commit until the very last moment the identity of the messenger and consequently the nature of the offering led some earlier interpreters to seek a religio-historical explanation. Rudolph Kittel, for example, found a transition from food offerings to fire offerings.[45] Such explanations do not commend themselves today, especially if, as my argument would suggest, the ambiguity between food and sacrifice is an artifice that fits within the book's larger literary designs.

The confusion that introduces the story of Gideon is less benign. In the reader's first encounter with Gideon the future leader is portrayed turning agricultural facilities to irregular uses. When the angel appears Gideon is found beating out the wheat in a winepress. The exposed location of the threshing floor, ideal for threshing and winnowing grain, would be a conspicuous target for the Midianite raiders, whose voracious appetite for plunder is compared to the locust:

Whenever the Israelites had sowed, the Midianites, Amalekites and the Easterners would come up against them. They would encamp against them and destroy the

---

[42] KB, 601 for details. R. J. Thompson observes that, 'it is a question, however, whether Gideon intended an offering from the first, or a meal for a stranger' (R. J. Thompson, *Penitence and Sacrifice in Early Israel Outside the Levitical Law* (Leiden: Brill, 1963), 88).

[43] It has been observed by Moore that there is a disproportionate amount of flour when compared to 1 Sam. 1.24 (Moore, *Judges*, 187). D. R. Ap-Thomas suggests emending *efah* to 'and he baked' (D. R. Ap-Thomas, 'The Ephah of Meal in Judges vi 19', *JTS* 41 (1940), 175–7). Emendation is unnecessary since it is likely that an analogy is being drawn with the divine visitation to Abraham in Genesis 18. Certainly there are a number of allusions to the Pentateuch in the chapter (O'Connel, *Rhetoric of the Book of Judges*, 148–9).

[44] Assis rightly observes the ambiguity in Gideon's actions: 'The ambiguity between a ritual offering and a human present seems to be intentional both here and in the episode of Manoah and his wife' (E. Assis, *Self-Interest or Communal Interest: An Ideology of Leadership in the Gideon, Abimelech and Jephthah Narratives (Judg. 6–12)*, VTSup, 106 (Leiden: Brill, 2005), 37).

[45] R. Kittel, *Studien zur hebräischen Archäologie und Religionsgeschichte*, Beiträge zur Wissenschaft vom Alten Testament, 1 (Leipzig: J. C. Hindrich, 1908), 97–103 (noted in Thompson, *Penitence and Sacrifice*, 88). For a more recent example of such attempts see Soggin, *Judges*, 121.

produce of the land as far as the vicinity of Gaza. They did not leave any sustenance in Israel, and no sheep, ox or donkey. They and their livestock would come up, bringing their tents, as thick as locusts; there was no counting their camels. They came into the land and wasted it. Israel was greatly impoverished because of Midian.   (6.3–5)

The animal simile is no accident, for human beings with animal appetites will prove to be a regular theme in the story of Gideon. Beating out grain by hand is a poor alternative to the threshing floor. It is an inefficient activity, which is only suitable for a small amount of grain (Ruth 2.17). No prominent landowner, who can command ten servants (Judg. 6.27), would ordinarily seek to process grain in this way. The scene not only serves to portray Gideon's timidity, but also points to a society in disarray.[46]

Gideon's improper use of agricultural facilities anticipates his moment of triumph over the Midianite foe. After the defeat of the Midianite army the two chief captains, Oreb and Zeeb, flee before Gideon's victorious army. The Israelites give chase, but the captains are captured and killed by the Ephraimites. The account appears at first glance to be aetiological: The Ephraimites 'captured the two commanders of Midian, Oreb and Zeeb. They killed Oreb at the rock of Oreb, and Zeeb they killed at the winepress of Zeeb' (7.25).[47] More recently the aetiological element has been recognized as somewhat artificial,[48] and the names have been viewed instead as puns. *Orev* 'raven' and *Zeev* 'wolf' suggest that the Midianites like their captains' namesakes are wild, predatory animals, rather than human beings.[49]

If humour rather than aetiology were the purpose, might there be any significance to the 'rock' and 'winepress' where the two kings are slain? In the Old Testament *yeqev*, 'winepress', is clearly an agricultural installation, signifying the two reservoirs hewn into an exposed piece of rock where grapes are pressed. *Tsur*, on the other hand, is the common Hebrew word for something

---

[46] Our argument that this confusion is deliberate would support the traditional reading of *gath* as 'winepress' rather than 'farm' (A. Lemaire, *Inscriptions hébraïques I, Les ostraca* (Paris: Les Editions du Cerf, 1977), 58) or 'fief' (D. Michaux-Colombot, 'La *gat* de Gédéon, pressoir ou fief?' *UF* 29 (1997), 579–98). Whilst Ugaritic *gt* means 'farm' or 'estate' (G. Del Olmo Lete and J. Sanmartín, *A Dictionary of the Ugaritic Language in the Alphabetic Traditions*, 2 vols. (Leiden: Brill, 2003), 1: 310–13), the other biblical uses of the common noun are to a winepress, as their conjunction with *darak* or parallelism with *yeqev* shows (Isa. 63.2; Joel 3.13; Lam. 1.15; Neh. 13.15). Michaux-Colombot's suggestion that *gath* in Judg. 6.11 occurred before a semantic shift of the term in Hebrew during the late pre-exilic period rests on a questionable dating of both Judges 6 and Isaiah 63.

[47] For attempts to identify these locations, see E. Gaß, *Die Ortsnamen des Richterbuchs in historischer und redaktioneller Perspektive*, Abhandlungen des deutschen Palästina-Vereins, 35 (Wiesbaden: Harrassowitz, 2005), 296–9).

[48] Boling, *Judges*, 151; see A. Scherer, *Überlieferungen von Religion und Krieg: Exegetische und religionsgeschichtliche Untersuchungen zu Richter 3–8 und verwandten Texten*, WMANT, 105 (Neukirchen-Vluyn: Neukirchener Verlag, 2005), 300–8.

[49] F. M. T. Böhl, 'Wortspiele im Alten Testament', *JPOS* 6 (1926), 196–212, esp. 203.

rocky, used of anything from a mountain to a boulder. On two occasions, however, *tsur* is associated with the production of oil. In the Song of Moses YHWH provides Israel with 'oil from flinty rock' (Deut. 32.13), and Job remembers how in better days 'the rock poured out oil' (29.6).[50] While it may be possible to explain the reference in Deuteronomy 32 by appeal to the poet's belief in the 'capacity of Israel's land to produce richly from unlikely places', such interpretations do not explain Job 29.6.[51] It might be more satisfactory to regard this use of *tsur* as a poetic way of describing an oil press.[52] One additional biblical text may support this suggestion: the call of Gideon in Judges 6. The angel of YHWH appears to Gideon while he is beating out wheat in a winepress (6.11). The location of the appearance is also described as 'under the oak at Ophrah'. After the angelic commission Gideon brings an offering to the angel, which again is described as being 'under the oak' (6.19). The angel directs Gideon to place the offering upon 'this rock (*sela'*)' (6.20). After Gideon has presented the offering a fire comes up from 'the rock (*tsur*)' and consumes it (6.21).[53] This 'rock' is the reservoir where Gideon has been beating out the grain.

The deaths of Oreb and Zeeb are both associated, then, with agricultural installations where the grape or olive harvest is crushed. When the Ephraimites arrive with the heads of Oreb and Zeeb and complain about not being invited to the battle, Gideon replies with an acerbic 'isn't the gleaning of the Ephraimites better than the vintage of Abiezer' (8.2), where Abiezer is a reference to Gideon's own family. Gideon's response to the Ephraimites is far more than Boling's banal attempt at rephrasing 'is not the mop-up work done by your tribe more significant than the performance of my contingent' or Polzin's suggestion that we have a statement equivalent to the modern proverb that 'a bird in the hand is worth two in the bush'.[54] Gideon's reply is a macabre pun on the deaths that the two Midianite leaders have met. The bodies of Oreb and Zeeb have been trampled and crushed like grapes in the press. How can Gideon's vintage of numerous Midianite corpses compare to the gleanings

---

[50] For the Hebrew note the recent discussion by Clines: D. J. A. Clines, *Job 21–37*, WBC, 18A (Nashville: Nelson, 2006), 935–6.

[51] J. G. McConville, *Deuteronomy*, Apollos Old Testament Commentary (Leicester: IVP, 2002), 455.

[52] This has been argued recently by Clines: 'The "rock" (צור) that flowed with streams of oil is most probably the olive press' (Clines, *Job 21–37*, 984).

[53] There seem to me to be no reasons for accepting W. Bluedorn's suggestion that presentation of the offering under the tree is cultically unacceptable, and must be placed on the rock (W. Bluedorn, *Yahweh Versus Baalism: A Theological Reading of the Gideon–Abimelech Narrative*, JSOTSup, 329 (Sheffield: Sheffield Academic Press, 2001), 86).

[54] Boling, *Judges*, 151; R. Polzin, *Moses and the Deuteronomist: A Literary Study of the Deuteronomistic History*, pt. 1: *Deuteronomy, Joshua, Judges* (Bloomington: Indiana University Press, 1980), 168.

of the late-arriving Ephraimites, who parade two bloody heads as a demonstration of their own rich harvest? We should not be surprised at Gideon's
morbid humour, after all, YHWH is occasionally portrayed crushing humans
on the battlefield like grapes in a press with blood like grape juice splattering
everywhere. The fullest exposition of this theme is found in Isaiah 63:

> Why are your robes red, and your garments like someone who has been treading
> the winepress? I have trodden the winepress alone...I trod them in my anger and
> trampled them in my wrath. I splattered their juice on my garments, and I stained all
> my robes...I trampled peoples in my anger, I made them drunk with my wrath, and I
> poured out their juice on the earth.   (vv. 1–6)[55]

The analogy between blood and grape juice is decidedly disturbing, used of
YHWH's enemies or the Midianites. It suggests the confusion of human flesh
with food and drink.

The utilization of puns continues with the introduction of two additional
Midianite kings that Gideon now begins to pursue after his meeting with
the Ephraimites. Zebah and Zalmunna are eventually caught by Gideon and
slaughtered by him (8.18–21). Their names, which mean respectively 'sacrifice'
and 'shelter refused', appear to allude to their death at Gideon's hand.[56] The
suggestion that these two kings are a 'sacrifice' (*zevach*) can hardly be thought
an accident in the context of the other puns that we have observed. The
Midianites are wild animals and thus their killing is akin to crushing grapes
or making a sacrifice.

As we have seen, comparing the killing of Israel's enemies to food or sacrifice is not novel. In the story of Gideon, however, we witness a troubling development. Like Adoni-bezeq Gideon is unable to distinguish human beings and
dishes, even when the former includes his fellow Israelites. Whilst pursuing
Zebah and Zalmunna, Gideon seeks aid from the townsmen of Succoth, but
is spurned by them. His macabre wit is now turned against his own people,
and he promises that on his return, 'I will thresh your flesh with thorns of the
wilderness and with briers' (8.7).[57] The fearful farmer who beat out his crop

---

[55] Cf. Joel 3.13 and Lam. 1.15.

[56] It has long been suggested that the forms of these names are deliberately humorous. An
earlier generation of scholars tended to assume that the names had been corrupted by the
Masoretic tradents and that behind the present vocalization lay genuine Midianite names and
historical individuals. Moore is representative: 'the pronunciation of the names has very likely
been perverted by malicious wit....M[asoretic Text], as so often in similar cases, by an inept
witticism makes the names mean *Victim* and *Protection refused*' (Moore, *Judges*, 218–19).

[57] The fulfilment of Gideon's vow in v. 16 presents a text-critical problem. The Masoretic
Text reads, 'he caused to know or he taught' (*wayyoda'*). The unusual form of the Hiphil and
the witness of the versions suggest corruption from an original *wayyadash* 'he threshed'. For the
relevant bibliography see O'Connel, *Rhetoric of the Book of Judges*, 469.

in secret has now become brazen with his new harvest.[58] If grain can be beaten in a winepress, there is no reason why human beings cannot be threshed.

The narrator retains the last laugh in this use of food puns, for what Gideon sows, his own family reaps in abundance. Gideon's son Abimelech initiates his short and brutal reign with an audacious slaughter of his own brothers.[59] According to the narrator, Abimelech 'killed his brothers, the sons of Jerub-baal, seventy men, on one stone' (9.5). The emphasis on 'one stone' is clear and calls for explanation. The closest intertextual allusion is 1 Sam. 14.33–4, where Saul sacrifices sheep and oxen on a single stone in the open countryside. As Boling argues, 'comparison with 1 Sam 14.33–34 suggests that it is regarded by the narrator as a particularly disastrous perversion of Yahwist sacrificial cultus'.[60] In addition, the use of the number 'seventy' creates a link within the book of Judges to the actions of Adoni-bezeq. The resulting comparison is hardly flattering to Abimelech.

There is an additional reason for this emphasis on the 'one stone'. According to Judges, the troubles for Gideon's family do not end with the slaughter of most of his progeny. After a devastating reign, Abimelech finally meets his end crushed by an upper millstone dropped from the tower of Thebez (9.53).[61] Mieke Bal suggests that the 'one woman' who drops the millstone is a symmetrical counterpart to Abimelech, who made much during his accession to the throne of being 'one' (9.2). Further, the woman kills him with a single millstone, as he killed his brothers on a single stone (*even*).[62] Since Job 41.24

---

[58] 'The similarity between the agricultural activities indicates the reversal that has occurred in Gideon's personality' (Assis, *Self-Interest or Communal Interest*, 93).

[59] Abimelech's reign has more in common with Israel's oppressors than with her judges. Amit suggests that Abimelech's reign is the punishment prior to the judgeship of Tola (Amit, *Book of Judges*, 40–3). This is to push the book into a tight Deuteronomistic framework which is actually beginning to disintegrate at this point.

[60] Boling, *Judges*, 171. See also 1 Sam. 6.14 and possibly compare 1 Kgs. 1.9. Assis makes a similar connection, but her comment that 'the cruelty of the killing on one stone emerges from the comparison with the slaughter of the cattle on a stone by Saul' is understated (Assis, *Self-Interest or Communal Interest*, 137 n. 11).

[61] Abimelech's death by a millstone belongs to the motif of death through unorthodox weapons that Judges frequently employs. Shamgar kills six hundred Philistines with an ox-goad (4.31); Samson slaughters a thousand men with the jawbone of a donkey (15.15); Jael shatters Sisera's skull with a tent peg (4.21; 5.26). Ehud's assassination of Eglon also occurs with an unusual weapon, a home-made dagger for a left-handed man (3.16). This is another mark of confusion.

[62] M. Bal, *Death and Dissymmetry: The Politics of Coherence in the Book of Judges* (Chicago: University of Chicago Press, 1988), 217; J. G. Janzen, 'A Certain Woman in the Rhetoric of Judges 9', *JSOT* 38 (1987), 33–7; T. A. Boogaart, 'Stone for Stone: Retribution in the Story of Abimelech and Shechem', *JSOT* 32 (1985), 45–56. Assis notes that this connection is already made in *Tanhuma Wayyera*, which sees here a theology of retribution (Assis, *Self-Interest or Communal Interest*, 169 n. 65). If there is an implicit link with Adoni-bezeq and his unusual treatment of seventy, this may be a sound judgement.

places 'stone' (*even*) in poetic parallelism with lower millstone, we might say that the death of Abimelech rounds off the slaughter of Gideon's sons. The two parts of the millstone at the beginning and end of Abimelech's reign fix Gideon's descendants like grain to be ground. By the end of the story all have been milled in gruesome fashion.

Jephthah

There is no doubt about the use of sacrificial imagery in the famous story of Jephthah's daughter in Judges 11.30–40. Before his battle with the Ammonites Jephthah vows to sacrifice as a burnt offering whoever meets him first from his house should he return in victory. The impetuous vow is soon regretted when he returns victorious to be greeted by his only daughter. She persuades her father that he must fulfil his vow, but asks for a two-month period in which to mourn her virginity. It is well-known that the story does not conclusively state that Jephthah sacrificed her at the end of this period. Nevertheless, most scholars believe this to be the most natural way to interpret 'he did to her as he had vowed' (11.39). The case is strengthened by the clarity of Jephthah's vow. 'The person coming forth (*hayyotse*) . . . I will offer up as a burnt offering' not only promises an immolation but anticipates it will be a human being and not an animal.[63] Jephthah's words also echo Gideon's promise to return in vengeance against Penuel (11.31; cf. 8.9), a connection that must be regarded as inauspicious. If Jephthah's daughter is indeed sacrificed then Judges seems no longer to hesitate on the threshold of contemplating humans as sacrificial victims. Many of the stories have alluded to the possibility that humans might be similar to sacrifices, but with Jephthah's vow metaphor becomes reality. Humans and animals are now hopelessly confused even in the mind of one of Israel's judges. Nor is the sacrifice offered to any alien deity, but to YHWH himself.[64]

For a long time readers of the story about Jephthah's daughter have resisted the possibility that she was sacrificed by her father, the abhorrence of human sacrifice to some of the writers in the Old Testament providing grounds for

---

[63] Moore is forthright: 'That a human victim is intended is, in fact, as plain as words can make it; the language is inapplicable to an animal and a vow to offer the first sheep or goat that he comes across—not to mention the possibility of an unclean animal—is trivial to absurdity' (Moore, *Judges*, 299).

[64] The overlap between sacrifice and human slaughter is further suggested by the wording of Jephthah's vow. According to Judg. 11.30, 'Jephthah made a vow to YHWH and he said, "If you will give the sons of Ammon into my hand . . .".' His words echo Israel's vow in Num. 21.2–3: 'Israel made a vow to YHWH and said, "If you will give this people into my hand . . .".' Whilst Israel promises to utterly destroy conquered Arad, Jephthah turns the vow inwards and offers one of Israel's own as a human sacrifice (Assis, *Self-Interest or Communal Interest*, 223).

believing that a divinely appointed judge would not have committed such an atrocity. Although the majority of scholars have held that this view cannot be maintained, some have made the case for the fulfilment of the vow through the perpetual virginity of Jephthah's daughter. In favour of such a position is the strong emphasis in the story on her virginity. Second, on two occasions the unambiguous statements that Jephthah sacrificed his daughter are qualified by an adjacent clause. The initial vow, 'I will present it as a burnt offering', is juxtaposed with 'it will be for YHWH (*wᵉhayah layhwh*)', which Marcus has argued denotes consecration (11.31).[65] The statement that Jephthah fulfilled his vow is further explained with 'she did not know a man' (11.39). In the light of important textual arguments on both sides of the debate, there may be much to Thomas Römer's suggestion that we maintain some of the ambiguity. 'Even if the arguments for a literal interpretation of the text are much stronger, it is not totally impossible to adopt a non-sacrificial reading. The ambiguity in Judg. 11.30–40 might then have been intended.'[66]

The two different possibilities for Jephthah's daughter correspond to two different valuations of sex and virginity, and two different valuations of sacrifice. If Jephthah's vow can be carried out through his daughter's perpetual virginity then we have an equation of equivalence set up between virginity and sacrifice. In both the body is consecrated to YHWH, either through protecting its virginal status or by immolating it on the altar. On the other hand, if Jephthah fulfils his vow by sacrificing his daughter a different equation of equivalence is being proposed between sex and sacrifice. In both the body is consumed, either through deflowering a virgin or by making the victim a holocaust. Whichever is to be preferred, sex and sacrifice are interrelated and confused, as also it is clear killing and sacrifice have been.

Samson: Boundaries Reaffirmed and Dissolved

We have seen how in the book of Judges the boundaries between food, killing, sex and sacrifice are increasingly transgressed, in contrast to the book of Joshua, where the boundaries are resolutely retained. This does not mean, however, that the book instantly plunges us into a confused morass from the very beginning. As we have seen, a sense of narrative progression is retained in the book. In the story of Adoni-bezeq the Israelites are not implicated in his confusion of warfare and the dining table. Adoni-bezeq's confession that he is suffering punishment in kind, a *lex talionis*, portrays Judah as a vehicle of divine justice. Jael, again, is the action of a non-Israelite, and one like Ehud's

---

[65] D. Marcus, *Jephthah and His Vow* (Lubbock, TX: Texas Tech Press, 1986).
[66] Römer, 'Sacrifice of Jephthah's Daughter', 35.

that can be celebrated because it leads to the execution of a leader of an oppressive nation. With Gideon a decisive shift takes place, the trampling of the heads of Midianite commanders soon turns into the threshing of Israelite cities in the Jordan valley. Abimelech's short reign with its undisguised brutality appears to be the nadir of Israel's experience until Jephthah proceeds to offer his daughter as a burnt offering to YHWH. The increased dissolution of Israelite society under the judges is also signalled in the Deuteronomistic cycle, which would otherwise be a bastion of stable judgement. The cycle becomes more disjointed as the book progresses. As Exum observes, 'the framework deconstructs itself, so to speak, and the cycle of apostasy and deliverance becomes increasingly murky'.[67]

In the context of this dissolution of the boundaries the story of Samson begins with what appears to be an attempt to fortify them. The sacrifice of Manoah echoes in many of its particulars the story of Gideon's sacrifice in Judges 6 but without its ambiguities. Manoah's wife discerns early on that the divine figure is an angel of God (13.6), and even though Manoah lacks his wife's perceptiveness, the angel prevents Manoah from bringing a meal, accepting only a sacrifice to YHWH (v. 16).[68] The message of the angel articulates a distinction between food and sacrifice. His appointment of Samson as a nazirite to God includes placing boundaries within the diet of the judge. He is not to eat anything unclean and he is not to drink anything intoxicating.[69]

There is some disagreement about the role the nazirite vow plays within the Samson cycle. For some, 'Samson's Nazirite status hardly functions in the story.'[70] The story tells of a heroic figure with legendary strength, whose Achilles heel is his hair, the source of his magical strength. The nazirite vow is a later element that gives the superhuman might a theological explanation. Thus, the vow serves only to explain the betrayal of Samson in chapter 16 and is absent from chapters 14–15. On the other hand, the vow has been given a more substantial role in the plot by others. The consumption of honey from

[67] Exum, 'Centre Cannot Hold', 412.

[68] J. C. Exum, 'The Theological Dimension of the Samson Saga', *VT* 33 (1983), 30–46, here 39.

[69] The nazirite vow under which Samson is placed differs in some of its details from that found in Num. 6.1–21. According to Judges 13 Samson is not to drink anything intoxicating, eat anything unclean, or cut his hair, whilst in Numbers 6 the Nazirite is not to drink anything intoxicating, cut his or her hair or touch a corpse (vv. 1–8). In addition Samson's nazirite status is lifelong, whilst the vows in Numbers 6 are for a limited duration. The scarcity of evidence for the nazirite in the Old Testament makes tracing an evolving tradition almost futile. Nevertheless, it is possible that Numbers and Judges reflect two variant understandings of the Nazirite vow separated by time or reflecting local variation. Consequently using Numbers 6 to interpret Samson's vow is questionable.

[70] J. Crenshaw, *Samson: A Secret Betrayed, a Vow Ignored* (Atlanta: John Knox Press, 1978), 73–4.

the carcass of a lion and the celebration of his wedding with a feast in chapter 14 can be viewed as initial steps in violating his vow.[71]

What is easily lost in this argument is the unusual consecration of Samson. Neither the nazirite vow as legislated for in Numbers nor any other deliverer figure in Judges knows consecration from birth. The vow is extended to include both Samson and his mother, and it is Samson's parents that are the recipients of the angelic revelation and the terms of the vow. Consequently, they have a role in policing the vow. It should be observed that Samson's parents continue to figure in the story into chapter 14. Initially they seek to maintain one of the boundaries that is not covered in the vow, that between endogamy and exogamy. For the first time a story about a judge touches upon the concerns of the Deuteronomistic framework. The chapter opens with Samson's desire to marry a Philistine from Timnah. Both father and mother oppose, 'Is there not a woman among the daughters of your kinsmen or all my people that you must take a wife from the uncircumcised Philistines?' (14.3).[72] Eventually they succumb to the insistent Samson, going down to Timnah to arrange the wedding (v. 4). The failure of Samson's parents to maintain the vow appears again in the famous story of the lion. Samson kills a young lion that attacks him, leaving the broken carcass beside the road. On a return journey he observes bees in the carcass and a supply of wild honey. Eagerly he eats and takes some home to his parents, despite the fact that the honey is unclean (cf. Lev. 11.24–5, 39). Samson thus violates his own vow, and by not telling his parents they are unintentionally implicated too.[73]

Samson's cavalier approach to the terms of his vow continues with his wedding feast. The Hebrew *mishteh* emphasizes the feast as a place at which much drinking took place. The bawdy atmosphere gives rise to a competitive bout of riddle exchange, which Samson initiates with the poetic couplet,

---

[71] McCann, for example, uses the nazirite legislation in Numbers to present Samson's life as a steady violation of every aspect of his vow. 'Sampson [*sic*] does not shun "wine and strong drink" (see 14:5, 10; cf. Num. 6.3); he does not avoid contact with a carcass (see 14:8; cf. Num. 6:6–8); and finally, he foolishly allows his hair to be cut (see 16:15–22; cf. Num 6:5–6)' (J. C. McCann, *Judges*, Interpretation (Louisville: John Knox Press, 2002), 99). McCann's reliance on Numbers is apparent in this quotation, including contamination by a corpse which would have been problematic for a military deliverer like Samson. It should be observed that by concentrating on the prescriptions in Numbers, McCann has omitted the consumption of unclean food. Arguably eating honey from a carcass would be deemed unclean food, and thus McCann's interpretation of the whole story can still be maintained by holding onto the particulars of Judges 13 (cf. J. Blenkinsopp, 'Structure and Style in Judges 13–16', *JBL* 82 (1963), 65–76).

[72] Following MT and avoiding any emendations of the personal suffixes on the basis of the versions (cf. Soggin, *Judges*, 239).

[73] This is particularly the case if Samson's mother is still bound by the nazirite obligations. It would be natural to assume that her nazirite obligations ceased after the birth of Samson. This is not, however, explicit in the angel's commission.

> Out of the eater came something to eat,
> out of the strong something sweet.

> (v. 14)

The riddle has perplexed interpreters, since it does not seem to accord to the rules for a good riddle. 'It was, in truth, a bad riddle, and quite insoluble without a knowledge of the accidental circumstances which suggested it.'[74] A common solution has been to argue that the answer to the riddle is a play on the Hebrew word for lion, *ari*, and a homophone, *ari*, an Arabic word for honey. Samson's companions would not need to have a knowledge of Samson's encounter with the lion, they would merely need to solve a play on words.[75] Since *ari* is unattested in Hebrew, however, this solution can be proposed only tentatively. Recently Azzan Yadin has argued that the problem stems from the translation of *chidah* as 'riddle'.[76] Instead, Samson is initiating a competition in *skolion*, a practice known from Greek symposia. 'A symposiast would recite a verse, challenging his fellow drinkers to "cap" it.'[77] One benefit of this proposal is it explains why the Philistines do not answer the riddle, but produce their own enigmatic couplet,

> What is sweeter than honey?
> What is stronger than a lion?

> (v. 18)

To which the frustrated Samson responds:

> If you had not ploughed with my heifer
> You would not have discovered my riddle.

> (v. 18)

However the riddle is to be explained, there is much to Steve Weitzman's observation that what is significant according to the narrative is that the puzzle is insoluble.[78] Even Samson's parents do not know of the encounter with the lion (vv. 10, 16) and when the riddle is solved Samson knows that his wife is the source (vv. 17–18).

Samson's initial riddle demonstrates an ability, like Gideon, to make food-related puns. The riddle also draws attention to the juxtaposition of food and death in the original encounter of the lion, 'out of the eater came something to

---

[74] Moore, *Judges*, 335.

[75] For a recent acceptance of this argument which references the earliest proponents of this solution: S. Segert, 'Paronomasia in the Samson Narrative in Judges XIII–XVI', *VT* 34 (1984), 454–61.

[76] A. Yadin, 'Samson's Ḥîdâ', *VT* 52 (2002), 407–26.   [77] Ibid., 419.

[78] S. Weitzman, 'The Samson Story as Border Fiction', *BibInt* 10 (2002), 158–74, here 165 n. 19.

eat'. In addition the couplet, well suited to the bawdy atmosphere of a drinking feast, has a barely disguised sexual innuendo. The answer to the riddle could easily be the incident with the lion and honey. It is equally suited, however, as a description of the semen of the bridegroom, sweet to the bride who 'tastes' it through intercourse. It could also be the vomit of the inebriated guests. In Samson's rhyme the disastrous collapsing of sex, food and death in Israel becomes inspiration for a riddle to entertain the Philistines. The Philistines are not to be outdone by Samson and when they discover the nature of the riddle they propose their own couplet. It has long been suggested that the solution to this riddle is love or sexual desire, for they are both sweet and strong. Since Songs 8.6 contains a proverbial saying that equates the strength of death and love, we might also speculate whether death itself is both strong and sweet. Certainly in the Old Testament death is not sweet to those who experience it, yet for Samson the death of many Philistines does prove sweet. Thus, the counter-riddle of the Philistines also combines food, death and sex. Unabashed sexual innuendo is also present in Samson's claim that his guests have been 'ploughing' with his heifer. In Samson's final riddle an animal and a human are again confused.

The strength of love or sexual desire may justifiably be taken as a *leitmotif* for the rest of Samson's time as judge. His love for Philistine women leads to his revenge attack on the crops of the Philistines and the slaughter at Lehi, the destruction of the gates of Gaza and finally his capture through the wiles of Delilah. Before we reach the denouement of Samson's life it is worth pausing with the battle at Lehi because here we have another rhyming riddle and the confusion of animals and humans. In this brief story (15.9–17) Samson kills a thousand men using an ass's jawbone as an impromptu weapon. When he is done he composes a ditty to celebrate his victory:

> With the jaw of an ass,
> Heap, heaps;
> With the jaw of an ass
> I have struck a thousand men.

(15.16)

The second line is extremely difficult, but possibly plays upon the word $ch^a mor$, which can mean 'ass' or 'heap'. The slaughtered Philistines are both heaped up and, to attempt a similar pun to Samson's, 'made asses of'. Again, Samson utilizes a riddle to make beasts of human beings.

Samson's end comes at a festival to Dagon, the Philistine deity. This final episode in Samson's life deserves close attention not only because it again illustrates the collapse of food, sex, death and sacrifice into one another, but also because of its relationship to the concerns of the Deuteronomistic framework.

This festival is described as an occasion when the Philistine leaders gathered 'to sacrifice a great sacrifice', *lizboach zevach-gadol* (v. 23). This unusual phrase occurs on only three other occasions. In Neh. 12.43 it is used of the sacrifices at the Jerusalem temple and in Ezek. 39.17 it is used of the carnage in the apocalyptic battle against Gog. The closest parallel is in 2 Kgs. 10.19 where Jehu calls the worshippers of Baal to 'a great sacrifice' in the temple of Baal. There, as also in Judges 16, the words have a double meaning. There will indeed be a great sacrifice, but not the one envisaged by the worshippers, a sacrifice of the worshippers and not of animals.[79] Naturally the festival to Dagon is an occasion for feasting, as implied by 'their hearts were merry' (v. 25),[80] and for entertainment. The latter is to be provided by Samson. The possibility, proposed by Susan Niditch, that this is sexual humiliation, a play on the word *schq / shchq*, is suggestive. As we have seen, the book of Judges frequently plays with double entendre, but it is difficult to be fully confident in this instance.[81] Even without this the narrative's relating of sacrifice, feasting and death is in agreement with the perspective we have seen elsewhere in the stories of the judges.

The conclusion of Samson's life also agrees with the Deuteronomistic framework in a way that no other story in the book of Judges does. Samson is the prime example of the Deuteronomistic fear that intermarriage will lead to cultic unfaithfulness. Samson's obsession with non-Israelite women eventually results in him being led, against his will, into the cultic feasting of the Philistines for their god, Dagon. With a new infusion of energy from YHWH Samson can bring the feast to a halt, but only by bringing the building down on top of himself.[82] Thus, with the very last judge the Deuteronomistic

---

[79] See, e.g., J. Gray, *I & II Kings*, OTL (London: SCM Press, 1964), 560; T. R. Hobbs, *2 Kings*, WBC, 13 (Waco: Word, 1985), 129. The failure of the commentators on Judges to draw attention to this intertextual link with 2 Kings 10, or to note the paronomasia is a surprising and unfortunate omission.

[80] The phrase is commonly used as an idiom for the satisfaction that comes from a meal (Deut. 28.47; 1 Sam. 25.36; Judg. 19.6, 9, 22; 2 Sam. 13.28; 1 Kgs. 21.7; 2 Kgs. 25.24; Isa. 65.14; Ruth 3.7; Esther 1.10; 5.9).

[81] S. Niditch, 'Samson as Culture Hero, Trickster, and Bandit: The Empowerment of the Weak', *CBQ* 52 (1990), 608–24, esp. 617. I am even less confident of Niditch's attempt to find in Samson's 'grinding' for the Philistines a sexual euphemism.

[82] This naturally raises the question of the extent to which 16.23–31 is the work of a Deuteronomistic editor. Kratz argues that vv. 23b–24, 28 are later Deuteronomistic supplements, removing from the story the explicit mention of YHWH or the gods of the Philistines (Kratz, *Composition of the Narrative Books*, 208). It is not clear to me that this sufficiently addresses the extent to which this section touches upon the Deuteronomists' concerns with exogamy and participation in non-Yahwistic festivals. One of the classic ways in which the Samson cycle has been regarded is as fairly late material in the book of Judges. 'It is harder to decide whether Dtr.'s account included the Samson stories (Judg. 13.2–16.31) or whether they are a later interpolation' (M. Noth, *The Deuteronomistic History*, JSOTSup, 15 (Sheffield: JSOT Press, 1981), 84). Our examination of the theme of food in the book of Judges demonstrates how the Samson cycle has

fears about feasting, intermarriage and idolatry finally fuse with the collapse of cultural categories that we have observed in the stories of the judges.

'Everyone Did what was Right in his Own Eyes': Judges 17–21

The book of Judges ends with a double conclusion that depicts the final dissolution of order in Israel. The story of Micah and the Danites (chs. 17–18) and the Levite and his concubine (chs. 19–21) depart from the cyclical pattern of Judges, which as we have seen was increasingly breaking down. No longer does Israel do evil and yhwh raises up a judge. As the book concludes, not even a deliverer can be found, for 'everyone does what is right in their own eyes' (17.6; 21.25). Besides sharing this judgement on Israel, the two stories have other similarities. Both relate a tale about an anonymous Levite who is related to both Ephraim and Bethlehem. Both anticipate positively the establishment of the monarchy, explaining the depravity of the period with the judgement 'in those days there was no king in Israel' (17.6; 18.1; 19.1; 21.25). Not just any king will do, and there are veiled polemics against the northern kingdom and Saul. Despite these shared concerns they are judged to have independent histories.[83]

The original independence of the stories is reflected in their subject matter. The story of Micah and the Danites relates how the Danites migrated from their allotted inheritance in the Philistine territory to settle Dan in the north of the country. During their migration they appropriate a cultic image and its attendant priest, and install both in Dan. The narrative concludes, 'they set up for themselves the image that Micah had made for the whole time that the house of God was in Shiloh' (18.31). The reference to what the Deuteronomists regarded as the central shrine during the pre-monarchic period suggests that the story of Micah and the Danites is primarily concerned with condemning cultic apostasy. The final location of the image at Dan, one of the cultic sites of the northern kingdom, and the negative portrayal of Micah as both devious and hapless, confirms the polemical intent of this story. Thus, the story of Micah and the Danites coheres with the Deuteronomistic condemnation of cultic apostasy.

The Deuteronomistic fears about apostasy are not limited to cult images; as we have seen, they also concern sex and food. These aspects are absent from chapters 17–18, but present in chapters 19–21, which themselves lack

---

material in common with the other stories about the Judges and also with the Deuteronomistic framework.

[83]   A. D. H. Mayes, 'Deuteronomistic Royal Ideology in Judges 17–21', *BibInt* 9 (2001), 243–58; Amit, *Book of Judges*, 310–57.

any reference to cultic apostasy. Again we will see in this story the collapse of food, sex, sacrifice and warfare into one another, bringing the book to its debilitating conclusion.

Judges 19 opens with an anonymous Levite whose concubine or secondary wife has returned to her father.[84] After some months he visits his father-in-law to seek her return. Despite the marital disharmony his father-in-law is overjoyed to see him and is lavish in his hospitality. As we have already seen with Jael's entertainment of Sisera the excessive hospitality strikes an uncertain note. Susan Niditch judges it to be model, whilst David Penchansky considers it a parody, in which the father-in-law preys on the Levite's weakness.[85] The excess again alerts the reader to something unusual, although unlike in the story of Jael and Sisera the gory outcome will be deferred. Nevertheless, the over-generosity of the father-in-law plays an important role in leading to the concubine's death. First, the delaying tactics of the host lead to the Levite leaving at an inauspicious mid-point in time. It is the fifth day when the Levite finally resolves to leave, half-way between the classic short period of three days and a week of seven days. They leave not when the day has just begun, but when the day is half spent. The delay means that the Levite and his concubine are caught needing shelter before they have reached their home in the Ephraimite hills. Second, the excessive generosity of the father-in-law contrasts with the lack of hospitality on offer in Gibeah. When the Levite and his concubine arrive, only an old man meets them and his concern to take them away from the open square is ominous. The situation is so unpromising that the Levite suggests he and his concubine will eat their own food, as long as shelter can be offered for the night.

The negative experience appears to have been dispelled when the old man takes them in and offers to supply all their needs. They enjoy a meal together and 'their hearts are merry' (19.22). The convivial picture is broken by riotous disorder outside the house and a demand from the men of Gibeah that they be given the man for sexual intercourse. The allusion to the events at Sodom is clear (Gen. 19), and as there, women are offered to the mob instead of the male guest. Whilst Lot offers his two virgin daughters, the old man offers his virgin daughter and the Levite's concubine. Despite this breach with the conventions of hospitality and the refusal of the mob, the Levite thrusts his own concubine out to be ravished. Whilst he remains safe, she is raped and murdered.

---

[84] For the meaning of *pilegesh* see, *inter alia*, S. Ackerman, *Warrior, Dancer, Seductress, Queen: Women in Judges and Biblical Israel* (New York: Doubleday, 1998), 235–6.

[85] D. Penchansky, 'Staying the Night: Intertextuality in Genesis and Judges', in D. N. Fewell (ed.), *Reading between Texts* (Louisville: Westminster John Knox Press, 1992), 77–88; S. Niditch, 'The "Sodomite" Theme in Judges 19–20: Family, Community, and Social Disintegration', *CBQ* 44 (1982), 365–78.

The contrasting experience at Gibeah creates a relationship between feasting and sex. Inside the male feasts, outside the female is raped. Judges 19 supports drawing this parallel in its use of the keyword *chazaq bᵉ-*, 'to seize'. Earlier in the story the Levite is 'seized' by his father-in-law and made to stay and feast (v. 4), now he seizes the daughter and thrusts her out to be raped (v. 25). The following morning when the Levite gets ready to leave he finds his concubine dead on the doorstep. He hauls her callously on to his donkey and returns to his home. At home he seizes her and cuts her into twelve pieces and distributes her around the tribes. The word 'seize' (*chazaq bᵉ-*) again links the two events.[86] She is seized in order to be violated, now she is seized in order to be dissected.

The account of the dissection suggests a number of important links that help characterize the event. The first is to the opening story in Judges where Adoni-bezeq mutilates his conquered foes. The book opens and closes with human mutilation. The second is to 1 Samuel 11 when Saul assembles the Israelite tribes by sending a dismembered pair of oxen along with a message to muster.

Saul took a yoke of oxen and dismembered them. He sent them throughout the entire Israelite territory by messengers, saying, 'Whoever does not come out after Saul and Samuel, so shall it be done to his oxen!' (1 Sam. 11.7)

Again, humans and animals are not distinguished. It is perhaps not insignificant that Saul's troops assemble at Bezeq, the only other occasion in the Old Testament that this location is known outside of Judges 1.4–7. In other words these three texts, Judges 1, Judges 19 and 1 Samuel 11, have been closely related to one another. A final intertextual connection is with Genesis 22, for the word for 'knife' (*maᵃkeleth*) is found only there and in Prov. 30.14. The Levite's action looks, then, like an act of sacrifice, paralleling the sacrifice of Isaac, and within the book of Judges the sacrifice of Jephthah's daughter. Yet, the word for 'knife' (*maᵃkeleth*) suggests food (*akal*) (cf. Prov. 30.14). Are the Israelite tribes being sent a dismembered sacrifice or a joint of meat?

As a result of the Levite's actions the tribes gather and attack the tribe of Benjamin, who refuse to give up the people of Gibeah. The extended account of the war against Benjamin tells of three battles before victory is achieved. The account not only echoes the assault on Ai (Joshua 7–8) where the Israelites were first defeated before ambushing the city, but also echoes the opening story of the book of Judges when the tribes consult YHWH about how to undertake the battle. The irony of Judges 20 is that holy war is now being pursued within Israel. The account of the battle is interesting because when

[86] Note also the use of 'send' (*shalach*; 9.25, 29).

the city is captured by the ambushing force it is set on fire. The Benjaminites turn and see 'the entire city going up to the heavens' (20.40). The word for 'entire', *kalil*, is a term also used for a burnt offering, and the sentence could also be translated 'the holocaust of the city rose up to heaven'. Although the Israelite ban included the idea of devoting a city to YHWH, that is completely destroying it, it is extremely unusual for sacrificial vocabulary to be employed in this context. Thus David Janzen rightly argues that in the Deuteronomistic History the ban is not a kind of sacrifice, though the Historian does portray it in terms rather like sacrifice.[87] Since this is a departure from Deuteronomy's careful distinction between ban and sacrifice, such occurrences demand careful attention, as is the case here. The unusual use of the sacrificial imagery here again confirms that the separate categories of warfare and sacrifice are being collapsed into one another.

CONCLUSION

With the dissolution of Israelite society in the final chapters the book of Judges reaches its catastrophic conclusion. The office of judge has ceased and there is no king to bring order in Israel. As Exum puts it, in the Israel of the judges 'disorder is...a fact of life'.[88] This disorder is revealed in the collapsing of recognized distinctions resulting in a veritable salgamundi of food, sacrifice, killing and sex. Increasingly the boundaries between cultural domains affirmed elsewhere in the Old Testament disintegrate. In a similar way the boundaries between animals and humans are increasingly crossed. Initially it is Israel's enemies that suffer from what appears to be wry national humour, but as the book progresses it is Israel herself that is caught up in the bewildering chaos.

In this examination of the book of Judges we have suggested that attention to food and an application of Mary Douglas's ideas of 'matter out of place' might provide a suggestive way of understanding the book of Judges. In particular, the confusion between the cultural domains of food, sacrifice, killing and sex and between the natural domains of humans and animals that are found in the stories about the judges explains the choice of these narratives rather than any others that may have been available. The collapse of these natural and cultural domains portrays a collapse of Israel's social structures. That is not to

[87] D. Janzen, *The Social Meanings of Sacrifice in the Hebrew Bible: A Study of Four Writings*, BZAW, 344 (Berlin: W. de Gruyter, 2004), 164–76.

[88] J. C. Exum, *Tragedy and Biblical Narrative: Arrows of the Almighty* (Cambridge: Cambridge University Press, 1992), 46.

say that there are not other aspects to the book of Judges. As Exum observes, 'the book of Judges exhibits an enigmatic complexity; so much transpires on different levels that multiple interpretations are inevitable, as the plurality of views in current scholarship illustrates'.[89] Nevertheless, the use of food within the book offers important insights into how the book instils its message.

Our examination of Judges also has implications for the way that Judges is used within the discussion of Israel's religio-historical development. The issue is not merely when we date the stories of the judges, with suggestions ranging from the pre-monarchic period to the Hellenistic period, but also the possibility that some of the cultic observations in the book may serve thematic and literary purposes. We must not ascribe great significance to every divergence from the religious practices that we find elsewhere in the Old Testament. We should hesitate, for example, before drawing wide-ranging conclusions about the peculiar nature of Gideon's offering, the prevalence of human sacrifice or the existence of a maturation festival for unmarried women. In the context of modern literary readings of the Bible the case for due consideration of these issues does not need to be overdone. We cannot, however, assume that beneath the thick strokes of the Deuteronomistic pen we have unrestrained access to early Israel. The stories have too many features in common to suggest that they reflect a disinterested collection of material that survived from an early period. The stories do demonstrate, however, a fascinating 'thinking together' of food, sex, killing and sacrifice apart from their Deuteronomistic framework.

[89] Exum, 'Centre Cannot Hold', 410.

5

Feasting Fit for a King: Food and the Rise
of the Monarchy

Food and taste are commonly perceived to be a conservative force within society. People eat what they are used to. Food taboos have often been understood as vestigial practices whose original logic was no longer perceived by those who kept them. The biblical food laws are a good example. The taboo against eating pork is usually thought to have been long-standing, and archaeology provides some measure of confirmation for this view. In their present formulation, however, the laws stem from scribal activities around the exilic period. The criteria of a cloven hoof and chewing the cud are later scribal classifications that appear to provide some logic for the traditional avoidance of pork by the ancient Israelites.

A conservative impulse is also depicted in Jeremiah's use of the Rechabites as an example of faithfulness (Jeremiah 35). Although now forced by the Babylonian invasion to live in an urban setting, the Rechabites appear originally to have been a non-sedentary tribe. They preserve certain features of their earlier existence.

We have obeyed our ancestor Jonadab son of Rechab in all that he commanded us, not to drink wine all our days, ourselves, our wives, our sons, and our daughters, and not to build houses to live in. We have no vineyard or field or seed; and we have lived in tents. We have heard and obeyed all that our ancestor Jonadab commanded us.

(Jer. 35.8–10)

Jeremiah's attempt to lure them with wine demonstrates that their allegiance to traditional ways is shown particularly in their distinctive diet.

The argument to be pursued here is that in ancient Israel food was also a force for social change, and not just a conservative and atavistic impulse. In particular I wish to argue that feasting played an important role in the development of early Israel into a monarchy in the early Iron Age. A critical examination of some of the social-scientific models that were developed to explain this significant historical transition reveals a number of deficiencies and lacunae that can benefit from attention to recent anthropological work

on feasting as a vehicle for social change. The purpose of this argument is not to replace the social-scientific models for Israel's development, but rather to augment them. Such an argument will depend not only on its ability to provide a more comprehensive model of the development of Israel's society, but also on its ability to account for the biblical and archaeological evidence for the early Iron Age period.

This chapter is closely linked to the following chapter. In this chapter a historical argument is presented for the development of the Israelite monarchy which draws on the relevant historical data—mostly biblical and archaeological evidence—and anthropological theory. This will demonstrate that in ancient Israel feasting was an important locus of political power, both as means of mobilizing support and labour, but also as means of displaying success. A significant factor in the emergence of a centralized monarchy was the control of food distribution by a small elite. The close relationship that existed between political power and the circulation of food was not unnoticed in ancient Israel. The recognition of this relationship provides the basis of the biblical evidence utilized in this chapter. Additionally, however, it stimulated certain literary motifs that are to be found in biblical literature. The following chapter, therefore, examines the relationship between monarchy and table on the literary level, giving particular attention to the table as the locus of divine and human judgement.

THE DEVELOPMENT OF ISRAEL FROM TRIBAL SOCIETY TO MONARCHY

In 1979 Gottwald published his ground-breaking work on the sociology of ancient Israel, *The Tribes of Yahweh*. In it Gottwald deploys social-scientific methodology on an unprecedented scale to pre-monarchic Israelite society.[1] Following in his wake a number of scholars sought to further the analysis of early Israelite society and, in particular, to explore the rapid development of the disparate Israelite tribes into a monarchy.[2] Earlier studies had been content to see the external Philistine threat as the decisive factor in the development of the monarchy. The new scholarship drew upon anthropological studies of state formation and sought to describe the internal dynamics that could lead to such a rapid adoption of monarchy. Three such studies were Frick's book

---

[1] Gottwald, *Tribes of Yahweh*.
[2] Most of the volumes in the 'Social World of Biblical Antiquity Series' were concerned with early Israel.

The Formation of the State in Ancient Israel, Coote and Whitelam's co-authored volume *The Emergence of Early Israel in Historical Perspective* and Schäfer-Lichtenberger's essay 'Sociological and Biblical Views of the Early State'.[3]

Frick: the Formation of the State

In his analysis of early Israel Frick utilizes a number of anthropological models for state formation.[4] A central presupposition for Frick in employing these models is a commitment to systems theory. In systems theory societies are viewed as made up of many interrelated elements such that significant variation in one part results in variation elsewhere. Thus a single cause alone cannot explain complex changes in society. In the case of Israel Frick is dissatisfied with explanations of Israel's development that attribute the change to an external Philistine threat.

The trajectory of Israelite society, according to Frick, is from a segmentary society to a small urban state through an intermediate stage of chieftainship. In its earliest stages Israel was a segmentary society. Relationships between the Israelite tribes and within the tribes are defined genealogically. In theory all the tribal units have an equal standing. The tribes themselves are also internally homogenous to a great extent. There is no permanent leadership at the tribal level. Although the distinction between a chieftainship and kingship is difficult to define, there are two ways in which chiefdoms differ from segmentary societies. First, in chiefdoms individuals are ranked within the community, and, second, local communities are regionally centralized. Such social differentiation together with the centralization of leadership in a single person counters the process of fissioning that is characteristic of segmentary societies. This differentiation is achieved as subordinate positions are awarded to other than close kin. Continued success of the chieftain depends upon maintaining his supporters through redistribution, ritual sanction and clientship. The chief accumulates wealth and redistributes it periodically to his supporters; theocratic claims provide religious legitimation for the chief; and, redistribution produces a body of loyal clients.

The single most important factor in stimulating social change according to Frick is the environmental challenges facing the Israelite farmers. The climate

---

[3] For a recent description and analysis of these works see P. McNutt, *Reconstructing the Society of Ancient Israel*, Library of Ancient Israel (Louisville: Westminster John Knox Press, 1999), 112–42. Disappointingly McNutt's work does not advance the study of this period aside from an undeveloped observation that the Solomonic period makes little or no contribution to these reconstructions of Israelite society.

[4] F. S. Frick, *The Formation of the State in Ancient Israel*, SWBA, 4 (Sheffield: Almond Press, 1985).

of Palestine means the timing of agricultural activities is crucial, and at certain points there is a labour shortage. 'For this reason it seems fair to conclude that the environment of early Israel tended to select for those technologies (terraces, etc.) and social organizational structures (segmentary society > chiefdom > state) that could maximize and extend the capabilities of the labor supply.'[5] The efficient utilization of labour would also lead to specialization.

When labour needs required a level of efficiency beyond that which could be supplied by productive specialization in the local household or residential group, an organizing principle based on hierarchical partitioning of society emerged and the chiefdom appeared. The chief and his clients organized and directed energy exchanges between the different segments of the society. Otherwise there would be very little security for individuals producing only a limited range of goods to satisfy their needs.[6]

The move towards monarchy was only achieved under David. Here there is an important shift in Frick's argumentation as warfare becomes the principal driver of societal change. David secured a large alliance with which he could conquer the plains of Palestine. This territory was allocated to David's supporters, strengthening the bonds between patron and client, and creating further wealth differentiation in early Israel.

Coote and Whitelam: the Emergence of Early Israel

Coote and Whitelam's work has much in common with Frick's.[7] There is a scepticism about the Philistines as a unilineal explanation of Israel's development. Anthropological theories and models are utilized alongside detailed attention to the material conditions that the Israelites faced in the environment of ancient Palestine. There is also agreement that Israel developed from a segmentary society to a chiefdom to a state. Coote and Whitelam are distinct in employing Braudel's *longue durée* perspective, and seeking to rely almost entirely on archaeological evidence without recourse to the biblical text. If we are to seek an interpretation for the rise of the monarchy other than the religious one proposed by the biblical authors we need, they argue, to view the events of the late Bronze Age and early Iron Age within the cyclical patterns of decline and regeneration of historical Palestine.

In tracing the processes that give rise to the Israelite state Coote and Whitelam appeal particularly to Carneiro's circumspection theory. The tribal groups that became Israel were circumscribed geographically by semi-arid steppe and desert, and socially by lowland city-states, hostile nomadic raiders and the Philistine pentapolis. Within this circumscribed area Israel was able to

---

[5] Ibid., 197.   [6] Ibid., 199.   [7] Coote and Whitelam, *Emergence of Early Israel*.

expand as her population initially grew. As the amount of unsettled land that was available declined, the population pressures remained and encouraged other changes. Coote and Whitelam explore three areas of change that took place in ancient Israel: expansion and intensification of the economic base, socio-economic stratification and political centralization. These are understood as interdependent areas: 'whatever triggers the process off sets in motion a multiple and complex feedback system involving and acting upon all forms of economic, social, political and religious organizations'.[8]

First, economic intensification occurred through the use of agricultural technology such as terracing and cisterns. Further developments took place as richer Israelites obtained larger land holdings and were able to invest in cash crops, such as olives and grapes. Second, socio-economic stratification was stimulated by the resumption of international trade which allowed an emerging elite to benefit from transit trade. According to Coote and Whitelam socio-economic differences were never entirely absent from early Israel, even if the society was more homogenous than that found in the city-states. The re-emergence of trade allowed some areas along trade routes to benefit to a greater degree than others. At a village level the varying economic fortunes of different families would have resulted in increasing stratification. Finally, political centralization took place as competition for arable land resulted in social conflict. This in turn led to territorial units that transcended the village, the number of which naturally decreased as the units increased in size. The threat of the Philistines also encouraged centralization as a means of redistributing the cost of defence. This was particularly advantageous to the emerging Israelite elite who wished to protect from the Philistines their stake in international trade. This was achieved, but the cost was borne not only by themselves, but also by their poorer compatriots.

Schäfer-Lichtenberger: Sociological and Biblical Views of the Early State

In common with Frick, and Coote and Whitelam, Schäfer-Lichtenberger's examination of the transformation of early Israel is informed by social-scientific studies, but in contrast to them archaeology plays no role and she has a far more positive view of the biblical materials as a repository of serviceable historical information for the early monarchic period.[9] Schäfer-Lichtenberger

---

[8]   Ibid., 145.
[9]   C. Schäfer-Lichtenberger, 'Sociological and Biblical Views of the Early State', in V. Fritz and P. R. Davies (eds.), *The Origins of the Ancient Israelite States* (Sheffield: Sheffield Academic Press, 1996), 78–105.

rejects the existence of a transitional stage of chieftainship. Geographical iso-
lation is a necessary condition for the development of chiefdoms and this
was never the case for early Israel. Consequently, she seeks to determine
whether the biblical texts show evidence of the characteristics of an early state.
There are seven characteristics of an early state that Schäfer-Lichtenberger
identifies. First, the population should be large enough to allow stratification
and specialization to develop; second, the state has a definite territory; third,
there is a centralized government; fourth, the state is politically independent;
fifth, there must exist a minimum of social stratification; sixth, there is a
level of production high enough to attain a surplus that can support the state
organization; seventh, rule is based on ideas of legitimation derived from an
existing ideology of reciprocity. The biblical descriptions of Saul and David's
reign are measured against these seven characteristics.

Critical Perspectives on the Models for Israel's Development

The choice presented by Coote and Whitelam, and by Schäfer-Lichtenberger,
between biblical and archaeological evidence is an invidious one. It is not
desirable to choose between sources of historical information, even if the
biblical material is problematicized by an extended redactional history and
its composition at some remove from the historical events described.[10] The
significant progress made by the analyses of Frick, Coote and Whitelam, and
Schäfer-Lichtenberger in describing the development of Israel during the early
Iron Age results not from choosing between historical sources, but from their
use of anthropological research. In each case early Israel is placed into a
comparative context, and the appearance of the monarchy is not treated as *sui
generis*. The utilization of a broad range of anthropological models produces
sophisticated accounts of the development of early Israelite society.

It is possible to critique such accounts on their use of anthropological models and to raise questions about the use of segmentation for the very earliest
Israelite society.[11] Other theories have been proposed for the early history of

[10] Thompson for one is not convinced that Coote and Whitelam's proposed model achieves
independence from the biblical texts (T. L. Thompson, *Early History of the Israelite People: From
the Written and Archaeological Sources*, SHCANE, 4 (Leiden: Brill, 1992), 155–6). Finkelstein, on
the other hand, finds works such as Coote and Whitelam's more accomplished theoretically than
archaeologically. He attempts to fill the deficit with a study of the changing nature of settlement
patterns in the Iron Age I period (I. Finkelstein, 'The Emergence of the Monarchy in Israel: The
Environmental and Socio-Economic Aspects', *JSOT* 44 (1989), 43–74).

[11] See, e.g., J. W. Rogerson, 'Was Early Israel a Segmentary Society?', *JSOT* 36 (1986), 17–26;
D. Fiensy, 'Using the Nuer Culture of Africa in Understanding the Old Testament: An Evaluation',
JSOT 38 (1987), 73–83. It is clear that even between the accounts examined there exists not a little
difference, such as on the question of the separate existence of chieftainship.

Israel, most recently Robert Miller's 'complex chieftains'.[12] My purpose is not
to defend such theories against all possible objections or even to advocate
them. It is the case that these theories still muster support amongst Old
Testament scholars. My aim is a relatively modest one: to identify a weakness
in the models examined and to demonstrate how feasting might go some
way to meeting that weakness. It may well be the case that the arguments
about feasting could with some changes be made against other models of
early Israelite society. Certainly I hope to draw attention to evidence often
overlooked.

Frick's work provides a useful point for setting out the problems that I wish
to identify, for his work exhibits a bifurcation between warfare and agriculture.
It is a major achievement of Frick's work to move geographical and climatic
information about Palestine from the area of prolegomena to form part of
a materialist and historical account of Israelite society. Yet the agricultural
realities that form the material matrix of the social possibilities remain at
a remove from the developments within Israelite society. It is warfare that
is most clearly related to social structure and thus social change. This can
be illustrated by considering Frick's discussion of the chief's reliance upon
redistribution, ritual sanction and clientship for his success. In every instance
Frick appeals to the chief's role in warfare. On redistribution Frick observes,
'among the common reasons that chief's initially attract supporters is because
they are successful in obtaining and distributing resources, because they are
successful as leaders in war, or because they are successful in being viewed
as "charismatic" persons'. The chief is 'an intensifier-redistributor-warrior'.[13]
Similarly in his discussion of ritual sanction Frick observes that there exists
a relationship between the sacral aspect of leadership and warfare. Unfortunately the nature of the relationship is not explained, but it is evident that war
is significant in the formation of the state. 'The role of warfare seen from such
a perspective is obviously significant in view of the "conquest" dimensions
of the story of early Israel as well as in assessing the exploits of Saul and
David in their role as war leaders.'[14] Clientship depends on successful accumulation. David's success must be related to his ability to gain more clients,
and, as we have already seen, this is in no small part due to his success as a
warrior.

How, then, does social structure relate to agricultural intensification and
technological progress? It is difficult not to gain the impression that the
relation is merely chronological. Thus, Frick argues that 'when labour needs

---

[12] Miller, *Chieftains*. 'Complex chieftainships' are networks of chieftainships that include not
only a principal chief but also sub-chiefs.
[13] Frick, *Formation of the State*, 79.   [14] Ibid., 85.

required a level of efficiency beyond that which could be supplied by productive specialization in the local household or residential group, an organizing principle based on hierarchical partitioning of society emerged and the chiefdom appeared'. Agricultural imperatives provide the initial changes in societal structure, but a warrior chieftain is needed to complete the process towards state formation. Not only this but the shift is explained in a manner that lacks the concrete detail that characterizes Frick's discussion of the chief as warrior or Israel's organization as an agricultural society. Thus, the development of early Israelite society is redescribed rather than resolved. Indeed, even allowing for the rather abstract anthropological language this 'organizing principle' looks suspiciously like a *deus ex machina*. What is it, and how does it operate?

Similar difficulties are evidenced in Coote and Whitelam's work. Their argument for the importance of international trade can be much more fully developed for the final stages of the transition towards monarchy than the earlier stages. It is also more thorough on external causation than the internal dynamics that led to social change. Where Frick relies on an 'organizing principle', Coote and Whitelam are apt to rely on 'the passage of time' as a means of explanation, particularly for the earliest period of Israel's existence. Thus, for the development of agricultural specialization Coote and Whitelam explain that, 'it was only *a matter of time* before the effects of depletion and overpopulation would lead to the political forms created by landed interests for the furtherance of their power'. Similarly, 'it is to be expected that, on the basis of comparative studies, socio-economic stratification increased in early Israel *over time*', and 'even slight initial differences ... would tend to be magnified *over time* by the varying economic fortunes of the different families, dependent on varying factors of production and economic relations'.[15] These statements are no doubt true, but they fall short of explaining the processes that led to specialization and increased stratification.

Our critical review of Frick, and of Coote and Whitelam, does not necessarily require that an alternative theory be offered to replace those offered by them, but it does highlight a critical deficiency common to both accounts. This deficiency is a failure to provide a convincing explanation of agricultural intensification by reference to social phenomena, rather than by appeals to time or nature. Since these models claim to illuminate our understanding of ancient Israel precisely by attending to her social world this must be judged a serious deficiency on their own terms. If this weakness is to be corrected we must attend, in Goody's terms, not only to production, but also to *distribution*. The strength of these social-world studies from the 1980s was their attendance

---

[15] Coote and Whitelam, *Emergence of Early Israel*, 152, 154, 156. Italics mine.

to production, the agricultural realities of existence in Palestine, but the additional step of analysing distribution was not carried through. In other words, how can agricultural surpluses be controlled and utilized in order to further technological advances, increase intensification, create societal cohesion and engender societal change?

Quite different problems attend Schäfer-Lichtenberger's work, but for our purposes it is only necessary to note one to which Schäfer-Lichtenberger herself draws attention. The sixth characteristic of a monarchy—the production of a surplus that can support the state organization—is the one that Schäfer-Lichtenberger acknowledges is most difficult to detect in the biblical record. For the reigns of Saul and David she observes that there are very few statements about the financing of the monarchy. The existence of an army, and additionally in the reign of David a conscripted labour force, harem and state cult, can be taken as indication of a surplus. In Saul's reign four sources of income can be identified: gifts, booty, income from Saul's household and service. The list is longer during David's reign, including tribute and forced labour.

In this chapter I will argue that some recent anthropological work on feasting, particularly as it gives attention to the relationship between feasting and social transformation, will prove useful in making good the identified deficiencies in the works of Frick, Coote and Whitelam, and Schäfer-Lichtenberger. Such work shows how agricultural surpluses are used by successful individuals to gather supporters, stimulate technological change and mobilize labour. It also allows us to revisit the biblical texts of Samuel and Kings and to appreciate the extent to which feasting is an important element in them.

FEASTING AND SOCIAL CHANGE

The importance of a broad anthropological examination of feasting for understanding aspects of the Old Testament was first appreciated, as we have already seen, by William Robertson Smith in his *Lectures on the Religion of the Semites*. In his lecture on animal sacrifices he argues for the commensal significance of the sacrificial feast. 'The one thing directly expressed in the sacrificial meal is that the god and his worshippers are *commensals*, but every other point in their mutual relations is included in what this involves.'[16] When men eat together they become kin and as such are bound to one another. In establishing the significance of the common meal Smith appeals primarily to Arab

---

[16] Smith, *Religion of the Semites, First Series*, 269.

examples, but he also observes that 'the Old Testament records many cases where a covenant was sealed by the parties eating and drinking together'.[17] The value of these observations can be recognized in the continued appeal by Old Testament scholarship to the 'covenant meal' when interpreting texts such as the covenant between Jacob and Laban (Gen. 31.54), and the meal eaten by the elders of Israel upon Mount Sinai (Exod. 24.9–11).

It is evident that the sacrificial feast as understood by Smith is socially transformative. The common meal effectively moves a stranger from outside the tribal group to within it. The visitor who is offered hospitality is afforded the same protection as any other member of the kin. The possibility of developing Smith's insight into the importance of feasts, in general and in their socially transformative aspects, has been greatly increased by recent attention given to the subject of feasting. Of particular importance is a collection of essays edited by Michael Dietler and Brian Hayden.[18]

All the essays reflect the belief that feasting is an important and neglected concept for understanding the way that ancient and modern societies function.

Feasting is emerging as one of the most powerful cross-cultural explanatory concepts for understanding an entire range of cultural processes and dynamics ranging from the generation and transformation of surpluses, to the emergence of social and political inequalities, to the creation of prestige technologies including specialized domesticated foods, and to the underwriting of elites in complex societies.[19]

Nevertheless, the essays exhibit a variety of disciplinary foci and theoretical perspectives. On the level of disciplinary focus some of the contributors approach the subject of feasting as ethnographers and examine contemporary societies, the remainder are historians or archaeologists who discuss societies from ancient Mesopotamia to modern America. One of the most important theoretical divides is between those who work within the framework of a materialist or cultural-ecological perspective and those who follow a culturalist perspective.[20] From the materialist perspective feasting is so widespread, persistent and costly that it must have some adaptive function and not result from self-gratification or increased prestige. From the culturalist perspective the goals are not universal, but culturally constructed. Mary Weismantel has discerned a further theoretical divide that is important for our discussion of

---

[17] Ibid., 271.

[18] M. Dietler and B. Hayden (eds.), *Feasts: Archaeological and Ethnographic Perspectives on Food, Politics and Power* (Washington: Smithsonian Institute Press, 2001).

[19] B. Hayden, 'Fabulous Feasts: A Prolegomenon to the Importance of Feasting', in Dietler and Hayden (eds.), *Feasts*, 23–64, here 24.

[20] M. Dietler and B. Hayden, 'Digesting the Feast—Good to Eat, Good to Drink, Good to Think: An Introduction', in Dietler and Hayden (eds.), *Feasts*, 1–20, esp. 12–16.

ancient Israel. Weismantel observes that whilst some of the contributors view feasting as a transhistorical phenomenon that can be investigated in almost every culture, some of the contributors are particularly concerned with the feast as a vehicle for social change at specific historical moments. In the latter cases 'the feast [is] a mechanism by which ambitious individuals may propel decentralized horticultural or foraging societies toward more centralized forms of political economy'.[21] The historical argument about the development of Israelite society focuses on the latter concern, yet because of the difficulties with the biblical material—particularly the question of whether it really portrays the historical period it purports to describe—we are more concerned at that point with feasting as a phenomenon in the established political economy of the monarchy. Thus, in the case of the biblical material we are closer to the former concern.

What is a feast? The question of definition is obviously important and, although the different contributors to Dietler and Hayden's volume have their own understandings, the collection does not seek a single definition. Whatever definition is chosen it should secure two distinctions. First, a feast must be distinguished from other general exchanges of food and drink. In other words the feast is an occasion when food and drink are consumed. Second, a feast must be distinguished from everyday domestic meals. The quantity of food, the number of participants, the length of the meal, the social distance of the participants are some of the criteria that can be used to define a feast.[22] One of the characteristic features of a feast is its combination of social, political and ritual elements. It is this combination that makes feasts such an interesting and important cultural practice for ethnographic analysis.

What are the practical benefits of feasting? Hayden suggests there are at least nine types of practical benefit that commonly result from feasts. First, a feast may be a means of mobilizing labour. Second, a feast creates cooperative relationships within groups. One consequence of this is often, conversely, to exclude other groups from these relationships. Third, feasts can be used to create cooperative support between social groups. Fourth, feasts are a context in which surpluses can be invested and profits generated. Fifth, the feast provides a context in which the success of a group or individual is advertised. This can be important for attracting mates, labour, allies or wealth exchanges. Sixth, feasts can be used to create political power through the creation of a network of reciprocal debts. Seventh, a feast can be used by elites as a means

---

[21] M. Weismantel, 'An Embarrassment of Riches: Review of Michael Dietler and Brian Hayden (eds.), *Feasts: Archaeological and Ethnographic Perspectives on Food, Politics and Power*', *Current Anthropology* 42 (2001), 141–2, here 142.

[22] See Dietler and Hayden, 'Digesting the Feast', 3.

of extracting and utilizing surpluses from the rest of the population. Eighth, a feast can be used to solicit favours from a more powerful figure. Finally, a feast may be a means of compensating for transgressions.[23]

It is evident that many of the practical benefits of feasting that Hayden outlines concern the creation and maintenance of social relationships. Successful providers can use feasts to maintain and gather supporters, and to enter into alliances and wealth exchanges with other elites. The ritual elements of feasts can further define and inculcate social and political distinctions. In Hayden's account, then, 'feasting and gift giving are probably *the* principal means for transforming surpluses in order to improve chances of survival and reproduction'.[24] Since feasts are an important exchange for transforming surplus into political power it is clear that feasting can not only be an important incentive for generating surpluses but also a significant part of the dynamic for stimulating technological and cultural change. Attention must be given not only to the benefits accruing to elites but also to those who cooperate with the aggrandizer. The giver of feasts needs a high degree of cooperation from his supporters. Undoubtedly this is partly created by religious ideology, but also by definite benefits to the supporters. These can include participation in feasts, access to valuable resources, social position and power, and receipt of sponsorship for their own feasts.[25]

One type of feast that does not primarily concern the creation and maintenance of social relationships is the work feast. This receives detailed theoretical attention in an essay by Michael Dietler and Ingrid Herbich.[26] They note its almost universal appearance in pre-monetary economies.

The use of feasts to mobilize collective labor has been a widespread and fundamental economic practice of societies around the world. In fact, variants of the practice are so strikingly omnipresent in the ethnographic and historical literature that a good case can be made for acknowledging it both as virtually a universal feature among agrarian societies and as the nearly exclusive means of mobilizing large voluntary work projects before the spread of the monetary economy and the capitalist commoditization of labor and creation of a wage labor market.[27]

In their analysis Dietler and Herbich describe a continuum of collective work events from work exchanges to work feasts. The ideal work exchange occurs between closely related persons, operates on a small scale, and is a reciprocal

---

[23] Hayden, 'Fabulous Feasts', 29–30.   [24] Ibid., 27.

[25] See J. R. Perodie, 'Feasting for Prosperity: A Study of Southern Northwest Coast Feasting', in Dietler and Hayden (eds.), *Feasts*, 185–214; L. L. Junker, 'The Evolution of Ritual Feasting: Systems of Prehispanic Philippine Chiefdoms', in Dietler and Hayden (eds.), *Feasts*, 267–310.

[26] M. Dietler and I. Herbich, 'Feasts and Labor Mobilization: Dissecting a Fundamental Economic Practice', in Dietler and Hayden (eds.), *Feasts*, 240–64.

[27] Ibid., 240.

arrangement. Our interest is primarily towards the other extreme of Dietler and Herbich's spectrum, a pole represented by the ideal work feast.[28] The work feast is the organization of a diverse work force, potentially very large, for a specific project. The work feast exchanges labour for lavish hospitality. Two variants may be distinguished, voluntary and obligatory. In the first the reputation of the host attracts a work force. In the second, often known as corvée labour, an institutionalized authority can compel the provision of labour. Even in this latter case continued consent from the work force requires generous provision. Whichever variant is found the work feast allows surpluses to be converted into other forms, such as building projects, whilst also potentially promoting the host's reputation as generous.

It has already been observed that a number of the contributors assign feasting an important role in driving social transformation. Hayden theorizes about the nature of feasts in hunter-gatherer societies, transegalitarian societies, and chiefdoms and early states. For a variety of reasons, including the inability to accumulate and store surpluses, feasting similar to that which takes place in more developed societies is unlikely to take place in hunter-gatherer societies. Survival needs predicate that food consumption will take place together between kin. With transegalitarian societies the full range of feasting develops, including food storage, wealth accumulation, alliance and work feasts.[29] With the transition from transegalitarian to stratified societies 'it is clear that major changes in feasting behaviour take place'.[30] Feasting can take place on a far larger scale and is utilized by chiefs for the collection of surpluses.

In a study of feasting in the American Northwest Coast James Perodie argues that 'feasts, potlatches, and related activities may have been significant

---

[28] Dietler and Herbich's continuum of collective work events corresponds to the spectrum of exchange developed by Sahlins (M. Sahlins, *Stone Age Economics* (London: Tavistock Press, 1972)). It is important in applying such models to the biblical texts that the integrity of the spectrum of exchange/collective work events be respected. The description of the two poles is heuristic, rather than typical. As Dietler and Herbich note, 'it is important to recognize that such culturally specific forms of C[ollective] W[ork] E[vents] may be located at various points along the abstract continuum according to local expectations about the relative degree of labor reciprocity obligations and scale of requisite hospitality. Moreover, in a given society, there may be no forms that closely approximate the polar extremes' (Dietler and Herbich, 'Feasts and Labor Mobilization', 245). For a critique of the use of Sahlins's theory of economic exchange within biblical studies along these lines see N. MacDonald, 'Driving a Hard Bargain? Genesis 23 and Models of Economic Exchange', in M. I. Aguilar and L. J. Lawrence (eds.), *Anthropology and Biblical Studies: Avenues of Approach* (Leiden: Deo, 2004), 79–96.

[29] Earle notes how ubiquitous feasting is in chiefdoms (T. Earle, 'The Evolution of Chiefdoms', in T. Earle (ed.), *Chiefdoms: Power, Economy and Ideology* (Cambridge: Cambridge University Press, 1991), 1–15, esp. 3)

[30] Hayden, 'Fabulous Feasts', 46.

factors in the transition from egalitarian to ranked societies'.[31] Sharing Hayden's materialist perspective he sees the feast as a mechanism for ambitious individuals to concentrate control of debts, alliances and wealth in their hands. An examination details how the various types of feasts accomplish the aims of these individuals. We have already considered Dietler and Herbich's analysis of work feasts. In their discussion of ethnographic examples from Kenya they observe that the organization of work feasts is only possible by those who have sufficient wealth. Adeptly managed by individuals it can lead to increased social and economic inequality even in societies with egalitarian ideologies.[32] As well as creating social inequalities, the feast is also the context for exhibiting these inequalities. In an essay on feasting in Polynesia, Patrick Kirch observes that in Hawaii feasting is mainly limited to elites and is characterized by daily consumption of food that is superior in terms of quality and quantity.[33] For African societies Dietler observes how a differentiated cuisine and style of consumption reaffirm and legitimize differences in social and economic status.[34]

Finally, an essay by Laura Junker examines ritual feasting in the Philippines.[35] Again Junker draws attention to its competitive nature and transformative role. The Philippines offers a particularly interesting example because low population density relative to productive land favours alliance-based political units, rather than chiefdoms that are territorially defined. Feasting plays an important role in defining the nature of these alliances. Junker observes the importance of international trade in the immediate pre-hispanic period. 'The emergence of larger and more complex chiefdoms in a number of regions of the Philippines in the two centuries prior to Spanish contact is associated with an increased involvement in the foreign porcelain trade and an expanded scale of ritual feasting.'[36]

The volume of essays edited by Dietler and Hayden suggests that there may be much to gain by integrating an analysis of feasting into the social-scientific models for the development of the early Israelite state.[37] The possibility that

---

[31] J. R. Perodie, 'Feasting for Prosperity: A Study of Southern Northwest Coast Feasting', in Dietler and Hayden (eds.), *Feasts*, 185–214, here 185.

[32] Dietler and Herbich, 'Feasts and Labor Mobilization', 249–56.

[33] P. V. Kirch, 'Polynesian Feasting in Ethnohistoric, Ethnographic, and Archaeological Contexts: A Comparison of Three Societies', in Dietler and Hayden (eds.), *Feasts*, 168–84.

[34] M. Dietler, 'Theorizing the Feast: Rituals of Consumption, Commensal Politics, and Power in African Contexts', in Dietler and Hayden (eds.), *Feasts*, 65–114.

[35] Junker, 'Evolution of Ritual Feasting'.   [36] Ibid., 268.

[37] It is certainly insightful to return to the anthropological material on state formation that Frick, Coote and Whitelam draw upon in their examination of the social development of early Israel. Claessen and Skalník draw attention to the close correlation between surplus production and more complex forms of socio-political organization in all the examples of early states studied. This can be used to stimulate further growth and makes for opulence and conspicuous

feasting might stimulate early state development in the ancient Near East has already been proposed by Alexander Joffe.[38] Beginning with some of Dietler's earlier work, he argues that 'the production, exchange, and consumption of alcoholic beverages form a significant element and regularity in the emergence of complex, hierarchically organized societies, along with the restructuring of labor and gender relations'.[39] Elites used the production and control of alcohol to secure allegiance and mobilize labour. Joffe's work is focused on societies in the fourth and third millennia BC.[40] His subsequent work on the emerging state of the Iron Age Levant, however, gives a much smaller role to feasting. This stems, in part, from Joffe's acceptance of the distinction between primary and secondary state formation, and a particular account of this distinction. For Joffe, the processes that lead to complex societies at the end of the second millennium BC are quite different, for what was needed was not 'new bureaucratic methods, but new social identities, novel ethnic categories and boundaries'.[41] The generation of new social identities and ethnic categories requires different social engines, though even here feasting may play some role. 'Religious rituals and other activities such as community feasting in the context of seasonal agricultural labor, not to mention common defense, fixed the ties, and identities which held communities together'.[42] Such an observation is a reminder of the continued relevance of W. R. Smith's work on commensality and covenant meals, but does suggest a much more subdued role for feasting than Joffe envisages for the emergence of the first states.

In contrast to Joffe, I wish to argue that feasting may have had a more central role, occupying a pivotal position between agricultural production, on the one hand, and international trade or warfare, on the other. A successful

consumption amongst the small elite (H. J. M. Claessen and P. Skalník, 'Limits: Beginning and End of the Early State', in H. J. M. Claessen and P. Skalník (eds.), *The Early State* (The Hague: Mouton, 1978), 619–35, esp. 627–8; cf. H. J. M. Claessen, 'The Early State: A Structural Approach', in H. J. M. Claessen and P. Skalník (eds.), *The Early State* (The Hague: Mouton, 1978), 533–96, esp. 549, 563–5). Fried also observes the importance of feasting in rank societies (M. H. Fried, *The Evolution of Political Society: An Essay in Political Anthropology* (New York: Random House, 1967), 116–18, 133–7, 179–81). Unfortunately Fried's views that social development results from conflict means that his discussion of stratified societies is concerned primarily with warfare, and feasting and food surpluses are almost entirely absent.

[38] A. H. Joffe, 'Alcohol and Social Complexity in Ancient Western Asia', *Current Anthropology* 39 (1998), 297–332.

[39] Ibid., 297.

[40] See also S. Pollock, 'Feasts, Funerals, and Fast Food in Early Mesopotamian States', in T. L. Bray (ed.), *The Archaeology and Politics of Food and Feasting in Early States and Empires* (New York: Kluwer Academic, 2003), 17–38.

[41] A. H. Joffe, 'The Rise of Secondary States in the Iron Age Levant', *Journal for the Economic and Social History of the Orient* 45 (2002), 425–67, here 425.

[42] Ibid., 438.

chieftain can utilize the feast to invest agricultural surpluses into attracting allies, advertising his and his tribes' success, and generating ritual sanction. Such an individual will be in the position to threaten tribal neighbours or successfully repel aggression. He will also be able to participate in and profit from international trade, further boosting his power and prestige. Thus, feasting plays a more important role in early Israelite society than just generating and maintaining communal bonds.

FEASTING AND SOCIAL CHANGE IN ANCIENT ISRAEL

Incorporating Feasting into Theories of Ancient Israel's Formation

There exists no reason to doubt the importance of feasting within the life of ancient Israel. Not only is feasting ubiquitous in human cultures, as we have seen, but numerous biblical texts attest to feasting activity. There are the principal biblical feasts of Passover, Unleavened Bread, the Feast of Weeks and the Feast of Tabernacles. That these have been related to events in Israel's salvation history, such as the Passover to the Exodus from Egypt, and their original agricultural significance minimized, has often been taken as evidence for the antiquity of the biblical feasts.

The economic wealth of Palestine, as the studies of Borowski, Frick and Hopkins suggest, lies principally in agricultural production. Stratification and the centralization of power in early Israel must have occurred as certain individuals found a way to exploit agricultural production and transform it into enduring power and status. The original possibilities probably lay, as Coote and Whitelam suggest, in unequal access to agricultural resources. It has been common to emphasize the existence of an egalitarian ideology in early Israel. There may be some justification in this, and early Israel probably did exhibit considerably less disparity in the distribution of wealth than was true of later periods. Nevertheless, the soils of Israel are not equally fertile and some areas are more easily managed than others. In addition, the vicissitudes of life see some families with more sons or with better health. A measure of wealth disparity seems almost inevitable. Inevitable or not there is no need to attribute growing social inequality to the passage of time alone. For some individuals good fortune meant the existence of surplus production that could be invested through feasting. As we have seen, such investments can lead to greater accumulation of power and prestige.

An important aspect of the agricultural exploitation of the highlands of Israel was the terracing of the hills. Terracing provided a number of

advantages, including the control of run-off water and the utilization of otherwise unserviceable land. These advantages could only be obtained through considerable labour. That this labour might have been marshalled through a work feast must certainly be considered a possibility. Even if terracing work was undertaken on the level of the clan some mechanism must be proposed for mobilizing and organizing this labour. In this way feasting could be seen as an important means of effecting technological progress and agricultural efficiency. An individual or family that could mobilize labour in this way would further increase its ability to generate surpluses. Labour could also be mobilized to terrace land for supporters, thus increasing the power of the organizer. The net result of this feasting activity would have been increased social stratification and a greater concentration of wealth.

Another important stage in early Israel's evolution was diversification into horticulture, the cultivation of vines and olive trees. This development beyond subsistence agriculture requires the existence of a context where oil and wine can be exchanged for cereals. In addition, this exchange context must be secure and stable since vines and olives require an investment of at least five to seven years before they can be harvested. The successful organizer of feasts was not only in a position to provide the original investment, but also controlled the context from which demand for oil and wine arose. In possession of a substantial surplus such an individual could underwrite the production of wine and oil that would further enhance the reputation of his feasts and increase his power and influence.

The individual that could mobilize labour would also be in a position to call on his supporters to defend territorial possessions or raid neighbours. Success in war would have further cemented the power of the individual by accumulating further wealth and distributing spoil amongst his followers. In the realm of international trade it is aggrandizing individuals who stand to benefit most from controlling trade routes and participating in trade themselves. In many of the cultures examined in the collection edited by Dietler and Hayden the feast was often the primary location for exchanging prestigious and valuable items.

There seems, then, to be a good case for attending to feasting as an important dynamic in pre-monarchic Israel that led to the concentration of wealth, an increase in stratification, and the intensification and technological development of agriculture. As such feasting can make good claim to have been an important factor in the appearance and development of chiefdoms and, ultimately, the Israelite monarchy. Up to this point, however, we have worked at a fairly general level, can archaeology and the Old Testament provide any support for the theory that feasting played such a role in ancient Israel?

Archaeological Evidence for Feasting in Early Israel

One of the concerns of Hayden and Dietler's edited volume on feasting is to explore the possibility of identifying feasting in the archaeological record. Consequently, Brian Hayden attempts to sketch a number of possible archaeological signatures of feasts.[43] These include evidence of recreational foods, food waste, preparation and serving vessels in unusual numbers or of unusual quality and size, significant food preparation facilities, special feasting facilities, an abundance of prestige items, ritualized vessels, ritual paraphernalia, significant food-storage facilities and unusual resource abundance. Can these signature features be found at any early Israelite sites that might indicate they were used as a significant location for feasting and resource redistribution?

A potential test case is the archaeological site of Khirbet Seilun or Shiloh. Miller has recently identified Shiloh as the centre of a 'complex chiefdom' in early Iron Age Palestine.[44] In addition, consumption of meat in ancient Israel could only take place if the animal had been offered as a sacrifice, especially for major communal feasts where ritualized action probably played a large role. Both archaeological and textual evidence suggest that Shiloh was an important cultic centre in early Israel. If we are to find signature features of feasting at any early Israelite site, then it is likely to be at Shiloh.

At Shiloh archaeological excavations revealed the presence of pillared buildings and a large number of silos in Iron Age I. In biblical texts Shiloh is an important cultic site in the period of the Judges where the Ark of the Covenant was kept during the priesthood of Eli. It is likely that this cult site occupied the highest part of the site, but unfortunately damage in this area means that there is little to recover. Nevertheless, 'the pillared buildings are among the most elaborate architectural remains found in any Iron I highland site'[45] and the silos exceed the needs of the local population.[46] Together with 'the richest assemblage of Iron I pottery known from the hill country',[47] there is enough to suggest to the excavator, Israel Finkelstein, that Shiloh was a significant cult site for the Samarian highlands.[48]

---

[43] Hayden, 'Fabulous Feasts', here 40–1.   [44] Miller, *Chieftains*.

[45] Bunimovitz, 'Area C: The Iron Age I Pillared Buildings and Other Remains', in I. Finkelstein (ed.), *Shiloh: The Archaeology of a Biblical Site* (Tel Aviv: Tel Aviv University, 1993), 15–34, here 33.

[46] B. Rosen, 'Economy and Subsistence', in I. Finkelstein (ed.), *Shiloh: The Archaeology of a Biblical Site* (Tel Aviv: Tel Aviv University, 1993), 62–7.

[47] Bunimovitz, 'Area C: The Iron Age I Pillared Buildings and Other Remains', 33–4.

[48] For the question of Shiloh as a central cult site for the whole of Israel, and the relationship of this to Noth's amphicytony theory, see I. Finkelstein, 'The History and Archaeology of Shiloh from the Middle Bronze Age II to Iron Age II', in I. Finkelstein (ed.), *Shiloh: The Archaeology of a Biblical Site* (Tel Aviv: Tel Aviv University, 1993), 371–89, esp. 385–8.

A large number of animal bones were recovered from the Iron Age I stratum. This, together with other unusual features suggests the site was an important location for feasting. Just under 23 per cent of these are cattle bones. This is an unusually high proportion compared to both earlier periods at Shiloh (between 8.5 and 11.8 per cent) and other sites in the Israelite highlands during the early Iron Age. Most of the animals slaughtered were adults, but a high percentage (28 per cent) were killed between the ages of two and three. The same pattern is to be found amongst the caprovines. Most animals were kept into adulthood, but some (12 per cent) were culled earlier. These figures of young animals are high compared to other highland sites in Iron Age I. In the middle and late Bronze Age a number of trunk bones were discovered, but in the Iron Age there is a higher level of the meat-rich fore and hind limbs.[49]

Animal bones are not the only evidence of food at Shiloh. In two of the silos a considerable amount of grain was discovered, mainly wheat but also barley. Additionally in the store house just under three hundred charred raisins were found.[50] The types of pottery vessels unearthed at Shiloh also appear in unusual proportions compared to other Iron Age I sites. In their survey of the pottery, Bunimovitz and Finkelstein observe that 'the Iron I assemblage from Shiloh is the richest found in any hill country site'.[51] The site yielded sixty complete or near-complete vessels, whilst vessels from Izbet Sartah, Giloh, Mount Ebal and Khirbet el-Dawwara only number thirty-five. However, Bunimovitz and Finkelstein note that a significant factor affecting these figures is that only Shiloh was destroyed, whereas the other sites were abandoned. Comparing the types of pottery excavated to those found at the other sites, they observe that whilst Shiloh has a very low level of bowls and kraters, the number of cooking pots is significantly higher than at the other sites. This pattern of pottery types differs from earlier periods at Shiloh. There are a significant proportion of collared-rim pithoi found in one area in buildings which probably functioned as storerooms.[52]

The early Iron Age remains from Shiloh, then, have a number of features that Hayden has identified as possible indicators of feasting activity. These include food-storage facilities, unusual quantities of certain food items, unusual numbers of preparation vessels and resource abundance above the capacity of the local area. Rosen rightly observes that 'the economic activity

[49] S. Hellwing, M. Sadeh and V. Kishon, 'Faunal Remains', in I. Finkelstein (ed.), *Shiloh: The Archaeology of a Biblical Site* (Tel Aviv: Tel Aviv University, 1993), 309–50.

[50] M. E. Kislev, 'Food Remains', in I. Finkelstein (ed.), *Shiloh: The Archaeology of a Biblical Site* (Tel Aviv: Tel Aviv University, 1993), 354–61.

[51] S. Bunimovitz and I. Finkelstein, 'Pottery', in I. Finkelstein (ed.), *Shiloh: The Archaeology of a Biblical Site* (Tel Aviv: Tel Aviv University, 1993), 81–196, here 153.

[52] Ibid.

at Iron Age I Shiloh was more complex than that in typical hill country subsistence communities', and argues that Shiloh was a redistribution centre.[53] Finkelstein also observes that 'in the early 11th century B.C.E. Shiloh served as a redistribution centre for an extensive hinterland. This makes Shiloh an important stage in the transition of the Iron Age I hill country population from a social system concentrated around small isolated groups into the formation of an early monarchic state'.[54] The redistribution centred at Shiloh took place, I would suggest, primarily by means of feasting, and such feasting may have been an important part of the social transformation of early Israel.

The Old Testament and Feasting in the Social Development of Early Israel

Despite their utilization of biblical material neither Frick nor Schäfer-Lichtenberger draw attention to feasting in the development of the Israelite monarchy. The lack of any explicit discussion of feasting necessitates, therefore, revisiting the stories of Israel's existence before, during and after the rise of the monarchy for evidence of feasting. However, we will have to be far more circumspect in our assessment of the historical value of the stories in Samuel and Kings than is the case in Schäfer-Lichtenberger's study. The final redaction of the stories in Samuel and Kings took place as part of a larger Deuteronomistic History sometime during or after the Babylonian exile. Although earlier sources are undoubtedly to be found in the Deuteronomistic History, the process of updating and editing these materials, and the difficulties in ascertaining their original extent, means that historical judgements can only be drawn from these books with hesitancy. Indeed, in the present many Old Testament scholars have little confidence that we can utilize biblical materials, especially the Deuteronomistic History, for historical purposes earlier than the eighth or ninth centuries BC, and for some even this would be too optimistic. What I shall hope to show is that there is a strong association of the king and his court with feasting within the stories of Samuel and Kings. While this has generally been overlooked by biblical interpreters, the biblical writers portray it as an important aspect of the Israelite monarchies. It appears that feasting is so characteristic of the monarchies—standing in contrast to the experience of the king's subjects—that it plays a role in Israelite portrayals of the nascence of the united monarchy. This is a minimal account that makes no claims that the biblical material stems from the period that the biblical narrative describes. Nevertheless, it does highlight the importance of feasting for the monarchy

---

[53] Rosen, 'Economy and Subsistence', esp. 366.
[54] I. Finkelstein, 'History and Archaeology', 387.

within the Iron Age political economy and strengthens the suggestion that recent anthropological work on feasting may helpfully augment models of Israel's early development.

The King's Table

The biblical account of the reign of Solomon offers the most detailed picture of food redistribution in the ancient Israelite economy.[55] It has long been recognized, however, that the strong Deuteronomistic and idealistic coloration problematize its utilization for assessing a possible Solomonic period. Nevertheless, some of the material in 1 Kings 1–11 appears to have been culled from annalistic sources available to the Deuteronomistic Historian.[56] As we will see, many of the passages that speak about food redistribution are those that have been most confidently recognized as old, even if the exact age is often impossible to determine.

We will begin, however, with an account that has often been judged late and legendary, the visitation of the Queen of Sheba in 1 Kings 10. Across 1 Kings 1–11 the nature of Solomon's wisdom varies considerably. In 1 Kings 3 it is exhibited through a perceptive judicial verdict, whilst in 1 Kings 5 it is demonstrated through proverbial wisdom and knowledge of the natural world. The Queen of Sheba, however, is amazed by what she sees in the temple and palace at Jerusalem.[57]

When the Queen of Sheba had seen all the wisdom of Solomon, the house that he built, the food of his table, the seating of his officials, the attendance of his servants, their clothing, his cup-bearers, and the offerings that he offered in the house of YHWH, there was no more spirit in her.   (1 Kgs. 10.4–5)[58]

---

[55] For a collection of essays on the Solomonic material from a variety of perspectives, see L. K. Handy (ed.), *The Age of Solomon: Scholarship at the Turn of the Millennium*, SHCANE, 11 (Leiden: Brill, 1997).

[56] Kratz, *Composition*, 164–5, 184–5.

[57] The exhibition of Solomon's wisdom has been associated primarily with the questions posed by the Queen. So Gray, 'the wisdom here is of a different kind from the administrative *savoir-faire* of ch. 3 and the encyclopaedic nature-lore of ch. 5, and is rather skill in riddles, probably word-plays in verse' (Gray, *I & II Kings*, 257). Verses 4–5a are then seen as something of a digression. So Jones, 'the mention of his house, administration and sacrifices in the Temple introduces a deviation from the main theme of the narrative' (G. H. Jones, *1 and 2 Kings*, NCBC, 2 vols. (Grand Rapids: Eerdmans, 1984), 1: 222).

[58] The seated *ʿavadav* are clearly Solomon's royal officials (cf. 1 Kgs. 1.9) and the *mᵉshartav* those waiting on them (cf. 2 Kgs. 4.42–4). Gray understands *mashqav* as a derivative noun, 'his drinking-service', since he reasons that the cup-bearers would have been included amongst Solomon's servants (Gray, *I & II Kings*, 258). However, 'his cup-bearers' makes good sense, and 2 Chronicles certainly understood *mashqav* as cup-bearers for it adds 'and their clothing' (9.4).

As Burney observes, the whole verse 'refers to Solomon's magnificent *display at his banquets*'.[59] For the Queen of Sheba, then, it is this along with Solomon's ability to answer all her questions (v. 3) that leads to her praise: 'The report I heard in my own land was true concerning your acts and your wisdom' (v. 6). Though a late reflection, 1 Kings 10 is interesting for it sees the royal food and feasting as central to Solomonic wisdom, and in this respect offers a complementary perspective to some of the sources that the Deuteronomistic Historian utilizes in 1 Kings 1–9.

The Queen of Sheba's awe at the sight of Solomon's table highlights its role in these chapters, an aspect too easily missed in discussions of 1 Kings 1–11. In particular it calls attention to the devotion of one whole chapter to the administration required to provision Solomon's court (1 Kings 4).[60] The list of Solomon's twelve district officials (*nitstsavim*) has often been regarded as one of the parts of 1 Kings 1–11 most likely to have been derived from early records, though how early is disputed.[61] These district officials were responsible for supplying the court with food. Each of these officials had charge over a district of Israel from which they were to supply the court for one month. These twelve district governors are accountable to Azariah son of Nathan, a member of Solomon's cabinet (4.5).

Azariah's place amongst the state officials highlights the importance of feasting within the Deuteronomistic Historian's portrayal of the Solomonic kingdom compared to the Davidic and Saulide kingdoms. The three lists of state officials (2 Sam. 8.15–18; 20.23–6; 1 Kgs. 4.1–6) have been ordered in such a way that the expanding kingdom and state bureaucracy under David and Solomon is mirrored by the growing list of officials.[62] The second list from David's reign includes only one addition to the first list: Adoram, the official responsible for the corvée. In Solomon's reign three additional officers make their appearance. The 'friend of the king' is a post already known from the narratives about David, but the nature of the role is unclear. The other two are Ahishar, who is in charge of the royal estate, and Azariah. Both of these state

---

[59] C. F. Burney, *Notes on the Hebrew Text of the Books of Kings* (Oxford: Clarendon Press, 1903), 143. Burney's italics.

[60] I. W. Provan wishes to see Solomon's table as proto-messianic. Whether this is the case or not it does allow him to recognize the importance of the table in the account of Solomon's reign. 'It is of some significance that it is *Solomon's* table that stands at the center of the account of his glorious and peaceful rule over Judah/Israel and the nations in 1 Kgs. 4' (I. W. Provan, *1 and 2 Kings*, New International Biblical Commentary (Peabody, MA: Hendrickson, 1995), 35).

[61] See, e.g., J. M. Miller, 'Separating the Solomon of History from the Solomon of Legend', in Handy (ed.), *Age of Solomon*, 1–24; H. M. Niemann, 'The Socio-Political Shadow Cast by the Biblical Solomon', in Handy (ed.), *Age of Solomon*, 252–99; T. N. D. Mettinger, *Solomonic State Officials: A Study of the Civil Government Officials of the Israelite Monarchy*, ConBOT, 5 (Lund: CWK Gleerup, 1971).

[62] Mettinger, *Solomonic State Officials*, 7–14.

officials are concerned with the production and royal control of agricultural surpluses.

The daily amount of food received by Azariah from the district governors was substantial: 'Thirty cors of fine flour and sixty cors of meal, ten fattened cattle, twenty pastured cattle, and a hundred sheep, besides deer, gazelles, roebucks and fatted fowl' (4.22). In addition the governors supplied the fodder for Solomon's stables: 'They brought to the required place barley and straw for the horses and chariots' (4.28). This was an even more substantial obligation since according to v. 26 there were 40,000 horses.[63] A cor is approximately 400 litres, and so Solomon's court received 12,000 litres of fine flour and twice the amount of meal. These figures would have been substantial for an ancient court which could have had other sources of income, such as tribute, which often came in the form of agricultural produce (Judg. 3.15; cf. Judg. 6.1–6), and the profit from substantial royal estates. Could the provision be judged realistic for any period in Israel's history? According to Fritz they are 'grossly exaggerated', whilst De Vries can describe them as 'entirely believable'.[64] Millard rightly draws attention to the generous provisioning at other courts in the ancient Near East. Sargon of Akkad provided for 5,400 men and the courts of Mari and Egypt consumed large amounts too.[65] Yet whilst such examples may provide a parallel to 1 Kings 4, they might just as easily be a *topos* imitated by the biblical author. The quantities of food certainly appear generous for Solomon's court and are not inconsistent with the rhetorical portrayal of Solomon in 1 Kings.

The mechanics of the supply system have also been judged suspect. Often questions about it have been conceived in terms of the Solomonic period that 1 Kings 1–11 purports to describe. Could such an organized supply system with its centralized control have existed in the time of Solomon? A very centralized system of twelve district governors was often deemed inconceivable at this stage in the Iron Age, even prior to more recent scepticism about the Solomonic empire. Yet questions can be raised in other respects. Is it conceivable that at different months districts with varying agricultural capabilities and populations could have provided identical supplies?[66] The portrayal certainly appears mechanical and rigid, though it might be argued that this is often a tendency of central bureaucracies, from whose perspective

---

[63] In 2 Chron. 9.25 there were only 4,000 horses.

[64] V. Fritz, *1 & 2 Kings*, Continental Commentaries (Minneapolis: Fortress Press, 2003), 54; S. J. De Vries, *1 Kings*, WBC, 12 (Waco, TX: Word Books, 1985), 73.

[65] A. Millard, 'King Solomon in His Ancient Context', in Handy (ed.), *Age of Solomon*, 30–53.

[66] Cf. Niemann, who writes, 'the rotational system of supply, each of the 12 men being responsible for one month, was mechanically thought up and does not take into account the reality of the agricultural calendar' (Niemann, 'Socio-Political Shadow', 284).

the historian writes. Whatever is made of the details we might also question whether large-scale circulation of foodstuffs might have taken place in the Israelite monarchies during the Iron Age. The ethnographical evidence for feasting suggests that redistribution on a significant scale is not unknown even for relatively rudimentary societies. Thus, we may posit, at least, that the redistribution of food by a centralized royal court was an important aspect of the Israelite political economy in the monarchic period.

The king's table was very important for creating and maintaining political support amongst the emerging elite. To be admitted to the table would have been an important marker of social status and influence. Texts in the Deuteronomistic History see members of the royal family and trusted advisors present at the table.[67] In the first instance the royal table consisted of the king and his family. In the Israelite monarchy political power was organized predominantly along family lines which meant that the privileged companions of the king were mainly family members. Certain ambitious individuals, however, may have been admitted into the circle of political power. A place at the royal table was an important step for such individuals, whilst also drawing them into the group of the king's political supporters. When Mephibosheth is invited to join the royal household his elevation is described as 'eating at the king's table like one of the king's sons' (2 Sam. 9.11).[68] The use of the expression 'the sons of the kings'[69] is suggestive for it is reminiscent of the expression 'the sons of El', known from Ugarit. The 'sons of El' are frequently presented in the Ugaritic texts banqueting with El.[70] These sons are not only El's table companions but also constitute the divine council, the body responsible for ruling the cosmos. At Ugarit and in the biblical texts, then, the royal feast is an important locus for the making of decisions and the exercise of political power.

The extension of the royal table beyond the immediate family is represented as occurring on a number of occasions in the time of the united monarchy. David is invited to Saul's table (1 Samuel 20), and David elevates Mephibosheth to the royal table (2 Samuel 9). Barzillai the Gileadite, who has his faithfulness to David rewarded by an invitation to the royal table in Jerusalem, declines because of his age and offers his son in his place (2 Sam. 19.31–40).

---

[67] Invited to Saul's table in 1 Samuel 20 were David, Jonathan and Abner. David's sons ate at his table (2 Sam. 9.11). The Queen of Sheba saw the king surrounded by his seated officials and royal servants (1 Kgs. 10.4–5). Jezebel kept the prophets of Baal and Asherah at her table (1 Kgs. 18.19).

[68] MT is clearly in error when it reads 'my table'. The Septuagint reads 'David's table'.

[69] 'The sons of the king' is also used of those who attend banquets hosted by Absalom and Adonijah, and both occasions may be presented as claims to the throne.

[70] For the divine banquet in the Ugaritic texts see J. B. Lloyd, 'The Banquet Theme in Ugaritic Narrative', *UF* 22 (1991), 169–93.

Between Mephibosheth and Barzillai comes the less auspicious case of Uriah the Hittite, who is received at David's table (2 Sam. 11.13) in the hope of getting him drunk so that he sleeps with his wife Bathsheba. Uriah's fate suggests that the dizzying elevation to the royal table could be a mixed blessing.

On the other hand, exclusion from the table clearly indicates disfavour or political exclusion, whilst absence can be interpreted as disloyalty. At the end of David's life Adonijah hosted a feast at En-rogel. Nathan protests to David:

> He has gone down today and sacrificed abundant oxen, fatlings and sheep. He has invited all the king's sons, the commanders of the army, and Abiathar the priest. They are now eating and drinking before him and saying 'Long live king Adonijah!' But he has not invited myself, your servant, Zadok the priest, Benaiah son of Jehoiada or Solomon your son.

Nathan and Bathsheba interpret Adonijah's feast as a coup, a perception that is underlined by their omission from the list of guests. Conversely, David's absence from Saul's table at the feast of the new moon in 1 Samuel 20 marks the final dissolution of the relationship between the king and his son-in-law.

The description of Solomon's table suggests that the royal feasts were distinguished from ordinary fare in at least four ways. First, individual portions were considerably larger than those enjoyed by most Israelites. Second, the quality of the food was higher. Sheep, cattle, deer, gazelles, roebucks and choice fowl were very unlikely to grace the table of most Israelites and certainly not on a daily basis. Third, the choice of foods was more varied. Fourth, the surroundings were more opulent. The Queen of Sheba is said to have seen the clothing worn at the table. Barzillai suggests male and female singers were present at the royal table (2 Sam. 19.35). This final distinguishing characteristic is paralleled in Amos's descriptions of aristocratic feasts which included beds of ivory and couches, bowls of wine and fine oil (Amos 6.4–7).

These dimensions of the feast could be manipulated to signal royal favour or status. Certain choice items can be used to indicate special status. The story of Saul's elevation to the monarchy describes how he received a thigh portion from Samuel (1 Sam. 9.23–4). Position and posture at the table indicated one's place in the political order.[71] The king and the highest ranked would be seated, servants and lower ranked would stand. At the feast of the new moon Saul was seated, as was Abner, who was Saul's cousin and commander of the army; Jonathan, on the other hand, stood (1 Sam. 20.25).[72] Joseph's brothers are

[71] For Ugaritic parallels see A. J. Ferrera and S. B. Parker, 'Seating Arrangements at Divine Banquets', *UF* 4 (1972), 37–9.

[72] The Septuagint read 'with Jonathan in front of him' (*proephthasen*), which may suggest an original *wayᵉqaddem* (KB, 1068). On the other hand, Gordon notes the MT's reading as a parallel to Baal's stance at the banqueting scene in the Ugaritic myths (R. P. Gordon, *I & II Samuel: A Commentary* (Carlisle: Paternoster Press, 1986), 167).

seated in order (Gen. 43.33); 'the eldest according to his birthright' would appear to suggest more than seating by age, but according to precedence. At the royal table proximity to the king understandably indicates status. Another way of indicating favoured status at the meal was to provide a larger portion. The Syriac translation has Hannah receiving a double portion from Elkanah at the annual feast (1 Sam. 1.5), whilst Benjamin received five times the amount of his brothers (Gen. 43.34).[73]

It is no surprise, then, that the Deuteronomistic Historian takes organizing a feast as a signal of royal ambitions. When Adonijah organized a feast for his brothers in the twilight of David's reign the suspicions of Nathan and Bathsheba are aroused, though as Fritz observes, 'Adonijah is not proclaimed king during the banquet.'[74] It may be that the narrator wishes to preserve a level of ambiguity on Adonijah's part; the feast appears like a preparatory gathering of political support for a later claim to the throne.[75] Nathan, however, interprets it as the moment of investiture, to which neither he, Zadok, Benaiah nor Solomon, David's designated heir, have been invited.

The basis for Nathan's concerns can be seen in those texts that see a festive meal as part of the king's coronation.[76] 1 Chron. 12.38–40 describes a feast at the inauguration of David's reign over the whole of Israel:

All these, fighting men arrayed in battle order, came to Hebron with one mind: to enthrone David over Israel. The rest of Israel were also of the same mind to make David king. They were there with David three days eating and drinking, for their kin had provided for them. Also their neighbours as far away as Issachar, Zebulun and Naphtali brought food on donkeys, camels, mules and oxen: abundant provisions of meal, cakes of figs, clusters of raisins, wine, oil, oxen and sheep, for there was rejoicing in Israel.

The theme of great joy is found at the enthronement of Solomon in 1 Chron. 22.21–2, during which time thousands of animals were sacrificed and the people ate and drank together. The purposes of such meals was, no doubt,

---

[73] Joseph's ordering of the brothers according to age reflects the natural order. The extraordinary size of Benjamin's portion subverts the natural order and indicates Benjamin to be the favoured younger child, a common theme in the patriarchal narratives (see J. D. Levenson, *The Death and Resurrection of the Beloved Son: The Transformation of Child Sacrifice in Judaism and Christianity* (New Haven: Yale University Press, 1993)).

[74] Fritz, *1 & 2 Kings*, 18.

[75] Such a meal could lack an explicit political purpose, as did Absalom's sheep-shearing feast to which the king and his sons were invited (2 Samuel 13). However, the possibility of hubris is suggested in a variant Hebrew reading represented at Qumran and in the Septuagint which adds the clause 'Absalom made a feast like the feast of a king' between vv. 27 and 28. We may have a foreshadowing of Absalom's subsequent rebellion.

[76] For the components of the coronation see M. Z. Brettler, *God as King: Understanding an Israelite Metaphor*, JSOTSup, 76 (Sheffield: Sheffield Academic Press, 1989).

commensal and rewarded faithful supporters.[77] Both descriptions belong to the Chronicler's special materials, and are probably his own distinctive creations. Not only do 'feasts punctuate high points in Israelite and Judean history' in Chronicles,[78] but also both accounts exhibit distinctive features of the Chronicler's theology. In addition, we should note the feast David gave for Abner at Hebron when he was gathering support for his attempt to gain rulership of northern Israel (2 Sam. 3.20–2).[79]

The same motif is found in the divine sphere where YHWH's kingship is celebrated through a communal meal. At Sinai Moses and the seventy elders of Israel celebrate a meal in the presence of YHWH (Exod. 24.9–11). The description of YHWH's appearance, which is reminiscent of Isaiah 6, suggests that YHWH is seated on a royal throne. The same idea is found in Isaiah's vision of the eschatological banquet for all nations (Isa. 25.6–10). The feast on Mount Zion is a continuation of the beginning of YHWH's reign described in 24.21–3. 'The Lord of Hosts now reigns on Mount Zion, revealing his glorious presence. On this mountain, namely Jerusalem, Yahweh inaugurates a festival to celebrate his coronation.'[80]

The Israelite Corvée

Thus far we have considered the foodstuffs obtained by the monarch through taxation, tribute, plunder and the royal estates only in relation to their consumption at the royal court by the king, his family and close advisors. Inscriptions from Palestine and elsewhere in the Near East indicate that food was frequently used as a means of paying labourers. It is conceivable that the author of the Solomonic material imagined the large flow of food to the king to have been utilized for a wider distribution beyond the court. This possibility is suggested by the two accounts of Solomon's exchange of agricultural produce for a supply of cedars of Lebanon from Hiram of Tyre. According to 1 Kgs. 5.11, in exchange for the cedars Solomon gave Hiram wheat and oil for his house (*betho*). In 4.7 Solomon's house was the entity for which the district governors were to provide. However, according to the parallel passage in 2

---

[77] The commensal intentions of the meal do not require it to be understood specifically as a 'covenant meal' (*contra* D. J. McCarthy, 'Social Compact and Sacral Kingship', in R. Ishida (ed.), *Studies in the Period of David and Solomon and Other Essays* (Tokyo: Yamakawa-Shuppansha, 1982), 75–92).

[78] G. N. Knoppers, *1 Chronicles 10–29*, AB, 12A (New York: Doubleday, 2004), 572.

[79] We might also compare Gaal son of Ebed who rebels against Abimelech. It is while he is feasting that he questions the appropriateness of Abimelech's rule over the Shechemites (Judg. 9.26–9).

[80] B. S. Childs, *Isaiah*, OTL (London: SCM Press, 2001), 184.

Chron. 2.9–10 Solomon provided wheat, barley, wine and oil for Hiram's servants employed to log the timber.[81] In terms of Dietler and Herbich's categories, the Chronicler's version could be taken to provide a terse description of a collective work event, perhaps even a work feast. A large labour project is effected through the exchange of labour for food. This is clearly important for understanding the many other examples of labour mobilizations envisaged in the Deuteronomistic History, the institution known as corvée (*mas*).[82]

The Old Testament contains a limited number of references to the corvée, with their distribution almost entirely restricted to the literature concerning the united monarchy and the pre-monarchic period.[83] When they were in the ascendancy the Israelite tribes are said to have subjected the Canaanites to corvée (Josh. 16.10; 17.13; Judg. 1.28, 30, 33, 35). In the time of David a position in the royal cabinet was created for the organizer of the corvée (2 Sam. 20.24), and in Solomon's reign the corvée was employed on numerous capital projects. 1 Kings 12 portrays the corvée obligations as a significant catalyst in the disintegration of the united kingdom.

The paucity of biblical references on the Israelite corvée means its mechanics have received little attention. There is general agreement that it entailed forced labour. 'One characteristic element we may . . . already take for granted: the involuntary aspect of the labor thus exacted'.[84] This is particularly apparent when the term *mas* is employed of the Hebrews' servitude in Egypt (Exod. 1.11), the oppression of the Canaanites in Joshua and Judges, or the future awaiting the Assyrian youth at the hands of the Babylonians (Isa. 31.8). However, the nature of this involuntary labour appears to be different from that envisaged in 1 Kings 1–11. According to 1 Kgs. 5.13–14, 'King Solomon conscripted a corvée from all Israel, and the corvée numbered thirty thousand men. He sent a shift of ten thousand of them every month. They were a month in Lebanon and a month at home.' Consequently, it is understandable then that Mendelsohn sought to distinguish between different uses of the term *mas*. It could be used of taxation, of the Israelite corvée and of total enslavement.

[81] Note that according to Ezra 3.7 food, drink and oil were given to Sidonians and Tyrians to transport cedars from Lebanon for use in the construction of the second temple.

[82] The risks of employing the word 'corvée', a term originating in a feudal context, has been noted by some scholars. I have retained the term for its convenience, hoping that the discussion will determine its significance in an ancient Israelite context.

[83] For discussion of the relevant biblical and ancient Near Eastern texts see Mettinger, *Solomonic State Officials*, 128–39; J. A. Soggin, 'Compulsory Labor under David and Solomon', in R. Ishida (ed.), *Studies in the Period of David and Solomon and Other Essays* (Tokyo: Yamakawa-Shuppansha, 1982), 259–68; A. F. Rainey, 'Compulsory Labor Gangs in Ancient Israel', *IEJ* 20 (1970), 191–202; I. Mendelsohn, 'State Slavery in Ancient Palestine', *BASOR* 85 (1942), 14–27; I. Mendelsohn, 'On Corvée Labor in Ancient Canaan and Israel', *BASOR* 167 (1962), 31–5.

[84] Soggin, 'Compulsory Labor', 259. Cf. 'there can be little doubt that the term is related to forced labour' (Mettinger, *Solomonic State Officials*, 129).

The former was based on the use in Esther 10.1, a use continued in later Hebrew. The latter two uses Mendelsohn argued could be distinguished by subtle differences in vocabulary. The Israelite corvée was simply *mas*, whilst total enslavement was described as *mas 'oved*, literally 'a corvée of slavery'.[85] Unfortunately this lexicographical argument cannot be maintained.[86] Nevertheless, Mendelsohn's instinct to distinguish between the labour of military captives and the labour of a peasant corvée was surely correct, but can only be determined with reference to the context. Unfortunately this insight has largely been overlooked.

The labour provided by the Israelites could not be described as voluntary.[87] According to the Deuteronomistic Historian the labour is an important factor in a growing resentment towards the Davidic monarchy. Nevertheless, 1 Kings does not see the people forced into labour as were military captives. Every two months in three they were free to pursue their own concerns. For the month of labour, however, their terms were probably not too different from those faced in captivity. They received board for their labour. We have already seen that Solomon's payments to Hiram went towards provisioning the labourers. Ancient Near Eastern texts that refer to the corvée also place a similar emphasis on the exchange of food for labour. Rainey notes that the Alakah corvée performed service far from home, was organized into labour battalions and was provisioned from the royal stores. Similarly a reference in the Amarna letters to a corvée at Meggido has a labour force gathered from a wide area who were provisioned by the king of Meggido.[88] Any Israelite corvée was probably organized along the same lines receiving only food and drink for their labours. Since none of their labour was invested in their own family-holdings and since there was probably some measure of social and political coercion, this labour could be viewed as oppressive and tantamount to the slavery experienced by captives.

The corvée, then, was an exchange between the elite and the Israelite population of labour for food. As such it highlights the importance of food redistribution, and hence the control and intensification of food production.

---

[85] Mendelsohn, 'State Slavery'.

[86] Rainey, 'Compulsory Labor Gangs'. It was rightly observed that *mas* and *mas 'oved* were used in parallel texts with no difference in meaning (e.g. Josh. 16.10 and 17.13). Mendelsohn was also forced into an unpersuasive argument that the unmodified uses of *mas* of the Canaanites and other foreign nations in Deut. 20.11; Josh. 17.13 and Judges 1 were to be understood as 'the payment of tribute'. This later meaning of *mas* is possibly to be found in Esther 10.1, but is hardly appropriate with the preposition *lᵉ*.

[87] I assume that the corvée was made up of Israelites. For a different view see C. L. Meyers, 'Kinship and Kingship: The Early Monarchy', in M. D. Coogan (ed.), *The Oxford History of the Biblical World* (Oxford: Oxford University Press, 1998), 165–205.

[88] Ibid.

Solomon's purchase of cedars from Hiram with foodstuffs demonstrates the way that food can be transformed into other objects, including buildings. The biblical texts do not give us any indication that feasting was an important dynamic in Solomon's food exchange, though comparative ethnographical evidence gathered in Dietler and Hayden's volume might suggest it. It may be judged probable for a male workforce away from home with generous supplies of food and possibly wine and beer. The potential of the feast for inspiring and rewarding workers is apparent in the story of David and Nabal (1 Samuel 25). The narrative is set in the reign of Saul and portrays two autonomous leaders operating in southern Judah on the fringes of the Negev. Nabal is a pastoralist with significant herds and consequently a number of servants, whilst David leads a group of bandits. The time of sheep-shearing appears to have been a traditional occasion for feasting (cf. 2 Sam. 13.23–9) and offered both leaders an opportunity to reward their followers.

Biblical Perspectives on the Development of the Israelite Monarchy

The biblical texts do not intend to provide an account of Israel's social development. Nevertheless, as we have seen, the information contained in them has often been utilized to create models of social change in Israel. Recent questions about the historicity of biblical texts has problematized such attempts in significant ways. Such accounts can indicate, at least, some of the dynamics within the ancient Israelite political economy that were appreciated by the ancient scribes. I have tried to show that there is evidence for the redistribution of foodstuffs, particularly through feasting, in the ancient Israelite monarchy. The biblical writers appear to have recognized this as an important part of the dynamic of the monarchy; unfortunately this has often been overlooked by modern scholars.

Not only was redistribution of foodstuffs part of the Israelite royal economy, but at least one Israelite writer identified this as the most striking characteristic of the monarchy in contrast to the tribal society of pre-monarchic Israel. According to 1 Sam. 8.11–17, Samuel warns the Israelites that the monarchy entails many undesirable consequences:

This is the way of a king that will reign over you. He will take your sons and set them in his chariots and upon his horses, and they will run before his chariots. He will appoint for himself some as commanders of thousands and commanders of fifties. Some will plough for him, and others will harvest; some will make weapons of war, and others will make his chariot equipment. He will take your daughters as flavourers, cooks and bakers. He will take the best of your fields, vineyards and olive orchards, and he will give them to his servants. He will require a tenth of your seed and your vineyards,

and he will give it to his officials and servants. He will take the best of your male and female servants, your cattle and donkeys, and put them to work. He will require a tenth of your flocks, and you will be his slaves.[89]

What Samuel describes is not individual acquisitions by the king but the entire royal political economy, which is directed towards warfare and consumption at the royal table. The importance of the king's table is apparent in the king's acquiring of the people's daughters for 'flavourers, cooks and bakers'. This has been obscured by translating the first term as 'perfumers'. *Raqqachoth* is used in the Old Testament of those who prepare spices, usually for ointments or incense, but on a few occasions it is used of adding spices to food or drink.[90] The daughters, then, play a pivotal role transforming the agricultural produce into edible food used to supply and reward the army. As the Samuel of the Deuteronomistic History recognizes, the king is the figure who controls and directs all this activity essential for the first-millennium state.

CONCLUSION

The land of Israel is not endowed with significant natural assets. It does have usable agricultural land that can be put to seed, planted with fruit trees or grazed by flocks. As the basis of the Israelite economy agriculture offers certain rewards to anyone who controls its production and the distribution of its fruits. In the wake of the collapse of civilized empires at the end of the second millennium BC, Israel and other small states arose in the Levant as ambitious individual chieftains and their families controlled the circulation of food and used this control to their own advantage. The natural poverty

[89] Veijola attributes this speech, incorporated into 1 Samuel by DtrN, to a Northern writer from the time of Solomon or later (Veijola, *Königtum*, 60–6)

[90] In Ezekiel's allegory of the siege of Jerusalem the prophet describes a cooking pot: 'Increase the logs, kindle the fire, boil the meat, *wᵉ harqach hammerqachah*, until the bones are charred' (Ezek. 24.10). The difficult *wᵉ harqach hammerqachah*, which can be translated 'mix the spices' or 'anoint the anointing mixture', is frequently deemed unintelligible and emended on the basis of the Greek to 'pour out the broth' (W. Zimmerli, *Ezekiel I*, Hermenia (Philadelphia: Fortress Press, 1979), 495; J. W. Wevers, *Ezekiel*, NCB (London: Nelson, 1969), 191; W. Eichrodt, *Ezekiel*, OTL (London: SCM Press, 1970), 334–5; H. Fuhs, 'Ez 24—Überlegungen zu Tradition und Redaktion des Ezechielbuches', in J. Lust (ed.), *Ezekiel and His Book: Textual and Literary Criticism and Their Interrelation*, BETL, 74 (Leuven: Leuven University Press, 1986), 266–82). On the other hand, Greenberg feels no compulsion to emend the text (M. Greenberg, *Ezekiel 21–37*, AB, 22A (New York: Doubleday, 1997), 501). In the Song of Solomon the woman speaks of giving her lover 'spiced wine' (*yayin hareqach*) (Songs 8.2). The incongruity of referring to perfumers is reflected in Ackroyd's suggestion that *raqqachoth* may be a euphemism for concubines (P. Ackroyd, *The First Book of Samuel*, CBC (Cambridge: Cambridge University Press, 1971), 72).

of these Levantine states and their small size relative to their Egyptian and Mesopotamian neighbours meant that their ascendancy could only be relatively short-lived. The resurgence of the Assyrian and then the Babylonian empires eventually led to the destruction of these small independent states. In their social development, however, from tribal societies to states, food and feasting played an important role, for which the biblical texts provide evidence.

The role that feasting played in the development of the Israelite state is not that of providing the initial stimulus to state formation. This traditional concern of biblical scholarship, still central to the arguments of Frick, Coote and Whitelam, can be addressed by appeal to a variety of different factors including external pressure, international trade, internal strife and population growth. Feasting, however, goes a long way to explaining the dynamics that are set in motion by initial stimuli. Feasting is at the heart of what Coote and Whitelam describe as 'a multiple and complex feedback system involving and acting upon all forms of economic, social, political and religious organizations' that is set in motion by the original stimuli and leads towards statehood.[91]

---

[91] Coote and Whitelam, *Emergence of Early Israel*, 145.

6

Taste and Discernment: the Literary Motif of Judgement at the Table

In ancient Near Eastern civilizations there was a close association between food and political power. As we have seen the ancient Israelite kingdoms were no different in this respect. This association finds frequent expression in the biblical texts. Job describes how the poor scavenge for food:

> [The wicked] thrust the needy from the path,
> the poor of the earth all hide themselves.
> They are wild asses in the desert,
> they go out to toil, scavenging for food
> in the wasteland for bread for their children.
> In the field they gather his fodder,
> and glean in the vineyard of the wicked ...
> Naked, they go about without clothes;
> hungry, they carry sheaves;
> between the terraces they press out oil,
> thirsty, they tread the winepresses.
>
> (Job 24.4–6, 10 11)

The rich, on the other hand, enjoyed a life of luxury, which provokes the ire of Amos:

> Those lying on beds of ivory,
> spread upon their couches,
> eating lambs from the flock
> and calves from the stall,
> strumming upon their harps like David,
> improvising on musical instruments,
> drinking from basins of wine.
> They anoint themselves with the finest oils,
> and feel no pain over the ruin of Joseph.
>
> (Amos 6.4–6)

These two selections are part of highly rhetorical speeches—Job's objections to divine injustice and Amos's denunciation of the Israelite nobility—which register a protest against this state of affairs. Though they should not be taken as straightforward portrayals of life in ancient Israel, they do suggest the existence of a disparity in food distribution.

The frequent objections to YHWH permitting this inequality can arise from at least two quarters. On the one hand, many psalms acclaim YHWH as creator who provides food for all of his creation (e.g. Psalm 104).[1] On the other hand, the Deuteronomic lawcode promises agricultural prosperity to those who obey the commandments and punishment to those who disobey (Deuteronomy 28). The apparent reversal of this in Israel's experience is cause for indignation.

In light of the relationship between food and justice it is perhaps not surprising that the table is frequently the context for YHWH's vindication of the just or his judgement of the wicked. The righteous poor being fed and the wicked going hungry are, in the ancient world, poignant images of justice being done.[2] The present chapter will consider the relationship between the table and divine judgement, first in the so-called Deuteronomistic History and then elsewhere in the Old Testament.

JUDGEMENT AND TABLE IN THE DEUTERONOMISTIC HISTORY

Hannah and Eli's Sons at Shiloh

The first book of Samuel opens, as did the book of Judges, with food and feasting. Judges begins with the arrogant Adoni-bezeq, whilst the protagonist in Samuel is the victimized Hannah. What both characters have in common is an affirmation placed upon their lips that the table is the context for divine vindication or judgement. As we have already seen, in the account of his defeat in Judges 1, Adoni-bezeq testifies to the appropriateness of his fate; the loss of his digits is recognized as a case of a divinely ordained *lex talionis*. Hannah's psalm of praise also describes acts of reversal that see the poor being vindicated:

---

[1] For discussion of some of the relevant Old Testament passages see Claassens, *God Who Provides*, 23–41.

[2] The continued potency of such ideas can be seen, for example, in the New Testament story of the rich man and Lazarus (Luke 16.19–31).

> Those who were full have hired themselves out for bread,
> but the hungry are fat with food.
> The barren has borne seven,
> but she who has many sons is forlorn...
> ʏʜwʜ makes poor and makes rich;
> brings down and also raises up.
> Raises the poor from the dust;
> he lifts the needy from the ash heap,
> to sit them with princes
> and make them inherit a seat of honour.
>
> (1 Sam. 2.5–6, 7–8)[3]

Hannah's song describes two ways in which the righteous will be vindicated that relate to the table. In the first the hungry receive food, whilst the full do without. The second is more opaque, describing the poor taking a seat amongst the powerful. Sitting with princes could either be a reference to sitting at the royal feast (cf. 1 Sam. 10.5) or sitting amongst the town judiciary (cf. Prov. 31.23). The first possibility should be preferred on two grounds.[4] First, those who constitute the town judiciary are usually described as elders, not princes. Second, Lam. 4.5 describes in similar terms a reversal in the opposite direction where the reference to feasting is explicit:

> Those eating delicacies perish in the streets;
> Those brought up in purple embrace ash heaps.[5]

It has frequently been observed that Hannah's song had a different setting and function than it now bears in its narrative context. In particular, it anticipates the establishment of the monarchy and there is little in the psalm that refers to Hannah's own situation. Gordon's comments are representative: 'This psalm...ranges far beyond the contemplation of Hannah's plight and vindication. Only in verse 5, indeed, does the subject of barrenness and

---

[3] In the difficult second line of v. 5 *hadal* is interpreted as 'to be fat' rather than 'to cease' and *ad* has been understood as a noun, 'food', see Gordon, *I & II Samuel*, 80.

[4] See Klein, who suggests the possibility that sitting means to dine (R. W. Klein, *1 Samuel*, WBC, 10 (Waco, TX: Word, 1983), 18). Note that the assembly of princes that surround the king in Prov. 25.6–7 is understood in a dining context in Luke 14.7–11.

Gottwald discerns in these verses the overthrow of kingship by the Hebrews (Gottwald, *Tribes of Yahweh*, 535–8) and Gordon appears to suggest exaltation to the divine throne, presumably by comparison with Psalm 113 (Gordon, *I & II Samuel*, 18). Both suggestions appear a little far-fetched.

[5] It should be noted, of course, that the Magnificat, which is clearly based on Hannah's Song and thus one of its earliest interpretations, makes the connection between the raising of the poor and sitting at the table explicit: 'he has brought down the powerful from their thrones | and exalted the lowly; | he has filled the hungry with good things, | but sent the rich away empty' (Luke 1.52–3).

birth-giving definitely materialize, though verse 1 may make its contribution.'[6] Watts rightly warns against too narrowly assessing the appropriateness of a psalm by its relation to the plot. The most likely explanation of psalms in narrative contexts in the Old Testament is that they 'were not used by ancient Hebrew writers for plot development, but for other narrative purposes such as thematic exposition and characterization'.[7] Indeed, as we shall see, Hannah's description of the exaltation of the poor to the royal table will appear on a number of occasions in Israel's subsequent history. Such observations should not obscure the fact that it is not only with its reference to the barren woman that Hannah's song suits its narrative context. Hannah's prayer and subsequent exaltation occur in the context of the annual feast, whilst the account of the fall of Eli's house, with which the Hannah story is interwoven, turns around the abuse of the priestly portion of food by Eli's sons.

The story of Hannah and the birth of Samuel unfolds in the context of the annual festival at Shiloh to which Elkanah and his family make pilgrimage. The reader is allowed to see the family only whilst they are at the Shiloh sanctuary year on year (1.3). This is the occasion for paying vows and bringing sacrifices to YHWH. At the completion of the sacrifice the family group share the flesh of the sacrificial animal. Thus, every episode of the story presupposes a celebratory feast at which meat and wine are consumed (cf. 1.13).

Our introduction to Elkanah's family presents the feast as an occasion for the publication of Hannah's failure as a wife and Israelite woman. Every year the apportioning of the sacrifice testifies to Hannah's barrenness and the fecundity of Elkanah's other wife, Peninnah. Peninnah receives portions for herself and her offspring. The Hebrew describing Hannah's portion is difficult (1.5) and many translations choose to follow the Syriac and read 'a double portion'.[8] This may be no more than an educated guess on the part of the ancient translator and it may be better to follow the Septuagint and emend the text as follows: 'He gave Hannah one portion; however, it was Hannah he loved, but YHWH had shut her womb.'[9] Elkanah's private devotion to Hannah

[6] Gordon, *I & II Samuel*, 78.
[7] J. W. Watts, *Psalm and Story: Inset Hymns in Hebrew Narrative*, JSOTSup, 139 (Sheffield: JSOT Press, 1992), 34.
[8] See, e.g., NIV, NRSV.
[9] S. R. Driver, *Notes on the Hebrew Text of the Books of Samuel* (Oxford: Clarendon Press, 1890), 7–8; Klein, *1 Samuel*, 2; Gordon, *I & II Samuel*, 73–4. It should be noted that the Septuagint has an additional clause before *plen hoti*: 'because she did not have a son' that would more naturally precede 'nevertheless, it was Hannah he loved' (S. D. Walters, 'Hanna and Anna: The Greek and Hebrew Texts of 1 Samuel 1', *JBL* 107 (1988), 385–412, here 390). It should also be noted that the expression for Benjamin's enlarged portion in Gen. 43.34 does not resemble 1 Sam. 1.5.

stands in tension with her annual public humiliation. The stage is set for the annual feast to be the location of her vindication.

Hannah's vindication occurs at the third annual feast recorded in the chapter when she appears with her long-awaited son and a thank offering. Although the Masoretic Text does not make an explicit reference to the annual feast, the Septuagint, supported by a Qumran manuscript, has a longer reading which does: 'The boy was with them. They came before YHWH, and his father killed the sacrifice as he did year by year before YHWH.' The annual sacrifice now becomes the occasion when Hannah celebrates the gift of a son with a new robe and receiving her own individual blessing from Eli which eventually brings still more offspring (1.20–1). Hannah has been raised from the dust and inherits a seat of honour at the feast.

Interwoven with the story of Hannah and her son is the account of Eli and his sons. The contrasting behaviour and destinies of the children is achieved through juxtaposition: Samuel is a faithful priest who will come to know YHWH (2.35; 3.7), whilst Hophni and Phinehas do not know YHWH and will be struck down (2.12, 34). The divinely effected trajectory for Hannah and her son is upwards, but for Eli and his family it is downwards. If Hannah can be seen to be the embodiment of the one who was poor but now 'sits with princes' and 'inherits a seat of honour' (2.8), then Eli's family are those who 'were full' but will be forced to 'hire themselves out for bread' (2.5).[10]

The sacrificial feasts at Shiloh are also where the sins of Eli's sons take place. Their abuse of the sacrificial system is motivated by gluttony. Exactly how Hophni and Phinehas deviated from the accepted practice is a little unclear,[11] certainly the seizure of meat before the fat has been burnt is considered a grievous sin (2.15). The fat was considered the choice part of the offering which had to be offered up to YHWH (2.29). It is striking that the narrative emphasizes Eli's role as much as his sons. The reader's introduction to Eli is inauspicious, for he is presented 'sitting on a throne' (1.9),[12] a posture that he maintains despite his sons' practices until he finally falls from it and dies

[10] *Contra* Miscall: 'Any associations [to 2.5] are of questionable importance, although the theme of eating and drinking pervades 1 Samuel' (P. D. Miscall, *1 Samuel: A Literary Reading* (Bloomington, IN: Indiana University Press, 1986), 16).

[11] It is possible that both the particular use of the fork in vv. 13–14 (which certainly deviates from the regulations in Leviticus) and the seizing of meat before the fat was burnt in v. 15 were forbidden. This would be suggested by the *gam* at the beginning of v. 15, yet since the priests insisted on taking the meat before boiling it is difficult to see how both could have been instances of malpractice.

[12] Polzin draws attention to the regal portrayal of Eli, who sits on a throne at the temple/palace (*hekal*) (R. Polzin, *Samuel and the Deuteronomist: A Literary Study of the Deuteronomic History*, Pt. 2: *1 Samuel* (Bloomington, IN: Indiana University Press, 1989), 23).

(4.18). The 'bringing down' of the rich that Hannah's song describes is literal and metaphorical in the case of Eli. It is no accident either that his final demise results from his weight: 'he was old and heavy' (4.18). Eli, as well as his sons, have benefited from the sacrifices of the Israelites. This is the implication of 2.29, which has both Eli and his sons fattening themselves on the choicest parts of the offerings.[13] Eli's connivance with his sons would be even stronger if NRSV's translation of this verse is correct, 'Why then look with greedy eye'; the Hebrew is too difficult to be confident in such a reading.[14] If there is an insistent criticism of Eli's house for fattening itself, a fattening which eventually plays its part in Eli's death, it may well be that there is more to YHWH's rebuke, 'Why do you honour (*te kabbed*) your sons more than me?' (2.29) and the naming of Phinehas's son Ichabod (4.21). In both cases there may be a play on *kbd*, which means 'honour, glory', but also 'heaviness'. Eli is found guilty of fattening himself and his sons before God and, as a result, the fatness his family has enjoyed will depart never to return. Eli's failure to prevent his sons' malpractice and his participation in it leads to the family losing its special status as priests and the resultant privileges. YHWH's retribution against the Elides is another instance of the punishment fitting the crime: access to the sacrificial meat is denied and instead the surviving family members have to beg just to receive a piece of bread (2.36). Hannah's song finds fulfilment, the full do hire themselves out for bread.

For both Hannah and Eli, then, the table is the context for divine vindication or for divine judgement. As each story opens, injustice occurs in relation to events of eating and drinking. It is the attitude to food demonstrated by Hannah and Eli that characterizes them as pious or impious. Hannah weeps and refuses to eat and drink, so distressed is she at her childless state; in contrast, Eli and his sons have appetites that cannot be controlled.[15] Hannah

---

[13] There is no need to accept the emendation of McCarter, who reads 'to let them eat' *le habrotem* for MT 'to fatten yourselves' *le have riª kem* (P. K. McCarter, *1 Samuel*, AB, 8 (New York: Doubleday, 1980), 87–8).

[14] The Hebrew here and in v. 32 appears to be corrupt; MT reads, 'Why do you kick my sacrifices and offerings that I commanded—habitation'. McCarter records a personal communication with F. M. Cross, who recommends emending to *tabbit...tsarat 'ayin* 'why do you look...with needy eye', hence NRSV's reading (McCarter, *1 Samuel*, 87). Gordon's pessimistic 'the problem...still awaits a solution' is not unfair (Gordon, *I & II Samuel*, 86).

[15] Hannah is said not to have eaten in 1.7 and she claims not to have been drinking in 1.15. After she receives blessing from Eli, Hannah returns to the family group and eats (1.18). On the other hand, 1.9 describes Hannah as rising up 'after she had eaten' (*oke lah*). The Septuagint's 'after they had eaten' (*meta to phagein autous*) is an unsurprising harmonization.

For refusing to eat 'as a signal of a troubled spirit' see D. M. Sharon, 'When Fathers Refuse to Eat: The Trope of Rejecting Food and Drink in Biblical Narrative', in A. Brenner and J. W. Van Henten (eds.), *Food and Drink in Biblical Worlds*, Semeia, 86 (Atlanta: Society of Biblical Literature, 1999), 135–48

is lifted up from hunger to celebration, whilst the Elides fall from thrones to the status of beggars. It is through food events that YHWH exhibits his justice.

Food and the Divine Election of Israel's Monarch

We have already observed that Hannah's song not only plays a role within its immediate narrative context, but also anticipates many of the themes found in the books of Samuel and consequently serves as a thematic overture. Central to the book is the establishment of the monarchy, which Hannah foresees in the conclusion of her song: 'He will give strength to his king, and exalt the horn of his anointed' (2.10). However, there are also anticipations of the rise to power of Saul and David in the assertion that YHWH 'raises the poor from the dust ... to sit them with princes and make them inherit a seat of honour' (2.8). In the case of both kings the narrative emphasizes their humble background and their rise to an honoured status at the table and, ultimately, to the royal throne itself.

The account of Saul's anointing begins by identifying him as the son of a 'man of wealth' and describing him having an unequalled physical presence (9.1). Saul's own self-presentation is modest: 'Am I not a Benjaminite, from the least of the tribes of Israel, and my clan is the smallest of all the clans of the tribes of Benjamin?' (9.21). When he is announced to all Israel there are some who question his ability to lead Israel (10.27). Importantly Saul's path to kingship does not merely involve anointing by YHWH's prophet, but takes place after Saul has been invited to a sacrifice at which he received an honoured place. Saul's arrival at Ramah searching for his lost donkeys is not a chance happening, Samuel has already been told that Israel's anointed will appear. Saul is given the principal position at the select group that dine (9.22). In addition special portions of the sacrifice have been reserved for him (9.23–4). The thigh and the fat tail are probably to be understood as delicacies; the priestly literature reserves them for God alone.[16] Saul's exaltation at this meal anticipates his elevation to the throne.

Saul's rise to the status of king can rightly be seen as an instance of Hannah's exaltation of the poor to a place amongst kings. On the other hand, Gordon observes that 'Saul's family was not in the depressed class' and that in Saul's self-deprecatory comments 'the motif of the ennobling of the lowly is probably not so prominent ... as is sometimes suggested'.[17] Nevertheless, the existence of two portrayals of Saul's status is interesting and suggests a tension between

---

[16] See, e.g., Exod. 29.22. The difficult *he'aleyha* is usually read as *haalyah* 'the fat tail' (Driver, *Books of Samuel*, 58).

[17] Gordon, *I & II Samuel*, 115.

a tradition about Saul's family and a literary and ideological purpose. The parallels with David's ascendancy suggest that the modest origins of both royal houses be understood as a display of the paradoxes of divine choice (cf. 1 Kgs. 16.2), which sees God exalting the unimportant.

David's modest origins are more clearly visible in the account of his anointing in 1 Samuel 16. Samuel is directed by God to go and anoint one of the sons of Jesse the Bethlehemite. Neither genealogical information is given nor any indication of Jesse's social status. The context for the anointing is again a sacrificial feast to which the elders as well as Jesse and his sons are invited. As the youngest son of the family David is not considered important enough to attend this significant social event. According to Samuel, however, the feast cannot begin until David has been brought (16.11). On his arrival he is anointed by Samuel.

We have already observed the association of the feast with kingship and in particular with the moment of coronation. The reigns of David (1 Chron. 12.38–40) and Solomon (1 Chron. 22.21–2) begin with feasting, as does Adonijah's abortive attempt at succeeding his father (1 Kings 1). These feasts of anointing should rightly be seen as anticipations of the coronation feast.[18] It is apparent also that these events are being portrayed as instances of divine justice in which God raises the insignificant to noble company and proleptically to the throne.

As we have observed with the house of Eli, the motif can also operate in reverse: eating and feasting can signal the end of the ruling dynasty. This is true of the first three dynasties of the northern kingdom, all of which end with animals feasting on the remains of the dynastic family (1 Kgs. 14.11; 16.4; 21.24). In the last case, the dynasty of Omri and Ahab, the inaugural feast of the new king, Jehu, and the macabre end of the old dynasty are juxtaposed.

The story of Jehu's accession to the throne has a number of features in common with the ascendancy of Saul and David. Elisha sends one of the 'sons of the prophets' to anoint Jehu as king over Israel. When he arrives Elisha's servant finds Jehu sitting (*yosh^{e}vim*) with the army commanders. The NRSV over-interprets *yosh^{e}vim* by rendering it as 'in council'.[19] In contrast, the ambiguity should be preserved allowing for the possibility that

---

[18] First noted by L. Schmidt, *Menschlicher Erfolg und Jahwes Initiative: Studien zu Tradition, Interpretation und Historie in Überlieferungen von Gideon, Saul und David*, WMANT, 38 (Neukirchen-Vluyn: Neukirchener Verlag, 1970), 84.

[19] Gray is similar: 'The commanders were "sitting", possibly "in session" as a council of war. Possibly the appearance of the prophet was a preconcerted signal for denouement of the military plot' (Gray, *I & II Kings*, 487). Gray's historical reconstruction of a political connivance between the prophetic group and Jehu finds no other basis in the text, and obscures the text's ambiguity.

the commanders and Jehu are eating together.[20] This is particularly the case since eating is so central to the accounts of the demise of the Omrides. After killing Joram, Jehu arrives at Jezebel's palace and has her thrown down from the building. According to Elijah's prophetic word Jezebel's body was to be consumed by dogs (1 Kgs. 21.23). The text effects this punishment by having Jehu enter the building to eat and drink whilst Jezebel's corpse remains outside. Only after he has finished his meal does Jehu's mind turn to the queen's body and how it should be dealt with appropriately: 'See to this accursed woman and bury her, for she is a king's daughter' (2 Kgs. 9.34). But by then it is too late and there is little that the street dogs have left. This literary artifice not only achieves the macabre juxtaposition of Jehu's eating with the consumption of Jezebel's body by dogs, but also portrays the enthronement meal of the new dynasty as the moment of Jezebel's judgement.[21] After killing Joram and Jezebel, Jehu deals with the rest of Ahab's descendants. Their killing is described on two occasions as a 'slaughtering' (*shachat*; 2 Kgs. 10.7, 14), a term more commonly used of cultic sacrifice. After Ahab's sons are killed their heads are placed in either cooking pots or baskets (*dudim*).[22] In either case these are containers usually used for bearing, and even cooking, food. When Jehu receives the heads he heaps them outside the city gate like grain. The final purge of everything associated with the Omride dynasty is the destruction of the worshippers of Baal. The grand moment of cultic worship is described as a 'great sacrifice', a description both deliberate and ironic, as we have already noted in our examination of the story of Samson.

Divine judgement against a dynasty is also enacted in the case of Elah son of Baasha. His short reign is ended by the conspiracy of his servant Zimri. The end comes at a banquet in which Elah is drunk (1 Kgs 16.9). Even the final end of the Judahite kingdom, Zedekiah's rebellion against the Babylonians, is described in language reminiscent of the feast. Like Ahab's seventy sons, his two sons are 'slaughtered' (*shachat*; 2 Kgs. 25.7) before his eyes.

There appears then to be a tendency to describe the beginning or end of a dynasty with language that alludes to the table. In the case of the beginning of the dynasty the feast appears to inaugurate a new reign. When a dynasty is brought to an end the deaths are associated with human or animal eating. Even when no eating event is present the motif of divine judgement at the table appears to exert some pressure to describe human deaths with language that alludes to consumption or sacrifice.

---

[20] For *yashav* with this sense see 1 Kgs. 13.20; 2 Kgs. 4.38; Isa. 65.4.

[21] For this as an enthronement meal see Fritz, *1 & 2 Kings*, 287.

[22] See KB, 215 and J. R. Lundbom, *Jeremiah 21–36*, AB, 21B (New York: Doubleday, 2004), 228.

Jehoiachin at Evil-Merodach's Table

The significance of food in the Deuteronomistic History's presentation of Israel and Judah's history is apparent in the final scene of the books of Kings. The concluding chapters describe the final years of the southern kingdom of Judah, the loss of its independence, the exiling of its kings and the scattering of its population between Babylonia and Egypt. In the final verses, however, there is a shift of perspective and we are given an after-history of one of the last major characters of the story, king Jehoiachin.[23]

Now it happened in the thirty-seventh year of the exile of Jehoiachin, king of Judah, on the twenty-seventh day of the twelfth month, Evil Merodach, king of Babylon, in the year that he began to reign, lifted up the head of Jehoiachin, king of Judah, from prison. He spoke kindly with him and he gave him a throne among the thrones of the kings who were with him in Babylon. So he took off his prison clothes and for the rest of his life ate regularly in his presence. His daily allocation of food was a permanent allocation given to him by the king for the rest of his life.   (2 Kgs. 25.27–30)[24]

These verses are a famous textual crux for it is unclear whether they promise a hopeful future beyond exile with the restoration of a member of the Davidic line to a position of influence or whether they are more muted with the former monarch pensioned off and spending the rest of his days a house guest of the Babylonian king.

The problem received prominence with Noth's proposal that Deuteronomy to 2 Kings formed a single historiographical work. Noth's own understanding of this work was that it attributed the fall of the Israelite kingdoms to their own sinfulness and their failure to obey the divine covenant. The conclusion gives no cause to hope. The final verses are 'only to provide a mitigating conclusion to the long account of the decline which [the Deuteronomistic History] had to give, not to conceal or leave in doubt the fact that the history of the Israelite and Judaean kings was in fact over'.[25] Von Rad, on the other hand, discerned a more optimistic perspective on the Davidic monarchy. According to 2 Samuel 7 God offered David an everlasting dynasty: 'Your house and your kingdom will be established forever before me; your throne will be firm forever' (2 Sam.

---

[23] Granoski helpfully compares this with the ending of other great works of literature. In some literary epilogues the *nachgeschichte* of the main characters is traced for the reader (J. J. Granowski, 'Jehoiachin at the King's Table: A Reading of the Ending of the Second Book of Kings', in D. N. Fewell (ed.), *Reading Between Texts: Intertextuality and the Hebrew Bible* (Louisville: Westminster John Knox Press, 1992), 173–90, here 177).

[24] For the translation of the different clauses and possible Akkadian parallels see E. Zenger, 'Die deuteronomistische Interpretation der Rehabilitierung Jojachins', *BZ* 12 (1968), 16–30. I have maintained a fairly literalistic translation.

[25] Noth, *Deuteronomistic History*, 27.

7.16). The end of 2 Kings is an indication to the reader 'that the line of David has not come to an irrevocable end'.[26]

More recent work on these verses has chosen not to embrace either extreme.[27] Since there is no mention of YHWH's activity, no allusion to Nathan's oracle in 2 Samuel 7 and no indication of repentance by Jehoiachin there can, according to some, be no suggestion of the restoration of the kingdom and the Davidic monarchy.[28] Comparison has been drawn with the demise of Saul's dynasty and David's actions towards Mephibosheth in 2 Samuel 9. In particular, both Jehoaichin and Mephibosheth are said to have 'eaten bread continually' at the tables of their respective overlords (2 Sam. 9.7; 2 Kgs. 25.29). Thus, as Mephibosheth's presence at David's table expressed the final demise of Saul's house so also the hopes of the Davidic dynasty come to an end with the last descendant living out his life at another king's largesse.[29] Noth was correct, then, to argue that these verses offered no hope to the discredited Davidic line. He was overly negative, however, for the history's readers are offered the prospect of a tolerable life under Babylonian hegemony.[30]

As suggestive as an allusion to the fate of Mephibosheth is, it is certainly not the only intertextual resonance that Jehoiachin's release has.[31] The apparent end of monarchy should be heard in conjunction with its first announcement in Hannah's song.[32] Jehoiachin's release from prison is another example of raising the 'poor from the dust' (1 Sam. 2.8). In the final verses of 2 Kings we

---

[26] G. von Rad, 'The Deuteronomic Theology of the History in I and II Kings', in *The Problem of the Hexateuch and Other Essays* (Edinburgh: Oliver & Boyd, 1966), 205–21, here 220.

[27] Levenson is more sanguine than most with Jehoiachin's release signalling within Israel's diaspora existence a messianic hope conditional on her repentance (J. D. Levenson, 'The Last Four Verses in Kings', *JBL* 103 (1984), 353–61). Also positive is Sharon, *Patterns of Destiny*, 195–9.

[28] See, e.g., C. T. Begg, 'The Significance of Jehoiachin's Release: A New Proposal', *JSOT* 36 (1986), 49–56; B. Becking, 'Jehoiachin's Amnesty, Salvation for Israel? Notes on 2 Kings 25, 27–30', in C. Brekelmans and J. Lust (eds.), *Pentateuchal and Deuteronomistic Studies*, BETL, 94 (Leuven: Leuven University Press, 1990), 283–93.

[29] Granowski, 'Jehoiachin at the King's Table'; J. Schipper, '"Significant Resonances" with Mephibosheth in 2 Kings 25.27–30: A Response to Donald F. Murray', *JBL* 124 (2005), 521–9.

[30] It would hardly be insignificant then that Jeremiah ends with the same narrative, for submission to the Babylonians was an important aspect of that prophet's message.

[31] For the recognition of the importance of exploring intertextual allusions to 2 Kgs. 25.27–30 see R. E. Clements, 'A Royal Privilege: Dining in the Presence of the Great King (2 Kings 25.27–30)', in R. Rezetko, T. H. Lim and W. B. Aucker (eds.), *Reflection and Refraction: Studies in Biblical Historiography in Honour of A. Graeme Auld*, VTSup, 113 (Leiden: Brill, 2007), 49–66. Clements explores the links to Psalms 18 and 72. In the new context of exile there is some hope. 'Israel would indeed live among the nations under the shadow of an heir of the ancient royal line. Jehoiachin's example was held up as exemplary' (64).

[32] It has been suggested that Hannah's song forms an *inclusio* with David's psalm in 2 Samuel 22. Might it be possible that an inclusio is also formed with the end of the books of Kings? Certainly none of the parallels between Hannah's song and David's psalm touch upon the allusions to food and eating in 1 Sam. 2.1–10 (see, e.g., Watts, *Psalm and Story*, 23 n. 3).

may have a demonstration of YHWH's justice to the ends of the earth in which he gives 'strength to his king and exalts the horn of his anointed one' (1 Sam. 2.10).[33] If Jehoiachin's experience in exile parallels those of Saul and David in their moments of anointing, we might have grounds for finding in Jehoiachin's taking his place at Evil-Merodach's table an anticipation of a future restoration of Jehoiachin and the Davidic dynasty to the Judahite throne.

In the cases of Saul and David, however, the elevation takes place by the hand of a prophet at YHWH's request, whilst the elevation of Jehoiachin is the action of a foreign king. As Begg observes, this final vignette in the book of Kings 'does not attribute Jehoiachin's release to Yahweh's initiative'.[34] Yet whilst this is true, the final fall of Jerusalem is not attributed to YHWH either, and it is altogether unlikely that the writer did not understand Jerusalem's capture as a moment of divine punishment. Indeed, the concluding chapters of Kings seem to be preparing the reader for the possibility that invading empires are evidence of YHWH's wrath. Rabshakeh's claim to be YHWH's tool is proved untrue (2 Kgs. 18.25), but the marauding groups that threaten Judah in her final years are attributed to divine action: '*Surely (ak)* this happened to Judah by the mouth of YHWH' (24.3).

It should also be noted that in 2 Kings 25 a subtle contrast is made between Zedekiah and Jehoiachin. When Zedekiah is defeated and captured Nebuchadnezzar 'spoke justice with him' (v. 6); in the case of Jehoiachin, by contrast, Evil-Merodach 'spoke kindly with him' (v. 28). The use of food language in the slaughter of Zedekiah's son has already been noted; in the narrative this immediately follows Nebuchadnezzar's sentence. For Jehoiachin the kindly words are followed by his elevation to the king's table and above the other kings. If the slaughter of Zedekiah's sons is indeed the indication of the end of his dynasty, then we may have further grounds for seeing in Evil-Merodach's gracious actions towards Jehoiachin the establishing of his dynastic line. As with the transition between Ahab's house and Jehu's, one dynasty finds itself slaughtered or sacrificed, whilst the other begins to eat palace food.

Mephibosheth and Human Justice at the Table

Why should the establishment and collapse of dynasties be particularly associated with events of eating? One answer clearly lies in the association of political

---

[33] Cf. Polzin, who draws attention to the anticipations of the whole history of monarchy in his analysis of Hannah's song, including the experience of Jehoiachin in Evil-Merodach's court. 'The throne of honour and the fattening food spoken of by Hannah may point to the glories of David and Solomon, but they also force us to contemplate the final table and throne of honor accorded the final Israel king, now luxuriantly subjugated to the king of Babylon' (Polzin, *Samuel*, 37).

[34] Begg, 'Jehoiachin's Release', 50.

power with feasting and eating well. The king is identified as the one who lays on feasts for his court. To hold a feast was often seen as a claim to kingship. The demise of a dynasty at the feast sees this association in ironic reversal. Another answer, however, lies in the assertion that YHWH himself is a king. As a human king exhibits his rule through providing for his people and raising his chosen courtiers to the royal table, so also YHWH does the same for his people. The table, then, becomes a window onto the heavenly banquet and the distribution of divine favour.

The biblical example, par excellence, of the table as the context for kingly favour is, of course, David's generosity towards Mephibosheth. After David has established himself upon the throne of Israel and Judah he seeks out the remaining descendants of Saul in order that he might show them 'kindness' (*chesed*).[35] Mephibosheth, the lame son of Jonathan, is discovered and David provides him with a permanent place at the royal table. Whether Mephibosheth is to provide his own food from his ancestral holdings or receives some of the king's fare is unclear. He is, however, the recipient of the king's generosity and another instance of the fulfilment of Hannah's prophetic song.[36]

It has often been observed that David's actions towards Mephibosheth are a fulfilment of his promise to Jonathan when they part in 1 Samuel 20. David makes a covenant with Jonathan that he will not cut off his kindness (*chesed*) to Jonathan's house forever (v. 15; cf. v. 8). What has not been noticed is that David's kindness at the table is contrasted with Saul's wrath at the table. This contrast is grounded in the use of the rare expression 'the king's table' (*sulchan hammelek*), which apart from these chapters otherwise occurs only at 1 Kgs. 4.27.[37] David excuses himself from the new moon festival in order to ascertain Saul's attitude towards him. On this occasion David is expected to dine with

---

[35] David's *chesed* towards Mephibosheth, Saul's descendant, is the context for his *chesed* towards Hanun the heir of Nahash the Ammonite (2 Samuel 10). Consequently it is not possible to detach 2 Samuel 9 from the wider literary context (*contra* G. Keys, *The Wages of Sin: A Reappraisal of the 'Succession Narrative'*, JSOTSup, 221 (Sheffield: Sheffield Academic Press, 1996), 74–81. In the story of 2 Samuel 10, however, Hanun scorns David's demonstration of *chesed* with his own act of inhospitality towards David's messengers, sexually humiliating them rather than welcoming them into the court. The contrast with David's hospitality in 2 Samuel 9 is clear.

[36] It has often been suggested that David's generosity was more calculated than the text suggests. By keeping Mephibosheth at the royal court in Jerusalem David could monitor his activities and prevent him becoming a focus of a pro-Saulide faction. As Gordon notes, if this were so 'the plan might easily have backfired' (Gordon, *I & II Samuel*, 248). More seriously we might question whether it is possible to attempt such a suspicious political reading of an event that we know only through an already heavily politicized account.

[37] In 1 Kgs. 4.27 the expression is fuller: King Solomon's table. It should also be noted that Saul calls David a 'son of death' (1 Sam. 20.31), whilst Mephibosheth describes himself as a 'man of death' (2 Sam. 19.28).

the king, with Abner and Jonathan also present. When Saul becomes aware of the absence he expresses his anger with David, culminating with him throwing his spear at his son Jonathan.

The kindness that David shows to Mephibosheth is at odds with the kinds of treatment that we might expect the scion of a former royal house to receive. The actions of Abimelech (Judges 9) and Jehu (2 Kings 9) illustrate the bloody outcomes of dynastic coups. Saul's own response to David is a recognition of this threat and an attempt to remove an alternative royal house before his own is threatened. David's actions towards Mephibosheth overthrow this expectation and with it the usual employment of the language of the table. Whilst Ahab's family are 'slaughtered' and 'consumed' through Jehu's actions, Mephibosheth is invited to join the royal table, albeit denuded of any independent political power. This action is described by David as 'the kindness of God' (*chesed elohim*; 2 Sam. 9.3). Although D. W. Thomas sought to argue that the reference to the divine should be understood as a superlative, 'great kindness', there seems no reason not to find here a comparison with the actions of God.[38] This is apt if, as we have suggested, an analogy is being drawn between human royal action at the table and divine royal action at the table. As David uses the table to demonstrate *chesed*, so too YHWH uses the table for this purpose.

Divine Judgement at the Table: Non-royal Variations on the Theme

The table as the context of divine justice occurs on a number of occasions for non-royal individuals. To be more precise, the judgement or vindication is in relation to non-royal individuals, even if royal figures feature in all the stories. We will consider the examples of Nabal and the man of God in 1 Kings 13. In addition, we will examine the story of Naboth, where the motif is inverted.

The story of Nabal (1 Samuel 25) revolves around the sheep-shearing feast. David demands a share of Nabal's wealth for the service of protection that he and his men have provided. Nabal, who is characterized as 'surly and mean', refuses to be party to what appears to be a protection racket by a band of outlaws. This is certainly a miscalculation, because David mobilizes his forces, a bloody end only being averted by the prompt actions of Abigail, Nabal's astute wife. She meets David on his way to attack Nabal and provides him with sufficient food and drink for David to feast his men. Abigail's success results not only from giving David the delayed payment but by her persuasive speech (vv. 24–31). In this speech considerable play is made on the word-pair

---

[38] D. W. Thomas, 'A Consideration of Some Unusual Ways of Expressing the Superlative in Hebrew', *VT* 3 (1953), 209–24; cf. Gordon, *I & II Samuel*, 248.

'good'–'evil' (vv. 26, 28, 30, 31), important words elsewhere in the narrative. Nabal has done evil in response to David's good, but David is persuaded against repaying this evil with evil. David is to avoid shedding the blood of his enemy and to trust himself to YHWH to bring good to him.

The wisdom of Abigail's counsel and David's acceptance of it is seen in the denouement of the narrative. However, the narrative continues with Abigail returning to the house where Nabal is feasting 'like a king'. When the feast ends and Nabal has relieved himself of all the wine he has drunk,[39] Abigail informs her husband of her conduct. As a result 'his heart died within him, and he became like a stone' (v. 37).[40] Ten days later he dies, an action attributed to the intervention of YHWH. David interprets Nabal's death within this framework of good and evil: 'Blessed be YHWH who has judged the case of my reproach at Nabal's hands and has restrained his servant from *evil*, and he has brought Nabal's *evil* upon his own head' (v. 39). David and the narrator understand what happens to Nabal at the end of the feast as an example of divine justice, a justice that is demonstrated at the table.

It is not, of course, entirely correct to describe Nabal as a non-royal individual. Although the text introduces him as a landowner in the south of the country, he acts in the context of 1 Samuel as a cipher for Saul. This is seen not only in the parallels between the story about Nabal and the stories about Saul that encompass it, but also in the description of Nabal as 'feasting like a king'.[41] Nabal's evil response to David is repaid upon him; so also the evil that is plotted against David by Saul is eventually returned upon Saul's head by YHWH. Saul's demise, though, takes place on the hills of Gilboa at the hands of the Philistines, and not at the feast like Nabal's.

In the story of the man of God from Judah in 1 Kings 13 the table is the site of both the man of God's transgression and an oracle of judgement from the Northern prophet. The narrative opens with the man of God commissioned

---

[39] For this understanding of 'while the wine was going out of Nabal' (*b^{e}tseth hayyayin minnaval*) see P. J. Leithart, 'Nabal and his Wine', *JBL* 120 (2001), 525–7. Leithart draws attention to how this motif plays an important role in the portrayal of Saul and Nabal in 1 Samuel 24–6.

[40] Boyle rightly warns against reading modern understandings of physiology into the biblical text. She argues against understanding this verse as a heart attack or a stroke, instead suggesting that it should be read with passages that speak about people hardening their heart. Whilst it is probably inappropriate to restrict a rich narrative text like 1 Samuel 25 to purely physiological explanations, it is not clear to me that Boyle has provided an adequate explanation for the expression 'his heart died within him', which is not the usual language for human obduracy (M. O. Boyle, 'The Law of the Heart: The Death of a Fool (1 Samuel 25)', *JBL* 120 (2001), 401–27).

[41] For 1 Samuel 24–6 as an example of narrative analogy see the studies of R. P. Gordon, 'David's Rise and Saul's Demise: Narrative Analogy in 1 Samuel 24–26', *Tyndale Bulletin* 32 (1980), 37–64 and J. D. Levenson, '1 Samuel 25 as Literature and as History', *CBQ* 40 (1978), 11–28.

to confront Jeroboam I and his novel cult. After the man of God has delivered his oracle against the Bethel cult and exercised miraculous powers, Jeroboam seeks to befriend him and offers him hospitality. This is refused, for according to the man of God: 'I was commanded by the word of God, "Do not eat food or drink water there; do not return by the way that you came"' (13.9). The rationale for this divine instruction is not articulated explicitly, but the emphasis on 'eating', 'drinking' and 'returning' in the narrative shows that a great deal is perceived to be at stake in this commandment. Provan suggests that a true prophet must not be obligated to anything except the word of YHWH. Jeroboam's hospitality is an attempt to buy the loyalty of the Judaean man of God.[42] This is appropriate only if the story is to be understood to be primarily concerned with the ascertainment of true and false prophecy.[43] On the other hand, if greater attention is paid to the story within the wider narrative frame of the reign of Jeroboam, the main characters can be seen to be representatives of their respective nations.[44] The prohibition against eating and drinking not only prevents any friendly interaction between the man of God from the southern kingdom of Judah and the northern king, Jeroboam, but also any complicity on the part of the man of God with Jeroboam's cultic apostasy. This is especially the case if, as Gray suggests, the meal to which Jeroboam invites the man of God is to take place at the dining hall of the sanctuary, where the sacrificial meat would be consumed (cf. 1 Sam. 1.18).[45] This might be compared to the fears that friendly overtures from Canaanites might result in Israelites compromising their loyalty to YHWH and joining in the worship of other gods (Exod. 34.15–16).[46] Such worship included participation in the sacrificial feasts.

[42] Provan, *1 and 2 Kings*, 114. Cf. De Vries, who writes, 'Yahweh's command not to eat, drink or return by the same road certainly seems arbitrary and irrational, but that is precisely the point: the man of God's complete subjection to the divine purpose can only be tested through laying on him conditions that may seem unreasonable and burdensome to him' (De Vries, *1 Kings*, 170–1).

[43] See, *inter alia*, T. B. Dozeman, 'The Way of the Man of God from Judah: True and False Prophecy in the Pre-Deuteronomic Legend of 1 Kings 13', *CBQ* 44 (1982), 379–93; D. W. Van Winkle, '1 Kings XIII: True and False Prophecy', *VT* 39 (1989), 355–70.

[44] See K. Barth, *Church Dogmatics II.2* (Edinburgh: T&T Clark, 1957), 393–409; D. Bosworth, 'Revisiting Karl Barth's Exegesis of 1 Kings 13', *BibInt* 10 (2002), 366–83; R. Boer, 'National Allegory in the Hebrew Bible', *JSOT* 74 (1997), 95–116, esp. 106–12.

[45] Gray, *I & II Kings*, 297.

[46] The comparison is even more apt if the 'Canaanites' in Exodus 34 are a cipher for those whose worship does not accord with strict Yahwism. The reshaping of elements of the Covenant Code in Exodus 34 in light of the sin of the Golden Calf (Exodus 32) has an important role in characterizing the Calf cult as a Canaanite phenomenon which involves feasting and sexual licence (see a more detailed discussion in MacDonald, 'Recasting the Golden Calf'). Since Jeroboam's cult was associated in Israel's history with the erection of Golden Calves the characterizing of the Calf cult in Exodus may be held to be insightful for understanding Jeroboam's cult.

Whichever understanding of the overall narrative and the divine command is to be preferred, it is clear that the command concerns loyalty
to YHWH, and that part of this loyalty is expressed through the refusal of
food and drink whilst the man of God is in the northern kingdom. The
importance of obedience to this command is apparent in the development
of the story when the old prophet from Bethel deceives the man of God
and persuades him that he is to share a meal with him at the prophet's
home. It is while they are at the table that the deceiving prophet receives an
authentic oracle of judgement from God concerning the man of God from
Judah. The table is both the location of the man of God's disobedience and
the divine judgement upon him. After he leaves the prophet's house he is
attacked on his return journey by a lion, who shows more restraint than the
man of God is capable of. The lion stands beside the body without eating
it (v. 28).[47]

In the case of Naboth we have an interesting inversion of this motif of
judgement at the table (1 Kings 21). Food plays a prominent role in the
narrative, as it does elsewhere in the stories of Elijah and Ahab's dynasty.[48]
The story opens with Ahab desiring Naboth's vineyard for a vegetable patch.
The contrast between the archetypal Israelite plant, the vine, often used as a
metaphor of the nation, and the vegetable foods that Ahab desires, creates
an important characterization of the two male figures in the story. One is
typically Israelite, the other insubstantial and associated with Egypt. When
Naboth refuses to sell the field to Ahab the petulant Israelite monarch takes
to his bed and will not eat. His fast is broken when Jezebel assures him that
she will obtain the field for him. Jezebel orders the elders of Naboth's city to
arrange a fast, with Naboth given a prominent position at the head of the
assembly. During the fast two scoundrels will accuse Naboth of blasphemy.
Conveniently the assembled elders can as easily be a court as part of the local
fast. The case is decided—there are the required two witnesses—and Naboth
summarily executed.

The reasons for the calling of the fast are not specified. It is most frequently
suggested that this is a communal fast to make penance for some sin. The
occasion for such an event would have been some pressing misfortune. This

---

[47] *Contra* Klingbeil, who writes, 'However, as instructed by YHWH he is *not to eat or drink*
in Israel (I Reg 13,7), and failing this—wrongly believing an elderly prophet from Bethel—he
gets *eaten* by a lion (I Reg 13,24f.)' (G. A. Klingbeil, '"Momentaufnahmen" of Israelite Religion:
The Importance of the Communal Meal in Narrative Texts in I/II Regum and Their Ritual
Dimension', *ZAW* 118 (2006), 22–45, here 40).

[48] D. A. Appler, 'From Queen to Cuisine: Food Imagery in the Jezebel Narrative', in A. Brenner
and J. W. Van Henten (eds.), *Food and Drink in the Biblical Worlds*, Semeia, 86 (Atlanta: Society
of Biblical Literature, 1999), 55–71.

leaves the queen's role in calling the fast unexplained.[49] It has been suggested that the purpose of the public fast was to ascertain the cause of the misfortune and that Naboth was placed at the head of the assembly in the position of the accused.[50] Such a use of the communal fast cannot be paralleled elsewhere in the Old Testament. It is possible that the 'fast' is a literary invention that bears no obvious relation to Israelite ritual or communal activity. In other words, it is no more than a literary and ironic inversion of the feast. Naboth is positioned like Saul in 1 Sam. 9.22 in the place of honour at the head of the table.[51] Yet at this table there is nothing to eat, and there is an accusation rather than acclamation. The table again becomes the context for judgement, when Naboth is accused of blasphemy and condemned by the surrounding city elders. Until Elijah intervenes with an oracle of judgement against Ahab's house, there is no evidence of divine justice. The judgement at the table is executed by the elders and Jezebel.

Judgement at the Table in the Book of Judges

Some of the stories in the book of Judges that we have already examined fit well the theme of justice exhibited at the table. The story of Adoni-bezeq is particularly apt since, although his punishment does not take place at the table of the Israelites, he draws a comparison to his own practice of having maimed kings scavenge for food under his table. As Adoni-bezeq recognizes, there is divine justice at work. In the song of Deborah the death of Sisera occurs whilst he is enjoying the drink of milk, a punishment that is seen as an exhibition of divine justice: 'so let all your enemies perish, O YHWH' (5.31). The death of Samson is also celebrated in the book of Judges as revenge for Philistine incursions. The death of Samson and the Philistines occurs at a 'great sacrifice', an expression that points to the festive occasion as well as the great slaughter that ensues.

In the so-called Deuteronomistic History, then, the table is frequently a locus for divine judgement and vindication. The literary motif is found in a number of stories and is even used to structure the account of the Israelite kingdoms, ultimately expressing the hope of the writers of 2 Kgs. 25.27–30 that the Israelite monarchy will be restored.

---

[49] For a discussion of the difficulties see most recently P. T. Cronauer, *The Stories about Naboth the Jezreelite: A Source, Composition, and Redaction Investigation of 1 Kings 21 and Passages in 2 Kings 9*, LHBOTS, 424 (London: T&T Clark, 2005), 138–43.

[50] Discussed and rightly rejected by Gray, *I & II Kings*, 440–1.

[51] Cronauer overlooks the similarity of 1 Sam. 9.22 to 1 Kgs. 21.9, 12 (Cronauer, *Naboth the Jezreelite*, 142). For Naboth's place as one of honour see Gray, *I & II Kings*, 391.

NARRATIVES ABOUT JUDGEMENT AT THE TABLE
ELSEWHERE IN THE OLD TESTAMENT

The theme of divine judgement at the table is found not only in the Deuteronomistic History, but also in other narrative material in the Old Testament. Some of this we will examine in the following chapter, particularly as it occurs in the diaspora novellas of the Second Temple period. For the moment we will examine two places in the Hebrew Bible where the motif may be expressed—the story of Joseph and the story of Job—and what light it may shed on details of those texts.

Joseph in Egypt

The story of Joseph and his brothers in Genesis 37–45 touches on food and eating on a number of occasions. As is well-known the wisdom of Joseph is demonstrated in his interpretations of Pharaoh's dreams in which he predicts the seven years of plenty that will be followed by seven years of famine. Food occurs on a number of other occasions, though this is usually overlooked by commentators. Two examples may be mentioned. First, while Joseph is in the pit and his brothers are deliberating his fate the narrator informs us that the brothers 'sat to eat bread' (37.25). This seemingly innocuous observation rarely receives attention. An exception is Westermann, who finds here no more than a literary pause: 'the pause that follows is a necessary preparation for the continuation of the action. The brothers sit to eat.'[52] Second, the restoration of Pharaoh's cup-bearer and the punishment of his baker takes place on a festive day. Wilson observes that the narrator provides 'some unnecessary detail—such as the mention of Pharaoh's birthday'. These merely serve to 'build suspense' for the climax of the chapter where the two officials receive their foreseen destiny (40.20–3).[53] The regular appearance of eating events in the story of Joseph raises the question of whether these references are merely narrative 'filler'.

The story of Pharaoh's two officials illustrates the conjunction of judgement and table (Genesis 40). Both have dreams that Joseph interprets as prophetic of their fate. The cup-bearer will be restored, which is described with the idiom 'have his head lifted up', whilst the baker will be executed, which is described

---

[52] C. Westermann, *Genesis 37–50: A Commentary* (Minneapolis: Augsburg, 1986), 41.

[53] L. Wilson, *Joseph Wise and Otherwise: The Intersection of Wisdom and Covenant in Genesis 37–50*, Paternoster Biblical Monographs (Milton Keynes: Paternoster, 2004), 119.

as 'having his head lifted from upon him'. The occasion of judgement for both is the feast (*mishteh*) during the celebration of Pharaoh's birthday.[54]

A more complex case is the episodes of eating that propel Joseph on his Egyptian journey and bring the story to its climax; these are respectively the brothers' meal around the pit (37.25) and the feast in Joseph's house (43.26–34). These two meals are connected with subtle intertextual allusions. First, both stories concern 'eating bread' (37.25; 43.25) whilst seated (37.25; 43.33).[55] Second, only here in the Joseph story do we have a reference to 'raising the eyes' (37.25; 43.29). Third, in both meals the brothers and Joseph are separated during the act of eating, either because Joseph is in the pit or because Egyptian conventions do not allow them to share a common table. The relationship between the two meals makes them into important inverted counterparts. At the first meal Joseph is condemned to a life of slavery by his brothers because of his dreams, at the second meal Joseph's elevation over his brothers finds full expression.

The meal in Joseph's house sees Joseph being completely vindicated before his brothers. This occurs in the first instance at the table where the brothers are ranked according to age, but the preference for the sons of Rachel is expressed through the vast portion that Benjamin receives (43.34). The favouritism that was shown to Joseph is thus affirmed. Joseph's vindication continues into chapter 44, which should not be separated from the meal at Joseph's house. This is for a couple of reasons. First, the brothers are sent away only to be recalled to Joseph's house. The text emphasizes the events taking place 'there' (44.14).[56] Judah's speech and Joseph's revelation of his identity all take place at Joseph's house, whose only significance in the narrative has been as the location of the meal. The departure is, thus, only an interlude in a narrative that takes place in Joseph's house. Second, the pretext of the cup, which is found in Benjamin's sack, maintains the festal context. Thus, the house where the feast took place becomes the location for a quasi-judicial accusation (44.15) and plea for mitigation (44.18–34). The result is that the brothers' guilt, so often expressed to themselves, is now fully exposed and Joseph vindicated before them.

[54] For the relation of the royal birthday to amnesties in Egypt see D. B. Redford, *A Study of the Biblical Story of Joseph*, VTSup, 20 (Leiden: Brill, 1970), 203–4.

[55] 'Eating bread' otherwise only occurs in 39.6 (in a slightly different expression). For the way in which 'food' is usually designated in the story of Joseph see ibid., 173.

[56] The suggestion that Joseph had not yet gone out to his place of work because it was early is banal (J. Skinner, *Genesis*, ICC (Edinburgh: T&T Clark, 1963), 484; cf. N. Sarna, *Genesis* בראשית: *The Traditional Hebrew Text with the New JPS Translation*, JPS Torah Commentary (Philadelphia: Jewish Publication Society, 1989), 305).

The Family of Job

The book of Job opens and closes with familial feasting (1.4–5; 42.11).[57] The possibility that sin and divine judgement might arise at the table is expressed in Job's actions after the feasts of his children. He reasons to himself that his children may have cursed God in their hearts during their feasting, and so offers sacrifices for them to absolve any inadvertent sin (1.4–5). Whilst this overly-scrupulous behaviour primarily demonstrates Job's excessive piety, it also prepares the reader for the destruction of the children as part of Job's trials (1.18–19). The death of all the children comes at the climax of the first set of trials, and the telling of it alludes to the possibility of a directed divine action. There are four disasters that come upon Job that are structured according to an 'alteration of human and "natural" (or "supernatural") calamities'.[58] The first and third disasters result from raids by Sabeans and Chaldeans. The second calamity results from 'fire of God from heaven' and the final calamity from 'a great wind'. Although we must be careful not to over-interpret the natural catastrophes,[59] the reader is led back to Job's actions and the question of whether the children have acted impiously or Job has not been as scrupulous as usual. Certainly Job attributes the disasters to divine action, though he does not ascribe guilt to anyone, including God (1.21–2).

At the end of the story Job's re-socialization is marked by a feast where family and friends are present (42.11). The description of the feast bears comparison with 2.11, which also sees friends coming to offer 'consolation and comfort'. In that case the three friends offer only accusations and condemnation. In 42.11 the feast is framed by statements about the restoration of Job's wealth. The comfort that the friends and family offer for 'the evil that YHWH had brought upon him' appears only to occur after Job has returned to material wealth.[60] It would seem that the feast is a statement of divine vindication, rather than a means of redressing the losses Job has suffered.[61]

---

[57] 'The meal [in Job 42.11] recalls the periodic feasts enjoyed by Job's sons before their unfortunate demise (1:5, 18)' (N. C. Habel, *Job: A Commentary*, OTL (London: SCM Press, 1985), 585).

[58] D. J. A. Clines, *Job 1–20*, WBC, 17 (Dallas: Word Books, 1989), 20.   [59] Ibid., 33.

[60] Habel speaks of 'their belated act of "consoling" and "comforting" ' (Habel, *Job*, 585).

[61] *Contra* Brueggemann, who argues that 'this human, communal action is stated as a response to God's evil. God may do evil, but redress is done through social process' (W. Brueggemann, 'Theodicy in a Social Dimension', *JSOT* 33 (1985), 3–25, here 19).

The estrangement of friends is also evidence of divine judgement (so Job 19.13).

JUSTICE AT YHWH'S TABLE

Alongside narratives that express divine judgement at the table, there are a number of uses of this motif in other parts of the Old Testament, especially in the psalms and the prophets. We will turn first to the cup of wrath, perhaps the most obvious instance of divine judgement at the table, before looking at positive uses of the cup. Finally we will consider the portrayal of eschatological judgement with language of feasting.

The Cup of Wrath and the Cup of Salvation

The imagery of the 'cup of wrath' is one of the most striking expressions of the idea of the table as the locus of divine judgement, becoming so emblematic that it can be referred to simply as the 'cup'. It is found frequently within the prophetic corpus (Isa. 51.17–22; Jer. 25.15–29; 48.26; 49.12; 51.7; Ezek. 23.31–4; Obad. 16; Hab. 2.15–17; Zech. 12.2) and also in the Psalms and the book of Lamentations (Pss. 60.3; 75.8; Lam. 4.21). Each of these texts envisages a cup filled with wine being passed to the nations, who are forced to drink its entire contents. The wine is a symbol of the judgement of YHWH which must be completely realized through the devastating punishment of the nation made to drink. Isa. 51.17 is typical,

> Rouse yourself, rouse youself
> Stand up, O Jerusalem,
> Who has drunk the cup of wrath from the hand of YHWH
> Drained to the dregs the chalice of reeling.

The recipient of the judgement may vary, sometimes it is Israel or Jerusalem, at other times other nations, but the bearer of the cup is always YHWH or his prophetic representative (Jer. 25.15, 28).[62]

The effect of the contents of the cup of wrath also varies. In some cases the cup causes drunken staggering. In Isaiah 51.17–22, for example, Jerusalem is portrayed as a drunken mother (cf. Zech. 12.2; Ps. 60.3).[63] She has no children

---

[62] T. Seidl, '*Der Becher in der Hand des Herrn*': *Studie zu den Prophetischen* '*Taumelbecher*'-*Texten*, Arbeiten zu Text und Sprache im Alten Testament, 70 (St Ottilien: EOS, 2001).

[63] Note, however, that some translate *sap ra'al* in Zech. 12.2 as 'threshold of reeling' rather than 'cup of reeling' (e.g. D. L. Petersen, *Zechariah 9–14 and Malachi: A Commentary*, OTL (Louisville: Westminster John Knox Press, 1995), 107). Translating *sap* as 'threshold' provides a good parallel to 12.3 and is an understanding attested already in LXX. However, Meyers and Meyers are right to note that *ra'al* is used of drunken reeling (cf. Isa. 51.17; Ps. 60.3), rather than

to guide her home,[64] and as a result she find herself physically humiliated by others. In other cases, the emphasis can also be on the psychological humiliation. Jeremiah 25.17 announces that Jerusalem and the cities of Judah will become a 'hissing and a curse' (cf. 49.12–13), whilst in Ezek. 23.32–3 Jerusalem is mocked and scorned. The same fate comes upon Moab when she is held in derision whilst she wallows in her vomit (Jer. 48.26). The two forms of humiliation are probably combined in the description of Edom receiving the cup, becoming drunk and exposing herself. In her loss of control she forsakes not only her possessions, but also her dignity (Lam. 4.21). The shame of being exposed is also to be found in Hab. 2.15–17, where comparison may be made to the experience of Noah in Genesis 9. In other cases the wine causes not only drunken staggering, but madness (Jer. 25.15–17; 51.7). The state of intoxication can be so overwhelming that the result is fatal (Jer. 25.27; cf. Obadiah 16).

Although the metaphor appears on a number of occasions in the Old Testament and across a range of books, its background is notoriously unclear. This is despite the fact that in Hab. 2.17 and Jer. 25.15–29, which are probably its earliest appearances, the meaning of the metaphor is taken as self-evident for the writer and his readers. The sudden appearance of this metaphor in Israelite literature at the beginning of the sixth century BC and its subsequent popularity is striking. Ancient Near Eastern parallels do not help, for although kings and gods are sometimes portrayed holding a cup aloft, these portrayals do not illuminate the metaphor of the 'cup of wrath'. The Near Eastern imagery is positive, and no one is made to drink.[65] Consequently it has been suggested that we have an inner-Israelite

stumbling caused by an object. It may be that this is an instance of *double entendre* (C. L. Meyers and E. M. Meyers, *Zechariah 9–14*, AB, 25C (New York: Doubleday, 1993), 313).

[64] The description is reminiscent of the responsibilities of a son in Aqhat: 'And let him have a son in (his) house … someone to grasp his hand when he is drunk, someone to support him when he is sated with wine' (*KTU* 1.17.i.25, 30–1; cf. *KTU* 1.114.15–19; translation from J. C. de Moor, *An Anthology of Religious Texts from Ugarit*, Nisaba, 16 (Leiden: Brill, 1987)).

[65] Although Gressmann first suggested that the metaphor had developed from the Israelite cultic meal (H. Gressmann, *Der Ursprung der israelitisch-jüdischen Eschatologie*, FRLANT, 6 (Göttingen: Vandenhoeck & Ruprecht, 1905), 129–36), he later saw a link to the fate-goddess Gudea (H. Gressmann, 'Der Festbecher', in A. Jirku (ed.), *Sellin-Festschrift: Beiträge zur Religionsgeschichte und Archäologie Palästinas* (Leipzig: A. Deichertsche, 1927), 55–62). This comparison is not especially illuminating since it involves a not insignificant shift from judgement to fate. Smothers compares the cup of wrath to the Esarhaddon treaties, where ratification occurs, *inter alia*, through drinking of a cup (T. G. Smothers, 'Excursus: The Cup of Wrath', in G. L. Keown, P. J. Scalise and T. G. Smothers (eds.), *Jeremiah 26–52*, WBC, 27 (Nashville: Thomas Nelson, 1995), 277–9).

The latest attempts to find non-Israelite precursors for the metaphor have been undertaken by Fuchs. (G. Fuchs, 'Das Symbol des Bechers in Ugarit und Israel', in A. Graupner, H. Delkurt and A. B. Ernst (eds.), *Verbindungslinien: Festschrift für Werner H. Schmidt zum 65. Geburtstag* (Neukirchen-Vluyn: Neukirchener, 2000), 65–84 and G. Fuchs, *Der Becher des Sonnengottes: Zur Entwicklung des Motivs 'Becher des Zorns'*, Beiträge zum Verstehen der Bibel, 4 (Münster:

development.[66] McKane sought to link the metaphor to the trial by ordeal in Numbers 5, but this is difficult to sustain. The woman who submits to the ordeal in Numbers 5 may be guilty or innocent, unlike the nations who receive the cup of wrath. It is also difficult to see the contents of the cup as poisonous. Although Jeremiah speaks of 'waters of poison' in Jer. 8.14; 9.15; 23.15 these seem to have no direct relation to the cup of wrath.[67]

In the light of more compelling parallels it is, perhaps, simplest to assume that Gressmann was correct in suggesting that the metaphor was a prophetic reversal of the Israelite cultic meal.[68] Indeed, it is not impossible that the metaphor originates within the Jeremianic tradition.[69] Not only is the metaphor employed on a number of occasions in the book, but the story is also told of how Jeremiah gathered the Rechabites to one of the chambers in the Jerusalem temple, which were used for cultic eating and drinking (cf. 1 Sam. 9.22; Ezek. 42.13), in order to give them wine to drink (Jer. 35). With the 'cup of wrath' metaphor the picture of the benevolent host and generous hospitality has been reversed so that we have an 'anti-banquet theme'.[70] The possibility that the banquet that is being inverted is a cultic event might well be suggested by the focus of the 'cup of wrath' on Jerusalem. It is Jerusalem that is given the cup in Ezek. 23.31–4 and Isa. 51.17–22. In Obadiah 16, on the other hand, the drinking that brings annihilation to the nations takes place at Jerusalem, and in Zech. 12.2 Jerusalem herself is the cup that the nations will drink.

It is possible that the cup of wrath is a parody of a positive tradition of the cup.[71] Certainly a cup received from YHWH is a matter of thanksgiving in some

---

Lit, 2003)). In her most recent work Fuchs argues that the cup was an image of the sun-god. Unfortunately many of the parallels that she cites are from the Greek world and the 'cup of wrath' texts show little or no influence of solar motifs as she recognizes: '[die] Spuren noch dunkel im Alten Testament erhalten sind' (125). Finally, the argument that *chemah* 'wrath' is better rendered 'glow' is difficult to sustain and, in large part, relies on a reading of Hab. 2.15 that involves a textual emendation that may not be necessary.

[66] H. A. Brongers, 'Der Zornesbecher', in J. F. Vink et al. (eds.), *The Priestly Code and Seven Other Studies*, OTS, 15 (Leiden: Brill, 1969), 177–92; K. -D. Schunck, 'Der Becher Jahwes: Weinbecher—Taumelbecher—Zornesbecher', in A. Graupner, H. Delkurt and A. B. Ernst (eds.), *Verbindungslinien: Festschrift für Werner H. Schmidt zum 65. Geburtstag* (Neukirchen-Vluyn: Neukirchener, 2000), 323–30.

[67] McKane also provides an account and critique of Ringgren's argument that we have a development of the intoxication of the 'god-king' at the New Year's Festival (W. McKane, 'Poison, Trial by Ordeal and the Cup of Wrath', *VT* 30 (1980), 474–92). This theory is rightly rejected by McKane.

[68] Gressmann, *Ursprung der israelitisch-jüdischen Eschatologie*, 129–36.

[69] B. Huwyler, *Jeremia und die Völker: Untersuchungen zu den Völkersprüchen in Jeremia 46–49*, FAT, 20 (Tübingen: Mohr Siebeck, 1997), 351 n. 78.

[70] McKane, 'Poison', 491.   [71] Schunck, 'Becher Jahwes'.

of the Psalms: 16.5; 23.5; 116.13. The most famous of these, of course, is the overflowing cup of Psalm 23.

> You arrange a table before me
> in the presence of my enemies.
> You anoint my head with oil;
> my cup is an overflow.

This verse marks a transition from the imagery of God as a shepherd in vv. 1–4 to God as a host in vv. 5–6. Both metaphors have in common the idea of divine provision for the psalmist. It has often been suggested that the imagery of host and table originates in a cultic meal at the Temple. Although the sacrifice is brought by the worshipper, YHWH himself is the host at the subsequent meal. What is interesting is that the table is seen as a place of vindication before the enemies of the psalmists with the anointing and overflowing cup as signs of divine favour. The table is, thus, the place where YHWH gives a judgement on the psalmist in the sight of everyone else in the Temple.

The uses of 'cup' in Pss. 16.5 and 116.13 do not touch directly on the theme of divine judgement at that table, though there are indications of the theme of vindication and judgement. In Psalm 16.5 we have a mix of metaphors that is somewhat perplexing. The cup interrupts the dominant land imagery: 'YHWH has allotted my portion and my cup. You hold my lot.'[72] The cup allotted by YHWH appears to contrast with the bloody libations offered by other worshippers to their gods (v. 4). Whilst they will receive sorrow, the psalmist will be rewarded with a delightful inheritance. In Ps. 116.13 'the cup of salvation' is in the hand of the psalmist, who raises it in praise of YHWH. Probably some ritual action is in view, but whether the cup has been received from YHWH or is offered to YHWH is unclear.[73] In either case the psalmist is portrayed celebrating an act of deliverance—which is also an act of vindication (vv. 6–7, 15–16)—before the festal throng gathered in the Temple.

The cup of wrath and the overflowing cup of the psalmist are evidence of the view that YHWH provides judgement and vindication at his table. The table is not only the locus of divine judgement, but the public exhibition of it. As was the case with the narratives of judgement at the table, these are no private meals. The vindication of the psalmist probably occurs in the Temple before

---

[72] Reading *manitha* 'you have allotted' for MT's *mᵉnath* 'portion'.

[73] Anderson outlines the possible meanings of the 'cup of salvation'. It could be: (1) a drink offering as part of a thank offering (cf. Num. 28.7); (2) a metaphor of deliverance and the opposite to the cup of wrath; (3) a cup connected with the ordeal; (4) the wine at thanksgiving meals. Anderson thinks that the first is most plausible, and the similarities between v. 13 and v. 17 would provide strong support for this suggestion (A. A. Anderson, *The Book of Psalms*, 2 vols., NCB (London: Oliphants, 1972), 794).

his enemies. Likewise in the cup of wrath passages the judgement of Jerusalem and her vindication through the subsequent judgement of the nations takes place before all.

Judgement and Table in the Future

Some of the uses of cup of wrath in the prophets associate the punishment of the nations with a future that is close to hand, sometimes using the 'day of YHWH' to describe this approaching event (e.g. Obadiah 15–16). It is not at all surprising that the relationship between table and judgement that we have discerned should also be expressed in texts concerning the future salvation of Israel and the judgement of God.

In Ezek. 39.17–20 we have a rather grisly example where the birds and wild animals are invited to feast on the remains of the armies of Magog. Instead of animals being consumed by humans, it is human flesh that is eaten by the wild animals. A similarly macabre twist can be found in Zeph. 1.7–8 where a sacrifice is being prepared. Sweeney notes that here in Zephaniah, 'two parties . . . are essential to the sacrifice, that is, the sacrifice itself and those who are to attend the sacrifice. Indeed, as the passage develops, the distinction between these two parties seems somewhat blurred, as those who are invited to observe or attend the sacrifice are indeed those who are themselves to be sacrificed'.[74] With both these passages the table is the locus of divine judgement because it is here that YHWH's enemies are killed and consumed.

A quite different perspective is found in Isa. 25.6–8, where YHWH's table is appropriated into the apocalyptic vision of Isaiah 24–7 and projected into the eschatological future. At the end of time a dinner will be thrown by YHWH where the righteous and the unrighteous receive their due:

> YHWH of hosts will prepare,
> for all nations on this mountain,
> a feast of rich food, a feast of fine wines,
> rich food filled with marrow, fine wines that are well-strained;
> and he will swallow on this mountain
> the shroud that covers all peoples
> and the covering that is spread over all nations.
> He will swallow death forever,
> and Lord YHWH will wipe away tears from all faces,
> and the disgrace of his people will be taken away from all the earth
> because YHWH has spoken.

[74] M. A. Sweeney, *Zephaniah*, Hermeneia (Minneapolis: Fortress, 2003), 78.

On the face of it the passage seems to represent an undifferentiated universal-
ism where everybody from all the nations partake in YHWH's feast with only
'death' singled out for punishment. This impression needs to be modified
in light of 24.21–3, which is clearly linked to it since 'this mountain' (25.6)
is a reference to 'Mount Zion' (24.23).[75] The eschatological vision includes
the punishment of divine and human powers, including kings (24.21). The
location of the eschatological meal is nowhere other than Jerusalem, where
YHWH reveals himself before the elders of Israel (24.23)[76] and vindicates the
nation before the assembled throng of nations (25.8). There is a universalistic
horizon, but it has significant particularistic elements to it.[77]

Although the eschatological meal of YHWH is a fresh departure within the
Old Testament, it by no means lacks appropriation of earlier material. This
includes the theme of a global pilgrimage to Zion and the coronation meal.
In relation to the latter we will also need to consider the question of whether,
in fact, we have a covenant meal as has been suggested recently by Hagelia.[78]
First, we turn to the theme of an international pilgrimage to Zion. The vision
of all nations gathering together on Mount Zion finds expression in Isaiah
2.1–5, where the nations make pilgrimage to Jerusalem. This vision is projected into the future, 'in the last days' (2.2). The nations come to Zion in order
to learn YHWH's law and there on the mountain YHWH judges between the
nations. The juridical character of 2.1–5 is very pronounced and complements
24.23–5, where the heavenly powers and earthly kings are punished.

The description of the feast in 25.6–8 is usually taken to be of a coronation
meal or a meal to celebrate YHWH's kingship. Although this idea has been
related to theories of an enthronement festival in pre-exilic Israel, it is
independent of those theories because the identification of YHWH as king
in 24.23–5 is clear. The alternatives to YHWH's lordship of the earth are
imprisoned and punished and YHWH takes over direct rule of the earth from
Zion. The meal that is attended by all peoples follows on from his assumption
of universal kingship.

There are both ancient Near Eastern parallels and biblical parallels to the
divine royal meal that is portrayed in these verses. In relation to the former the

[75] H. Wildberger, 'Das Freudenmahl auf dem Zion', *TLZ* 33 (1977), 373–83, here 374.
[76] Willis suggests that the unique reference to YHWH's elders has in view the members of
the divine council, rather than the elders of Israel (T. M. Willis, 'Yahweh's Elders (Isa 24,23):
Senior Officials of the Divine Court', *ZAW* 103 (1991), 375–85). Two observations tell against
this suggestion. First, the members of the divine council are never referred to as elders elsewhere
in the Old Testament. Second, in the important parallel in Exod. 24.9–11 God is manifest to the
elders of Israel.
[77] See also the punishment of Moab in 25.10–12, which is connected to 25.6–8 by reference
to 'this mountain' (25.10).
[78] H. Hagelia, 'Meal on Mount Zion: Does Isa 25:6–8 Describe a Covenant Meal?' *SEÅ* 68
(2003), 73–96.

coronations of Marduk in *Enuma Elish* and Baal in the Ugaritic texts have often been noted. In both cases a myth celebrates the assumption of the national god to universal kingship which entails the defeat of cosmic opposition and a festive meal. It has rightly been observed that the participants in these meals are always other divine beings, and the human participants in 25.6–8 are a significant development within this ancient Near Eastern motif. The biblical parallels include the coronation texts that we have already examined in the previous chapter, where the assumption of a human king to the throne is often marked by a celebratory feast.

One of the most significant biblical parallels to the eschatological meal in Isaiah 25 is Exod. 24.9–11. After the delivery of the terms of the covenant to Moses the elders of Israel are invited up onto mount Sinai. There they see the God of Israel and eat in his presence. In relation to Isaiah 25, the consumption of a meal in the divine presence is striking as also is the emphasis on the elders. A further parallel is observable, for Exod. 24.9–11 appears to describe YHWH in terms that allude to his kingship. According to 24.10 'under his feet there was something like a pavement of sapphire as clear as the heavens'. This description of the heavenly pavement is reminiscent of Ezekiel's description of the enthroned YHWH who sits on a sapphire throne placed upon a frosted heavenly expanse (Ezekiel 1).[79]

The question must be addressed of whether Exodus 24 portrays a 'covenant meal' and whether this is also the case for Isaiah 25. Certainly ratification of a covenant through commensal eating and drinking is known in the Old Testament (e.g. Gen. 26.26–30; 31.43–53) and it has been suggested that this is the significance of the meal in Exod. 24.11.[80] Yet, Smend rightly warns against interpreting every meal in close proximity to a covenant as a covenant meal.[81] Eating and drinking are not synonymous with covenant making. Indeed, in Exodus 24 the ratification of the covenant appears to be limited to vv. 3–8 and takes place between YHWH and the people, and not with the elders as representatives of the people.[82] Exodus 24.9–11, on the other hand, concentrates on the theophanic appearance of YHWH in kingly splendour.[83] The meal is a

---

[79] See T. C. Vriezen, 'The Exegesis of Exodus xxiv 9–11', in M. A. Beek et al. (eds.), *The Witness of Tradition*, OTS, 17 (Leiden: Brill, 1972), 100–33.

[80] M. Noth, *Exodus*, OTL (London: SCM Press, 1962), 196; Vriezen, 'Exegesis of Exodus xxiv 9–11'.

[81] Smend, 'Essen und Trinken'.

[82] Verses 1–2, 9–11 and 3–8 were distinguished in the traditional historical-critical analysis of this chapter, see, *inter alia*, E. W. Nicholson, 'The Origin of the Tradition in Exodus xxiv 9–11', *VT* 26 (1976), 148–60.

[83] For Exod. 24.9–11 as a theophany see E. W. Nicholson, 'The Interpretation of Exodus xxiv 9–11', *VT* 24 (1974), 77–97; E. W. Nicholson, 'The Antiquity of the Tradition in Exodus xxiv 9–11', *VT* 25 (1975), 69–79; Nicholson, 'Origin of the Tradition in Exodus xxiv'. Nicholson believes that 'eating and drinking' is only an indication that the elders rejoiced or worshipped in the presence of YHWH. There are two problems with this suggestion. First, the comparison that Nicholson

celebration of this kingship eaten by the elders in the presence of YHWH. It is not necessary, then, to interpret Exod. 24.11 as a covenant meal, and this is even more true of Isa. 24.21–3; 25.6–8, which lacks any explicit reference to a covenant.[84]

The eschatological meal in Isa. 25.6–8 is, therefore, rightly seen as a meal that celebrates YHWH's kingship over the earth. Consequently all the nations are invited to the meal. This meal is the context for divine judgement, most especially in relation to 'death', which is consumed by YHWH. We must not, though, assume that the annihilation of death means judgement is absent for the peoples of the earth. As we have seen, the heavenly powers and the earthly kings are judged and punished. Israel, on the other hand, is vindicated before all. We can conclude, then, that the table in Isaiah 25 belongs to the motif of judgement and vindication at the table, but in this case it is projected uniquely into the eschatological future.

CONCLUSION

In the Old Testament the table is the locus for judgement and vindication. Possibly this idea developed from the royal table as the place where favour was shown to the servants of the king. To be raised to sit at the table amongst

---

is making is to quite distinctive Deuteronomic expressions which belong to Deuteronomy's rhetoric of feasting (see Chapter 3). These cannot without significant qualification be adduced as parallels to a tradition that Nicholson is seeking to argue is 'of great antiquity' (Nicholson, 'Antiquity of the Tradition in Exodus xxiv', 70). Second, the rejoicing that is to accompany the feast is always made explicit. In other words, 'eating and drinking' are not used as a cipher for rejoicing in the examples that Nicholson adduces. Nicholson's later argument that 'eating and drinking' is a cipher for 'live' is equally problematic (Nicholson, 'Origin of the Tradition in Exodus xxiv', 148–50).

Nicholson does not, then, provide a satisfactory account of the 'eating and drinking' in Exod. 24.11. He resists the suggestion that what is in view is a royal banquet, and his controversy with Vriezen at this point is instructive. Vriezen argued that Exod. 24.9–11 utilized royal imagery as part of a larger argument that 24.11 referred to a covenant meal. According to him 24.11 portrays a royal king eating with his vassals. Nicholson argues that 24.9–11 belongs to a theophany tradition and does not allude to a covenant meal. 'Accordingly, it cannot be maintained, in my opinion, that what is here described resembles a royal banquet held by a king for his vassals' (Nicholson, 'Origin of the Tradition in Exodus xxiv', 156). Yet, *contra* both Vriezen and Nicholson, the recognition of an allusion to YHWH's kingship and, possibly, a coronation meal does not entail subscribing to the view that this meal is also a covenant meal.

[84] Despite attempts to argue that Isa. 25.6–8 is a covenant text, Hagelia rightly observes that 'it lacks some of the distinctive marks of a covenant text' (Hagelia, 'Meal on Mount Zion', 16). His arguments turn especially on establishing intertextual links with Isa. 24.5–6; 28.15, 18 and 55.1–5. Yet it is not clear that all these links are well founded or that covenant can be transferred from them to Isa. 25.6–8.

the 'sons of the king' was a great honour. Nevertheless, the table was also a place for competitive struggles and could also be the place at which shaming or dishonour took place. Since YHWH is also portrayed as a king in the Old Testament it is not surprising that the table becomes a locus for his judgements. The structure of the books of Samuel and Kings may reflect this notion in order to suggest the possibility of a future hope for the Davidic king, understated as this may appear to an uninitiated reader. The theme of judgement at the table is also apparent in the prophetic metaphor of the cup of wrath and the overflowing cup of Psalm 23. Perhaps most influential on later Jewish and Christian thinking is the portrayal of the end of time as a feasting occasion when the wicked are punished and the righteous vindicated on Mount Zion (Isa. 25.6–8).

7

You Are How You Eat: Food and Identity
in the Post-exilic Period

The role of food in generating and sustaining national identities is well docu-
mented in literature on food and foodways.[1] French and English cuisine, for
example, often function as dialogical opposites and as such are seen not only
to represent different food cultures, but to embody national characteristics.
French food aimed at innovative and sophisticated recipes which began as
an imitation of the royal court. English food, on the other hand, sought
rusticity and plainness embodied in the housewife ideal of a Mrs Beaton,
or even a Delia Smith. The different cuisines find expression in alternative
ideals of manners at the table. This contrast can take on an abbreviated
form where the English describe the French as 'frogs legs' and the French,
the English as *les rosbifs*. As an important element of national characterization what matters is not only the food that one eats (and also shuns),
but also the manners that accompany it. Together they form a grammar of
identity.[2]

In the present chapter we will examine the role of food in the identity
of post-exilic Jews. That food had an important role alongside other factors
such as circumcision and the keeping of the Sabbath has long been observed
in Old Testament scholarship, but its role has tended to be limited to the
dietary laws. We will see that the dietary laws come to particular prominence
within Judaism only in the Maccabean period in response to Hellenizing.
Nevertheless, when this does occur it is alongside other expressions of Jewish
food culture. In particular, attention will be given to the characterization of
the Persians as gluttonous others in order to develop an ethic of moderation.
As the title of this chapter suggests it is not a case of 'you are what you eat',
but also 'you are how you eat'. In addition, it will be argued that this portrayal
of the Persians probably derives from the perception of the Persians by the

---

[1] An earlier version of some of this chapter appeared as 'Food and Drink in Tobit and Other
"Diaspora Novellas"', in M. R. J. Bredin (ed.), *Studies in the Book of Tobit*, LSTS, 55 (London:
T&T Clark, 2006), 165–78.
[2] For a thorough and nuanced history of French and English cuisine and their interrelationship, see Mennell, *All Manners of Food*.

Greeks. Thus, the relationship to Greek influences is complex as, indeed, are Jewish responses to the Achaemenid empire.

In this chapter particular attention will be given to food-related literary motifs as they are found in a number of diaspora novellas from the Second Temple period, such as Esther, Daniel, Judith, the story of the Three Guardsmen in 1 Esdras, and Tobit.[3] These stories offer an interesting field for the study of food because of the greater freedom writers of fiction have in their use of material than is often the case with other genres. In her work on food in Roman literature, Emily Gowers justifies her use of fiction in the following way:

> In fiction the author has most control over his choice of material. The sifting process involved gives us a better idea of the applications of food or its use as a focus for other ideas than, say a book on dietetics, a farming manual, or a cookery book. . . . Another advantage of fictional evidence is the writer's use of metaphor, which picks out correspondences across wide fields of experience.[4]

In the case of the Jewish tales from the Second Temple period it will be seen that the authors of these works use a limited selection of ingredients derived from both Israelite and Greek sources, but in doing so they create at least one novel combination.

---

[3] For the description 'diaspora novellas' see A. Meinhold, 'Die Gattung der Josephgeschichte und des Estherbuches: Diasporanovelle I', *ZAW* 87 (1975), 306–24 and A. Meinhold, 'Die Gattung der Josephgeschichte und des Estherbuches: Diasporanovelle II', *ZAW* 88 (1976), 72–93. Meinhold restricts 'diaspora novellas' to short tales in a diaspora setting where a single Jew rises to a position of influence. Tobit does not belong to this genre because it does not have a court setting, even though it is set in the Jewish diaspora.

In his discussion of these works, Lawrence Wills prefers to describe them as 'Jewish novels'. 'Jewish novels, for example, are shorter than modern novels or even Greek and Roman novels...[but] the term novella, for instance, in the modern idiom generally refers to carefully crafted literary works that are too short to be novels and too long to be short stories and that are often seen as derived forms of the more rambling novel... In the study of ancient literature and culture, novella is often used for oral narratives that are short and entertaining, set in the real world instead of the make believe world of fairy tale, and focused on a single unexpected turn of events' (L. M. Wills, *The Jewish Novel in the Ancient World* (Ithaca: Cornell University Press, 1995), 7). In terms of their size, Daniel, Esther, Tobit and Judith are closer to novellas, as Wills recognizes. A significant issue for Wills in the use of 'novella' for these Jewish tales is his belief that they were transparently fictional to their readers. In my view, the appearance of significant Jewish protagonists in the late Mesopotamian empires and the presence of historical anachronisms, such as 'Nebuchadnezzar the Assyrian' are more likely to reflect historical confusion on the part of the authors than the use of 'a set of narrative "facts" that would have been instantly recognized by the audience as historical impossibilities' (3). It is all very well appealing, as Wills does, to Herodotus' concern to distinguish between history and myth, but by what authorities could audiences judge the historical plausibility of the claims being made by these narratives?

[4] Gowers, *Loaded Table*, 12.

FOOD CONSCIOUSNESS IN POST-EXILIC JUDAISM

The Dietary Laws in Post-exilic Judaism

The importance of the dietary laws for sustaining the identity of displaced Judahites during the Babylonian exile has often been noted. The defeat of the last Israelite kingdom and the destruction of Jerusalem and its temple was a significant crisis for the exiled community, some of whom found a way to maintain their belief in YHWH through a set of practices that could be performed outside of Palestine. In particular, a number of observances, such as the Sabbath, circumcision and the food laws, became important boundary markers between the exiles and their neighbours in Babylonia. Rainer Albertz's observations are typical,

> Alongside circumcision, during the exile the traditional dietary customs probably for the first time played a part in establishing identity, even if we know little about them in detail. Here too the development will have begun from the Babylonian exiles, who in a foreign land suddenly found that some of the dietary customs they had previously taken for granted were a peculiarity of their people. . . . Even if many dietary customs and regulations go well back into the pre-exilic period, and their original significance escapes us, it is probable that the detailed casuistry in the defining of clean and unclean animals to be found in Deut. 14 and in an even more refined form in Lev. 11 arose from this need in the exilic situation. They gave the exilic family an important mark of identity with the aid of which they could demonstrate in everyday life whether or not they still counted themselves among the people of Judah and held fast to their religious traditions.[5]

That the dietary laws reached their final form in the exilic, or more probably post-exilic, period is generally accepted, but we should be careful not to draw too much from this historical-critical result. First, as Albertz notes, the dietary laws as we now have them were probably not composed *de novo* but represent, at least in part, existing Israelite customs. The prophet Hosea threatens the northern kingdom with defilement in exile: 'They shall not dwell in the land of YHWH, but Ephraim shall return to Egypt and they shall eat unclean food in Assyria' (Hos. 9.3). It is unclear whether the defilement is caused by eating a food that is deemed unclean or by the consumption of food in 'an unclean land' (Amos 7.17), which belonged to other gods (1 Sam. 26.19).[6] Ezekiel also refers to notions of clean and unclean food: 'As for you take wheat, barley, beans, lentils, millet and spelt, place them in a vessel and make bread for

---

[5] R. Albertz, *A History of Israelite Religion in the Old Testament Period*, vol. 2: *From the Exiles to the Maccabees* (London: SCM Press, 1994), 408.

[6] The latter possibility is strengthened by the parallel in Amos 7.17 and the unique reference to Palestine as 'the land of YHWH' in Hos. 9.3.

yourself.... You shall eat it as a barley cake, baking it with human dung in their sight. Yнwн says, "So shall the sons of Israel eat their bread, unclean among the nations"' (Ezek. 4.9, 12–13). The problem appears not to have been the bread with its various ingredients, but the cooking with human dung as is clear from the subsequent exchange between God and Ezekiel (Ezek. 4.13–15).[7] This regulation is not found in the Pentateuchal laws about clean and unclean food, though the other regulations to which Ezekiel refers are known: 'I have not eaten a carcass or a torn animal ... nor has an abominable thing come into my mouth' (Ezek. 4.14). Thus, the regulations known from the prophetic books appear to differ in some ways from what we have in Leviticus 11 and Deuteronomy 14, but do evidence the existence of notions of clean and unclean food in the pre-exilic period. Second, the exilic and early post-exilic period saw the final codification of all of the lawcodes of the Pentateuch. Although the food laws appear, quite exceptionally, in both priestly and Deuteronomic versions, it may be mistaken to give these laws special prominence as expressions of Jewish identity. There are many other legal prescriptions that also receive their final literary codification at this time.

Hesitation at this point is warranted when we consider what evidence exists for the dietary laws having such an important role in the exilic and post-exilic periods. This proves to be relatively thin prior to the time of the Maccabees. In the Hebrew Bible the prohibition of pork appears only in Isaiah 65–6 outside Leviticus 11 and Deuteronomy 14. In Isa. 65.3–4 the prophet accuses his hearers of continually provoking yнwн. They are those 'who sit inside tombs and spend their nights in secret places; who eat the pig's flesh, and whose vessels hold broth of abominable things'. In the following chapter the end is announced of 'those who eat pig's flesh, the detestable thing, and the mouse' (66.17). The context, which describes acts of necromancy and incubation (65.3–4), suggests that it is not the consumption of pork as such that angers the prophet, but rather the consultation of the dead (cf. 66.3). Nevertheless, some of the language of Isa. 65.3–4 and 66.17 echoes that found in Leviticus and it may be that the prophet is drawing upon priestly prohibitions, including Leviticus 11.[8]

---

[7] King and Stager make the rather perplexing observation that 'this unusual mixture of foodstuffs, which is legally unclean (Lev. 19:19; Deut. 22:9) and may reflect a scarcity of food, is described as siege food' (King and Stager, *Life in Biblical Israel*, 66). Lev. 19.19 and Deut. 22.9 refer to mixing crops in a field or breeding animals, and can only be transferred to cooking by analogy.

[8] For translation and discussion, see S. Ackerman, *Under Every Green Tree: Popular Religion in Sixth-Century Judah*, HSM, 46 (Atlanta: Scholars Press, 1992), 165–212; B. B. Schmidt, *Israel's Beneficent Dead: Ancestor Cult and Necromancy in Ancient Israelite Religion and Tradition*, FAT, 11 (Tübingen: Mohr Siebeck, 1994), 260–2.

The relationship of the Torah's dietary laws to the story of Daniel and his friends in the Babylonian royal court is also problematic. According to Daniel 1, Daniel and his friends keep themselves from defilement through eating vegetables and water, rather than their apportioned rations from the royal table. R. H. Charles argued that the dietary laws are in view: 'the faithful had to abstain from the food of the heathen, not only because the Levitical laws as to clean and unclean animals were not observed by the heathen in the selection and preparation of their food, but also because the food so prepared had generally been offered to idols'.[9] As Charles perceived, though, Daniel's scruples cannot be explained on the basis of the dietary laws alone. The passage describes the concern as one of 'defilement', and whilst meat may be defiled (Mal. 1.7, 12) there is no Pentateuchal law that prohibits the consumption of wine.[10] Consequently Goldingay argues that 'pagan food and drink may simply epitomize the pagan uncleanness associated with exile...Daniel's abstinence thus symbolizes his avoiding assimilation'.[11]

Daniel's practice represents an extreme position among Jews in his refusal to eat the royal food. The same level of discipline is found in the story of Judith. Judith refuses Holofernes' fare and provides her own clean food, which she carries to the Assyrian camp in a bag (Jdt. 10.5; 12.1–3).[12] In this way she prevents herself being defiled, a danger that she asserts is now present within the town of Betuliah because of the siege: 'since their food supply is exhausted and their water has almost given out, they have planned to kill their livestock and have determined to use all that God by his laws has forbidden them to eat. They have decided to consume the first fruits of the grain and the tithes of the wine and oil, which they had consecrated and set aside for the priests who minister in the presence of our God in Jerusalem—things it is not lawful for any of the people even to touch with their hands' (Jdt. 11.12–13).[13] On the other hand, other prominent Jews were not as scrupulous in their relation to court food. Jehoiachin, as we have seen, ate at the king's table in Babylon (2 Kgs. 25.27–30). The Esther of the Masoretic Text also exhibits no qualms

---

[9] R. H. Charles, *A Critical and Exegetical Commentary on the Book of Daniel* (Oxford: Clarendon Press, 1929), 19.

[10] J. J. Collins, *Daniel*, Hermeneia (Minneapolis: Fortress Press, 1993), 142.

[11] J. E. Goldingay, *Daniel*, WBC, 30 (Dallas: Word Books, 1989), 19.

[12] The description of the bread as 'pure' (*katharon*) may be an indication that it is ritually clean, or a description of its quality (see C. A. Moore, *Judith*, AB, 40 (Garden City, NY: Doubleday, 1985), 201).

[13] This example from Judith is particularly interesting for the development it evidences from pre-exilic notions that eating in a foreign land were defiling. It is evident that for the writer of Judith, Jews in exile and in diaspora (Judith in the Assyrian camp) are on the same level as those who live in the land (the Jews in Betuliah). The obligation to obey the law in respect to the food laws is placed on all equally regardless of location.

about receiving portions of food in the palace (Esther 2.9) or participating in the many celebratory banquets. It is only in the Old Greek version that Esther is portrayed as someone who refused to participate in the royal feasts or drink the king's wine (14.16). In the words of David Clines, the additions to the story of Esther that are evidenced in the Old Greek 'assimilate the book of Esther to a scriptural norm'.[14] Tobit belongs outside the royal sphere, but he also expresses his piety, already apparent before his exile to Nineveh, through his avoidance of Gentile food (Tob. 1.10–11). Fitzmyer understands this as the fulfilment of the Jewish dietary regulations, but since such actions prove Tobit to be 'duly mindful of God' (1.12), what may be in view is a general avoidance of assimilation rather than obedience to a specific commandment.[15] The book of *Jubilees* makes no mention of the dietary laws, despite the importance of various other features of Jewish identity in the book.[16] The solitary reference to food identity is in Isaac's blessing of Jacob, where he exhorts him to obey the commandments of Abraham: 'Separate from the nations, and do not eat with them. Do not act as they do, and do not become their companion; for their actions are something that is impure, and all their ways are defiled and something abominable and detestable. They offer their sacrifices to the dead, and they worship demons. They eat in tombs, and everything they do is empty and worthless' (22.16–17).[17] It is commensality that exercises *Jubilees*, not the food laws.

These texts demonstrate the importance of the developing food conscious-ness amongst Jews in the Second Temple period, although not all can be directly related to the dietary laws. The stories of Tobit and Daniel may be pre-Maccabean,[18] and there are grounds for thinking that broader concerns about food and assimilation are in view rather than the specific issues of Leviticus 11 and Deuteronomy 14. The book of *Jubilees*, which probably dates

---

[14] D. J. A. Clines, *The Esther Scroll: The Story of the Story*, JSOTSup, 30 (Sheffield: JSOT Press, 1984), 169.

[15] J. A. Fitzmyer, *Tobit*, Commentaries on Early Jewish Literature (Berlin: de Gruyter, 2003), 113.

[16] This is especially notable in the light of VanderKam's observation that, 'several writers have understood the book to be directed against the influences of Hellenism, particularly what is understood to be the tendency of its Jewish adherents to drop the distinctive traits of Judaism in favor of a more accommodating form of religion' (J. C. VanderKam, 'The Origins and Purposes of the Book of Jubilees', in M. Albani, J. Frey and A. Lange (eds.), *Studies in the Book of Jubilees*, Texte und Studien zum antiken Judentum, 65 (Tübingen: Mohr Siebeck, 1997), 3–24, here 16).

[17] J. C. VanderKam, *The Book of Jubilees*, Corpus scriptorum Christianorum orientalium, 511 (Leuven: Peeters, 1989), 131.

[18] For the date of Tobit see the recent discussion by Fitzmyer, *Tobit*, 50–4. The date of Daniel 1 cannot be separated from questions about the literary integrity of the whole book. For the question of the age of the stories in Daniel and their relationship to the visions, see, e.g., Collins, *Daniel*, 24–38.

from some point in the middle of the first century BC,[19] also lacks a concern with the dietary laws. In this respect the heightened concern of Greek Esther compared to Hebrew Esther may be significant as evidence that it is only in the Maccabean period that the dietary laws become such an important marker of Jewish identity.

The importance of the dietary laws from the Maccabean period onwards finds clearest expression in the stories of the Maccabees. According to 1 Maccabees the crisis initiated by Antiochus IV Epiphanes included a number of elements, not least the defilement of the Jerusalem temple through the sacrifice, and presumably also the consumption, of 'swine and other unclean beasts' (1.47). The Jewish resistance to these decrees included the refusal to eat unclean food, even though this meant death (1.62–3). The succinct formulations in 1 Maccabees find extended narrative rehearsal in the account of the Maccabean martyrs in 2 Maccabees 6.18–7.24. The aged sage Eleazer refuses to eat pork, not only spitting it out when it was forced into his mouth, but refusing the pleas of his compatriots to eat other meat pretending that it is pork (6.18–28). 'But he, welcoming death with honour rather than life with pollution, went up to the rack of his own accord, spitting out the flesh, as all ought to go who have the courage to refuse things that it is not right to taste, even for the natural love of life' (6.19–20). In the story of the mother and her seven sons it is again the consumption of pork that is the symbol of apostasy: 'It happened also that seven brothers and their mother were arrested and were being compelled by the king, under torture with whips and thongs, to partake of unlawful swine's flesh' (7.1). Each submits himself to death, allowing their own flesh to be cooked, rather than eating unclean flesh. The significance of the food laws for Jewish identity in a Hellenistic context continues to be apparent in literature from after the second century BC. Thus, for example, in 4 Maccabees the actions and words of the Maccabean martyrs are expounded at length and in the *Letter of Aristeas*, of all the material in the Torah, it is the food laws that receive particular attention.[20]

In sum, there is clear evidence of a developing food consciousness in Second Temple Judaism, but the role of the Torah's dietary laws in this

---

[19] For dating see J. A. Goldstein, 'The Date of the Book of Jubilees', *Proceedings of the American Academy for Jewish Research* 50 (1983), 63–86; R. H. Charles, *The Book of Jubilees* (London: A. and C. Black, 1902), lviii–lxiii; J. C. VanderKam, *Textual and Historical Studies in the Book of Jubilees*, HSM, 14 (Missoula: Scholars Press, 1977), 207–85.

[20] 4 Maccabees is probably to be dated to the first century AD (see D. A. deSilva, *4 Maccabees*, Septuagint Commentary Series (Leiden: Brill, 2006), xiv–xvii). The *Letter of Aristeas* may tentatively be dated to sometime during the first century BC. Note, however, that my colleague Jim Davila raises the possibility that vv. 82–171 were a later interpolation, since they are not cited by Josephus (J. R. Davila, 'The Letter of Aristeas', http://www.st-andrews.ac.uk/~www_sd/aristeas.html, accessed 17 May 2007).

food consciousness should not be over-emphasized. No doubt many obser-vant Jews in the Second Temple period kept to the dietary restrictions in Leviticus and Deuteronomy, but it is only in a Hellenistic environment and, in particular, through the Maccabean crisis that the dietary laws become such important touchstones of Jewish identity. As Collins observes, 'the aversion to foreign food was intensified by the experience of the Maccabean era'.[21] In addition, the food consciousness of the Second Temple period was far broader than a concern with permitted and prohibited foods. In what fol-lows I wish to argue that it was also expressed through a certain attitude to food that contrasted with that believed to be displayed by their political overlords.

PERSIAN CONSPICUOUS CONSUMPTION

The diaspora novellas display a fascination with the culinary practices of the Persian nobility. The most important expression of the distinctive Persian taste was the feast. The book of Esther, in particular, utilizes the Persian feast as a motif in a most sustained manner. Michael Fox observes that, 'the book opens with a banquet, the denouement occurs at a banquet, and the crisis eventuates in a perennial banquet'.[22] The description of the opening banquet depicts a lavish Persian court. The feast for the officials lasts 180 days and is followed by a feast for all the people of Susa lasting seven days. Interestingly the extravagance of the meals is conveyed not by a description of the food, but the overall aesthetic experience:

There were white cotton curtains and blue hangings tied with cords of fine linen and purple to silver rings and marble pillars. There were couches of gold and silver on a mosaic pavement of porphyry, marble, mother-of-pearl, and coloured stones. Drinks were served in goblets of different kinds, and the royal wine was lavished according to the bounty of the king. (1.6–7).

The feast is an exercise in what has been described as 'conspicuous consump-tion', and food is not the only item to be consumed. It is this appreciation of beauty as part of the feast that leads to the plot's development. For Xerxes also wants his guests to feast their eyes on his wife (1.11). Banquets, then, are a

---

[21] Collins, *Daniel*, 143.

[22] M. V. Fox, *Character and Ideology in the Book of Esther*, 2nd edn (Grand Rapids: Eerdmans, 2001), 156. 'Esther's author constructed a tale whose beginning, middle and conclusion center upon the motif of feasting. In addition each of these banquet pairs recalls the others, simul-taneously paralleling and contrasting with them' (S. B. Berg, *The Book of Esther*, SBLDiss, 44 (Missoula: Scholars Press, 1979), 35).

public display of the wealth one possesses and the honour in which one is to be held (1.4).

In Judith, Holofernes appears as a Persian satrap, with his tent serving as dining room. As Pierre Briant observes: 'The best description of a Persian general's tent appears in the book of Judith, namely, the tent of Holofernes.'[23] That the rigours of the campaign were not to interfere with the enjoyment of the table is clear at the start of the book when the Assyrian army is mustered. The narrator shows little interest in describing the army and its regiments, but does grant a couple of verses to describing the provisions that the Persian host took with them.

He took along a vast number of camels and donkeys and mules for transport, and innumerable sheep and oxen and goats for food; also ample rations for everyone, and a huge amount of gold and silver from the royal palace.   (Jdt. 2.17–18)

This is, in the words attributed to Napoleon, 'an army that marches on its stomach'. At the height of the campaign when Judith is captured she is escorted into Holofernes' tent. It is far from the austere experience that we might expect for the height of a military campaign. 'Holofernes was resting on his bed under a canopy that was woven with purple and gold, emeralds and other precious stones. When they told him of her, he came to the front of the tent, with silver lamps carried before him' (10.21–2). Entranced by her beauty Holofernes has a table laid out with silverware, delicacies and wine (12.1–3). Again the concern of a diaspora novella writer with the total aesthetic experience is striking.

The aesthetic excesses of the table of the Mesopotamian empires are also to be found in the book of Daniel. In Belshazzar's feast the display of wealth and beauty takes an iniquitous turn with the Babylonians' profanation of the gold and silver vessels from the Jerusalem temple (Dan. 5.1–4). In 1 Esdras it is a royal Persian feast that provides the occasion for the story of the three guardsmen (3.1–4.42). Again it is the size of the banquet that is noted: 'Now King Darius gave a great banquet for all that were under him, all his household, and all the nobles of Media and Persia, and all the satraps, commanders and governors that were under him in the one hundred and twenty-seven satrapies from India to Ethiopia' (3.1–2). How exactly the feast relates to the contest of wits between the guardsmen is unclear within the logic of story. According to 1 Esdras, it is while Darius is sleeping off the effects of the feast that the guardsmen challenge themselves to find the strongest thing

---

[23] P. Briant, *From Cyrus to Alexander: A History of the Persian Empire* (Winona Lake, IN: Eisenbrauns, 2002), 347. It need hardly be noted that Judith's portrayal is at odds with the presentation of Holofernes as an *Assyrian* general under the command of the *Babylonian* Nebuchadnezzar. Judith's confusion at this point is well known.

in the world.[24] It is, though, somewhat strange that the guardsmen themselves promise an extravagant reward from Darius to the one who proves to be the wisest. Josephus finds this perplexing and narrates the story with the king waking in the night as a result of his overeating. Unable to return to sleep he seeks diversion from his guardsmen. During this conversation he offers a prize to the one who shows himself wisest.[25] However the story is pursued, both versions emphasize the size of the feast and the consequences of the king's excessive appetite.

Persian Feasts through Greek Eyes

This fascination with the excesses of the Persian table was not restricted to Jewish writers. There are a number of parallels in Greek literature that are well known and have been the focus of a number of studies. Pierre Briant writes:

> Of all the symbols of this power to impose tribute, the Greeks were particularly impressed by the splendour and luxury of the king's table. In the polemical portrait of the Great King drawn in the *Agesilaus*, Xenophon writes: 'The Persian king has vintners scouring every land to find some drink that will tickle his palate; an army of cooks contrives dishes for his delight'. Many Greek authors returned to this theme, often stating that the Great King regularly rewarded those who brought new foodstuffs for his table with prizes and payment. The king's table in its sumptuousness and variety was in fact considered emblematic of the political and material might of the Great King.[26]

Herodotus tantalizes his readers with reports that animals as big as oxen or horses were roasted whole,[27] and notes the Persian devotion to wine and how they made decisions when drunk that they reconsidered when sober and vice versa. Polyaenus describes how after his victory Alexander the Great was served according to the style of the Persian king. The menu he tells us was inscribed on a bronze pillar and ran to no fewer than forty-seven items, including wheat, barley, sheep, cattle, pigeons, fresh milk, whey, garlic, onion, cumin, dill, sesame, grape jelly, salt, parsley, various oils and wine. The allocations for his soldiers are also enumerated.[28] Greek writers also record that 'when the king and court were on the road, the entire kitchen staff went with them'.[29]

In their enumeration of the items on the menu, the Greek writers show an interest in culinary details that escapes the writers of the diaspora novellas.

---

[24] For failure to sleep after a large feast, cf. Esther 6.1.   [25] *Ant.* 9.3.1–9.
[26] Briant, *Cyrus*, 200.
[27] Herodotus, *History* I.133. Cf. Aristophanes, *Acharnians* 85–9, cited in Athenaeus, *Deipnosophists* IV.131.
[28] Polyaenus, *Strategems* IV.3.32.   [29] Briant, *Cyrus*, 292.

Nevertheless, amongst Greek writers too there is a strong interest not only in the king's fare and his taste for novel dishes, but the whole aesthetic spectacle. They describe the attendant female musicians and artists, the royal furnishings and furniture, and the luxurious vessels. Herodotus describes the Persian camp as 'tents adorned with gold and silver, and couches gilded and silver-plated; and golden bowls and cups and other drinking vessels; and sacks they found on wains, wherein were seen cauldrons of gold and silver'.[30] Athenaeus quotes Parmenion's inventory of booty taken from the Persians, 'gold cups, weight seventy-three Babylonian talents, fifty-two minae; cups inlaid with precious stones, weight fifty-six Babylonian talents, thirty-four minae'.[31]

The Greek descriptions of Persian meals provide a fascinating picture of the role of food and drink in the Achaemenian court. Feasting appears to have played an important role in the Persian imperial ideology as an exhibition of wealth, power and status. As such the practice was probably disseminated through the Persian imperial bureaucracy as Nehemiah's governor feasts would appear to suggest. The importance of feasting is no surprise given that the Persians were heirs to a long history of feasting in Near Eastern empires. Texts from earlier periods indicate the importance of feasting within Mesopotamian imperial economies, as do the portrayals of banqueting scenes in reliefs and on seals.[32] The biblical descriptions of royal feasts that we examined in Chapter 5 indicate that the ideology of royal feasting was widely shared.

Nevertheless, despite the ubiquity of the royal feast in the ancient Near East we should take note of Sancisi-Weerdenburg's warning about taking these descriptions in Greek writers at face value, even though it is somewhat over-stated: 'It may legitimately be suspected that these statements do not serve to

---

[30] Herodotus, *History* IX.80 (translation from Herodotus, *Herodotus IV*, trans. A. D. Godley, Loeb Classical Library (London: William Heinemann, 1924)).

[31] Athenaeus, *Deipnosophists* XI.781–2 (translation from Athenaeus, *Athenaeus V*, trans. C. B. Gulick, Loeb Classical Library (Cambridge, MA: Harvard University Press, 1933)).

[32] J. M. Sasson, 'The King's Table: Food and Fealty in Old Babylonian Mari', in C. Grottanelli and L. Milano (eds.), *Food and Identity in the Ancient World*, History of the Ancient Near East Studies, 9 (Padua: Sargon, 2004), 179–215; J.-M. Dentzer, *Le motif du banquet couché dans le Proche-Orient et le mode grec du VIIe au IVe siècle avant J.C.* (Rome: École Française de Rome, 1982); R. D. Barnett, 'Assurbanipal's Feast', *Eretz Israel* 18 (1985), 1–6; H. Frankfort, *Cylinder Seals: A Documentary Essay on the Art and Religion of the Ancient Near East* (London: Macmillan, 1939), 77–8, 197, 272; Pollock, 'Feasts'; F. Pinnock, 'Considerations on the "Banquet Theme" in the Figurative Art of Mesopotamia and Syria', in L. Milano (ed.), *Drinking in Ancient Societies: History and Culture of Drinks in the Ancient Near East* (Padua: Sargon, 1994), 15–26; D. Schmandt-Besserat, 'Feasting in the Ancient Near East', in M. Dietler and B. Hayden (eds.), *Feasts: Archaeological and Ethnographic Perspectives on Food, Politics and Power* (Washington: Smithsonian Institution Press, 2000), 391–403. For a discussion of some aspects of banqueting practice taken over by the Persian empire from its Mesopotamian predecessors, see S. Parpola, 'The Leftovers of God and King: On the Distribution of Meat at the Assyrian and Achaemenid Imperial Courts', in C. Grottanelli and L. Milano (eds.), *Food and Identity in the Ancient World*, History of the Ancient Near East Studies, 9 (Padua: Sargon, 2004), 281–312.

convey information on Persia, but rather serve as an implicit or explicit means of comparison with Greek customs.'[33] Such explicit comparisons are found when, in contrast to what they saw as Persian indulgence and decadence, the Greeks characterize themselves as moderate at the table. Herodotus, for example, tells of how Pausanias of Sparta ordered a dinner to be prepared after he had defeated the Persian army. In the camp of the conquered Persians his servants prepare the meal in Persian style.

Pausanias, when he saw golden and silvern couches richly covered, and tables of gold and silver, and all the magnificent splendour before him, and for a jest bade his own servants prepare a dinner after Laconian fashion. When the meal was ready and was far different from the other, Pausanias fell a-laughing, and sent for the generals of the Greeks. They being assembled, Pausanias pointed to the fashion after which either dinner was served, and said: 'Men of Hellas, I have brought you hither because I desired to show you the foolishness of the leader of the Medes; who, with such provision for life as you see, came hither to take away from us ours, that is so pitiful.'[34]

The rich descriptions of Persian feasts were not merely intended to tickle the imagination of Greek readers, they also passed clear moral judgement.

Persians as Drunks and Gluttons

The excesses of the Persian feasts function in a similar way in the diaspora novellas, though in them it is especially the excessive consumption of wine that forms the point of contrast. Thus, in the story of Esther, the omission of food from the menu is not unimportant. Drunkenness is an important aspect of the book's characterization of the Persian king, a characterization that is important for the development of the plot. In Xerxes' feasts, then, it is natural for readers to assume that many items were consumed, yet it is only wine that is mentioned. Indeed, the use of the term *mishteh* throughout Esther suggests that the feast's primary function is as an occasion to consume wine. As Clines notes, in Esther 'banqueting has been presented to us as the Persian pastime *par excellence*', with the focus almost exclusively on drinking.[35] Xerxes is portrayed as a man making decisions according to a mood fuelled by drink. It is when he is 'merry with wine' (Esther 1.10) that he decides to

[33] H. Sancisi-Weerdenburg, 'Persian Food: Stereotypes and Political Identity', in J. Wilkins, D. Harvey and M. Dobson (eds.), *Food in Antiquity* (Exeter: University of Exeter Press, 1995), 286–302, here 287. Briant makes the observation that details in Polyaenus, for example, 'confirm that he had (indirect) access to a certain amount of original information'. Additionally some verification for the size of meals can be confirmed from the Persepolis tablets (Briant, *Cyrus*, 288, 290).

[34] Herodotus, *History*, IX.82 (translation according to Herodotus, *Herodotus IV*).

[35] Clines, *Esther*, 36.

put Vashti on display. Her refusal, possibly stemming from the debauchery that characterized the men's feast,[36] leads to the crisis that sees Esther become queen. Similarly his anger with Haman comes after drinking at the table. This judgement of the king's conduct may also be found in 3.15, where Haman and Xerxes are settling down for a drink. The king is unaware of or unconcerned by the confusion that is simultaneously engulfing the city of Susa.

In Judith it is again the unrestrained drinking that captures the imagination of the author. The deadly second feast, during which Holofernes hopes to seduce Judith, is portrayed as being so excessive that the guards retire to their beds and Holofernes drinks himself into a stupor. Indeed, Holofernes is said to have drunk 'more than he had ever drunk in any one day since he was born' (Jdt. 12.20). In the book of Daniel, Belshazzar's hubris is the result of his excessive drinking in some versions. According to Theodotion and possibly the Masoretic Text, Belshazzar 'was drinking wine in the presence of the thousand' and it was while under its influence that he ordered the Jerusalem temple vessels to be fetched.[37] Meadowcraft rightly notes that, 'although it is not specifically against the excesses of a Gentile court setting that God is complaining, perhaps there is an undercurrent of Jewish thought at work which expects bad things to happen in such scenes of dissipation, and sees them as images of human pride'.[38]

A similar portrayal arises in the story of the three guardsmen in 1 Esdras. As we have already observed, the account of Darius's vast feast has a rather unclear relationship to the competition between the guardsmen. Whilst the description of the feast gives attention only to its size, the speeches of the guardsmen reiterate the caricaturing of Persian indulgence we have found elsewhere. Thus, the speech of the first guardsman extols the strength of wine, which affects both rich and powerful. It makes not only the poor witless, but also the king (3.21). The ability of wine to befuddle the judgement is an apt critique of the Persian feasts as portrayed in other diaspora novellas. The speech of the second guardsman portrays the strength of a king who commands and it is done. Yet the commands are incoherent (4.8–9) and the speech ends with the king sitting at the table, eating and drinking before finally falling asleep. In the meantime his servants have to stand waiting for him—as indeed the guardsmen of the story have done—while he sleeps

---

[36] Berlin rightly draws attention to the Greek texts that suggest wives were dismissed from the feasts when the king and his nobles wished to indulge in licentiousness (A. Berlin, *Esther* (Philadelphia: Jewish Publication Society, 2001), 11).

[37] Theodotion's translation understands Belshazzar to be influenced by the wine, whilst the Septuagint attributes the reason to pride alone. Meadowcroft discusses the possible interpretations of MT's *bit'em hamra* (T. J. Meadowcroft, *Aramaic Daniel and Greek Daniel: A Literary Comparison*, JSOTSup, 198 (Sheffield: Sheffield Academic Press, 1995), 59–60).

[38] Meadowcroft, *Aramaic Daniel*, 58.

off the effects of the meal and drink (vv. 10–12). In the third speech the power of women is praised.[39] Like wine, women can make men witless. The speech closes with undisguised mockery of the king: 'I have seen him with Apame, the king's concubine and daughter of the honourable Bartacus. She sits at the king's right hand, seizes his crown from the head of the king and places it on her own, and she slaps him with her left hand. To all this the king can only gape open-mouthed. If she smiles at him, he laughs; if she is angry with him, he flatters her so that she will make up' (4.29–31). Again, this would be apt commentary on the portrayal of women at Persian feasts in the other diaspora novellas.[40] The competition, thus, turns into a contemptuous mocking of the Persian king, particularly when he is at the table. According to the speeches the king is a drunk, gluttonous, double-minded, and dancing to the tune of his concubine. The portrayal of the king in 1 Esdras is congruent with the portrayal of foreign powers found in Daniel, Esther and Judith: an effeminate army that cannot go to war without being accompanied by all the comforts of the dining room, imperial courts that are always filled with drunken courtiers, and kings making foolish drink-fuelled decisions.

The Jewish attitude to food, on the other hand, is one characterized by moderation. A favoured approach is to juxtapose Persian feasting with Jewish fasting. In Esther while the king and Haman enjoy the continual cycle of feasts, Esther and the Jews undertake a three day fast, taking neither food nor water (Esther 4.16). As Clines observes, this is a particularly severe fast.[41] The constant fasting of the widow Judith contrasts with the drunkenness of Holofernes. Daniel too is a man who eats modestly and fasts despite his elevated position in the Babylonian and Persian courts. The moral superiority of fasting not only is revealed in the final ends of the main characters in the

---

[39] Presumably in the original story, the three speeches took as their theme wine, the king and women. The speech about 'truth' (4.34–40) is clearly an addition. Not only do we have a gap between the two speeches (4.33–4), but there is an imbalance as the third guardsman now has two suggestions for what is 'greatest'. The greatness of truth is much more appropriate on the lips of Zerubbabel and, thus, vv. 34ff. (along with v. 13) are probably part of the editing of the story to become part of 1 Esdras. 'It seems likely that we have here a popular story, only later elaborated to fit its present context, by identifying the third youth as Zerubbabel and developing his answer to allow a place for truth as well as for women' (R. J. Coggins, 'Commentary on 1 Esdras', in R. J. Coggins and M. A. Knibb, *The First and Second Books of Esdras*, CBC (Cambridge: Cambridge University Press, 1979), 1–75, here 23; *contra* Torrey, who argues that all of 3.1– 4.42 (except for the reference to Zerubbabel) originally belonged to a non-Jewish wisdom story (C. C. Torrey, 'The Story of the Three Youths', in *Ezra Studies* (New York: Ktav, 1970), 37–61)).

[40] Coggins observes on these verses, 'a similar tension between the power of the king and that of women is illustrated by the story in Esther 1 (cp. especially verses 18–20)' (Coggins, '1 Esdras', 29).

[41] Clines, *Esther*, 35–6.

novellas, but is apparent even from their appearance. Daniel and his three friends have a better physique after only ten days on their vegetarian diet. Judith is portrayed like a female St Antony, for despite her rigorous fasting she loses none of her beauty and charm (Jdt. 8.7). The implicit equation of the moral and the aesthetic is interesting and relatively unusual in the Old Testament.[42]

None of the diaspora novellas, however, envisages the extreme asceticism that is associated with early Christianity.[43] Feasting is also appropriate and during Israel's festivals a moral imperative. Despite her mourning for her husband Judith breaks her fast for the Sabbath, new moon and other festivals (8.6). Yet even Jewish feasting is characterized by moderation. In the book of Esther the fasting of the Jews is turned into feasting when Haman and the other enemies of the Jews are destroyed. But whereas the Persian feasts are characterized by their drunkenness, with food making almost no appearance, the feast of Purim is an occasion for exchanging gifts of food. Despite Purim's association in Judaism with much drinking, the book of Esther makes no mention of the Jews drinking during the feast. In Judith Achior's appearance in Bethulia is celebrated with a feast, but whilst Holofernes' feast results in a night of drunkenness, the feast in Uzziah's house becomes a night of prayer (6.21).

The book of Tobit has no reflections on Persian court life, but takes a similar attitude to food. Tobit's appetite is overridden on numerous occasions. Unlike his compatriots he does not partake of the food of the Gentiles (Tob. 1.10–11). He shares his bread with the hungry (1.17). When he sits at the table for the Feast of Weeks and observes how much food has been prepared, he delays his meal while Tobiah finds a poor Jew to share the meal. When Tobiah discovers a corpse, the meal is set aside so the appropriate duties for the dead can be observed (2.1–6). When his wife brings him a goat as a reward from her employer, Tobit insists that it be returned as he suspects it has been stolen (2.11–14).[44] This approach to life is inscribed in the wisdom instructions that Tobit gives to Tobiah before he departs (4.5–19):

---

[42] In contrast, the equation of beauty with goodness and evil with ugliness is common in Western thinking. Note expressions such as 'as ugly as sin' (C. McGinn, *Ethics, Evil and Fiction* (Oxford: Clarendon Press, 1997)).

[43] For a comparison of Jewish and Christian attitudes to fasting see V. E. Grimm, *From Feasting to Fasting, the Evolution of a Sin: Attitudes to Food in Late Antiquity* (London: Routledge, 1996).

[44] Tobit probably originated in the Hellenistic period, but it is interesting to note that in the Persian empire the king's servants were often paid with food, rather than with silver (I. Gershevitch (ed.), *The Cambridge History of Iran*, vol. 2: *The Median and Achaemenian Periods* (Cambridge: Cambridge University Press, 1985), 600–9). The Persepolis Tablets give some idea of relative values in the Persian period. A sheep was equivalent to three months' ration of wheat.

Do not drink wine to excess or let drunkenness go with you on your way. Give some of your food to the hungry, and some of your clothing to the naked. Give all your surplus as alms, and do not let your eye begrudge your giving of alms. Place your bread on the grave of the righteous, but give none to sinners.   (vv. 15–17)[45]

The well-instructed Tobiah himself prioritizes family over his stomach when he concludes an agreement to marry Sarah before settling down to a meal with her father (7.11; cf. Gen. 24.33).[46]

THE DEVELOPING FOOD CONSCIOUSNESS
IN HISTORICAL PERSPECTIVE

The characterization of the Persian 'other' especially in the diaspora novellas is an important and interesting development in the food consciousness of Judaism. We have already observed the well-known fact that food and attitude to food is an important means of national stereotyping in the modern period. This use of food was known in the ancient world too. Nemet-Nejat notes, for example, that the Sumerians boasted about their developed cuisine, and compared their diet favourably to the vulgar palates of other groups.[47] Despite this, the characterization of others through food is relatively infrequent in earlier parts of the Old Testament. Egypt, one of the most important ideological 'others' in the Old Testament, is characterized as a place of abundant food, but it is of an insubstantial kind consisting primarily of vegetables (Exod. 16.3; Num. 11.5; cf. Prov. 15.17).[48] As we have already seen, the Ammonites and Moabites are remembered in the book of Deuteronomy as inhospitable during Israel's wilderness journeys, forming a contrast with the portrayal of the Israelites as those who show hospitality to the poor and vulnerable.

The existence of a parallel Greek tradition that characterizes the Persian 'other' through 'conspicuous consumption' naturally raises questions of

[45] For a discussion of the difficult v. 17 see N. MacDonald, ' "Bread on the Grave of the Righteous" (Tob. 4.17)', in M. R. J. Bredin (ed.), *Studies in the Book of Tobit*, LSTS, 55 (London: T&T Clark, 2006), 99–103.

[46] For the significance of food in Tobit see N. S. Jacobs, ' "You Did Not Hesitate to Get Up and Leave the Dinner": Food and Eating in the Narrative of Tobit with Some Attention to Tobit's Shavuot Meal', in G. G. Xeravits and J. Zsengellér (eds.), *The Book of Tobit: Text, Tradition, Theology*, JSJSup, 98 (Leiden: Brill, 2005), 121–38. Jacobs notes the importance of delayed eating (128).

[47] K. R. Nemet-Nejat, *Daily Life in Ancient Mesopotamia* (Peabody, MA: Hendrickson, 2002), 160.

[48] Appler, 'Queen to Cuisine'.

influence. The Jewish motif has distinctive elements—we have already noted its emphasis on drinking—but there can be little doubt that the Jewish use of this motif is derived from Greek use. First, it is intrinsically more likely that the writers of diaspora novellas were influenced by Greek writers than vice versa. Second, although some of the classical writers we have utilized lived in the first centuries AD, we have already in the fifth and fourth century BC writers Herodotus and Xenophon a well-developed interest in the conspicuous consumption of the Persians. The diaspora novellas, on the other hand, stem from no earlier than the Hellenistic period. Third, as we have observed, the Persians were heirs to an imperial ideology widespread in the ancient Near East in which the magnificence and opulence of the royal table played an important role. The stories of the Solomonic table show that this ideology was known in ancient Israel and, in addition, the splendour of Solomon's feasts was a cause for celebration and not just critique. Conspicuous consumption by the ruler and his court was an alien institution only to the Greeks and thus it seems most likely that it was only in the encounter of Greek and Persian culture that the table of the foreign king became a source of fascination and ridicule.

An Ethic of Moderation

Despite its Greek origins it is clear that the motif resonates with themes from the Old Testament, and has been appropriated in a distinctive way. The criticism of Persian conspicuous consumption can be compared with the prophetic critique of excessive opulence enjoyed by the nobility in Israel. Amos, for example, utters a lament over,

> Those lying on beds of ivory,
> spread upon their couches,
> eating lambs from the flock
> and calves from the stall,
> strumming upon their harps like David,
> improvising on musical instruments,
> drinking from basins of wine.
> They anoint themselves with the finest oils,
> and feel no pain over the ruin of Joseph.
>
> (6.4–6)[49]

---

[49] 'The sumptuous provision of beef and lamb, and young and tender animals as well, points to eating on a scale far beyond the means of the ordinary worker or farmer.... The excessive behaviour described here was its own condemnation' (F. I. Andersen and D. N. Freedman, *Amos*, AB, 24A (New York: Doubleday, 1989), 562–3).

Isaiah similarly condemns those who are always at feasts with wine and song (5.11–12).[50] The diaspora novellas are heirs to this caustic critique, but their caricature is of non-Israelite overlords rather than their own elites. It is unlikely that Jews would have been in a position to enjoy the feasts, despite stories about Jewish youths flourishing in the Persian courts, and the primary intention is probably the encouragement of an ethic of moderation.

This Jewish alternative to Persian feasting—a moderation at the table that is particularly exhibited through fasting—has also been influenced by Jewish traditions. Fasting was probably known in Israel from earliest times, but it is in the post-exilic period that fasting becomes particularly important within Jewish practice. In particular, it is probably only after the destruction of Jerusalem that regular and specific fast days began to be observed.[51] It is likely that fasting became a particularly appropriate expression of Jewish piety not only because it could be practised apart from the Temple, but also because it communicated physically the state of affliction endured by the one fasting.[52] The fast draws attention to the suffering and anguish being endured with the hope that this may produce a response from God.

In the diaspora novellas fasting is consciously contrasted to Persian feasting. If feasting is a sign of wealth and status, fasting is an appeal to a different court where humility and self-denial are valued.[53] This is most apparent in the prayer that Esther utters during her fast according to the Greek versions. Esther begins with an appeal to the divine king: 'My Lord, our king, you alone are my helper'. Her prayer cites her abhorrence of the royal apparel, splendour, feasts and food (14.3–19). This is expressed in her actions while fasting:

---

[50] Criticism of those who are gluttons and drunkards is also found in legal prescriptions (Deut. 21.18–21) and wisdom sayings (Prov. 23.20–1).

[51] J. Milgrom, 'Fasting and Fast Days: In the Bible', *EncJud II*, 6: 719–21; H. A. Brongers, 'Fasting in Israel in Biblical and Post-Biblical Times', in H. A. Brongers et al., *Instruction and Interpretation: Studies in Hebrew Language, Palestinian Archaeology and Biblical Exegesis*, OTS, 20 (Leiden: Brill, 1977), 1–21; D. L. Smith-Christopher, 'Hebrew Satyagraha: The Politics of Biblical Fasting in the Post-exilic Period (Sixth to Second Century B.C.E.)', *Food and Foodways* 5 (1993), 269–92.

[52] In an extensive treatment Lambert demonstrates that fasting in the biblical period was not an expression of penitence. 'There is little evidence for the category of the penitential fast, whether as an act of atonement for sin or even as an external sign of internal contrition. Rather, fasting and its accompanying rites of weeping, rending clothes, donning sackcloth, and applying ashes function as a physical manifestation and communicative expression of anguish and affliction. "See," the one fasting declares, "how awful is my state!" ' (D. Lambert, 'Fasting as a Penitential Rite: A Biblical Phenomenon?', *HTR* 96 (2003), 477–512).

[53] In a stimulating study Smith-Christopher argues that fasting was an expression of political and spiritual resistance during the Persian period. In particular, Smith-Christopher notes control of the body by others who are politically marginalized, such as medieval women and hunger strikers in Northern Ireland (Lambert makes the same comparison, apparently independently of Smith-Christopher) (Smith-Christopher, 'Hebrew Satyagraha').

Esther the queen fled to the Lord in deathly anxiety. She took off her splendid garments, and all the signs of her rank, and clothed herself with distress and mourning.
She covered her head with ashes and dung, instead of expensive perfume. She utterly
abased her body, covering with humiliation every sign of her adornment and delight.

(14.1–2)

Judith also prays to God as 'King of all of your creation', the one who has all
power and might in his hand (Jdt. 9.11–14). For Judith the transformation
is the reverse of that undertaken by Esther as she exchanges her usual life of
prayer and fasting for the task of enchanting Holofernes:

She removed the sackcloth she had been wearing and took off her widow's dress. She
bathed herself with water and anointed herself with oil. She arranged her hair, put on
a tiara, and dressed herself in festive garments... She put sandals on her feet and put
on her anklets, bracelets, rings, earrings and all the rest of her jewellery.   (10.3–4)

Thus, fasting is the negation of feasting, and the physical humiliation that
accompanies it is the negation of the aesthetic excesses of the Persian feast.

The significance of fasting as a way of appealing to the heavenly king rather
than the earthly monarch can be found earlier than Esther and Judith. Smith-
Christopher draws attention to Ezra's fast on the banks of the Ahava. Ezra
refuses the escort offered by Artaxerxes because 'we had told the king that the
hand of our God is good to all who seek him' (Ezra 8.22). Instead the people
fast and pray for protection on the way.[54] The language of 'seeking' suggests
an appeal to a royal throne, and is found elsewhere in relation to prayer and
fasting (2 Sam. 12.6; Dan. 9.3; 2 Chron. 20.3–4).[55]

Such moderation aims at the control not only of food, but also of sex.
The Persian table is portrayed as an aesthetic feast where it is not only food
that is consumed, but also human beauty. The great feast that opens the
book of Esther sees the king wanting to exhibit his wealth and status through
the abundance of his provision and by displaying his wife. In Belshazzar's
feast the queen is absent (Dan. 5.10) and only the harem women are present
(5.2). If a similar scene is to be imagined in Esther 1 it is not surprising that
Vashti resisted being the entertainment for Xerxes' guests. She is just another
aesthetic delight to tickle the palate of the king and his court.

---

[54] Smith-Christopher, 'Hebrew Satyagraha', 272–4.

[55] Wagner notes that in the Old Testament there are two different formulas with the verb
biqqesh: 'to seek ʏʜᴡʜ' and 'to seek the face of ʏʜᴡʜ'. 'It is difficult to say which of these
two formulas is more original, whether it be the shorter indirect phrase "seeking God" or the
longer direct phrase using *panim*, "seeking the face of God". The latter is more descriptive and
immediately understandable. In the secular realm, it is used in referring to the king, "seek the
face of the king" (Prov. 29:26; cf. 1 K 10:24; 2 Ch. 9:23)' (S. Wagner, 'בקשׁ *biqqēsh*', *TDOT* 2:
229–41, here 236–7). Note also Esther's request in the context of the feast (Esther 5.3).

In the book of Judith the confusion of food, sex and death, that we argued was present in the book of Judges, is developed. In particular, it has been observed that Judith appears to be modelled on both Deborah and Jael.[56] The comparison to Jael is particularly interesting since both Sisera and Holofernes are killed in a tent by a female assassin. The moment of death coincides with a food-event and includes allusions to sexual intercourse between the slain general and his killer. In Judith the events take place in Holofernes' tent with the general on his couch, which functions as a place for eating and sleeping. Holofernes intends his tent to be not only the place where he shares a meal with Judith, but also the place of sexual conquest. Judith appears in all respects to comply: 'Who am I, to refuse my lord? Whatever pleases him I will do at once, and it will be a joy to me until the day of my death' (12.14). The humour is working on a number of levels. Judith's unwillingness to refuse Holofernes suggests that she will submit not only to being entertained at a banquet but also in bed. On the other hand, the reader is surely meant to ask who is the 'lord' to whom she offers such complete obeisance, and why do we have an allusion to death? A similar ambiguity is expressed in Judith's statement that 'today is the greatest day in my whole life' (Jdt. 12.18). What Holofernes hears is that Judith is enjoying the feast and the prospect of sexual intimacy with him, what Judith celebrates is the prospect of killing her enemy.[57] Such humour, if that is what it is, takes a macabre turn when she leaves the camp with Holofernes' head in her *food bag* (13.10). The consumer of Judith's beauty is now himself consumed. In Judith then Holofernes is presented as a man with a voracious appetite, whether that concerns food or a beautiful woman. In contrast, Judith remains chaste following the death of her husband and spends her time in constant prayer and fasting.

The book of Tobit lacks the potency of the Persian 'other' but makes a similar point. Tobiah demonstrates his control over his appetite when he seeks to conclude the marriage with Sarah before sitting down to the feast that has been prepared. After Tobiah has exorcized the demon that has troubled Sarah, the two of them pray together. Before God Tobiah affirms that his marriage to Sarah is due to sincerity and not to lust (Tob. 8.7), a statement confirmed by his reference to her as his kinswoman.

---

[56] See, e.g., Ackerman, *Warrior*, esp. 61–6; S. A. White, 'In the Steps of Jael and Deborah: Judith as Heroine', in D. J. Lull (ed.), *Society of Biblical Literature 1989 Seminar Papers* (Atlanta: Scholars Press, 1989), 570–8.

[57] A similar ambiguity is found in 12.4. There is a discussion about whether Judith's supply of clean food will be sufficient for her time amongst the Assyrian army. Judith replies to Holofernes, 'As surely as you live, my lord, your servant will not use up the things I have with me before the Lord carries out by my hand what he has determined to do.' What the Lord will carry out, however, is not the conquest of Betuliah by Holofernes, as Judith has suggested in her speech to him, but the death of Holofernes and the defeat of his army.

Moderation is important because, as we have seen, divine judgement is exhibited at the table. In the diaspora novellas this theme from older Hebrew literature is combined with the Greek motif of Persian indulgence. The table is not only the locus of divine judgement and vindication, but also the place in which human righteousness or unrighteousness is most characteristically exemplified, through attitudes to food. The idea of the table as the context both for human sinning and for divine judgement is not absent from the earlier Old Testament stories—consider the stories of Hannah and Eli, or Joseph and his brothers. Nevertheless, the theme of Persian indulgence has sharpened the connection. Thus, Belshazzar demonstrates his impiety at the table when he asks for the temple vessels from Jerusalem. He is judged by God at the place of his impiety when the writing appears on the wall: 'that very night Belshazzar, the Chaldean king, was killed' (Dan. 5.30). Holofernes shows his voracious appetite through his inappropriate desire for the widow Judith and his excessive drinking. At the very place where his unrighteousness is revealed, his head is lost. For Judith the opposite is the case. Her righteousness and purity is vindicated through her victory over Holofernes. For Haman the first feast that Esther prepares becomes an occasion for self-congratulation and hubris. He returns home to wife and friends to boast of the honour he is held in. Spurred on by his own pride and the encouragement of his friends he constructs the gallows intended for Mordecai. In the subsequent meal, however, Haman's plans are undone when Esther reveals her Jewish heritage. The king's judgement is expressed at the dining couch (7.8; cf. 1.6) and Haman is hanged on the gallows prepared for Mordecai. Thus, in Esther also, the table is where Haman demonstrates his impiety and, at the very same time, experiences divine judgement.

CONCLUSION

It is well known that there is a developing food consciousness in post-exilic Judaism. Typically it is the dietary laws that are mentioned in this context, although, as we have seen, they only play a central role from the Maccabean period onwards. Alongside, and even prior to the Maccabean period, there are other aspects of the Jewish food consciousness that are taking shape. These characterize Jews as moderate at the table through contrasting themselves with their imperial overlords who frequently exhibit a voracious appetite. Jews fast and feast, as events and the calendar dictate, eating neither too much nor too little. The Persians, on the other hand, are indulgent, eating and drinking too

much. As a result they are hasty in their decisions, reckless in their conduct and impious.

Although the food laws and the ethic of moderation appear to be two distinct streams in the developing food consciousness within Judaism, they will very soon be brought together in the allegorical interpretation of the food laws in Philo.

At the same time he [Moses] also denied to the members of the sacred Commonwealth unrestricted liberty to use and partake of the other kinds of food. All the animals of land, sea or air whose flesh is the finest and fattest, thus titillating and exciting the malignant foe pleasure, he sternly forbade them to eat, knowing that they set a trap for the most slavish of the senses, the taste, and produce gluttony, an evil very dangerous both to soul and body. For gluttony begets indigestion which is the source and origin of all distempers and infirmities. Now among the different kinds of land animals there is none whose flesh is so delicious as the pig's, as all who eat it agree, and among the aquatic animals the same may be said of such species as are scaleless. Having skilled gifts for inciting to self-control those who have a natural tendency to virtue, he trains and drills them by frugality and simple contentedness and endeavours to get rid of extravagance. He approved neither of rigorous austerity like the Spartan legislator, nor of dainty living, like him who introduced the Ionians and Sybarites to luxurious and voluptuous practices. Instead he opened up a path midway between the two.[58]

Thus, for Philo the dietary laws teach moderation.

Although moderation is valued by Jewish writers, the use of Persian feasts in the diaspora novellas creates a certain ambiguity, for conspicuous consumption is not abrogated, it is merely shifted from the mouth to the eyes and the mind. Readers of these novels are titillated with stories of an extravagant world beyond their own experience. The attitude that the authors seek to cultivate is, we might say, a response of *mysterium tremendum et fascinans*. This is apparent in the baroque style of the narrative of Esther. The descriptions of the palace feasts with all their aesthetic excesses are intended to mesmerize the reader, but at the same time the Jews are portrayed as putting a different value on the pleasures of the table. The same perspective is a more explicit ingredient in the text of Judith. After the Assyrians flee Judith receives Holofernes' possessions as spoil. This includes his tent, silver dinnerware, beds, bowls and furniture (Jdt. 15.11). A strange gift, one might think, for the people to offer a widow noted for her fasting. The noble Judith finds a solution, for she offers the articles to God in Jerusalem (16.19).

Finally, we may observe that the examination of the conspicuous consumption of the Persians in the diaspora novellas problematizes the frequent assumption that Jewish responses to the Persians were always positive. The

---

[58] *Spec. Leg.* 4.100–2 (translation from Philo, *Philo VIII*).

Persians who appear in the novellas are portrayed as gluttons and buffoons. Nevertheless, as I have suggested, this presentation probably originates in a Hellenistic milieu. Not only would this have implications for dating of the diaspora novellas in the Hellenistic period and a Hellenistic provenance (including Esther) but it would imply that the negative stereotyping postdates Persian hegemony. The question must be left open of whether the literature is intended to model Jewish moderation, with Persian consumption acting merely as a foil, or whether it might have in view other forms of foreign feasting, such as feasting by Hellenistic overlords or the Greek symposium.

Conclusion

In the foregoing chapters we have attempted to show that food and drink, eating and drinking in the Old Testament is a worthwhile and important subject for examination. This is because acts of eating and drinking are always more than simply feeding a physical body. In the words of our title, bread is not bread alone.

Our examination of food in the Old Testament has by no means been exhaustive. There remain many aspects of the subject that could be profitably examined. In particular large parts of the Old Testament corpus have scarcely been touched, including most of the prophetic corpus and the wisdom literature. It is to be hoped that this book might stimulate more studies in the small, but growing, area of research on food in the Old Testament.

Hopefully the value of this study lies not only in its contribution to the study of the Old Testament and its capacity to stimulate further work in the area, but also in its contribution to other areas of study. In particular, the Old Testament has, consciously or unconsciously, had a considerable influence on Western civilization. From the Middle Ages to the modern day the valuation and symbolic assessment of food has been influenced by the Old Testament alongside other influences. Food historians may well find that the Old Testament offers more food for thought than a mere reference to the forbidden fruit of the Garden of Eden or the abomination of the pig.

It would hardly be possible even to begin sketching the possible trajectories of influence that the Old Testament employment of food may have had. Nevertheless, in this conclusion it may be valuable to suggest some areas in which the Old Testament may have influenced New Testament writers in their thinking about food. This is of obvious value for many prospective readers for whom—as for this writer—the Old Testament is the first part of a two-part canon. In addition, it was an important part of the New Testament writers' self-perception that what they practised and believed was 'according to the Scriptures'. 'According to the Scriptures' meant not only the Old Testament's capacity to speak of the promised Christ, but also its role as instruction from God, covering every area of life, including food and eating. This demands some reflection because meals played an important role in New Testament

literature and in the early Christian communities, a fact increasingly recognized in the number of significant studies by New Testament scholars on the many food-related problems within nascent Christianity.

THE CONTEXT OF EARLY CHRISTIAN THINKING ABOUT FOOD

Despite the importance of meals for the early Christians and the concern evident throughout the New Testament to relate the life of Jesus and the practice of the believing community to their Scriptures, a number of the studies of New Testament meals marginalize the role of the Old Testament. Two examples indicative of this trend may be given: Dennis Smith's *From Symposium to Eucharist* and Willi Braun's *Feasting and Social Rhetoric in Luke 14*.[1]

In *From Symposium to Eucharist* Smith interprets early Christian meals as examples of Graeco-Roman meals and, as such, rarely appeals to the Old Testament. Smith's work does allow for the existence of a 'Jewish banquet' within the common Graeco-Roman banqueting tradition. Yet, even in this case Smith wants to assert the dominance of Graeco-Roman patterns. 'To be sure, there were distinctive features in the Jewish tradition, but the form taken by Jewish meals in the Greco-Roman period on any particular occasion or in any particular setting was that of the Graeco-Roman banquet. Furthermore, the ideology of the meal was also that of the Greco-Roman banquet.'[2] The distinctive features of the Jewish banquet include the dietary laws as an expression of Jewish separatism and the ideology of the messianic banquet. Even the messianic banquet, however, 'represented a mythologization of the festive or joyous banquet that was a part of the common banquet tradition.'[3] The same logic holds for Smith's discussion of the combination of worship and joy in the Christian festive meals. Although noting the importance of this idea in the Deuteronomic command to 'rejoice before the Lord', he subsumes it under the pleasure of philosophical discourse at the symposium and the valuation of *euphrosyne*, 'festive joy', in Graeco-Roman banquets.[4] The danger of approaching the material on New Testament meals in this way is, as Hurtado notes, that 'Smith does not consider other relevant and cogent options.'[5] The

---

[1] Smith, *Symposium*; Braun, *Feasting*. Note also Corley, who sees Jewish meals in the context of Graeco-Roman banqueting traditions (Corley, *Private Women*, esp. 66–74).

[2] Smith, *Symposium*, 171.   [3] Ibid., 171.   [4] Ibid., 284.

[5] L. Hurtado, 'Review of Dennis Smith, *From Symposium to Eucharist: The Banquet in the Early Christian World* (Minneapolis: Fortress Press, 2003)', *JBL* 122 (2003), 781–5, here 783.

particular instance that Hurtado highlights is Smith's argument that 'unto my remembrance' in the Pauline and Lucan tradition of the Eucharist indicates the influence of Epicurean memorial meals. Yet, as Hurtado observes, 'the expression is not used in the funerary meals but *is* found in the LXX (e.g., Lev 24:7; Pss 37:1; 69:1; Wis 16:6) and in Jewish and Christian writers influenced by the biblical tradition (e.g., Josephus, Justin), and the idea of commemoration is a profound feature of the Passover meal tradition with which Jesus' death was associated very early (e.g., 1 Cor 5:7)'.[6] What Hurtado does not highlight is that the 'relevant and cogent options' that Smith elides are nearly always those that make appeal to the Jewish heritage of early Christian meals.

Braun's *Feasting and Social Rhetoric in Luke 14* is if anything even more insistent in its appeal to Graeco-Roman parallels at the expense of Jewish parallels. This approach is justified by his argument that the author of Luke–Acts belongs 'within the roster of first century Greco-Roman *littérateurs*' and was destined to be read by a literate and relatively wealthy urban elite.[7] Braun employs a similar method to Smith when the evidence forces him to accept the likelihood of a strong Jewish influence: he enfolds the Jewish influence into a 'wider' Graeco-Roman tradition. Thus, when discussing Jesus' saying about the invitation of dinner guests in Luke 14.12–14, Braun allows that there may be a similarity to the messianic banquet but with qualifications: 'There is no need to deny that Luke's hospitality rule alludes to motifs related to the Jewish messianic banquet (cf. 14.15), but its formulation is more patently a synecdoche of Greco-Roman conventions and their critique in the Cynic sources of which Lucian's dialogues are the most instructive examples.'[8] Accepting the usefulness of comparing Luke's meals to other Hellenistic meals, Esler rightly questions 'whether Braun is giving sufficient credit to Luke's Israelite traditions (as evident in his occasional uses of heavily Septuagintal language which Braun curiously denies—p. 49) or to his moral and theological seriousness'.[9] In particular, Esler notes that the reversal theme in Jesus' teaching about banquets (Luke 14.7–11) is not just a common Hellenistic *topos*, but an important part of Luke's theology. Indeed, as we shall see, it is not just an important Lucan emphasis, but one derived from the Old Testament and frequently linked to meals.

The reasons for a one-sided focus on Graeco-Roman parallels to New Testament meals are, perhaps, not difficult to discern. On the one hand, the appeal to a Graeco-Roman context reflects an attempt to correct the perceived failings of earlier New Testament scholarship, which was equally one-sided in

---

[6] Ibid., 783–4.   [7] Braun, *Feasting*, 9.   [8] Ibid., 61.
[9] P. F. Esler, 'Review of Willi Braun, *Feasting and Social Rhetoric in Luke 14* (Society for New Testament Studies Monograph Series, 85; Cambridge: Cambridge University Press, 1995)', *JTS* 49 (1998), 229–33, here 230.

interpreting the New Testament against a Jewish background. On the other hand, New Testament scholars have been poorly served when it comes to studies on food and eating in the Jewish and Israelite background to Christian meals. The rich scholarly discussion of the symposium and Graeco-Roman eating habits makes for a much more available resource, and New Testament specialists cannot be faulted too harshly for utilizing this.

The latter problem is readily illustrated in Blomberg's *Contagious Holiness*.[10] Blomberg recognizes the difficulties with the discussion of meals in New Testament scholarship, taking particular exception to Smith's *From Symposium to Eucharist*. Offering a correction to Smith's one-sided appeal to Graeco-Roman parallels, he is, nevertheless, forced to do most of his research on food in the Old Testament on his own. Blomberg's interest in the gospel accounts of Jesus' meals with 'sinners' leads to a focus only upon questions of commensality. This concern is aptly summarized in the title of Blomberg's chapter on Old Testament meals: 'forming friendships but evading enemies'.[11] This is just a small part of the perspectives on food and eating found in the Old Testament.

It is evident that the question of Graeco-Roman and Jewish influence upon early Christian thinking about food must not be presented as false alternatives. It is not necessary to choose between the influence of Graeco-Roman banqueting traditions or Jewish food traditions upon the New Testament writers. Nor is it necessary, as Smith and Braun do, to collapse Jewish meal traditions into Graeco-Roman traditions, as though the former can always be explained as a specific instance of the latter. As we have already seen in the last chapter, Jewish ideas about food and eating were being influenced by Hellenistic ideas from an early stage *at the very same time* as Jewish eating habits were becoming sharper community dividers. The question of differentiation and assimilation of Graeco-Roman meal traditions within Judaism is complex and multifaceted in the time before the rise of early Christianity.

THE INFLUENCE OF THE OLD TESTAMENT ON EARLY CHRISTIAN THINKING ABOUT FOOD

The ways in which the Old Testament influenced the New Testament writers in their thinking about food and meals demands a full-scale examination, responsive to the detailed interpretative issues that exegesis of the New Testament requires. All that can be offered here is a series of exploratory

---

[10] Blomberg, *Contagious Holiness*.   [11] Ibid., 32–64.

suggestions. There is no need to give attention to the topics that often receive attention, such as dietary laws and the messianic banquet. It is well known that the dietary laws were an important religious and ethnic marker for Judaism during the Graeco-Roman period and their significance for Gentile converts was an important point of disagreement within the nascent church. The messianic banquet has its origin in the vision of a festive meal in Isaiah 25. It was a motif that was developed in different ways across a variety of literature in Second Temple Judaism, including the writings of the New Testament.

I will examine three areas in which Old Testament themes are developed in the New: the Lucan theme of reversal, the juxtaposition of table and court in Mark, and the Pauline presentation of the Lord's Supper in 1 Corinthians.

The Lucan Theme of Reversal and the Table

It has frequently been observed that Luke is fond of the theme of reversal, in which the positions of the rich and poor are changed, particularly at the end of the age. Additionally it has been noted that this theme of reversal is linked with another of Luke's favourite themes, the meal.[12]

The reversal of the experience of poor and rich is frequently projected onto the messianic banquet. In Jesus' teaching in 13.22–30, those who had enjoyed table fellowship with Jesus—presumably the social elites with whom Jesus feasted (14.1)—will find themselves excluded from the messianic banquet, which will instead be opened up to all comers from every direction. This reversal of expectations is summarized with Jesus' concluding observation that 'some are last who will be first, and some are first who will be last' (13.30). Those who are excluded from the eschatological feast are frequently portrayed as eating and drinking well in the present. The unfaithful servant in 12.42–8 misappropriates the food to be shared amongst the servants and gets himself drunk when he believes his master to be delayed. When the master returns he receives a beating (12.48) rather than being served at the table (12.37). The doomed generations of the days of Noah and Lot were also characterized by their eating and drinking before catastrophe came upon them (17.26–30). The poor, who do without in the present, will find all their desires fulfilled in the Kingdom. Thus, Lazarus desires the scraps that fall from the table of the rich man who dines sumptuously every day. When Lazarus dies he receives his reward with Abraham, whilst the rich man descends to Hades (16.19–31).

---

[12] For the meal in Luke, see *inter alia*, J. P. Heil, *The Meal Scenes in Luke–Acts: An Audience-Oriented Approach*, SBLMS, 52 (Atlanta: Society of Biblical Literature, 1999); H. Moxnes, 'Meals and the New Community in Luke', *SEÅ* 51 (1987), 158–67; Braun, *Feasting*; Smith, *Symposium*, 253–72.

The example of Lazarus is generalized in the Lucan beatitudes where the poor are promised the Kingdom of God and the hungry are promised satisfaction (6.20–1).

This theme of reversal finds expression in the present order when Jesus teaches at the house of a leading Pharisee (Luke 14). Guests at a feast should choose the less honourable seats so that they are not shamed when they are ejected from the place of honour but are exalted when the host invites them to take a better position (14.7–10). Instruction about social wisdom turns into a universal statement about the values of the Kingdom with Jesus' concluding observation about the fate of those who exalt themselves: 'all who exalt themselves will be humbled, and those who humble themselves will be exalted'. Jesus' advice does not end with those who are invited to banquets, but even extends to those who give them. True generosity is not shown by inviting those who will repay with return invitations, but by throwing open the banquet to the disenfranchised of society (14.12–14). Instructions about the present order dissolve into the eschatological vision of the Kingdom of God when Jesus tells a parable about the Kingdom where these novel values are exemplified (14.15–24). Those who are expected to be at the banquet are excluded and the messianic banquet is opened to the poor, maimed, blind and lame.

The Kingdom values receive their earliest exposition in the Magnificat: 'he has brought down the powerful from their thrones, and lifted up the humble; the hungry he has filled with good things, but the rich he sent away empty' (1.52–3). As we have already observed, these verses are formulated on the basis of Hannah's prayer in 1 Samuel 2. Here it is apparent that Luke's interwoven themes of reversal and the table are not primarily borrowings from a Graeco-Roman milieu, but deeply embedded in the Old Testament portrayal of the table as the context for divine judgement and vindication. In the stories of the monarchy found in Samuel and Kings it is the 'poor and humble', such as Saul, David and Mephibosheth, that are raised to prominence at the table through divine action. Luke has taken this theme and combined it with the theme of the messianic banquet as the place where all injustices will finally be put right.

Table and Court in Mark

Although meals are a theme not as central to Mark as they are to Luke, it is possible that the juxtaposition of table and judgement may not be original to Luke, but originate with Mark. Certainly Mark seems to play with the idea in 10.37–44. James and John ask Jesus for the right to sit at his right hand and left hand in the Kingdom. The significance of these seats is not clear: 'the seats at

his *right hand and . . . left* could be either adjacent thrones (cf. Luke 22.30) or the seats of honour at the messianic banquet'.[13] The parallel in Luke allows for both possibilities: 'so that you may eat and drink at my table in my kingdom, and sit upon thrones judging the twelve tribes of Israel' (Luke 22.30). The kingship that Jesus exercises is not one that values the exercise of authority, rather greatness is demonstrated in service. The word for 'service', *diakonos*, calls to mind table service. Again, the implications are drawn out more clearly in Luke's version of Jesus' words: 'For who is greater, the one who sits at the table, or the one serving? Is it not the one sitting? But I am in your midst as one who serves' (Luke 22.27).

In Mark 10.37–44, then, we 'find that court and banquet table are brought together'.[14] Again, this is reminiscent of the juxtaposition of court and table in some of the literature of the Old Testament.

The Lord's Supper in 1 Corinthians

The New Testament descriptions of the Lord's Supper have long been recognized to draw upon Old Testament imagery, particularly in relation to the Passover. The Pauline version in 1 Corinthians has a number of distinctive elements, including the importance of memory and the theme of judgement.

It is, perhaps, no surprise that we should return to the place of memory in the Pauline version of the Lord's Supper, since we have already observed Lawrence's discussion of food and memory in 1 Corinthians and examined the relationship between food and memory in Deuteronomy. Although Smith seeks to associate the Pauline version of the Lord's Supper with Graeco-Roman memorial meals the more compelling parallels are to be found in the Old Testament. Although the phrase 'unto the remembrance' is found elsewhere in the Septuagint, it has often been observed that the instructions about the feast of Passover–Unleavened Bread in Exodus 13.3–16 emphasize the importance of memory (vv. 3, 9, 16). This version of the Passover regulations is usually attributed to a Deuteronomic writer,[15] because it has terminological

[13] M. D. Hooker, *The Gospel According to St Mark*, Black's New Testament Commentaries (London: A&C Black, 1991), 246.

[14] Smith, *Symposium*, 246. Smith gives other examples: 12.38–9; 13.9 (Smith, *Symposium*, 246–9). In the case of 12.38–9 one must assume that the *protokathedria* in the synagogue were used for legal rulings or judgement. This is not impossible, but would need justification. In the case of 13.9 Smith writes, 'the primary imagery here is the alien worlds of the synagogue and the throne room of the king. But table fellowship imagery functions in this rhetoric as well' (Smith, *Symposium*, 249). I can find no justification for this latter assertion.

[15] For a brief account, see B. S. Childs, *Exodus: A Commentary*, OTL (London: SCM Press, 1974), 184–6.

and conceptual similarities with Deuteronomy. The conceptual similarities include the strong linkage between meals and memory. In his emphasis on the Lord's Supper as a feast in which Jesus is remembered, Paul draws upon Deuteronomic thought. The utilization of an embodied practice of eating to link past, present and future, as Lawrence discussed, is consonant with Deuteronomic conceptuality of festive meals.

The judgement that takes place at the Lord's Supper is one that relates to the conduct exhibited at the Christian communal meals. Paul requires that the Corinthian Christians give due heed to whether their conduct at the meals is appropriate or whether they have been showing contempt for the body of Christ and humiliating those who have nothing (1 Cor. 11.20–2). The communal meals are, thus, the place at which unrighteousness is being exhibited and where judgement will be forthcoming. Those who eat and drink without showing due regard for the body of Christ are said to drink judgement upon themselves (11.29). As a result the community has known some of its number to have perished or become ill (11.30).

With the coordination of judgement and table we again return to a theme that we have already seen in Luke and Mark. In the case of 1 Corinthians too there is a strong allusion to the messianic banquet and the theme of final judgement. Those who subject themselves to judgement will escape the final judgement and will not be condemned with the world (11.31–2). By passing discriminating judgement upon themselves the Corinthian Christians anticipate the eschatological judgement and avoid the final condemnation. In his own way, then, Paul reflects the idea that we found in the diaspora novellas where the table is not only the place where righteousness or unrighteousness is exemplified, but also where it is brought under judgement.

Bibliography

Ackerman, S., *Under Every Green Tree: Popular Religion in Sixth-Century Judah*, HSM, 46 (Atlanta: Scholars Press, 1992).

—— *Warrior, Dancer, Seductress, Queen: Women in Judges and Biblical Israel* (New York: Doubleday, 1998).

Ackroyd, P., *The First Book of Samuel*, CBC (Cambridge: Cambridge University Press, 1971).

Aharoni, Y., *The Land of the Bible: A Historical Geography*, 2nd edn. (London: Burns & Oates, 1979).

—— *Arad Inscriptions* (Jerusalem: Israel Exploration Society, 1981).

Alter, R., 'A New Theory of Kashrut', *Commentary* 68 (1979), 46–52.

—— *The Art of Biblical Narrative* (New York: Basic Books, 1981).

Amit, Y., 'Judges 4: Its Content and Form', *JSOT* 39 (1987), 89–111.

—— *The Book of Judges: The Art of Editing*, BIS, 36 (Leiden: Brill, 1999).

Anbar, M., 'The Story about the Building of an Altar on Mount Ebal: The History of its Composition and the Question of the Centralization of the Cult', in N. Lohfink (ed.), *Das Deuteronomium: Entstehung, Gestalt und Botschaft*, BETL, 68 (Leuven: Leuven University Press, 1985), 304–9.

Andersen, F. I. and Freedman, D. N., *Amos*, AB, 24A (New York: Doubleday, 1989).

Anderson, A. A., *The Book of Psalms*, 2 vols., NCB (London: Oliphants, 1972).

Anderson, G. A., *Sacrifices and Offerings in Ancient Israel: Studies in their Social and Political Importance*, HSM, 41 (Atlanta: Scholars Press, 1987).

Ap-Thomas, D. R., 'The Ephah of Meal in Judges vi 19', *JTS* 41 (1940), 175–7.

Appler, D. A., 'From Queen to Cuisine: Food Imagery in the Jezebel Narrative', in A. Brenner and J. W. van Henten (eds.), *Food and Drink in the Biblical Worlds*, Semeia, 86 (Atlanta: Society of Biblical Literature, 1999), 55–71.

Arensberg, B. and Rak, Y., 'Jewish Skeletal Remains from the Period of the Kings of Judaea', *PEQ* 117 (1985), 30–4.

Assis, E., *Self-Interest or Communal Interest: An Ideology of Leadership in the Gideon, Abimelech and Jephthah Narratives (Judg. 6–12)*, VTSup, 106 (Leiden: Brill, 2005).

Assmann, J., *Moses the Egyptian: The Memory of Egypt in Western Monotheism* (Cambridge, MA: Harvard University Press, 1997).

Athenaeus, *Athenaeus V*, trans. C. B. Gulick, Loeb Classical Library (Cambridge, MA: Harvard University Press, 1933).

Aufderheide, A. C. and Rodriguez-Martin, C., *The Cambridge Encyclopaedia of Human Palaepathology* (Cambridge: Cambridge University Press, 1998).

Bal, M., *Death and Dissymmetry: The Politics of Coherence in the Book of Judges* (Chicago: University of Chicago Press, 1988).

Barnett, R. D., 'Assurbanipal's Feast', *Eretz Israel* 18 (1985), 1–6.

Barth, K., *Church Dogmatics II.2* (Edinburgh: T&T Clark, 1957).

Bartlett, J. R., *Edom and the Edomites*, JSOTSup, 281 (Sheffield: JSOT Press, 1989).

Becker, U., *Richterzeit und Königtum*, BZAW, 192 (Berlin: de Gruyter, 2000).

Becking, B., 'Jehojachin's Amnesty, Salvation for Israel? Notes on 2 Kings 25, 27–30', in C. Brekelmans and J. Lust (eds.), *Pentateuchal and Deuteronomistic Studies*, BETL, 94 (Leuven: Leuven University Press, 1990), 283–93.

Begg, C. T., 'The Significance of Jehoiachin's Release: A New Proposal', *JSOT* 36 (1986), 49–56.

Bennett, H. V., *Injustice Made Legal: Deuteronomic Law and the Plight of Widows, Strangers and Orphans in Ancient Israel* (Grand Rapids: Eerdmans, 2002).

Berg, S. B., *The Book of Esther*, SBLDiss, 44 (Missoula: Scholars Press, 1979).

Berlin, A., *Esther* (Philadelphia: Jewish Publication Society, 2001).

Binger, T., *Asherah: Goddesses in Ugarit, Israel and the Old Testament*, JSOTSup, 232 (Sheffield: Sheffield Academic Press, 1997).

Blair, E. P., 'An Appeal to Remembrance: The Memory Motif in Deuteronomy', *Int* 15 (1961), 41–7.

Blenkinsopp, J., 'Structure and Style in Judges 13–16', *JBL* 82 (1963), 65–76.

—— 'Memory, Tradition, and the Construction of the Past in Ancient Israel', *BTB* 27 (1997), 76–82.

Blomberg, C. L., *Contagious Holiness: Jesus' Meals with Sinners*, NSBT (Downers Grove: InterVarsity Press, 2005).

Bluedorn, W., *Yahweh Versus Baalism: A Theological Reading of the Gideon–Abimelech Narrative*, JSOTSup, 329 (Sheffield: Sheffield Academic Press, 2001).

Boer, R., 'National Allegory in the Hebrew Bible', *JSOT* 74 (1997), 95–116.

Böhl, F. M. T., 'Wortspiele im Alten Testament', *JPOS* 6 (1926), 196–212.

Boling, R. G., *Judges*, AB, 6A (New York: Doubleday, 1975).

Boogaart, T. A., 'Stone for Stone: Retribution in the Story of Abimelech and Shechem', *JSOT* 32 (1985), 45–56.

Borowski, O., *Agriculture in Ancient Israel* (Winona Lake: Eisenbrauns, 1987).

—— *Daily Life in Biblical Times* (Atlanta: Society of Biblical Literature, 2003).

Bosworth, D., 'Revisiting Karl Barth's Exegesis of 1 Kings 13', *BibInt* 10 (2002), 366–83.

Boyle, M. O., 'The Law of the Heart: The Death of a Fool (1 Samuel 25)', *JBL* 120 (2001), 401–27.

Braulik, G., 'Leidensgedächtnisfeier und Freudenfest: "Volksliturgie" nach dem deuteronomischen Festkalender (Dtn 16,1–17)', in *Studien zur Theologie des Deuteronomiums*, SBA, 2 (Stuttgart: Katholische Bibelwerk, 1988), 95–121.

—— *Deuteronomium II 16:18–34:12*, NEB (Würzburg: Echter, 1992).

Braun, W., *Feasting and Social Rhetoric in Luke 14*, SNTSMS, 85 (Cambridge: Cambridge University Press, 1995).

Brenner, A., 'A Triangle and a Rhombus in Narrative Structure: A Proposed Integrative Reading of Judges 4 and 5', in A. Brenner (ed.), *A Feminist Companion to Judges* (Sheffield: Sheffield Academic Press, 1993), 98–109.

Brenner, A. and van Henten, J. W., 'Our Menu and What Is Not On It: Editor's Introduction', in A. Brenner and J. W. van Henten (eds.), *Food and Drink in the Biblical Worlds*, Semeia, 86 (Atlanta: Society of Biblical Literature, 1999), ix–xvi.

—— 'Food and Drink in the Bible: An Exciting New Theme', in J. W. Dyk et al. (eds.), *Unless Someone Guide Me...: Festschrift for Karel A. Deurloo*, Amsterdamse Cahiers voor Exegese van de Bijbel en zijn Tradities Supplement Series, 2 (Maastricht: Uitgeverij Shaker Publishing, 2001), 347–54.

Brettler, M. Z., *God as King: Understanding an Israelite Metaphor*, JSOTSup, 76 (Sheffield: Sheffield Academic Press, 1989).

—— 'Never the Twain shall Meet? The Ehud Story as History and Literature', *HUCA* 62 (1991), 285–304.

Briant, P., *From Cyrus to Alexander: A History of the Persian Empire* (Winona Lake, IN: Eisenbrauns, 2002).

Brongers, H. A., 'Der Zornesbecher', in J. F. Vink et al. (eds.), *The Priestly Code and Seven Other Studies*, OTS, 15 (Leiden: Brill, 1969), 177–92.

—— 'Fasting in Israel in Biblical and Post-Biblical Times', in H. A. Brongers et al., *Instruction and Interpretation: Studies in Hebrew Language, Palestinian Archaeology and Biblical Exegesis*, OTS, 20 (Leiden: Brill, 1977), 1–21.

Broshi, M., 'The Diet of Palestine in the Roman Period: Introductory Notes', in M. Broshi (ed.), *Bread, Wine, Walls and Scrolls*, JSPSup, 36 (London: Sheffield Academic Press, 2001), 121–43.

—— 'Wine in Ancient Palestine: Introductory Notes', in M. Broshi (ed.), *Bread, Wine, Water and Scrolls*, JSPSup, 36 (London: Sheffield Academic Press, 2001), 144–72.

Brueggemann, W., 'Theodicy in a Social Dimension', *JSOT* 33 (1985), 3–25.

—— *The Land: Place as Gift, Promise, and Challenge in Biblical Faith*, 2nd edn. (Minneapolis: Fortress Press, 2002).

Bulmer, R., 'Why is the Cassowray not a Bird?' *Man* 2 (1967), 5–25.

Bunimovitz, S., 'Area C: The Iron Age I Pillared Buildings and Other Remains', in I. Finkelstein (ed.), *Shiloh: The Archaeology of a Biblical Site* (Tel Aviv: Tel Aviv University, 1993), 15–34.

Bunimovitz, S. and Finkelstein, I., 'Pottery', in I. Finkelstein (ed.), *Shiloh: The Archaeology of a Biblical Site* (Tel Aviv: Tel Aviv University, 1993), 81–196.

Burney, C. F., *Notes on the Hebrew Text of the Books of Kings* (Oxford: Clarendon Press, 1903).

—— *The Book of Judges* (London: Rivingtons, 1918).

Butler, T. C., *Joshua*, WBC, 7 (Waco, TX: Word, 1983).

Carroll, M. P., 'One More Time: Leviticus Revisited', in B. Lang (ed.), *Anthropological Approaches to the Old Testament*, Issues in Religion and Theology, 8 (Philadelphia: Fortress Press, 1985), 117–26.

Chan, K.-K., 'You Shall not Eat These Abominable Things: An Examination of Different Interpretations on Deuteronomy 14.3–20', *East Asian Journal of Theology* 3 (1985), 88–106.

Charles, R. H., *The Book of Jubilees* (London: A. and C. Black, 1902).

Charles, R. H., *A Critical and Exegetical Commentary on the Book of Daniel* (Oxford: Clarendon Press, 1929).

Childs, B. S., *Memory and Tradition in Ancient Israel*, SBT, 37 (London: SCM Press, 1962).

—— *Exodus: A Commentary*, OTL (London: SCM Press, 1974).

—— *Isaiah*, OTL (London: SCM Press, 2001).

Claassens, L. J. M., *The God Who Provides: Biblical Images of Divine Nourishment* (Nashville: Abingdon Press, 2004).

Claessen, H. J. M., 'The Early State: A Structural Approach', in H. J. M. Claessen and P. Skalník (eds.), *The Early State* (The Hague: Mouton, 1978), 533–96.

Claessen, H. J. M. and Skalník, P., 'Limits: Beginning and End of the Early State', in H. J. M. Claessen and P. Skalník (eds.), *The Early State* (The Hague: Mouton, 1978), 619–35.

Clements, R. E., 'A Royal Privilege: Dining in the Presence of the Great King (2 Kings 25.27–30)', in R. Rezetko, T. H. Lim and W. B. Aucker (eds.), *Reflection and Refraction: Studies in Biblical Historiography in Honour of A. Graeme Auld*, VTSup, 113 (Leiden: Brill, 2007), 49–66.

Clines, D. J. A., *The Esther Scroll: The Story of the Story*, JSOTSup, 30 (Sheffield: JSOT Press, 1984).

—— *Job 1–20*, WBC, 17 (Dallas: Word Books, 1989).

—— *Job 21–37*, WBC, 18A (Nashville: Nelson, 2006)

Cody, A., ' "Little Historical Creed" or "Little Historical Anamnesis"?' *CBQ* 68 (2006), 1–10.

Coggins, R. J., 'Commentary on 1 Esdras', in R. J. Coggins and M. A. Knibb, *The First and Second Books of Esdras*, CBC (Cambridge: Cambridge University Press, 1979), 1–75.

Collins, J. J., *Daniel*, Hermeneia (Minneapolis: Fortress Press, 1993).

—— 'The Zeal of Phinehas: The Bible and the Legitimation of Violence', *JBL* 122 (2003), 3–21.

Connerton, P., *How Societies Remember* (Cambridge: Cambridge University Press, 1989).

Coote, R. B. and Whitelam, K. W., *The Emergence of Early Israel in Historical Perspective*, SWBA, 5 (Sheffield: Almond Press, 1987).

Corley, K., *Private Women, Public Meals: Social Conflict in the Synoptic Tradition* (Peabody, MA: Hendrickson, 1993).

Crenshaw, J., *Samson: A Secret Betrayed, a Vow Ignored* (Atlanta: John Knox Press, 1978).

Cronauer, P. T., *The Stories about Naboth the Jezreelite: A Source, Composition, and Redaction Investigation of 1 Kings 21 and Passages in 2 Kings 9*, LHBOTS, 424 (London: T&T Clark, 2005).

Crüsemann, F., *The Torah: Theology and Social History of Old Testament Law*, trans. A. W. Mahnke (Edinburgh: T&T Clark, 1996).

Dar, S., *Landscape and Pattern: An Archaeological Survey of Samaria, 800 BCE–636 CE*, 2 vols. (Oxford: BAR, 1986).

—— 'Food and Archaeology in Romano-Byzantine Palestine', in J. Wilkens, D. Harvey and E. Dobson (eds.), *Food in Antiquity* (Exeter: University of Exeter Press, 1995), 326–36.

Davies, E. W., 'Land: Its Rights and Privileges', in R. E. Clements (ed.), *The World of Ancient Israel: Sociological, Anthropological, and Political Perspectives* (Cambridge: Cambridge University Press, 1989), 349–69.

de Moor, J. C., *An Anthology of Religious Texts from Ugarit*, Nisaba, 16 (Leiden: Brill, 1987).

—— 'Seventy!' in M. Dietrich and I. Kottsieper (eds.), '*Und Mose schrieb dieses Lied auf*': *Studien zum Alten Testament und zum Alten Orient*, AOAT, 250 (Münster: Ugarit-Verlag, 1998), 199–203.

deSilva, D. A., *4 Maccabees*, Septuagint Commentary Series (Leiden: Brill, 2006).

De Vries, S. J., *1 Kings*, WBC, 12 (Waco, TX: Word Books, 1985).

Del Olmo Lete, G. and Sanmartín, J., *A Dictionary of the Ugaritic Language in the Alphabetic Traditions*, 2 vols. (Leiden: Brill, 2003).

Dentzer, J.-M., *Le motif du banquet couché dans le Proche-Orient et le mode grec du VIIe au IVe siècle avant J.C.* (Rome: École Française de Rome, 1982).

Dietler, M., 'Theorizing the Feast: Rituals of Consumption, Commensal Politics, and Power in African Contexts', in Dietler and Hayden (eds.), *Feasts*, 65–114.

Dietler, M. and Hayden, B., 'Digesting the Feast—Good to Eat, Good to Drink, Good to Think: An Introduction', in Dietler and Hayden (eds.), *Feasts*, 1–20.

Dietler, M. and Hayden, B. (eds.), *Feasts: Archaeological and Ethnographic Perspectives on Food, Politics and Power* (Washington: Smithsonian Institute Press, 2001).

Dietler, M. and Herbich, I., 'Feasts and Labor Mobilization: Dissecting a Fundamental Economic Practice', in Dietler and Hayden (eds.), *Feasts*, 240–64.

Douglas, M., *Purity and Danger: An Analysis of the Concepts of Pollution and Taboo* (London: Routledge, 1966).

—— 'Deciphering a Meal', in *Implicit Meanings* (London: Routledge, 1975), 249–75.

—— 'Self-Evidence', in *Implicit Meanings* (London: Routledge, 1975), 276–318.

—— 'The Forbidden Animals in Leviticus', *JSOT* 59 (1993), 3–23.

—— *Natural Symbols: Explorations in Cosmology* (London: Routledge, 1970; rev edn. 1996).

—— *Leviticus as Literature* (Oxford: Oxford University Press, 1999).

—— 'Impurity of Land Animals', in M. Poorthuis and J. Schwartz (eds.), *Purity and Holiness: The Heritage of Leviticus* (Leiden: Brill, 2000), 33–45.

—— 'The Compassionate God of Leviticus and his Animal Creation', in M. O'Kane (ed.), *Borders, Boundaries, and the Bible*, JSOTSup, 313 (London: Sheffield Academic Press, 2002), 61–73.

—— *Jacob's Tears: The Priestly Work of Reconciliation* (Oxford: Oxford University Press, 2004).

Dozeman, T. B., 'The Way of the Man of God from Judah: True and False Prophecy in the Pre-Deuteronomic Legend of 1 Kings 13', *CBQ* 44 (1982), 379–93.

Driver, S. R., *Notes on the Hebrew Text of the Books of Samuel* (Oxford: Clarendon Press, 1890).

Duhaime, J., 'Lois alimentaires et pureté corporelle dans le Lévitique: L'approche de Mary Douglas et sa réception par Jacob Milgrom', *Religiologiques* 17 (1998), 19–35.

Earle, T., 'The Evolution of Chiefdoms', in T. Earle (ed.), *Chiefdoms: Power, Economy and Ideology* (Cambridge: Cambridge University Press, 1991), 1–15.

Eichrodt, W. *Ezekiel*, OTL (London: SCM Press, 1970).

Eilberg-Schwartz, H., 'Creation and Classification in Judaism: From Priestly to Rabbinic Conceptions', *History of Religions* 26 (1987), 357–81.

Ellison, R., 'Diet in Mesopotamia: The Evidence of the Barley Ration Texts (c. 3000–1400 B.C.)', *Iraq* 43 (1981), 35–45.

—— 'Some Thoughts on the Diet of Mesopotamia from c. 3000–600 B.C.', *Iraq* 45 (1983), 146–50.

Esler, P. F., 'Review of Willi Braun, *Feasting and Social Rhetoric in Luke 14* (Society for New Testament Studies Monograph Series, 85; Cambridge: Cambridge University Press, 1995)', *JTS* 49 (1998), 229–33.

Exum, J. C., 'The Theological Dimension of the Samson Saga', *VT* 33 (1983), 30–46.

—— 'The Centre Cannot Hold: Thematic and Textual Instabilities in Judges', *CBQ* 52 (1990), 410–31.

—— *Tragedy and Biblical Narrative: Arrows of the Almighty* (Cambridge: Cambridge University Press, 1992).

Feeley-Harnik, G., *The Lord's Table: The Meaning of Food in Early Judaism and Christianity* (Washington: Smithsonian Institution Press, 1981).

Feliks, Y., 'Jewish Agriculture in the Period of the Mishnah', in Z. Baras (ed.), *Eretz Israel from the Destruction of the Second Temple to the Muslim Conquests* (Jerusalem: Yad Ben Zvi, 1982), 419–41.

Ferrera, A. J. and Parker, S. B., 'Seating Arrangements at Divine Banquets', *UF* 4 (1972), 37–9.

Fiensy, D., 'Using the Nuer Culture of Africa in Understanding the Old Testament: An Evaluation', *JSOT* 38 (1987), 73–83.

Finkelstein, I., 'The Emergence of the Monarchy in Israel: The Environmental and Socio-Economic Aspects', *JSOT* 44 (1989), 43–74.

—— 'The History and Archaeology of Shiloh from the Middle Bronze Age II to Iron Age II', in I. Finkelstein (ed.), *Shiloh: The Archaeology of a Biblical Site* (Tel Aviv: Tel Aviv University, 1993), 371–89.

Firmage, E. B., 'The Biblical Dietary Laws and the Concept of Holiness', in J. A. Emerton (ed.), *Studies in the Pentateuch*, VTSup, 41 (Leiden: Brill, 1990), 177–208.

Fitzmyer, J. A., *Tobit*, Commentaries on Early Jewish Literature (Berlin: de Gruyter, 2003).

Fotopoulos, J., *Food Offered to Idols in Roman Corinth: A Socio-Rhetorical Reconsideration of 1 Corinthians 8:1–11:1*, WUNT, II/151 (Tübingen: Mohr Siebeck, 2003).

Fox, M. V., *Character and Ideology in the Book of Esther*, 2nd edn. (Grand Rapids: Eerdmans, 2001).

Foxhall, L. and Forbes, H. A., '*Sitometreia*: The Role of Grain as a Staple Food in Classical Antiquity', *Chiron* 12 (1982), 41–90.

Frankel, D., 'The Deuteronomic Portrayal of Balaam', *VT* 46 (1996), 30–42.

Frankfort, H., *Cylinder Seals: A Documentary Essay on the Art and Religion of the Ancient Near East* (London: Macmillan, 1939).

Frayn, J. M., 'Wild and Cultivated Plants: A Note on the Peasant Economy of Roman Italy', *Journal of Roman Studies* 65 (1975), 32–9.

—— *Subsistence Farming in Roman Italy* (London: Centaur Press, 1979).

Frick, F. S., *The Formation of the State in Ancient Israel*, SWBA, 4 (Sheffield: Almond Press, 1985).

Fried, M. H., *The Evolution of Political Society: An Essay in Political Anthropology* (New York: Random House, 1967).

Fritz, V., *1 & 2 Kings*, Continental Commentaries (Minneapolis: Fortress Press, 2003).

Fuchs, G., 'Das Symbol des Bechers in Ugarit und Israel', in A. Graupner, H. Delkurt and A. B. Ernst (eds.), *Verbindungslinien: Festschrift für Werner H. Schmidt zum 65. Geburtstag* (Neukirchen-Vluyn: Neukirchener, 2000), 65–84.

—— *Der Becher des Sonnengottes: Zur Entwicklung des Motivs 'Becher des Zorns'*, Beiträge zum Verstehen der Bibel, 4 (Münster: Lit, 2003).

Fuhs, H., 'Ez 24—Überlegungen zu Tradition und Redaktion des Ezechielbuches', in J. Lust (ed.), *Ezekiel and His Book: Textual and Literary Criticism and Their Interrelation*, BETL, 74 (Leuven: Leuven University Press, 1986), 266–82.

Galling, K., 'Das Gemeindegesetz in Deuteronomium 23', in W. Baumgartner (ed.), *Festschrift Alfred Bertholet zum 80. Geburtstag* (Tübingen: Mohr, 1950), 176–91.

Gammie, J. B., *Holiness in Israel*, OBT (Minneapolis: Fortress Press, 1989).

Garnsey, P., *Famine and Food Supply in the Graeco-Roman World: Response to Risk and Crisis* (Cambridge: Cambridge University Press, 1990).

—— *Food and Society in Classical Antiquity*, Key Themes in Ancient History (Cambridge: Cambridge University Press, 1999).

Gaß, E., *Die Ortsnamen des Richterbuchs in historischer und redaktioneller Perspektive*, Abhandlungen des deutschen Palästina-Vereins, 35 (Wiesbaden: Harrassowitz, 2005).

Gaster, T. H., *Thespis: Ritual, Myth and Drama in the Ancient Near East* (New York: Harper & Row, 1950).

Geller, M. J., 'Diet and Regimen in the Babylonian Diet', in C. Grottanelli and L. Milano (eds.), *Food and Identity in the Ancient World*, History of the Ancient Near East Studies, 9 (Padua: Sargon, 2004), 217–42.

Gershevitch, I. (ed.), *The Cambridge History of Iran*, vol. 2, *The Median and Achaemenian Periods* (Cambridge: Cambridge University Press, 1985).

Goldingay, J. E., *Daniel*, WBC, 30 (Dallas: Word Books, 1989).

Goldstein, J. A., 'The Date of the Book of Jubilees', *Proceedings of the American Academy for Jewish Research* 50 (1983), 63–86.

Goody, J., *Cooking, Cuisine and Class: A Study in Comparative Sociology*, Themes in the Social Sciences (Cambridge: Cambridge University Press, 1982).

Gordon, R. P., 'David's Rise and Saul's Demise: Narrative Analogy in 1 Samuel 24–26', *Tyndale Bulletin* 32 (1980), 37–64.

—— *I & II Samuel: A Commentary* (Carlisle: Paternoster Press, 1986).

Gorringe, T. J., *The Education of Desire: Towards a Theology of the Senses* (London: SCM Press, 2001).

Gottwald, N. K., *The Tribes of Yahweh: A Sociology of the Religion of Liberated Israel, 1250–1050 BCE* (Sheffield: Sheffield Academic Press, 1979; 2nd edn. 1999).

Gowers, E., *The Loaded Table: Representations of Food in Roman Literature* (Oxford: Oxford University Press, 1993).

Granowski, J. J., 'Jehoiachin at the King's Table: A Reading of the Ending of the Second Book of Kings', in D. N. Fewel (ed.), *Reading Between Texts: Intertextuality and the Hebrew Bible* (Louisville: Westminster/John Knox Press, 1992), 173–90.

Gray, J., *I & II Kings*, OTL (London: SCM Press, 1964).

Greenberg, M., *Ezekiel 21–37*, AB, 22A (New York: Doubleday, 1997).

Gressmann, H., *Der Ursprung der israelitisch-jüdischen Eschatologie*, FRLANT, 6 (Göttingen: Vandenhoeck & Ruprecht, 1905).

——'Der Festbecher', in A. Jirku (ed.), *Sellin-Festschrift: Beiträge zur Religionsgeschichte und Archäologie Palästinas* (Leipzig: A. Deichertsche, 1927), 55–62.

Grimm, V. E., *From Feasting to Fasting, the Evolution of a Sin: Attitudes to Food in Late Antiquity* (London: Routledge, 1996).

Guillaume, P., *Waiting for Josiah: The Judges*, JSOTSup, 385 (London: T&T Clark International, 2004).

Habel, N. C., *Job: A Commentary*, OTL (London: SCM Press, 1985).

——*The Land is Mine: Six Biblical Land Ideologies*, OBT (Minneapolis: Fortress Press, 1995).

Hadley, J. M., *The Cult of Asherah in Ancient Israel and Judah: Evidence for a Hebrew Goddess*, University of Cambridge Oriental Publications, 57 (Cambridge: Cambridge University Press, 2000).

Hagelia, H., 'Meal on Mount Zion: Does Isa 25:6–8 Describe a Covenant Meal?' *SEÅ* 68 (2003), 73–96.

Halbe, J., *Das Privilegerecht Jahwes*, FRLANT, 114 (Göttingen: Vandenhoeck & Ruprecht, 1975).

Hallberg, L., Sandström, B. and Aggett, P. J., 'Iron, Zinc and Other Trace Elements', in J. S. Garrow and W. P. T. James (eds.), *Human Nutrition and Dietetics*, 9th edn. (Edinburgh: Churchill Livingstone, 1993), 174–207.

Halstead, P., 'Plough and Power: The Economic and Social Significance of Cultivation with the Ox-drawn Ard in the Mediterranean', *Bulletin of Sumerian Agriculture* 8 (1995), 11–22.

Handy, L. K. (ed.), *The Age of Solomon: Scholarship at the Turn of the Millennium*, SHCANE, 11 (Leiden: Brill, 1997).

Harris, M., *Cannibals and Kings: The Origins of Cultures* (New York: Random House, 1977).

——*Cultural Materialism: The Struggle for a Science of Culture* (New York: Random House, 1979).

——*Good to Eat: Riddles of Food and Culture* (London: Allen & Unwin, 1986).

Hartley, J. E., *Leviticus*, WBC, 4 (Nashville: Thomas Nelson, 1992).

Hasel, G. F., 'יעף yʿp I', in *TDOT* 6:148–56.

Hayden, B., 'Fabulous Feasts: A Prolegomenon to the Importance of Feasting', in M. Dietler and B. Hayden (eds.), *Feasts: Archaeological and Ethnographic Perspectives on Food, Politics and Power* (Washington: Smithsonian Institution Press, 2001), 23–64.

Heil, J. P., *The Meal Scenes in Luke–Acts: An Audience-Oriented Approach*, SBLMS, 52 (Atlanta: Society of Biblical Literature, 1999).

Hellwing, S., Sadeh, M. and Kishon, V., 'Faunal Remains', in I. Finkelstein (ed.), *Shiloh: The Archaeology of a Biblical Site* (Tel Aviv: Tel Aviv University, 1993), 309–50.

Hendel, R. S., *Remembering Abraham: Culture, Memory, and History in the Hebrew Bible* (New York: Oxford University Press, 2005).

Henisch, B. A., *Fast and Feast: Food in Medieval Society* (University Park: Pennsylvania State University Press, 1976).

Herodotus, *Herodotus IV*, trans. A. D. Godley, Loeb Classical Library (London: William Heinemann, 1924).

Hertzberg, H. W., *I and II Samuel*, OTL (London: SCM Press, 1964).

Hobbs, T. R., *2 Kings*, WBC, 13 (Waco: Word, 1985).

Hooker, M. D., *The Gospel According to St Mark*, Black's New Testament Commentaries (London: A&C Black, 1991).

Hopkins, D. C., *The Highlands of Canaan: Agricultural Life in the Early Iron Age*, SWBA, 3 (Sheffield: JSOT Press, 1985).

Houston, W. J., *Purity and Monotheism: Clean and Unclean Animals in Biblical Law*, JSOTSup, 140 (Sheffield: JSOT Press, 1993).

—— 'Towards an Integrated Reading of the Dietary Laws of Leviticus', in R. Rendtorff and R. A. Kugler (eds.), *The Book of Leviticus: Composition and Reception* (Leiden: Brill, 2003), 142–61.

—— 'The Character of YHWH and the Ethics of the Old Testament: Is *Imitatio Dei* Appropriate', *JTS* 58 (2007), 1–25.

Hurtado, L., 'Review of Dennis Smith, *From Symposium to Eucharist: The Banquet in the Early Christian World* (Minneapolis: Fortress Press, 2003)', *JBL* 122 (2003), 781–5.

Huwyler, B., *Jeremia und die Völker: Untersuchungen zu den Völkersprüchen in Jeremia 46–49*, FAT, 20 (Tübingen: Mohr Siebeck, 1997).

Jacobs, N. S., ' "You did not Hesitate to Get Up and Leave the Dinner": Food and Eating in the Narrative of Tobit with some Attention to Tobit's Shavuot Meal', in G. G. Xeravits and J. Zsengellér (eds.), *The Book of Tobit: Text, Tradition, Theology*, JSJSup, 98 (Leiden: Brill, 2005), 121–38.

Janzen, D., *The Social Meanings of Sacrifice in the Hebrew Bible: A Study of Four Writings*, BZAW, 344 (Berlin: de Gruyter, 2004).

—— 'Why the Deuteronomist Told about the Sacrifice of Jephthah's Daughter', *JSOT* 29 (2005), 339–57.

Janzen, J. G., 'A Certain Woman in the Rhetoric of Judges 9', *JSOT* 38 (1987), 33–7.

Jenks, A. W., 'Eating and Drinking in the Old Testament', in *ABD* 2: 250–4.

Joffe, A. H., 'Alcohol and Social Complexity in Ancient Western Asia', *Current Anthropology* 39 (1998), 297–332.

Joffe, A. H., 'The Rise of Secondary States in the Iron Age Levant', *Journal for the Economic and Social History of the Orient* 45 (2002), 425–67.

Jones, G. H., *1 and 2 Kings*, NCBC (2 vols.; Grand Rapids: Eerdmans, 1984).

Junker, L. L., 'The Evolution of Ritual Feasting: Systems of Prehispanic Philippine Chiefdoms', in M. Dietler and B. Hayden (eds.), *Feasts: Archaeological and Ethnographic Perspectives on Food, Politics and Power* (Washington: Smithsonian Institute Press, 2001), 267–310.

Keys, G., *The Wages of Sin: A Reappraisal of the 'Succession Narrative'*, JSOTSup, 221 (Sheffield: Sheffield Academic Press, 1996).

King, P. J. and Stager, L., *Life in Biblical Israel*, Library of Ancient Israel (Louisville: Westminster John Knox Press, 2001).

Kirch, P. V., 'Polynesian Feasting in Ethnohistoric, Ethnographic, and Archaeological Contexts: A Comparison of Three Societies', in Dietler and Hayden (eds.), *Feasts: Archaeological and Ethnographic Perspectives on Food, Politics and Power* (Washington: Smithsonian Institute Press, 2001), 168–84.

Kislev, M. E., 'Food Remains', in I. Finkelstein (ed.), *Shiloh: The Archaeology of a Biblical Site* (Tel Aviv: Tel Aviv University, 1993), 354–61.

Kittel, R., *Studien zur hebräischen Archäologie und Religionsgeschichte*, Beiträge zur Wissenschaft vom Alten Testament, 1 (Leipzig: J. C. Hindrich, 1908).

Klawans, J., *Impurity and Sin in Ancient Judaism* (Oxford: Oxford University Press, 2000).

Klein, R. W., *1 Samuel*, WBC, 10 (Waco, TX: Word, 1983).

Klingbeil, G. A., ' "Momentaufnahmen" of Israelite Religion: The Importance of the Communal Meal in Narrative Texts in I/II Regum and Their Ritual Dimension', *ZAW* 118 (2006), 22–45.

Knierim, R. P., 'Food, Land and Justice', in *The Task of Old Testament Theology: Substance, Methods and Cases* (Grand Rapids: Eerdmans, 1995), 225–43.

Knoppers, G. N., *1 Chronicles 10–29*, AB, 12A (New York: Doubleday, 2004).

Koehler, L., 'Problems in the Study of the Language of the Old Testament', *JSS* 1 (1956), 3–24.

Kratz, R. G., *The Composition of the Narrative Books of the Old Testament*, trans. J. Bowden (London: T&T Clark, 2005).

Kunin, S. D., *We Think What We Eat: Neo-Structuralist Analysis of Israelite Food Rules and Other Cultural and Textual Practices*, JSOTSup, 412 (London: Continuum, 2004).

Lambert, D., 'Fasting as a Penitential Rite: A Biblical Phenomenon?', *HTR* 96 (2003), 477–512.

Lambert, W. G., 'Donations of Food and Drink to the Gods in Ancient Mesopotamia', in J. Quaegebeur (ed.), *Ritual and Sacrifice in the Ancient Near East*, Orientalia Lovaniensia Analecta, 55 (Leuven: Peeters, 1993), 191–201.

Lawrence, L. J., *Reading with Anthropology: Exhibiting Aspects of New Testament Religion* (Milton Keynes: Paternoster Press, 2005).

Leithart, P. J., 'Nabal and his Wine', *JBL* 120 (2001), 525–7.

Lemaire, A., *Inscriptions hébraïques I, Les ostraca* (Paris: Les Editions du Cerf, 1977).

Levenson, J. D., '1 Samuel 25 as Literature and as History', *CBQ* 40 (1978), 11–28.

—— 'The Last Four Verses in Kings', *JBL* 103 (1984), 353–61.

—— *The Death and Resurrection of the Beloved Son: The Transformation of Child Sacrifice in Judaism and Christianity* (New Haven: Yale University Press, 1993).

Lévi-Strauss, C., *Totemism* (Boston: Beacon Press, 1963).

—— 'The Culinary Triangle', *Partisan Review* 33 (1965), 586–95.

—— *The Raw and the Cooked* (New York: Harper & Row, 1969).

—— *From Honey to Ashes* (New York: Harper & Row, 1973).

—— *The Origin of Table Manners* (New York: Harper & Row, 1978).

—— *The Naked Man* (New York: Harper & Row, 1981).

Levinson, B. M., *Deuteronomy and the Hermeneutics of Legal Innovation* (Oxford: Oxford University Press, 1998).

—— 'The Hermeneutics of Tradition in Deuteronomy: A Reply to J. G. McConville', *JBL* 119 (2000), 269–86.

Lichtheim, M., *Ancient Egyptian Literature: A Book of Readings*, vol. 1: *The Old and Middle Kingdoms* (Berkeley: University of California Press, 1973).

Lindars, B., *Judges 1–5* (Edinburgh: T&T Clark, 1995).

Lloyd, J. B., 'The Banquet Theme in Ugaritic Narrative', *UF* 22 (1991), 169–93.

Lohfink, N., '"I am Yahweh, Your Physician" (Exodus 15:26): God, Society and Human Health in a Postexilic Revision of the Pentateuch (Exod. 15:2b, 26)', in N. Lohfink (ed.), *Theology of the Pentateuch: Themes of the Priestly Narrative and Deuteronomy* (Edinburgh: T&T Clark, 1994), 35–95.

—— 'The Small Credo of Deuteronomy 26:5–9', in N. Lohfink (ed.), *The Theology of the Pentateuch: Themes of the Priestly Narrative and Deuteronomy* (Edinburgh: T&T Clark, 1994), 265–89.

Lundbom, J. R., *Jeremiah 21–36*, AB, 21B (New York: Doubleday, 2004).

Macalister, A., 'Food', in *A Dictionary of the Bible*, ed. J. Hastings (Edinburgh: T&T Clark, 1899), 2: 27–43.

McCann, J. C., *Judges*, Interpretation (Louisville: John Knox Press, 2002).

McCarter, P. K., *1 Samuel*, AB, 8 (New York: Doubleday, 1980).

McCarthy, D. J., *Old Testament Covenant: A Survey of Current Opinions*, Growing Points in Theology (Oxford: Basil Blackwell, 1972).

—— 'Social Compact and Sacral Kingship', in R. Ishida (ed.), *Studies in the Period of David and Solomon and Other Essays* (Tokyo: Yamakawa-Shuppansha, 1982), 75–92.

McConville, J. G., *Law and Theology in Deuteronomy*, JSOTSup, 33 (Sheffield: JSOT Press, 1984).

—— 'Deuteronomy's Unification of Passover and Massot: A Response to Bernard M. Levinson', *JBL* 119 (2001), 47–58.

—— *Deuteronomy*, Apollos Old Testament Commentary (Leicester: IVP, 2002).

McCree, W. T., 'The Covenant Meal in the Old Testament', *JBL* 45 (1926), 120–8.

MacDonald, N., *Deuteronomy and the Meaning of 'Monotheism'*, FAT, II/1 (Tübingen: Mohr Siebeck, 2003).

MacDonald, N., 'Driving a Hard Bargain? Genesis 23 and Models of Economic Exchange', in M. I. Aguilar and L. J. Lawrence (eds.), *Anthropology and Biblical Studies: Avenues of Approach* (Leiden: Deo, 2004), 79–96.

—— ' "Bread on the Grave of the Righteous" (Tob. 4.17)', in M. R. J. Bredin (ed.), *Studies in the Book of Tobit*, LSTS, 55 (London: T&T Clark, 2006), 99–103.

—— 'Food and Drink in Tobit and Other "Diaspora Novellas"', in M. R. J. Bredin (ed.), *Studies in the Book of Tobit*, LSTS, 55 (London: T&T Clark, 2006), 165–78.

—— 'Recasting the Golden Calf: The Imaginative Potential of the Old Testament's Portrayal of Idolatry', in S. C. Barton (ed.), *Idolatry: False Worship in the Bible, Early Judaism, and Christianity* (London: T&T Clark, 2007), 22–39.

—— 'Genesis 19 and 2 Samuel 10: An Unexplored Parallel', paper given at International SBL, Vienna, 2007.

—— *What Did the Ancient Israelites Eat? Diet in Biblical Times* (Grand Rapids: Eerdmans, 2008).

McGinn, C., *Ethics, Evil and Fiction* (Oxford: Clarendon Press, 1997).

McKane, W., 'Poison, Trial by Ordeal and the Cup of Wrath', *VT* 30 (1980), 474–92.

McKinlay, J. E., *Gendering Wisdom the Host: Biblical Invitations to Eat and Drink*, JSOTSup, 216 (Sheffield: Sheffield Academic Press, 1996).

McLaren, D. S. et al., 'Fat-soluble Vitamins', in J. S. Garrow and W. P. T. James (eds.), *Human Nutrition and Dietetics*, 9th edn. (Edinburgh: Churchill Livingstone, 1993), 208–38.

McNutt, P., *Reconstructing the Society of Ancient Israel*, Library of Ancient Israel (Louisville: Westminster John Knox Press, 1999).

Macht, D. I., 'An Experimental Pharmacological Appreciation of Leviticus 11 and Deuteronomy 14', *Bulletin of the History of Medicine* 27 (1953), 444–50.

Marcus, D., *Jephthah and His Vow* (Lubbock, TX: Texas Tech Press, 1986).

Matthews, V. H., 'Hospitality and Hostility in Judges 4', *BTB* 21 (1991), 13–21.

Mayes, A. D. H., *Deuteronomy*, NCB (London: Oliphants, 1979).

—— 'Deuteronomy 14 and the Deuteronomic World View', in F. García Martínez et al. (eds.), *Studies in Deuteronomy: In Honour of C. J. Labuschagne on the Occasion of His 65th Birthday*, VTSup, 53 (Leiden: Brill, 1994), 165–81.

—— 'Deuteronomistic Royal Ideology in Judges 17–21', *BibInt* 9 (2001), 243–58.

Meadowcroft, T. J., *Aramaic Daniel and Greek Daniel: A Literary Comparison*, JSOTSup, 198 (Sheffield: Sheffield Academic Press, 1995).

Meinhold, A., 'Die Gattung der Josephgeschichte und des Estherbuches: Diasporanovelle I', *ZAW* 87 (1975), 306–24.

—— 'Die Gattung der Josephgeschichte und des Estherbuches: Diasporanovelle II', *ZAW* 88 (1976), 72–93.

Mendelsohn, I., 'State Slavery in Ancient Palestine', *BASOR* 85 (1942), 14–27.

—— 'On Corvée Labor in Ancient Canaan and Israel', *BASOR* 167 (1962), 31–5.

Mennell, S., *All Manners of Food: Eating and Taste in England and France from the Middle Ages to the Present*, 2nd edn. (Urbana: University of Illinois Press, 1996).

Mennell, S., Murcott A. and van Otterloo, A. H., 'The Sociology of Food: Eating, Diet and Culture', *Current Sociology* 40 (1992), 1–152.

Merendino, R. P., *Das deuteronomische Gesetz: Eine literarkritische, gattungs- und über-lieferungsgeschichtliche Untersuchung zu Dt 12–26*, BBB, 31 (Bonn: Peter Hanstein, 1969).

Mettinger, T. N. D., *Solomonic State Officials: A Study of the Civil Government Officials of the Israelite Monarchy*, ConBOT, 5 (Lund: CWK Gleerup, 1971).

Meyers, C. L., 'Kinship and Kingship: The Early Monarchy', in M. D. Coogan (ed.), *The Oxford History of the Biblical World* (Oxford: Oxford University Press, 1998), 165–205.

Meyers, C. L. and Meyers, E. M., *Zechariah 9–14*, AB, 25C (New York: Doubleday, 1993).

Michaux-Colombot, D., 'La *gat* de Gédéon, pressoir ou fief?' *UF* 29 (1997), 579–98.

Milgrom, J., 'The Biblical Diet Laws as an Ethical System', *Int* 17 (1963), 288–301.

—— 'Fasting and Fast Days: In the Bible', *EncJud II*, 6: 719–21.

—— 'Ethics and Ritual: The Foundations of the Biblical Dietary Laws', in E. B. Firmage, B. G. Weiss and J. W. Welch (eds.), *Religion and Law: Biblical-Judaic and Islamic Perspectives* (Winona Lake, IN: Eisenbrauns, 1990), 159–91.

—— *Leviticus 1–16*, AB, 3 (New York: Doubleday, 1991).

—— 'Two Biblical Hebrew Priestly Terms: Sheqetz and Tame", *MAARAV* 6 (1992), 107–16.

Millard, A., 'King Solomon in His Ancient Context', in L. K. Handy (ed.), *The Age of Solomon: Scholarship at the Turn of the Millennium*, SHCANE, 11 (Leiden: Brill, 1997), 30–53.

Miller, J. M., 'Separating the Solomon of History from the Solomon of Legend', in L. K. Handy (ed.), *The Age of Solomon: Scholarship at the Turn of the Millennium*, SHCANE, 11 (Leiden: Brill, 1997), 1–24.

Miller, R. D., II, *Chieftains of the Highland Clans: A History of Israel in the Twelfth and Eleventh Centuries B.C.* (Grand Rapids: Eerdmans, 2005).

Mintz, S. W., *Sweetness and Power: The Place of Sugar in Modern History* (New York: Penguin Books, 1985).

Mintz, S. W. and Du Bois, C. M., 'The Anthropology of Food and Eating', *Annual Review of Anthropology* 31 (2002), 99–119.

Miscall, P. D., *1 Samuel: A Literary Reading* (Bloomington, IN: Indiana University Press, 1986).

Mitchell, G., *Together in the Land: A Reading of the Book of Joshua*, JSOTSup, 134 (Sheffield: Sheffield Academic Press, 1993).

Moore, C. A., *Judith*, AB, 40 (Garden City, NY: Doubleday, 1985).

Moore, G. F., *Judges*, ICC (Edinburgh: T&T Clark, 1895).

Moskala, J., *The Laws of Clean and Unclean Animals in Leviticus 11: Their Nature, Theology and Rationale, an Intertextual Study*, Adventist Theological Society Dissertation Series (Berrien Springs, MI: Adventist Theological Society Publications, 2000).

—— 'Categorization and Evaluation of Different Kinds of Interpretation of the Laws of Clean and Unclean Animals in Levicitus 11', *Biblical Research* 46 (2001), 5–41.

Moxnes, H., 'Meals and the New Community in Luke', *SEÅ* 51 (1987), 158–67.

Naveh, J., 'The Aramaic Ostraca from Tel Arad', in Y. Aharoni, *Arad Inscriptions* (Jerusalem: Israel Exploration Society, 1981), 153–76.

Nelson, R. D., *Deuteronomy*, OTL (Louisville: Westminster John Knox Press, 2002).

Nemet-Nejat, K. R., *Daily Life in Ancient Mesopotamia* (Peabody, MA: Hendrickson, 2002).

Neumann, J., 'On the Incidence of Dry and Wet Years', *IEJ* 5 (1955), 137–53.

Nicholson, E. W., 'The Interpretation of Exodus xxiv 9–11', *VT* 24 (1974), 77–97.

—— 'The Antiquity of the Tradition in Exodus xxiv 9–11', *VT* 25 (1975), 69–79.

—— 'The Origin of the Tradition in Exodus xxiv 9–11', *VT* 26 (1976), 148–60.

Niditch, S., 'The "Sodomite" Theme in Judges 19–20: Family, Community, and Social Disintegration', *CBQ* 44 (1982), 365–78.

—— 'Eroticism and Death in the Tale of Jael', in P. L. Day (ed.), *Gender and Difference in Ancient Israel* (Minneapolis: Fortress Press, 1989), 43–57.

—— 'Samson as Culture Hero, Trickster, and Bandit: The Empowerment of the Weak', *CBQ* 52 (1990), 608–24.

—— *War in the Hebrew Bible: A Study in the Ethics of Violence* (Oxford: Oxford University Press, 1993).

Niemann, H. M., 'The Socio-Political Shadow Cast by the Biblical Solomon', in L. K. Handy (ed.), *The Age of Solomon: Scholarship at the Turn of the Millennium*, SHCANE, 11 (Leiden: Brill, 1997), 252–99.

Nihan, C., *From Priestly Torah to Pentateuch: A Study in the Composition of the Book of Leviticus*, FAT, II/25 (Tübingen: Mohr Siebeck, 2007).

Noth, M., *Exodus*, OTL (London: SCM Press, 1962).

—— *The Deuteronomistic History*, JSOTSup, 15 (Sheffield: JSOT Press, 1981).

O'Connel, R. H., *The Rhetoric of the Book of Judges*, VTSup, 63 (Leiden: Brill, 1996).

O'Dowd, R. P., 'Memory on the Boundary: Epistemology in Deuteronomy', in M. Healy and R. Parry (eds.), *The Bible and Epistemology: Biblical Soundings on the Knowledge of God* (Milton Keynes: Paternoster, 2007), 3–22.

Olson, D. T., *The Death of the Old and the Birth of the New: The Framework of the Book of Numbers and the Pentateuch*, BJS, 71 (Chico: Scholars Press, 1985).

—— *Deuteronomy and the Death of Moses: A Theological Reading*, OBT (Minneapolis: Fortress Press, 1994).

Origen, *On First Principles*, trans. G. W. Butterworth (New York: Harper & Row, 1966).

Parpola, S., 'The Leftovers of God and King: On the Distribution of Meat at the Assyrian and Achaemenid Imperial Courts', in C. Grottanelli and L. Milano, *Food and Identity in the Ancient World*, History of the Ancient Near East Studies, 9 (Padua: Sargon, 2004), 281–312.

Penchansky, D., 'Staying the Night: Intertextuality in Genesis and Judges', in D. N. Fewell (ed.), *Reading between Texts* (Louisville: Westminster John Knox Press, 1992), 77–88.

Perlitt, L., *Bundestheologie im Alten Testament*, WMANT, 36 (Neukirchen-Vluyn: Neukirchener Verlag, 1969).

—— 'Wovon der Mensch lebt (Dtn 8:3b)', in *Deuteronomium-Studien*, FAT, 8 (Tübingen: Mohr Siebeck, 1994), 74–96.

Perodie, J. R., 'Feasting for Prosperity: A Study of Southern Northwest Coast Feasting', in M. Dietler and B. Hayden (eds.), *Feasts: Archaeological and Ethnographic Perspectives on Food, Politics and Power* (Washington: Smithsonian Institute Press, 2001), 185–214.

Petersen, D. L., *Zechariah 9–14 and Malachi: A Commentary*, OTL (Louisville: Westminster John Knox Press, 1995).

Philo, *Philo VIII*, trans. F. H. Colson, Loeb Classical Library (Cambridge, MA: Harvard University Press, 1960).

Pinnock, F., 'Considerations on the "Banquet Theme" in the Figurative Art of Mesopotamia and Syria', in L. Milano (ed.), *Drinking in Ancient Societies: History and Culture of Drinks in the Ancient Near East* (Padua: Sargon, 1994), 15–26.

Pollock, S., 'Feasts, Funerals, and Fast Food in Early Mesopotamian States', in T. L. Bray (ed.), *The Archaeology and Politics of Food and Feasting in Early States and Empires* (New York: Kluwer Academic, 2003), 17–38.

Polzin, R., *Moses and the Deuteronomist: A Literary Study of the Deuteronomistic History*, pt. 1: *Deuteronomy, Joshua, Judges* (Bloomington: Indiana University Press, 1980).

—— *Samuel and the Deuteronomist: A Literary Study of the Deuteronomic History*, pt. 2: *1 Samuel* (Bloomington: Indiana University Press, 1989).

Preuss, H. D., תּוֹעֵבָה *tôʿēḇâ*, *TDOT* 15: 591–604.

Pritchard, J. B., *Winery, Defenses and Soundings at Gibeon* (Philadelphia: Pennsylvania University Museum, 1964).

Propp, W. H. C., *Exodus 1–18: A New Translation with Introduction and Commentary*, AB, 2 (New York: Doubleday, 1999).

Provan, I. W., *1 and 2 Kings*, New International Biblical Commentary (Peabody, MA: Hendrickson, 1995).

Rad, G. von, 'The Form-Critical Problem of the Hexateuch', in *The Problem of the Hexateuch and Other Essays* (Edinburgh: Oliver & Boyd, 1966), 1–78.

—— 'The Deuteronomic Theology of the History in I and II Kings', in *The Problem of the Hexateuch and Other Essays* (Edinburgh: Oliver & Boyd, 1966), 205–21.

Rainey, A. F., 'Compulsory Labor Gangs in Ancient Israel', *IEJ* 20 (1970), 191–202.

—— 'Three Additional Texts', in Y. Aharoni, *Arad Inscriptions* (Jerusalem: Israel Exploration Society, 1981), 122–5.

Ramírez Kidd, J. E., *Alterity and Identity in Israel*, BZAW, 283 (Berlin: de Gruyter, 1999).

Redford, D. B., *A Study of the Biblical Story of Joseph*, VTSup, 20 (Leiden: Brill, 1970).

Reisner, G. A., Fisher, C. S. and Lyon, D. G., *Harvard Excavations at Samaria, 1908–1910*, vol. 1 (Cambridge, MA: Harvard University Press, 1924).

Renfrew, J. M., *Palaeoethnobotany: The Prehistoric Food Plants of the Near East and Europe* (London: Methuen, 1973).

Richter, W., *Traditionsgeschichtliche Untersuchungen zum Richterbuch*, BBB, 18 (Bonn: Peter Hanstein, 1966).

Rogerson, J. W., 'Was Early Israel a Segmentary Society?', *JSOT* 36 (1986), 17–26.

Rogerson, J. W., 'Anthropology and the Old Testament', in R. E. Clements (ed.), *The World of Ancient Israel: Sociological, Anthropological and Political Perspectives* (Cambridge: Cambridge University Press, 1989), 17–38.

Römer, T. C., 'Why Would the Deuteronomists Tell about the Sacrifice of Jephthah's Daughter?' *JSOT* 77 (1998), 27–38.

Rosen, B., 'Subsistence Economy of Stratum II', in I. Finkelstein (ed.), *'Izbet Ṣarṭah*, BAR International, 299 (Oxford: BAR, 1986), 156–85.

—— 'Wine and Oil Allocations in the Samaria Ostraca', *Tel Aviv* 13–14 (1986–7), 39–45.

—— 'Economy and Subsistence', in I. Finkelstein (ed.), *Shiloh: The Archaeology of a Biblical Site* (Tel Aviv: Tel Aviv University, 1993), 362–7.

—— 'Subsistence Economy in Iron Age I', in I. Finkelstein and N. Na'aman (eds.), *From Nomadism to Monarchy: Archaeological and Historical Aspects of Ancient Israel* (Jerusalem: Israel Exploration Society, 1994), 339–51.

Ross, J. F., 'Food', in *The Interpreter's Dictionary of the Bible* (New York: Abingdon Press, 1962–76), 2: 304–8.

Rost, L., 'Das kleine geschichtliche Credo', in L. Rost (ed.), *Das kleine Credo und andere Studien zum Alten Testament* (Heidelberg: Quelle & Meyer, 1965), 11–25.

Sahlins, M., *Stone Age Economics* (London: Tavistock Press, 1972).

Sancisi-Weerdenburg, H., 'Persian Food: Stereotypes and Political Identity', in J. Wilkins, D. Harvey and M. Dobson (eds.), *Food in Antiquity* (Exeter: University of Exeter Press, 1995), 286–302.

Sanders, P., *The Provenance of Deuteronomy 32*, OTS, 37 (Leiden: Brill, 1996).

Sarna, N., *Genesis* בראשית: *The Traditional Hebrew Text with the New JPS Translation*, JPS Torah Commentary (Philadelphia: Jewish Publication Society, 1989).

Sasson, A., 'The Pastoral Component in the Economy of Hill Country Sites in the Intermediate Bronze and Iron Ages: Archaeo-Ethnographic Case Studies', *Tel Aviv* 25 (1998), 3–51.

Sasson, J. M., 'The King's Table: Food and Fealty in Old Babylonian Mari', in C. Grottanelli and L. Milano (eds.), *Food and Identity in the Ancient World*, History of the Ancient Near East Studies, 9 (Padua: Sargon, 2004), 179–215.

Schäfer-Lichtenberger, C., 'Sociological and Biblical Views of the Early State', in V. Fritz and P. R. Davies (eds.), *The Origins of the Ancient Israelite States* (Sheffield: Sheffield Academic Press, 1996), 78–105.

Schaper, J., 'The Living Word Engraved in Stone: The Interrelationship of the Oral and the Written and the Culture of Memory in the Books of Deuteronomy and Joshua', in S. C. Barton, L. T. Stuckenbruck, and B. G. Wold (eds.), *Memory in the Bible and Antiquity: The Fifth Durham–Tübingen Research Symposium (Durham, September 2004)*, WUNT, 212 (Tübingen: Mohr Siebeck, 2007).

Scherer, A., *Überlieferungen von Religion und Krieg: Exegetische und religions-geschichtliche Untersuchungen zu Richter 3–8 und verwandten Texten*, WMANT, 105 (Neukirchen-Vluyn: Neukirchener Verlag, 2005).

Schipper, J., ' "Significant Resonances" with Mephibosheth in 2 Kings 25.27–30: A Response to Donald F. Murray', *JBL* 124 (2005), 521–9.

Schmandt-Besserat, D., 'Feasting in the Ancient Near East', in M. Dietler and B. Hayden (eds.), *Feasts: Archaeological and Ethnographic Perspectives on Food, Politics and Power* (Washington: Smithsonian Institute Press, 2001), 391–403.

Schmidt, B. B., *Israel's Beneficent Dead: Ancestor Cult and Necromancy in Ancient Israelite Religion and Tradition*, FAT, 11 (Tübingen: Mohr Siebeck, 1994).

Schmidt, L., *Menschlicher Erfolg und Jahwes Initiative: Studien zu Tradition, Interpretation und Historie in Überlieferungen von Gideon, Saul und David*, WMANT, 38 (Neukirchen-Vluyn: Neukirchener Verlag, 1970).

Schmitt, E., *Das Essen in der Bibel: Literaturethnologische Aspekte des Alltäglichen*, Studien zur Kulturanthropologie, 2 (Münster: Lit, 1994).

Scholliers, P. (ed.), *Food, Drink and Identity: Cooking, Eating and Drinking in Europe since the Middle Ages* (Oxford: Berg, 2001).

Schunck, K.-D., 'Der Becher Jahwes: Weinbecher—Taumelbecher—Zornesbecher', in A. Graupner, H. Delkurt and A. B. Ernst (eds.), *Verbindungslinien: Festschrift für Werner H. Schmidt zum 65. Geburtstag* (Neukirchen-Vluyn: Neukirchener Verlag, 2000), 323–30.

Scrimshaw, N., Taylor, C. E. and Gordon, J. E., *Interactions of Nutrition and Infection* (Geneva: World Health Organization, 1968).

Segert, S., 'Paronomasia in the Samson Narrative in Judges XIII–XVI', *VT* 34 (1984), 454–61.

Seidl, T., *'Der Becher in der Hand des Herrn': Studie zu den prophetischen 'Taumelbecher'-Texten*, Arbeiten zu Text und Sprache im Alten Testament, 70 (St Ottilien: EOS, 2001).

Senn, F. C., 'Anamnesis', in *The New Dictionary of Sacramental Worship*, ed. P. E. Fink (Collegeville: Liturgical Press, 1990), 42–3.

Sharon, D. M., 'When Fathers Refuse to Eat: The Trope of Rejecting Food and Drink in Biblical Narrative', in A. Brenner and J. W. van Henten (eds.), *Food and Drink in Biblical Worlds*, Semeia, 86 (Atlanta: Society of Biblical Literature, 1999), 135–48.

—— *Patterns of Destiny: Narrative Structures of Foundation and Doom in the Hebrew Bible* (Winona Lake, IN: Eisenbrauns, 2002).

Shutt, R. J. H., 'Letter of Aristeas', in J. H. Charlesworth (ed.), *The Old Testament Pseudepigrapha*, vol. 2: *Expansions of the 'Old Testament' and Legends, Wisdom and Philosophical Literature, Prayers, Psalms, and Odes, Fragments of Lost Judeo-Hellenistic Works* (New York: Doubleday, 1985), 7–34.

Simoons, F. J., *Eat Not This Flesh: Food Avoidances in the Old World* (Madison: University of Wisconsin Press, 1961).

Skinner, J., *Genesis*, ICC (Edinburgh: T&T Clark, 1963).

Smend, R., 'Essen und Trinken—Ein Stück Weltlichkeit des Alten Testaments', in H. Donner, R. Hanhart, and R. Smend (eds.), *Beiträge zur alttestamentliche Theologie* (Göttingen: Vandenhoeck & Ruprecht, 1977), 447–59.

Smith, D. E., *From Symposium to Eucharist: The Banquet in the Early Christian World* (Minneapolis: Augsburg Fortress, 2003).

Smith, M. S., *The Memoirs of God: History, Memory, and the Experience of the Divine in Ancient Israel* (Minneapolis: Fortress Press, 2004).

Smith, M. S., *The Rituals and Myths of the Feast of the Goodly Gods of KTU/CAT 1.23: Royal Constructions of Opposition, Intersection, Integration, and Domination*, Resources for Biblical Study, 51 (Atlanta: Society of Biblical Literature, 2006).

Smith, P., 'An Approach to the Palaeodemographic Analysis of Human Skeletal Remains from Archaeological Sites', in A. Biran and J. Aviram (eds.), *Biblical Archaeology Today, 1990: Proceedings of the Second International Congress on Biblical Archaeology* (Jerusalem: Israel Exploration Society, 1993), 2–13.

Smith, P. and Kolska-Horowitz, L., 'Culture, Environment and Disease: Palaeo-Anthropological Findings for the Southern Levant', in C. L. Greenblatt (ed.), *Digging for Pathogenes* (Rehovot: Balaban, 1998), 201–39.

Smith, W. R., *Lectures on the Religion of the Semites: Their Fundamental Institutions*, 3rd edn. (London: A. & C. Black, 1927).

——*Lectures on the Religion of the Semites: Second and Third Series. Edited with an Introduction and Appendix by John Day*, JSOTSup, 183 (Sheffield: Sheffield Academic Press, 1995).

Smith-Christopher, D. L., 'Hebrew Satyagraha: The Politics of Biblical Fasting in the Post-exilic Period (Sixth to Second Century B.C.E.)', *Food and Foodways* 5 (1993), 269–92.

Smothers, T. G., 'Excursus: The Cup of Wrath', in G. L. Keown, P. J. Scalise and T. G. Smothers (eds.), *Jeremiah 26–52*, WBC, 27 (Nashville: Thomas Nelson, 1995), 277–9.

Soggin, J. A., *Judges*, OTL (London: SCM Press, 1981).

——'Compulsory Labor under David and Solomon', in R. Ishida (ed.), *Studies in the Period of David and Solomon and Other Essays* (Tokyo: Yamakawa-Shuppansha, 1982), 259–68.

——*Israel in the Biblical Period: Institutions, Festivals, Ceremonies, Rituals*, trans. J. Bowden (Edinburgh: T&T Clark, 2001).

Stager, L. E., 'Ashkelon and the Archaeology of Destruction: Kislev 604 BCE', *Eretz Israel* 25 (1996), 61–74.

Stavrakopoulou, F., *King Manasseh and Child Sacrifice: Biblical Distortions of Historical Realities*, BZAW, 338 (Berlin: de Gruyter, 2004).

Stone, K., *Practicing Safer Texts: Food, Sex and Bible in Queer Perspective*, Queering Theology Series (London: T&T Clark International, 2005).

Stone, L. G., 'Ethical and Apologetic Tendencies in the Redaction of the Book of Joshua', *CBQ* 53 (1991), 25–36.

Stuart-Macadam, P. L., 'Nutritional Deficiency Diseases: A Survey of Scurvy, Rickets and Iron-Deficiency Anemia', in M. Y. Işcan and K. A. R. Kennedy (eds.), *Reconstruction of Life from the Skeleton* (New York: Liss, 1989), 201–22.

Sutton, D. E., *Remembrance of Repasts: An Anthropology of Food and Memory* (Oxford: Berg, 2001).

Sweeney, M. A., *Zephaniah*, Hermeneia (Minneapolis: Fortress, 2003).

Tambiah, S. J., 'Animals are Good to Think and Good to Prohibit', *Ethnology* 7 (1969), 423–59.

Thomas, D. W., 'A Consideration of Some Unusual Ways of Expressing the Superlative in Hebrew', *VT* 3 (1953), 209–24.

Thompson, R. J., *Penitence and Sacrifice in Early Israel Outside the Levitical Law* (Leiden: Brill, 1963).

Thompson, T. L., *Early History of the Israelite People: From the Written and Archaeological Sources*, SHCANE, 4 (Leiden: Brill, 1992).

Tigay, J., *Deuteronomy* דברים: *The Traditional Hebrew Text with the New JPS Translation*, JPS Torah Commentary (Philadelphia: Jewish Publication Society, 1996).

Torrey, C. C., 'The Story of the Three Youths', in *Ezra Studies* (New York: Ktav, 1970), 37–61.

VanderKam, J. C., *Textual and Historical Studies in the Book of Jubilees*, HSM, 14 (Missoula: Scholars Press, 1977).

—— *The Book of Jubilees*, Corpus scriptorum Christianorum orientalium, 511 (Leuven: Peeters, 1989).

—— 'The Origins and Purposes of the Book of Jubilees', in M. Albani, J. Frey and A. Lange (eds.), *Studies in the Book of Jubilees*, Texte und Studien zum antiken Judentum, 65 (Tübingen: Mohr Siebeck, 1997), 3–24.

Van Neer, W. et al., 'Fish Remains from Archaeological Sites as Indicators of Former Trade Connections in the Eastern Mediterranean', *Paléorient* 30 (2004), 101–48.

Van Winkle, D. W., '1 Kings XIII: True and False Prophecy', *VT* 39 (1989), 355–70.

Veijola, T., *Das Königtum in der Beurteilung der deuteronomistischen Historiographie: Eine redaktionsgeschichtliche Untersuchung*, Annales Academiæ Scientiarum Fennicæ, 198 (Helsinki: Soumalainen Tiedeakatemia, 1977).

—— 'The History of the Passover in the Light of Deuteronomy 16,1–8', *Zeitschrift für altorientalische und biblische Rechtsgeschichte* 2 (1996), 53–75.

Ventner, P. M., 'The Dietary Regulations in Deuteronomy 14 within Its Literary Context', *Hervormde Teologiese Studies* 58 (2002), 1240–62.

Vriezen, T. C., 'The Exegesis of Exodus xxiv 9–11', in M. A. Beek, et al. (eds.), *The Witness of Tradition*, OTS, 17 (Leiden: Brill, 1972), 100–33.

Wagenaar, J. A., 'The Cessation of Manna: Editorial Frames for the Wilderness Wandering in Exodus 16.35 and Joshua 5.10–12', *ZAW* 112 (2000), 192–209.

Wagner, S., 'בקש *biqqēsh*', *TDOT* 2: 229–41.

Walters, S. D., 'Hanna and Anna: The Greek and Hebrew Texts of 1 Samuel 1', *JBL* 107 (1988), 385–412.

Wapnish, P., 'Archaeozoology: The Integration of Faunal Data with Biblical Archaeology', in A. Biran and J. Aviram (eds.), *Biblical Archaeology Today, 1990: Proceedings of the Second International Congress on Biblical Archaeology* (Jerusalem: Israel Exploration Society, 1993), 426–42.

Watts, J. W., *Psalm and Story: Inset Hymns in Hebrew Narrative*, JSOTSup, 139 (Sheffield: JSOT Press, 1992).

Webb, B. G., *The Book of Judges: An Integrated Reading*, JSOTSup, 46 (Sheffield: Sheffield Academic Press, 1987).

Weinfeld, M., *Deuteronomy and the Deuteronomic School* (Oxford: Clarendon Press, 1972).

Weinfeld, M., *Deuteronomy 1–11: A New Translation with Introduction and Commentary*, AB, 5 (New York: Doubleday, 1991).

Weismantel, M., 'An Embarrassment of Riches: Review of Michael Dietler and Brian Hayden (eds.), *Feasts: Archaeological and Ethnographic Perspectives on Food, Politics and Power*', *Current Anthropology* 42 (2001), 141–2.

Weitzman, S., 'The Samson Story as Border Fiction', *BibInt* 10 (2002), 158–74.

Wellhausen, J., *Prolegomena to the History of Israel* (Edinburgh: Adam & Charles Black, 1885).

Wells, J. B., *God's Holy People: A Theme in Biblical Theology*, JSOTSup, 305 (Sheffield: Sheffield Academic Press, 2000).

Wenham, G. J., *The Book of Leviticus*, New International Commentary of the Old Testament (Grand Rapids: Eerdmans, 1979).

—— 'The Theology of Unclean Food', *Evangelical Quarterly* 53 (1981), 6–15.

Westermann, C., *Genesis 1–11: A Commentary* (Minneapolis: Augsburg, 1984).

—— *Genesis 37–50: A Commentary* (Minneapolis: Augsburg, 1986).

Wevers, J. W., *Ezekiel*, NCB (London: Nelson, 1969).

White, K. D., *Roman Farming: Aspects of Greek and Roman Life* (Ithaca: Cornell University Press, 1970).

White, S. A., 'In the Steps of Jael and Deborah: Judith as Heroine', in D. J. Lull (ed.), *Society of Biblical Literature 1989 Seminar Papers* (Atlanta: Scholars Press, 1989), 570–8.

Wildberger, H., 'Das Freudenmahl auf dem Zion', *TLZ* 33 (1977), 373–83.

Wilkins, J., *The Boastful Chef: The Discourse of Food in Ancient Greek Comedy* (Oxford: Oxford University Press, 2000).

Wilkins, J., Harvey, D. and Dobson, E. (eds.), *Food in Antiquity* (Exeter: University of Exeter Press, 1995).

Wilkins, J. M. and Hill, S., *Food in the Ancient World* (Malden, MA: Blackwell, 2006).

Wilkinson, J., *Jerusalem Pilgrims: Before the Crusades*, 2nd edn. (Warminster: Aris & Phillips, 2002).

Willis, T. M., 'Yahweh's Elders (Isa 24,23): Senior Officials of the Divine Court', *ZAW* 103 (1991), 375–85.

—— ' "Eat and Rejoice before the Lord": The Optimism of Worship in the Deuteronomic Code', in M. P. Graham, R. R. Marrs and S. L. McKenzie (eds.), *Worship and the Hebrew Bible: Essays in Honour of John T. Willis*, JSOTSup, 284 (Sheffield: Sheffield Academic Press, 1999), 276–94.

Wills, L. M., *The Jewish Novel in the Ancient World* (Ithaca: Cornell University Press, 1995).

Wilson, L., *Joseph Wise and Otherwise: The Intersection of Wisdom and Covenant in Genesis 37–50*, Paternoster Biblical Monographs (Milton Keynes: Paternoster, 2004).

Yadin, A., 'Samson's Ḥîdâ', *VT* 52 (2002), 407–26.

Zakovitch, Y., 'Sisseras Tod', *ZAW* 93 (1981), 364–74.

Zenger, E., 'Die deuteronomistische Interpretation der Rehabilitierung Jojachins', *BZ* 12 (1968), 16–30.

—— *Israel am Sinai: Analysen und Interpretationen zu Exodus 17–34* (Altenberge: CIS Verlag, 1982).

Zimmerli, W., *The Old Testament and the World* (Atlanta: John Knox Press, 1976).

—— *Ezekiel I*, Hermenia (Philadelphia: Fortress Press, 1979).

Zohary, D. and Hopf, M., *Domestication of Plants in the Old World: The Origin and Spread of Cultivated Plants in West Asia, Europe, and the Nile Valley*, 2nd edn. (Oxford: Clarendon Press, 1994).

Index of Names

Aharoni, Y. 65 n. 42
Albertz, R. 198
Amit, Y. 115
Anderson, A. A. 190 n. 73
Anderson, G. A. 113 n. 29, 114 n. 31
Ap-Thomas, D. R. 117 n. 43
Assis, E. 117 n. 43, 121 n. 60, 121 n. 62

Bal, M. 121
Barthes, R. 33
Begg, C. T. 177
Becker, U. 101 n. 5
Berlin, A. 208 n. 36
Berg, S. V. 203 n. 22
Binger, T. 9 n. 29
Blair, E. P. 71
Blenkinsopp, J. 75 n. 15
Blomberg, C. L. 222
Bluedorn, W. 119 n. 53
Boling, R. G. 116 n. 41, 119, 121
Borowski, O. 54–5, 56, 62 n. 36, 149
Bourdieu, P. 33
Boyle, M. O. 180 n. 40
Braudel, F. 137
Braulik, G. 81 n. 35
Braun, W. 221
Brenner, A. 7–8
Brettler, M. Z. 114
Briant, P. 204–5, 207 n. 33
Broshi, M. 61 n. 30, 61 n. 32, 62 n. 34
Brueggemann, W. 186 n. 61
Bulmer, R. 25–6
Bunimovitz, S. 152
Burney, C. F. 116 n. 41, 155

Carneiro, R. L. 137
Charles, R. H. 200
Childs, B. S. 71
Claassens, L. J. M. 10
Claessen, H. J. M. 147 n. 37
Clements, R. E. 176 n. 31
Clines, D. J. A. 119 n. 52, 201, 207, 209
Cody, A. 78
Coggins, R. J. 209 n. 40
Collins, J. J. 104 n., 203
Connerton, P. 72, 75, 87, 96

Coote, R. B. 136, 137–8, 141–2, 147 n. 37,
    149, 165
Cronauer, P. T. 183 n. 51
Cross, F. M. 171 n. 14

Dar, S. 48–9, 52, 53–64
Davila, J. R. 202 n. 20
de Moor, J. C. 111 n. 22
De Vries, S. J. 156
Dietler, M. 143–8, 150, 151, 161, 163
Douglas, M. 4 n. 13, 14–15, 17–28, 29–30,
    33–44, 72, 88 n. 51, 102, 132
Driver, S. R. 20 n. 9
Du Bois, C. M. 34 n. 53
Duhaime, J. 36 n. 57
Durkheim, É. 19

Earle, T. 146 n. 29
Ellison, R. 66
Esler, P. F. 221
Exum, J. C. 101, 124, 132, 133

Feeley-Harnick, G. 5 n. 14
Finkelstein, I. 139 n. 10, 151–3
Fitzmyer, J. A. 201
Forbes, H. A. 61 n. 30
Fox, M. V. 203
Foxhall, L. 61 n. 30
Frankel, D. 95
Fried, M. H. 148 n. 37
Frick, F. S. 135–7, 140–2, 147 n. 37, 149, 153,
    165
Fritz, V. 156, 159
Fuchs, G. 189 n. 65

Galling, K. 89
Garnsey, P. 14, 33–4, 55, 66
Goldingay, J. E. 200
Goody, J. 8, 141
Gordon, R. P. 158 n. 72, 168, 171 n. 14, 172,
    178 n. 36
Gottwald, N. K. 31, 135, 168 n. 4
Gowers, E. 197
Granowski, J. J. 175 n. 23
Gray, J. 173 n. 19, 181
Greenberg, M. 164 n. 90

Subject Index

Index of Biblical Citations

258

Index of Biblical Citations

11.9–12   21
11.13–19   21–2
11.20–3   21
11.24–5   125
11.27–31   21–2
11.39   125
11.41–4   21
11.42–5   43
12–15   23, 39 n. 62
18   103
19   41
19.19   199 n. 7
19.34   91
21–2   41
24.7   221
24.19   42

Numbers
5   189
6   124 n. 69
6.1–8   124 n. 69
6.3   125 n. 71
6.5–6   125 n. 71
6.6–8   125 n. 71
11   111 n. 20
11.4   83
11.5   211
20.14–21   91
21.2–3   122 n. 64
21.10–20   90 n. 54
25   107
28.7   190 n. 73
28.26   77 n. 19

Deuteronomy
1–11   83
1–3   107 n. 14
2   89–90
2.6   90
2.7   94
2.8–9   90 n. 54
2.8   90
2.18   90 n. 54
2.28–9   89, 90 n. 54
2.28   91
2.29   90 n. 54, 95 n. 69
3   194 n. 83
4.13   98
4.20   91
5.12–15   92 n. 60
5.15   91–2
5.21   83
5.22   98
6.3   84

6.4–9   96
6.10–19   84
6.10–12   84
7   75 n. 16, 108
7.1–5   79
7.8   91
7.18   70
7.25–6   87
8   54, 56, 75, 84
8.2–5   85, 94
8.2–4   84
8.3   97
8.7–9   54, 84
8.7–10   53
8.8–9   62
8.9   94
8.11   84
8.14   84–5
8.15–16   95 n. 69
8.15   84
8.18   84
8.19   84
9.21   79 n. 25
10.4   98
10.12–22   93
10.19   93
10.21   70
11   66
11.5   95 n. 69
11.9   84
11.13–17   84
12–26   83
12–15   39 n. 62
12   75 n. 17, 86
12.2–4   86
12.7   79, 105
12.8–12   100 n. 5
12.12   93
12.18–19   93
12.20   83
12.21   83
12.29–13.1   86 n. 42
12.29–31   86
12.30   86 n. 42
12.31   87
13   86, 88
13.9   86
13.12–18   86
13.14   87
14   14, 17, 36, 38, 39 n. 62, 43, 75 n. 17, 88, 198–9, 201
14.3–21   87
14.26   79